A 'CONSTITUTION FOR THE OCEANS'

The UN Convention on the Law of the Sea, signed in 1982, was the culmination of half a century of legal endeavour. Earlier attempts to create a treaty regime governing the oceans – at League of Nations and United Nations conferences held in 1930, 1958 and 1960 – had all failed to settle the breadth of the territorial sea, and in two cases failed to settle anything at all. During the negotiations, legal concepts were formulated and reformulated: straight baselines inspired archipelagic baselines; fishing conservation zones became exclusive economic zones; innocent passage through straits metamorphosed into transit passage through straits; and seabed common heritage was replaced by the parallel system of seabed exploitation. Many of the issues that animated the delegates during the negotiations – ocean pollution, overfishing, naval mobility, continental shelf claims and the impact of seabed mining – continue to exercise policymakers and lawyers to this day.

KIRSTEN SELLARS writes about sovereignty and the creation of public international law. Her previous publications include *'Crimes against Peace' and International Law* (2013), and the edited volume, *Trials for International Crimes in Asia* (2016).

A 'CONSTITUTION FOR THE OCEANS'

The Long Hard Road to the UN Convention on the Law of the Sea

KIRSTEN SELLARS

CAMBRIDGE
UNIVERSITY PRESS

CAMBRIDGE
UNIVERSITY PRESS

Shaftesbury Road, Cambridge CB2 8EA, United Kingdom

One Liberty Plaza, 20th Floor, New York, NY 10006, USA

477 Williamstown Road, Port Melbourne, VIC 3207, Australia

314–321, 3rd Floor, Plot 3, Splendor Forum, Jasola District Centre, New Delhi – 110025, India

103 Penang Road, #05-06/07, Visioncrest Commercial, Singapore 238467

Cambridge University Press is part of Cambridge University Press & Assessment,
a department of the University of Cambridge.

We share the University's mission to contribute to society through the pursuit of
education, learning and research at the highest international levels of excellence.

www.cambridge.org
Information on this title: www.cambridge.org/9781108840149

DOI: 10.1017/9781108879040

When citing this work, please include a reference to the DOI 10.1017/9781108879040

First published 2025

A catalogue record for this publication is available from the British Library.

A Cataloging-in-Publication data record for this book is available from the Library of Congress

ISBN 978-1-108-84014-9 Hardback

CONTENTS

FOREWORD

States need oceans. Oceans are a conduit for communications, commerce and cargoes; an arena for naval exercises and manoeuvres; a hunting ground for trawlers, seiners and trollers; a source of oil, tin and coal; a repository for nuclear waste and submarine detection devices; and a harbinger of breakthroughs in climatology and the biological sciences. Moreover, the relationship between states and oceans has always been complex and disruptive, giving the lie to the old idea that the sea was a realm of purity, abundance and freedom. Marine pollution is as old as coastal cities, laws curbing overfishing date back to the fourteenth century, and the apparently untrammelled 'freedom of the seas' has long been qualified by sanctions against delinquent vessels.

Between 1973 and 1982, delegates gathered at the third United Nations conference on the law of the sea to try to reach agreement on a comprehensive treaty governing states' entitlements and interactions in the oceans. The task facing them was monumental. As the Canadian external affairs secretary Mark MacGuigan explained,

> [T]he Conference is not merely an attempt to codify technical rules of law. It is a resource Conference; it is a food Conference; it is an environmental Conference; it is an energy Conference; it is a conservation Conference; it is an economic Conference; it is a maritime-boundary-delimitation Conference; it is a territorial-limitation and jurisdictional Conference; it is a transportation, communications and freedom-of-navigation Conference; it is a Conference which regulates all the uses of the oceans by humanity. Most important it is a Conference which provides for the peaceful settlement of disputes concerning the oceans. It is, in other words, a Conference dedicated to the rule of law among nations.[1]

[1] GOAR, A/36/PV.6 (21 September 1981), pp. 65–66.

The resultant UN Convention on the Law of the Sea, signed in 1982,[2] was the culmination of half a century of diplomatic endeavour: three previous international conferences had either failed to settle the breadth of the territorial sea – the cornerstone of the maritime zone system – or failed to settle anything at all. The sticking point was sovereignty, but the delegates persisted, and the aggregation of their sovereigntist impulses eventually resulted in fine-spun international law. Reflecting on the alchemy that transforms politics into law, the Algerian Mohammed Bedjaoui, one-time legal adviser to the Front de libération nationale, reached across the political divide for the words of the conservative Australian solicitor-general, Kenneth Bailey: 'One must not forget that propaganda can create pressures, that pressures can create content and that content can create law.'[3] This book traces the tortuous transition from one to the other, beginning in 1930 with the failed attempt to create a treaty governing territorial waters, and ending with the signing of the UN convention, governing almost all aspects of states' activities within the oceans.

British Decline

The initial stimulus to codify the law of the sea came in the years following the First World War, as the maritime powers anticipated the emergence of customary international law inimical to their navigational freedoms. Over the latter part of the previous century, *Pax Britannica* had maximised the United Kingdom's high seas mobility by imposing narrow territorial seas, subject to innocent passage, to minimise coastal states' interference with foreign vessels. Custom followed power, shaped by British commerce and enforced by the Royal Navy. But by the turn of the century, Britain's grip on international affairs had begun to loosen. States started to push against the existing system by seeking wider territorial seas and jurisdiction over adjacent security zones, customs zones, and fishing and conservation areas. It was expected that custom would evolve in response, enhancing the rights of less powerful coastal states and restricting the sea-going reach of the great powers. This was becoming a concern for Britain and the United States (the latter about to

[2] United Nations Convention on the Law of the Sea (signed 10 December 1984, EIF 16 November 1994) 1833 UNTS 397 [hereafter, UNCLOS].

[3] M. Bedjaoui, *Towards a new international economic order* (Paris: UNESCO/Holmes & Meier, 1979), p. 183, fn. 1.

replace the former as the leading power), and led to their first attempt, in 1930, to codify the law of the sea.

The perception that custom might work against navigational freedoms would continue to preoccupy the most powerful states. In 2004, the American rear-admiral William Schachte, while testifying in favour of the United States becoming a party to the 1982 convention, looked back over the legal antecedents and argued that it was unwise to rely solely on custom for the protection of their interests. One reason, he said, was that passage through straits used for international navigation and passage through archipelagic sea lanes were governed not by custom but by regimes that were the specific 'creations of the convention'.[4] In any case, custom did not always accord with the US Navy's priorities:

> if you examine the evolution of customary international law in the 20th century, you'll find that it [in]volved the erosion, not the preservation, of navigational rights and freedoms. In the mid-1950s – it was concluded by the major maritime powers that the best way to stop that erosion was through the adoption of a universally recognized treaty that established limits on coastal nation jurisdiction and preserved traditional navigational rights and freedoms.[5]

The decades after the war were indeed crucial. From the late forties onwards, the United States, for all its commanding influence and powers of enforcement, found itself caught in a spiral of discord over the law of the sea. In contrast to Britain, which earlier had been able to rely on custom arising from *Pax Britannia*, the United States could not depend on custom generated by *Pax Americana* to underwrite its maritime activities. Instead, it was compelled to look to treaty law. One reason for this was that the global problems of shipping congestion, marine pollution and overfishing had reached critical mass, and treaty law was in theory better able than custom to provide swift and detailed responses to them. Another reason was that the countries of the global South, their numbers bolstered by the newly independent states, were making more extensive claims to coastal waters and their resources. Custom (as Schachte noted) was thus evolving to erode, not preserve, the maritime powers' navigational rights.

This dependence on the treaty-making process brought the American negotiators into direct contact with less powerful actors, who had every

[4] US Senate committee on armed services, *Military implications of the United Nations convention on the law of the sea* (8 April 2004), p. 112.

[5] Ibid.

intention of jettisoning 'worn-out imperialisms' such as the three-nautical-mile territorial sea and transforming international law to serve their own interests.[6] As the Philippines delegate Arturo Tolentino – who campaigned for decades for recognition of a special regime governing archipelagic waters – said of one conference:

> [It] has become a battleground between the conflicting or divergent interests of developed and developing nations, and between the old order and new concepts. It has become the site of rebellion by small states against the dominance of the big maritime powers in laying down the rules of the sea. It has become a forum of insurgency against some established concepts.[7]

Here in a nutshell was the problem facing the United States: despite its immense power, it could neither revert to custom on navigation, because state practice was changing it, nor, faced with the 'insurgency', could it be confident of securing agreement to a treaty enshrining the oceanic order over which it hoped to preside.

Science and Technology

The law of the sea conferences were intimately connected, and can only be properly understood in relation to one another. The 1958 conference produced five conventions (including a protocol on dispute settlement), yet it failed to settle the essential question of the breadth of the territorial sea, just as the 1930 conference had failed to do, and for the same reason. The follow-up conference in 1960, convened to address this issue and the question of fishery limits, collapsed without resolving either. The final conference of 1973–1982 at last achieved agreement on these, while at the same time producing a convention that rewrote many of the provisions set down in the conventions agreed in 1958.

Why were states so set upon revising agreements they had concluded only a decade or so earlier? On one hand, the impulse was political: newly independent states who had not participated in the creation of the 1958 conventions wanted to remake the law to reflect their own interests. On the other hand, it was a response to new developments in science and

[6] 'Address by Dr. Alberto Ulloa, chairman of the delegation of Peru' (29 March 1950), p. 4: vol. 8355, 10600-BH-40, pt. 1.2, RG 25, Library and Archives Canada [hereafter, LAC].

[7] A. M. Tolentino, *The Philippines and the law of the sea: a collection of articles, statements, and speeches* (Manila: Secretariat to the Cabinet Committee on the Law of the Sea Treaty by the Development Academy of the Philippines Press, c. 1982), p. 66.

technology, which were in the process of transforming naval priorities and the operation of the ocean-based mining, fishing, logistics, and oil industries.

Throughout the twentieth century, innovations such as radar, the stern chute, deep-water drilling, helicopters, net-hauling power blocks, seismic surveying and satellite surveillance would each exert an influence on the legal regimes governing fishing, navigational safety, the movement of naval forces, and offshore oil industries. One of the most significant developments was in the field of energy production. The chemical processes known as thermal cracking (invented at the turn of the century) and catalytic cracking (developed in the thirties), broke down or 'cracked' crude oil molecules into smaller and more useful hydrocarbon molecules. These new processes would be used by the emerging petrochemical industry to produce new products – diesel, petrol and plastics – that would transform the sea-going world, with diesel-fuelled combustion engines replacing coal-fuelled steam engines, nylon replacing cotton in fishing nets, polyethylene replacing gutta-percha in undersea cable coating, and polypropylene replacing hemp in rope.

The age of oil, cracked and uncracked, was inevitably reflected in the law of the sea conventions. After the war, states looking to extend their jurisdiction over offshore oil fields would articulate the concept of the continental shelf: this idea was first internationally recognised by the 1958 continental shelf convention, and then elaborated within the 1982 convention. The petrochemical industry's demand for oil also transformed global logistics, with large oil tanker fleets being put to sea, which prompted states affected by pollution and oil-spills to agitate for provisions to protect the marine environment. Meanwhile, the introduction of diesel greatly extended the reach of vessels, including those of industrial fishing fleets, whose incursions into others' coastal waters prompted the affected states to campaign for another concept – the exclusive economic zone, which was first recognised by the 1982 convention.

The second major innovation in twentieth-century energy production was nuclear power. The substantive 1958 conventions made no direct reference to nuclear activities in the oceans, but by the time they came into force events had already overtaken them, and the United States was regularly deploying nuclear-propelled submarines armed with intercontinental ballistic missiles. These submarines possessed far greater range and lethality than diesel-electric submarines armed with torpedoes, and they would become central to nuclear deterrence. This shift was reflected in the 1982 convention. Explicit references to nuclear-related activities were confined to two articles dealing with the movement of 'nuclear-powered ships and ships carrying nuclear or other inherently dangerous or noxious substances' through the territorial sea,[8] but this belied the degree to which the convention was permeated by the powers' preoccupation with the movement of their own nuclear submarines and the placement of underwater tracking devices to monitor those of other nations. This heavily influenced the provisions on straits used for international navigation, passage through archipelagos, navigation rights in the exclusive economic zone, and non-resource-related rights on the continental shelf.

*

Although change was afoot, driven by decolonisation and technology, some patterns remained constant. The literature tends to focus on the divisions between East and West, and between North and South. These were certainly important, but they tend to be presented in a way that obscures some of the contradictions and conflicting pressures that existed at the time.

On East–West relations, some commentators suggest that the law of the sea was a product of the Cold War. This is only partly true. The superpowers' security concerns about each other did indeed exert a strong influence over the proceedings: throughout the post-war decades, both sides, acutely aware of their capacity for mutual destruction, focussed on deterrence. This led to *détente*, and with the Cold War in abeyance from the late sixties onwards, conditions were now conducive to collaboration on navigational rights. Both the United States and the USSR exploited the thaw by agitating for a legal regime that would maximise the range and movement of their nuclear submarines – the lynchpin of deterrence. The final conference was a product of this collaboration: they pushed for the negotiations to be held in the first place and then played a leading role within them, working in tandem to suppress unwelcome initiatives from the 'group of seventy-seven' (G77). This collaboration continued until their shared navigational objectives had been secured: after that, the recriminations returned, but around issues such as seabed mining which were not directly connected to naval mobility.

The respective roles of the North and South at the law of the sea conferences were also less straightforward than is sometimes suggested. It is certainly true that all three post-war law of the sea conferences were

[8] Articles 22(2) and 23, UNCLOS, 406.

dominated by the division between the 'industrial' and 'developing' states (to use here, as elsewhere in the book, the terminology of the time). Most of the former clung to the status quo by trying to rein in the expansion of territorial seas and adjacent zones; and most of the latter championed newer approaches – calling for wider territorial seas, exclusive economic zones, and the recognition of archipelagic waters. One unacknowledged result of these differences was that after the collapse of the 1960 conference, with Chile, Ecuador and India playing a decisive role in the final vote, the states of the North, especially those in Anglo-American alliance, started to lose confidence in the United Nations as a forum for concluding treaties that adequately reflected their interests. Their response to this problem was to switch from voting (which favoured majorities) to agreement by consensus (which favoured minorities). The 1973–1982 conference was the first major international gathering attended by almost every state to use consensus as the primary mechanism for reaching decisions.

Yet alongside this split on North-South lines, the negotiations were also shaped by bitter struggles *within* these two groups. The rifts between the industrial states of the North over tactics relating to the breadth of the territorial sea and fishing zones reverberated throughout the 1958 conference, while their disputes over seabed mining production featured prominently during the final years of the 1973–1982 negotiations. Within the G77, meanwhile, the coastal states found themselves at odds with the landlocked and geographically disadvantaged states over their different blueprints for development – whether to ensure economic security by exploiting the exclusive economic zone or by reaping the rewards of international seabed common heritage. The group's campaign for the new international economic order had thus already been undermined by these disputes well before the debt crisis of the eighties put paid to the prospect of greater parity between North and South.

As a consequence, the modern law of the sea did not arise fully formed like Venus from the waves; it emerged piecemeal and imperfect out of a process shaped by inter-state conflict, driven by political will and characterised by trade-offs and concessions.

The Invisible Side

Daniel Bethlehem, a former legal adviser to the British Foreign and Commonwealth Office, has argued that to understand international law, and to 'reach considered conclusions on whether conduct is lawful or unlawful', one must look beneath the surface of the final text and examine the factors that influenced its construction.[9] Some of this is visible, manifested as state practice and collated in yearbooks.[10] But much of it is not. This is 'the invisible life of international law, that part of international law that is not readily open to the public gaze'[11] – the behind-the-scenes and often undisclosed contribution of diplomats, ministers and government legal advisers to the formation of law. This contribution, he says, has a tremendous bearing on international law:

> It may not be visible, but it is there, it is weighty, it has effects, and it can, with sufficient scholarship and informed inquiry, be deduced and identified.[12]

This book's approach is to make at least some of the invisible visible. It is based primarily on documents from government archives, with the aim of shedding light on the internal factors influencing officials at crucial points during the negotiations. In this hidden realm of encrypted correspondence, internal reports and classified memoranda, one finds frank assessments of other states' motives, interests and tactics. These are often in marked contrast to the public pronouncements and calculated gestures of the conference floor, and they provide a useful context for assessing the successes and failures of the constituent parts of the conventions.

Inevitably, the accessible archival materials cover some internal debates more thoroughly than others. The available documents about the breadth of the territorial sea and fishing zones are ample, while those concerning the navigational requirements of naval vessels in straits are patchy, and those addressing submarine detection devices are positively threadbare. By the same token, some periods of the negotiations are better covered than others. Many repositories of materials on the most recent final conference – which ended just over four decades ago – remain closed: the final chapters therefore rely heavily on documents released by Western archives under the thirty-year rule. Fortunately, these files contain enough 'foreign' material – reports, transcripts and comments from other delegations – that, although acquired according to the priorities

9 D. Bethlehem, 'The secret life of international law', *Cambridge Journal of International and Comparative Law* 1 (2012), 23, 24.

10 Ibid.

11 Ibid.

12 Ibid., 36.

of the archive-holding states, nevertheless help to construct a more rounded perspective on the issues under discussion.

The book focusses almost entirely on the treaty-making process, switching attention to other sources of law only when they had a decisive bearing on it – the *Corfu Channel* and *Fisheries* cases being especially influential. Within these parameters, it also concentrates on those issues on which the differences between states were most pronounced, because they most clearly reveal the interests and intentions of the main players, and the strategies by which they sought to achieve their objectives. By laying bare the inner workings of the process, one can consider historical events in a distinctive and, one hopes, illuminating way.

I am extremely grateful to the archivists (and digitisers) of nearly twenty archives located around the world. I am especially grateful to those at Archivo Central at the Ministerio de Relaciones Exteriores del Perú, the National Archives of Singapore, and the University of Virginia Law School Library, as well as to Alex G. Oude Elferink and Golu Kumar, who generously made documents available to me at the height of the pandemic when it was impossible to visit the archives in person. To all, thank you.

Finally, my thanks to the delegates at the final law of the sea conference for coining the book's title;[13] to the University of London's Institute of Advanced Legal Studies and the Australian National University's Coral Bell School of Asia Pacific Affairs for hosting me as a visiting fellow at crucial stages of writing; to Joe Ng at Cambridge University Press for shepherding the book through the process; and to Ed Barrett, as always.

Kirsten Sellars
London
May 2023

[13] United Nations Law of the Sea Conference, 1973–1982 [hereafter, UNLOSC III], vol. 17: T. Koh, A/Conf.62/SR.185 (6 December 1982), pp. 13, 14; F. Zegers and A. J. Jacovides, A/Conf.62/SR.189 (8 December 1982), pp. 66, 71; and G. Papoulias, A/Conf.62/SR.191 (8 December 1982), p. 110.

ABBREVIATIONS

AAD	Access to Archival Databases (NARA)
AALCC	Asian-African Legal Consultative Committee
ASW	anti-submarine warfare
CIAHC	Central Intelligence Agency Historical Collections
EEZ	exclusive economic zone
FCO	Foreign and Commonwealth Office (UK)
FRUS	*Foreign Relations of the United States*
G5	Group of Five
G77	Group of Seventy-Seven
GAOR	General Assembly Official Records
ICJ	International Court of Justice
ICNT	Informal Composite Negotiating Text
ILC	International Law Commission
IMCO	Inter-governmental Maritime Consultative Organization
IMO	International Maritime Organization
IOR	India Office Records (UK)
LAC	Library and Archives Canada
LDCs	less developed countries
LLGDS	landlocked and geographically disadvantaged states
LN	League of Nations
LNTS	*League of Nations Treaty Series*
MRE del Perú	Archivo Central, Ministerio de Relaciones Exteriores del Perú
NAA	National Archives of Australia
NAI	National Archives of India
NARA	National Archives and Records Administration (US)
NATO	North Atlantic Treaty Organization
NMML	Nehru Memorial Museum and Library (India)
NRC	National Research Council (US)
OPEC	Organization of the Petroleum Exporting Countries
PRAAD	Public Records and Archives Administration Department (Ghana)
RRPL	Ronald Reagan Presidential Library

SEATO	Southeast Asia Treaty Organization
SOSUS	Sound Surveillance System (US)
TNA	The National Archives (UK)
UNCLOS	United Nations Convention on the Law of the Sea
UNGA	United Nations General Assembly
UNLOSC I, II, III	First, second and third UN Law of the Sea Conferences
UNTS	*United Nations Treaty Series*
UVLSL	University of Virginia Law School Library

1

End of the Old Order

The Attempt to Create a Convention on Territorial Waters

On 20 March 1929, during the era of Prohibition, master John Randell stood on the deck of the British schooner *I'm Alone*, anchored off the coast of Louisiana, and delivered a short, sharp lecture on the law of the sea to the American coastguard officers trying to board his vessel. 'You have no jurisdiction,' he shouted, 'I am on the high seas.'[1]

According to a later American indictment issued against *I'm Alone*'s owners and associates for unlawful conspiracy to import liquor into the country, the schooner, registered in Canada, had made numerous trips to the United States between 1927 and 1929. Some had started in Belize, British Honduras, where it would take on cargos of liquor, one listed as '1326 sacks of whiskey, gin and rum and 92 kegs of malt'.[2] From Belize, it would sail north across the Gulf of Mexico, then anchor off the coast of Louisiana near Vermilion Bay. There, it was alleged, it was met on different occasions by the motorboats *Venus*, *May*, *City of Rome*, *Laura Lead* and *Nicholas*,[3] whose crews identified themselves to Randell by presenting him with the matching half of a torn dollar bill.[4] These boats, known in the rum-running business as 'pullers', transported the liquor back to shore, where it was transported to warehouses, disguised and then distributed northwards from the railhead at Abbeville, Louisiana.[5]

1 UK Embassy Washington to UK Foreign Office (29 March 1929), p. 1: FO 371/13513, The National Archives, Kew, UK [hereafter, TNA].

2 Copy of indictment, *United States v Dan Hogan et al.* (no. 5623) US District Court for the Lake Charles Division of the Western District of Louisiana (16 December 1929), pp. 3–4: FO 371/14276, TNA.

3 Ibid., p. 4.

4 'I'm Alone skipper describes cruises', *New York Times* (30 December 1934).

5 Copy of indictment, *United States v Dan Hogan et al.* (no. 5623) US District Court for the Lake Charles Division of the Western District of Louisiana (16 December 1929), p. 4: FO 371/14276, TNA.

On this occasion, coastguard officers on the cutter *Wolcott* first spotted *I'm Alone* between ten and fifteen nautical miles off the coast – accounts differed – and instructed it by megaphone to heave to.[6] After Randell refused to allow them to board, *Wolcott* fired a warning shot across the bows, whereupon it took off in the direction of Mexico with *Wolcott* in pursuit. On the way, *Wolcott* shot through *I'm Alone*'s sails and rigging, but its gun jammed and it radioed for help. Another coastguard vessel, *Dexter*, joined the chase, and caught up with *I'm Alone* two days later, on the morning of 22 March, some 215 miles southeast of New Orleans in the Gulf of Mexico, with *Wolcott* following behind. *Dexter* instructed *I'm Alone* to heave to, Randell again refused to allow officers to board, and *Dexter* opened fire with a three-inch gun and rifles, hitting the schooner with 'some sixty or seventy shells'.[7] As *I'm Alone* went down, the crew took to the water in heavy seas, and Leon Mainguy, a French national, drowned. The others were transported to New Orleans in manacles, whereupon criminal charges were issued against them.[8]

A few days later, the US Treasury issued a statement indicating that the coastguards had intercepted the 'notorious rum smuggler' *I'm Alone* under the terms of the Tariff Act of 1922, and had given chase in accordance with the doctrine of hot pursuit.[9] Section 581 of the Tariff Act declared a four-league (i.e. twelve-mile) customs zone extending outwards from the United States' coast, empowering the authorities to hail, stop, inspect, search and examine a vessel, and if it attempted to escape, to 'pursue and arrest' those involved using 'all necessary force to compel compliance'.[10] When introduced, section 581 had antagonised the British, who saw no reason why their flagged vessels should be compelled to abide by American Prohibition laws beyond US territorial waters.[11] Thereafter, whenever the coastguard intercepted British-flagged vessels in the claimed zone beyond the three-mile limit, the British

[6] Hereafter, references to 'miles' should be taken to mean 'nautical miles'.

[7] 'The Canadian minister (Massey) to the secretary of state' (9 April 1929): *Foreign Relations of the United States* [hereafter, *FRUS*], *Papers relating to the foreign relations of the United States*, 1929, vol. 2, doc. 811.114 I'm Alone/76.

[8] For one account of the incident, see the summary of US Treasury statement, UK Embassy Washington to UK Foreign Office (26 March 1929), pp. 1–2: FO 371/13513, TNA.

[9] Ibid.

[10] Tariff Act of 1922, 42 Statutes at Large (1922), 858, 979. Section 581 applied these powers to 'any vessel', while section 586 made explicit reference to 'any vessel from a foreign port or place' (ibid., 980).

[11] Grey of Fallodon, UK House of Lords, *Hansard* (28 June 1923), vol. 54, col. 730.

protested on much the same lines as Randell: these were high seas, beyond the reach of the coastal state.

Shortly after the Treasury pronouncement on *I'm Alone*, the State Department stepped in and proposed that the schooner had in fact been intercepted under the Convention respecting the Regulation of the Liquor Traffic, concluded between Britain and the United States in 1924[12] – in other words, *not* the Tariff Act. This convention, designed to reduce the friction between the two countries over section 581, entitled British ships to lawfully carry sealed cargoes of alcohol through American territorial waters and ports provided that they were listed as sea stores or destined for elsewhere.[13] In return, the British would raise no objection to the American authorities boarding and, if justified, seizing British vessels suspected of unlawfully importing liquor, provided this happened at no greater distance than that 'traversed in one hour' from the United States' coast.[14] (This vague term got around Britain's reluctance to validate a four-league or twelve-mile contiguous zone, which they feared would set an unwelcome precedent.[15]) The convention also provided for hearings before two commissioners for compensation for the loss or injury of British vessels seized in a manner 'improper or unreasonable'.[16]

Whatever the legal basis for the interception, a case against the crew of *I'm Alone* seemed to be pending. But then the unexpected happened: on 9 April, the American authorities withdrew the charges against all of them and they were released.[17] The US Justice Department explained that the case had been dropped for lack of evidence of acts of conspiracy 'on shore or within marginal three mile limit', but that this in no way reflected on the legality of the coastguards' interception and pursuit of *I'm Alone*.[18] In London, British officials expressed their doubts about this latter claim, speculating that unnamed parties in Washington had instructed the coastguard to 'get rid of this troublesome boat', and had then decided

[12] Convention between the United States of America and the United Kingdom respecting the Regulation of the Liquor Traffic [hereafter, Liquor Convention] (signed 23 January 1924, EIF 2 May 1924) 27 LNTS 181.

[13] Article 3, ibid., 184.

[14] Article 2, ibid., 182–184.

[15] R. H. Hadow to C. W. Dixon (29 August 1929), p. 2: FO 371/13515, TNA.

[16] Article 4, Liquor Convention, 184.

[17] UK Embassy Washington to UK Foreign Office (11 April 1929), p. 1: FO 371/13513, TNA.

[18] Ibid.

against bringing the case lest their equally troublesome instruction came to light.[19]

The Doctrine of Hot Pursuit

States strongly resent other states' attempts to seize, never mind sink, their vessels on the high seas, especially during peacetime, and Herbert Hoover's new administration braced itself for a protest. Because *I'm Alone* was a Canadian-registered British vessel,[20] both Britain and Canada, then a British dominion, had a strong interest in the matter, and it was decided that the Canadians would raise a formal complaint with the Americans. On the day the charges against the crew were withdrawn, Canada's minister plenipotentiary to the United States, Vincent Massey, lodged a protest with Secretary of State Henry Stimson, indicating that he had reluctantly reached the conclusion that 'on the evidence now available, the pursuit and sinking of the vessel appears not to have been authorized either by the terms of the [Liquor] Convention of January 1924 or by the rules of international law'.[21]

The incident raised three legal issues. The first was whether *I'm Alone* was covered by the Liquor Convention when first intercepted by *Wolcott*. This could be settled by establishing two facts: the schooner's distance from the coast and its speed when it fled, both being necessary to calculate whether it was intercepted within an hour's sailing from the United States' coast, as specified by the convention. One difficulty was the 'one hour's sailing distance' formula, which the Canadian external affairs legal adviser John Read described as 'elastic, vague and unworkable'.[22] Another difficulty arose from the various claims about the schooner's position and speed made by the US authorities or by Randell and other crew members. Even so, if it could be shown that *I'm Alone* was outside treaty limits when intercepted, the American case would presumably 'fall [t]o the ground'.[23]

19 R. L. Craigie minute (10 April 1929): FO 371/13513, TNA.

20 *SS 'I'm Alone' (Canada / United States)* (1935) III RIAA 1609, 1617.

21 'The Canadian minister (Massey) to the secretary of state' (9 April 1929): *FRUS*, *Papers relating to the foreign relations of the United States*, 1929, vol. 2, doc. 811.114 I'm Alone/76.

22 'Memorandum' (29 August 1929), p. 4: FO 371/13515, TNA.

23 UK High Commission Ottawa, 'Memorandum' (28 August 1929), p. 2: FO 371/13515, TNA.

The next legal question was whether the doctrine of hot pursuit could be applied to a pursuit started outside territorial waters but within treaty limits. The Canadians and British argued that it could not; the doctrine applied to pursuit commencing only from territorial waters, not from elsewhere.[24] This position was consistent with the existing doctrine, evidenced by the approach taken during the contemporaneous territorial waters debates before and during the 1930 League of Nations conference on the codification of international law.[25] There, guidance documents set out the four criteria governing hot pursuit: it had to begin in territorial waters, had to be initiated in response to infringements of a state's laws and regulations, had to be uninterrupted, and had to cease if the pursued vessel entered its own or a third state's territorial waters.[26] The Canadians pointed out that the pursuit of *I'm Alone* did not begin in American waters, and argued that it was not uninterrupted because *Dexter* had taken over the lead from *Wolcott* during the pursuit.[27]

The State Department's legal advisers countered that unless the Liquor Convention was read as providing for hot pursuit from within treaty limits, it would be 'worthless'.[28] Stimson elaborated a little, stating that the effect of the convention was to extend American jurisdiction over certain categories of British ships, and that if the Americans' right to pursue them from within the treaty limit into the high seas were denied, 'it would seem that the advantages purported to be granted by the treaty are illusory, since it would always be open to offending vessels to refuse

[24] See, for example, 'The Canadian minister (Massey) to the secretary of state' (9 April 1929): *FRUS, Papers relating to the foreign relations of the United States*, 1929, vol. 2, doc. 811.114 I'm Alone/76.

[25] Bases 5 and 26, drafted in 1929 as the starting point for the discussion about territorial waters at the conference, recognised the contiguous zone but did not recognise hot pursuit from it; the conference discussion about hot pursuit from the contiguous zone was inconclusive; and draft article 11 produced in the rapporteur's final report referred to hot pursuit commencing from internal waters or the territorial sea, but not from the contiguous zone. (League of Nations (LN), *Conference for the Codification of International Law – vol. III – minutes of the second committee*, C.351 (b). M.145 (b) (1930), pp. 179, 181; and ibid., annex V, appendix 1, p. 216; and W. H. Hancock, 'Report on international conference' (u.d., c. May 1930), pp. 32–33: FO 372/2639, TNA.)

[26] Basis 26, LN, *Conference for the Codification of International Law – vol. III*, p. 181.

[27] 'The Canadian minister (Massey) to the secretary of state' (9 April 1929): *FRUS, Papers relating to the foreign relations of the United States*, 1929, vol. 2, doc. 811.114 I'm Alone/76.

[28] UK Embassy Washington to UK Foreign Office (9 April 1929), p. 1: FO 371/13513, TNA.

to stop when signalled, and flee to the high seas'.[29] As for the Canadian contention that the pursuit had been interrupted, Stimson countered that both *Wolcott* and *Dexter* were present at the pursuit's end, acting as a single unit 'of the same force and under one command'[30] – an idea that has endured, now applying to hot pursuits involving two or more naval vessels or a combination of naval vessels and military aircraft.[31]

The third legal issue concerned the proportionality of the coastguard's response to *I'm Alone*'s attempts to escape. The arrest of a vessel usually involves some form of compulsion, implied or otherwise; but sinking it, as the British pointed out, was 'drastic'.[32] Leon Mainguy's drowning added to the gravity of the incident. The precise question arising from the convention, however, was whether the destruction of *I'm Alone* was 'improper or unreasonable'.[33] The Foreign Office argued that it must be:

> From the Naval point of view the alleged continued firing at the vessel after she was crippled was indefensible: it would seem that she could have been forced to heave to without pushing the attack home to the point of sinking the vessel and en[d]angering the lives of all her crew; there must surely have been a period prior to the vessel's actual sinking during which she must have been quite helpless and which should have been used for the taking off of her crew rather than for the continued bombardment.[34]

Esmé Howard, the British ambassador in Washington, added that when settling the dispute, it was important to highlight the use of rifles and machine guns against *I'm Alone*, to 'put a curb on the homicidal tendencies of the Coast Guard'.[35]

Stimson gave two different responses. The first was that because Randell had refused to let the coastguards board, and because heavy seas prevented them from boarding by force, they faced a choice: they could

29 'The secretary of state to the Canadian minister (Massey)' (17 April 1929): *FRUS*, *Papers relating to the foreign relations of the United States*, 1929, vol. 2, doc. 811.114 I'm Alone/111.

30 Ibid.

31 Article 111(6)(b), UNCLOS, 439.

32 UK High Commission Ottawa, 'Memorandum' (28 August 1929), p. 2: FO 371/13515, TNA.

33 Article 4, Liquor Convention, 184.

34 UK Foreign Office to UK Embassy Washington (28 March 1929), pp. 2–3: FO 371/13513, TNA.

35 UK Embassy Washington to UK Foreign Office (4 April 1929), pp. 3, 4: FO 371/13513, TNA.

either sink the schooner or let it escape.[36] But then Stimson contradicted himself, arguing that the coastguards had *no choice*: their sinking of the schooner was 'in the circumstances, inevitable'.[37] In this second argument, he shifted the focus away from 'improper or unreasonable' compulsion and towards *necessary* compulsion to bring *I'm Alone* to a halt.

After the exchange of notes between Massey and Stimson, two commissioners were appointed to decide whether there was basis for the payment of compensation for loss or injury, as specified by the convention. The case was not concluded until 1935, but before then, the Foreign Office under-secretary Hugh Dalton was alarmed to receive a note from the Scottish Unionist MP Samuel Chapman saying that he would be bringing John Randell to visit in the hope that 'you can very kindly help him somehow or other'.[38] Dalton wrote back strongly discouraging Chapman from bringing Randell anywhere near the Foreign Office because there was 'no shadow of doubt that he was on a smuggling venture when his schooner came to grief', and that 'the extensive participation of British subjects and ships in this illegal traffic has in the past placed His Majesty's Government in a most embarrassing position vis-à-vis the Government of the United States'.[39]

A 'Bad Patch' at The Hague

On 13 March 1930, just as the *I'm Alone* process was getting under way, the League's conference on the codification of international law opened in The Hague. This was vested with responsibility for producing treaties on three outstanding international legal questions: territorial waters, state responsibility, and nationality. In the committee considering territorial waters, two crucial issues proved contentious: the breadth of territorial waters and the recognition of the contiguous zone. Some states were pushing their jurisdictions outwards into the oceans, and the British, as the self-proclaimed guarantor of the freedom of the seas, took a hard line against this. Their intransigence contributed to the committee's failure to agree on either outstanding issue, let alone produce a draft treaty. The

[36] 'The secretary of state to the Canadian minister (Massey)' (17 April 1929): *FRUS, Papers relating to the foreign relations of the United States*, 1929, vol. 2, doc. 811.114 I'm Alone/111.
[37] Ibid.
[38] S. Chapman to E. H. J. Dalton (13 December 1930), pp. 1–2: FO 371/14277, TNA.
[39] E. H. J. Dalton to S. Chapman (19 December 1930), p. 2: FO 371/14277, TNA.

conference broke up on 12 April, having produced only one agreement on a different issue – the conflict of nationality laws. At the Foreign Office, Hugh Dalton, shrugging off Britain's own part in the conference's outcome, wrote a few months later, 'We have struck a bad patch lately. All recent conferences have ended in either complete, or substantial, failure.'[40]

This breakdown of the negotiations on territorial waters testified to Britain's decline as the leading maritime power. The First World War had left it crippled with debts and had deepened its dependency on invisible earnings. After the war, it was compelled to share its naval crown with the United States – an idea that would have been unthinkable a few decades earlier – while its grip on commercial shipping was being prized loose, line by line, by its European competitors.[41] The façade of British omnipotence, propped up by displays of force in the colonies, was starting to crack. By the time the conference opened in 1930, Britain still retained a huge navy and merchant marine, but its maritime policy was essentially a holding operation, designed to manage its threadbare assets and shrinking influence in the face of growing competition.

In the domain of international law, the British, having long relied on custom to legitimise their global activities, had mixed feelings about efforts to inscribe the law of the sea in a treaty. On one hand, it was necessary. On the other, they resented having to negotiate with others. This came to the surface over the conference's territorial waters committee, which they thought was 'a particularly unfavourable forum' for the airing of opinions on maritime affairs.[42] One problem, it seems, was reading the motives of the other powers, some of whom seemed to positively welcome the progressive development of the law. Another problem was that the proceedings would be run on democratic lines, where 'many States having little or no maritime interests' would be in possession of a vote.[43] If given a choice, the British would have preferred to settle law of the sea issues by judicial decision on a case-by-case basis before the Permanent Court of International Justice, where the vote-wielding states' views would not be represented to the same degree, and

[40] E. H. J. Dalton (7 July 1930): FO 372/2640, TNA.

[41] E. H. Marker, 'Jurisdiction outside territorial waters' (u.d., c. 27 March 1930), p. 4: FO 372/2638, TNA.

[42] G. R. Warner, 'Memorandum for the Cabinet' (u.d., c. 8 March 1930), p. 4: IOR L/E/9/471, India Office Records, British Library, London [hereafter, IOR].

[43] Ibid.

because it was more the sort of forum 'to whom the British view of the law might well commend itself'.[44]

In advance of the conference, the British established an interdepartmental committee to advise the Cabinet on the approach to take during the negotiations. This committee took the view that if they conceded the principle of the three-mile limit, an unstoppable deluge of new claims would follow, to the detriment of British naval operations, freight shipping and long-distance fishing. Treasury solicitor Maurice Gwyer wrote:

> It is a matter of importance both to the Navy and to the Mercantile Marine that territorial waters should be as small in area as possible; British security in time of war depends on sea power, and in foreign waters British sea power cannot be exercised; British merchant ships ply their trade on all seas, and their interests lie in the utmost possible restriction of the areas in which any measure of control may be exercised by coastal States. Furthermore, as the population of this country consumes large quantities of fish . . . it is to the interests of this country that the foreign waters from which our fishing vessels are excluded shall be as small in area as possible.[45]

The problem, of course, was that this three-mile limit was not universally acknowledged. On the one hand, a score of states, including Belgium, Britain, France, Germany, Japan, the Netherlands and the United States, who between them commanded a global network of colonies, dominions and dependencies, had by the turn of the century adopted this narrow limit. [46] On the other hand, some of the smaller independent states – especially in Scandinavia and Latin America – were as likely to claim four- or six-mile territorial waters as they were to claim three. As Britain's global authority started to recede, as European security began to disintegrate, and as the use and exploitation of the oceans accelerated, adherence to three miles loosened, even among the powers. Some

[44] Ibid., pp. 4, 5.

[45] M. L. Gwyer, 'Interdepartmental committee on the codification of international law: final report' (u.d., c. 21 January 1930), p. 2: IOR L/E/9/471, IOR.

[46] G. J. Mangone, *Law for the world ocean – Tagore law lectures* (London: Stevens & Sons, 1981), p. 22. Another author, Bernard Heinzen, stated that twenty of twenty-one states accepted a three-mile zone in 1900 – *ergo*, it was custom ('The three-mile limit, preserving the freedom of the seas', *Stanford Law Review* 11 (1959), 597–664, 597, 632–634). Yet he overlooked the claims of around a dozen Latin American states, plus those of Bulgaria, China, Ethiopia, Japan, Korea, Morocco, Persia, the Philippines, Portugal, Romania and Siam, and suggested that Sweden and Norway were three-mile claimants when in fact they claimed four miles.

smaller states sought protection by claiming wider territorial waters *and* contiguous zones to go with them.

For the British, as the leading advocate of a binary maritime world made up of just high seas and territorial waters beyond internal waters, claims to contiguous zones were almost as unwelcome as claims to wider territorial waters. One reason was tactical: recognition of the contiguous zone would inevitably lead to more extensive jurisdictional claims. Another was practical: the Admiralty wished to avoid situations in which a foreign state could establish a contiguous zone to 'prevent . . . interference with its security by foreign ships' – interference, this note implied, being the Royal Navy's stock-in-trade.[47] (As an indication of the scale of its activities, Royal Navy warships had made at least twenty interventions threatening or using force along the coast and in the rivers of China in 1927 alone.[48])

Of all the British government departments concerned with maritime affairs, the Board of Trade, custodian of Britain's global commerce, made the most forceful case against concessions to the idea of the contiguous zone. Its argument was that if the zone were to be recognised, it would become another weapon in the arsenal of protectionism. Norman Hill, a leading figure in the shipping industry, referenced the 1927 world economic conference's finding that import tariffs were a major barrier to free trade, and concluded that it would be disastrous if coastal states were encouraged to bring new maritime areas in behind their customs frontiers.[49] One example of this was the United States' Tariff Act, which, as well as troubling British shipping with its four-league customs zone, had raised tariffs to protect its struggling agricultural and business sector. Hill thought that rather than validating the contiguous zone, it would be better to leave issues ill-defined, or if necessary, dealt with by way of exception.[50]

The Board also feared that recognition of the contiguous zone would encourage coastal states to further discriminate against British freight carriers. As officials pointed out, Britain, including its dominions, then possessed around a third of the world's total shipping and around half of

[47] M. L. Gwyer, 'Interdepartmental committee on the codification of international law: final report' (u.d., c. 21 January 1930), p. 5: IOR L/E/9/471, IOR.
[48] J. Cable, *Gunboat diplomacy 1919–1991: political applications of limited naval force* (Basingstoke: Macmillan, 3rd ed., 1994), p. 9.
[49] N. Hill, 'Territorial waters' (7 November 1929), p. 1: FO 372/2636, TNA.
[50] Ibid., pp. 1, 2.

its ocean-going tonnage, which made it a far bigger 'target to foreign interference' than other states.[51] Yet despite the gigantic scale of Britain's operations, its commercial shipping was going through a crisis, with the freight index falling by a fifth and operating costs rising by 70 per cent in the seventeen years since 1913.[52] This was partly due to the onset of the Depression, and partly due to other states' subsidised shipping industries eating into Britain's share of the market.[53] These competitors were not above discriminating in favour of their own cargo or passenger vessels, with the Board, perhaps ignoring the beam in its own eye, giving examples:

> Before the war Germany built up her mercantile marine by diverting to her own ships a great part of the emigration stream from Eastern Europe. With the help of her so called control stations designed ostensibly to prevent the introduction of cholera into Germany, it was not difficult for her to discover that passengers intending to travel by British ships were infected persons ... After the war Italy strove to prevent her emigrants from travelling to Australia on any but Italian ships and it was only the joint action of the British, Australian and Indian governments coupled with threat of retaliation that secured for British ships equality of treatment with Italian ships in this matter. Spain and Poland have penalised our shipping and we are at this moment endeavouring to get rid of some of the flag discrimination practiced by Portugal.[54]

The recognition of the contiguous zone – covering sanitation, customs, fiscal and immigration issues – would, the Board thought, enable its European competitors to extend their 'powers of mischief' to the further disadvantage of the British shipping industry.[55]

Yet for all their opposition to the zone, the British had to proceed with caution. One reason was that they had no wish to alienate some of the others in the three-mile group, especially the United States. Another reason was their fear that if it were put to the test, an international court would side with US chief justice John Marshall, who in *Church v Hubbart* (1804) had argued that a nation's 'power to secure itself from injury may

[51] E. H. Marker, 'Jurisdiction outside territorial waters' (u.d., c. 27 March 1930), p. 2: FO 372/2638, TNA.
[52] Ibid., p. 4.
[53] N. Hill, 'Shipping subsidies as an international problem', *International Affairs* (London) 12 (1933), 327, 339.
[54] E. H. Marker, 'Jurisdiction outside territorial waters' (u.d., c. 27 March 1930), p. 3: FO 372/2638, TNA.
[55] Ibid.

certainly be exercised beyond the limits of its territory'.[56] A final reason was that Britain itself had previously made jurisdictional claims beyond its territorial limits ('e.g. under the Hovering Acts'), and it might be hard to persuade foreign governments that what was once justifiable for the British was now unjustifiable when claimed by others.[57]

The Crucial Questions

When Ramsay MacDonald's Labour Party cabinet ministers met the day before the opening of the codification conference, they considered two questions: 'Whether our delegates are to refuse to admit any claims to territorial waters exceeding 3 miles even if this should result in the Conference failing'; and 'Whether our delegates should refuse to agree to the establishment . . . of a more extended limit of jurisdiction up to 12 miles for certain purposes, such as the prevention of liquor smuggling'.[58] William Graham, the president of the Board of Trade, argued that it would be better for the conference to produce no convention on territorial waters than one that permitted expanded maritime zones.[59] Impressed by this, the Cabinet adopted an unaccommodating stance. Its decision was cabled to Maurice Gwyer, now head of the British delegation, in The Hague:

> You should adhere strongly to principle of three mile limit. Any departure whatever from this principle should be on basis of bilateral agreements subject to adequate safeguards.[60]

While this decision did not exclude special, expedient bilateral arrangements with its allies, it pre-empted the prospect of creating a multilateral convention that allowed for more extensive maritime claims. In the Cabinet view, it would have to be either a three-mile limit without a contiguous zone, or no convention at all.

When the conference committee began its work, Gilbert Gidel, the French delegate and authority on the law of the sea, suggested for

[56] M. L. Gwyer, 'Interdepartmental committee on the codification of international law: final report' (u.d., c. 21 January 1930), p. 4: IOR L/E/9/471, IOR (quoting, not entirely accurately, from *Church v Hubbart* (1804) 6 US 187, 234).

[57] Ibid.

[58] UK Cabinet decision 15(30) (12 March 1930): IOR L/E/9/471, IOR.

[59] E. H. Marker, 'Jurisdiction outside territorial waters' (u.d., c. 27 March 1930), p. 1: FO 372/2638, TNA.

[60] UK Foreign Office to M. L. Gwyer (13 March 1930): IOR L/E/9/471, IOR.

precision's sake that delegates distinguish between the different shades of jurisdiction, proposing 'internal waters', 'territorial waters' and 'adjacent waters'.[61] Responding, the Colombian delegate José Luis Arango suggested that instead of 'territorial waters' they use 'national sea' or 'jurisdictional sea', while the Cuban delegate Carlos de Armenteros proposed another alternative, 'territorial sea'.[62] (The latter term appeared in the conference regulations and the final report but would not gain legal traction until the early fifties.)

Whatever the terminology, the discussion was confined to the law applicable to maritime zones during peacetime, not to issues relating to war – a deliberate adjustment of focus after states' long-standing preoccupation with the codification of the laws of naval warfare. It was understood, however, that wartime and peacetime regimes were not mutually exclusive: the peacetime law of the sea would continue to apply to relations between neutrals, and between neutrals and belligerents during conflicts. Furthermore, the breadth of territorial waters, if decided, would apply during both peace and war.[63]

The fate of the negotiations in the committee hinged on the three most important bases of discussion, covering the breadth of territorial waters and the recognition of the contiguous zone. These stated:

> **Basis of Discussion No. 3.**
> The breadth of the territorial waters under the sovereignty of the coastal State is three nautical miles.
>
> **Basis of Discussion No. 4.**
> Nevertheless, the breadth of the territorial waters under the sovereignty of the coastal State shall, in the case of the States enumerated below, be fixed as follows: – [to be endorsed by the committee]
>
> **Basis of Discussion No. 5**
> On the high seas, adjacent to its territorial waters, the coastal State may exercise the control necessary to prevent, within its territory or territorial waters, the infringement of its Customs or sanitary regulations or interference with its security by foreign ships. Such control may not be exercised more than twelve miles from the coast.[64]

61 LN, *Conference for the Codification of International Law – vol. III*, p. 30.
62 Ibid., pp. 36, 32.
63 M. L. Gwyer, 'Interdepartmental Committee on the Codification of International Law: final report' (u.d., c. 21 January 1930), p. 16: IOR L/E/9/471, IOR.
64 LN, *Conference for the Codification of International Law – vol. III*, p. 179.

Basis 3 set out the rule: three-mile territorial waters. Basis 4 set out the exception: some states could claim wider territorial waters based on 'historic right or geographical or economic necessity' if the conference agreed to their doing so.[65] Basis 5 moved beyond territorial waters, recognising a high seas zone adjacent to them, limited to twelve miles from the coast, in which states could exercise limited control over foreign vessels.

Before examining the disagreements between states about the breadth of territorial waters, there was one thing that united them: the premise that all coastal states possessed them. As Basis 1 indicated:

> A State possesses sovereignty over a belt of sea round its coasts; this belt constitutes its territorial waters.[66]

This statement set off a long discussion about the character of the state's possession of them. The Colombian José Luis Arango, for example, portrayed the state's authority in territorial waters as a kind of jurisdiction short of sovereignty:

> Strictly speaking, the State has no 'sovereignty' over the waters of the sea around its coasts; it has only a body or group of rights over those waters, a kind of 'competence' or 'jurisdiction' (I would emphasise those two words). This competence or jurisdiction, however, necessarily accords the coastal state a certain right of ownership or dominion limited by international law, which is placed above all sovereignty.[67]

Others stressed that the state *did* possess sovereignty over territorial waters, exactly as Basis 1 stated. Maurice Gwyer, for example, expressed his surprise that the word 'sovereignty' had 'occasioned such terror' among the forty sovereign states in attendance.[68] He did not share their fears because he assumed that they all agreed that the state exerted precisely the same rights over territorial waters as those exercised over its land territory (territorial waters being 'subject, of course, to such reservations as may be prescribed hereafter in the Convention').[69] Implicit in this view was the idea that the possession of territorial waters sprang from sovereignty, a state being no more able to abdicate its

[65] M. L. Gwyer, 'Interdepartmental committee on the codification of international law: final report' (u.d., c. 21 January 1930), p. 2: IOR L/E/9/471, IOR.
[66] LN, *Conference for the Codification of International Law – vol. III*, p. 179.
[67] Ibid., p. 36.
[68] Ibid., p. 37.
[69] Ibid.

command over them than over its land territory. As the Egyptian delegate Abdel Hamid Badawi said, 'I do not think . . . that a State could conceivably refuse to admit that it has sovereignty over its own territorial waters.'[70]

Un-splendid Isolation

In the conference committee, it was clear that states would find it difficult to agree on bases 3, 4 and 5 on the breadth of territorial waters and the contiguous zone, so the discussion of these was postponed until after most of the other bases (on passage, ports, bays, islands, straits and more) had been considered. By the end of March, halfway through the negotiations, the German committee chair M. Göppert decided it was time to grasp the nettle. He invited delegates from 'the more important Powers' – among them, Britain, France and Italy – to a private meeting to consider territorial waters.[71] After this discussion, Gwyer thought that the chance of reaching agreement was remote, especially with the Italians:

> The French would, I think, be willing to admit the Scandinavian claim [to four-mile territorial waters] as an exceptional case, provided that no other exceptions were made; but the attitude of the Italian Delegation, who demand a belt of six miles for all purposes, has hitherto been a fatal obstacle. The Italian Delegation have tentatively suggested a six mile belt for the whole of the Mediterranean.[72]

The matter was sent back to the committee, where the issue was finally discussed on 3 April 1930. At the start of this meeting, the Italian delegate Amedeo Giannini – backed by Greece, Portugal, Spain, Sweden and Yugoslavia – tried to force a vote on territorial waters, offering a choice between three or six miles, the principle of the latter being 'not three miles'.[73] After an inconclusive discussion, this move was eventually blocked by the Japanese delegate Mushanokōji Kintomo, who suggested that instead of taking a vote, each delegation should simply state their nation's view on the breadth of territorial waters.[74] The ensuing discussion revealed with brutal clarity that the British could not command a

[70] Ibid., p. 23.
[71] M. L. Gwyer to UK Foreign Office (1 April 1930), p. 5: IOR L/E/9/471, IOR.
[72] Ibid., pp. 5–6.
[73] LN, *Conference for the Codification of International Law – vol. III*, p. 119.
[74] Ibid., p. 123.

simple majority, never mind the required two-thirds, for the three-mile limit.

The approach of the latter was based on two connected premises: that the breadth of territorial waters should be restricted to three miles, and that this should apply uniformly to all. Gwyer might simply have stated, as he did in an internal report, that the three-mile limit was 'the one and only rule which international law recognises or which it should recognise'.[75] But in the committee, in the face of abundant evidence to the contrary, he had to choose his words more carefully. He explained that three miles was the minimum viable breadth for territorial waters: no 'civilised' nation, as he put it, had ever claimed it should be less.[76] And while he did not know much about the origin of the rule, it was certainly of long standing:

> It has been said, in my own country that the rules of the common law, as distinguished from those of Acts of Parliament, find their ultimate origin in the bosom of God. I am not prepared to make so high a claim as that for the three-mile rule, but I do say that it is a rule now of very respectable antiquity.[77]

He argued that over the centuries the three-mile limit had acquired 'growing support from the great majority of maritime nations',[78] and that this group now possessed around 80 per cent of the world's shipping tonnage.[79] As a result, 'the general concurrence of the maritime nations of the world is a matter which I think cannot reasonably be left out of account'.[80] His hint that the views of those possessing the greatest shipping tonnage should be accorded special consideration earned him a sharp rebuke from the next speaker, Amedeo Giannini, who said: 'I am quite aware of the size of the British Empire and of the United States, but . . . [h]ere, we believe in the equality of States, so that the British case is worth no more than my own.'[81]

Another British premise was that all territorial waters should be of the same uniform breadth. Gwyer did not make much of a case for this in

[75] M. L. Gwyer, 'Interdepartmental committee on the codification of international law: final report' (u.d., c. 21 January 1930), p. 2: IOR L/E/9/471, IOR.
[76] LN, *Conference for the Codification of International Law – vol. III*, p. 140.
[77] Ibid.
[78] Ibid.
[79] Ibid., pp. 140–141.
[80] Ibid., p. 141.
[81] Ibid., p. 142.

committee, merely stating that if every nation were able to choose their own breadth, it 'would produce a state of chaos, and the codification of international law on this subject would go backwards rather than forwards'.[82] But other states, pointing to Basis 4, disagreed. What was stopping them from fixing the limit of their territorial waters according to their own circumstances, provided it was within the limits of reasonableness and in conformity with international law? Norway, claiming four miles, argued that it was 'neither possible nor desirable' to fix a uniform breadth,[83] while Sweden, also claiming four miles, stated that a uniform breadth could only justly be imposed on states whose circumstances were the same.[84] Yugoslavia, claiming six miles, proposed that every state should have the right to fix the limit up to a maximum of six miles.[85] And the USSR (whose breadth of territorial waters was unclarified, but who had claimed a twelve-mile 'marine customs area' in 1909 and a twelve-mile fishing zone in 1927),[86] suggested that the conference declare that established rights of usage, in their varied forms, should not be overturned.[87]

At the conclusion of the debate, the British Admiralty's representative, W. H. Hancock, totted up the various countries' positions. Eleven states supported the three-mile limit without a contiguous zone, these being Britain; its dominions Australia, Canada, the Irish Free State and South Africa; its colony India; plus China, Denmark, Greece, Japan and the Netherlands (with around half prepared to support a zone if necessary).[88] Eight more states claimed three-mile territorial waters plus a contiguous zone: Belgium, Chile, Egypt, Estonia, France, Germany, Poland and the United States.[89] Four Scandinavian states – Finland, Iceland, Norway and Sweden – claimed four-miles with or without a contiguous zone. And twelve states, almost all from Latin America and the south and east of Europe, claimed six miles with or without a contiguous zone, these being Brazil, Colombia, Cuba, Italy, Latvia, Persia, Portugal, Romania, Spain,

82 Ibid., p. 20.
83 LN, *Conference for the Codification of International Law – bases of discussion – vol. II – territorial waters*, C.74.M.39 (1929), p. 30.
84 LN, *Conference for the Codification of International Law – vol. III*, p. 137.
85 Ibid., p. 145.
86 'Russian territorial waters' (14 December 1953), pp. 2, 3: FO 371/1665, TNA.
87 W. H. Hancock, 'Report on international conference' (u.d., c. May 1930), p. 9: FO 372/2639, TNA.
88 Ibid., p. 8.
89 Ibid.

Turkey, Uruguay and Yugoslavia.[90] (Hancock did not here mention the USSR, but a later report indicated that the Soviet delegate supported those states claiming more than three miles.[91])

Hancock concluded from this that while it was impossible for Britain to secure the required two-thirds of the vote for three-mile territorial waters without a contiguous zone, it might have been possible to round up enough votes for three-mile territorial waters plus a contiguous zone.[92] This seems very doubtful: with nineteen likely supporters among forty delegations, Britain still would have had to find at least five or six votes from among the Scandinavian four-milers (some of whom had claimed four miles for longer than Britain had claimed three) and the impoverished six-milers (who would lose half their breadth if they reverted to three), as well as relying on abstentions and no-shows to make up the numbers. What the figures really showed, as the Belgian jurist Charles de Visscher would later note, was that the three-mile limit had been 'shattered'.[93] The question was, what would take its place?

The Allure of the Contiguous Zone

The debate about the contiguous zone proved just as contentious. The central question was whether the zone's features were derived primarily from the high seas or from territorial waters. The British position was that waters beyond three miles were high seas, except where a bilateral treaty recognised an exception (the Liquor Convention, for example). But as Gilbert Gidel was at pains to point out, the zone was also determined by its relationship with the coastal state. For one thing, it could be defined as an adjunct to territorial waters, hence Gidel's proposal that the contiguous zone be called 'adjacent waters'. For another, it met the state's need to prevent or punish infringements of certain laws or regulations committed, or expected to be committed, *within its sovereign domain*. These enforcement rights were restricted – Gidel stated that a nation 'only enjoys special, limited and incomplete rights for particular purposes'[94] – but even so, contiguous zones were being put to more uses

90 Ibid., p. 9.

91 'Russian territorial waters' (14 December 1953), p. 4: FO 371/1665, TNA.

92 W. H. Hancock, 'Report on international conference' (u.d., c. May 1930), p. 9: FO 372/2639, TNA.

93 C. de Visscher, and P. E. Corbett (trans.), *Theory and reality in public international law* (Princeton, NJ: Princeton University Press, 2015), p. 212.

94 LN, *Conference for the Codification of International Law – vol. III*, p. 31.

in 1930 than were later permitted, allowing not only for the prevention and punishment of infringements of customs, fiscal, immigration or sanitary laws and regulations,[95] but also for the protection of national security and the conservation of fish stocks.

In 1930, the delegates expressed most interest of all in using the contiguous zone as a buffer against the ultimate threat to national integrity – military assault. Fears of another war hung heavy over the proceedings, and allusions to the rights of neutrals percolated through the committee's debates.[96] Gwyer reported that national defence 'seemed to be at the back of the minds of most of the Delegates who spoke', and especially the French, 'who are preoccupied with the question of [incursions from] the air'.[97] He also suggested that instead of calling for security zones, states facing imminent danger should rely instead on the doctrine of self-defence; after all, 'no country in the world would criticise that State for going beyond its territorial waters in order to repel that attack'.[98]

Yet states were already claiming security zones during this period, and they fell into two distinct clusters. One cluster was made up of independent but vulnerable non-European states who considered themselves at risk of incursions by the maritime powers. They already included Chile, Ecuador and Honduras, who each claimed four marine leagues within which to maintain state security and enforce fiscal regulations;[99] plus El Salvador, who joined them in 1933;[100] China, who in 1931 claimed twelve miles ostensibly to prevent smuggling but in fact 'to put a stop to Japanese vessels continually entering Chinese territorial waters';[101] and Persia, who in 1934 claimed twelve miles for the execution 'of laws and agreements relating to security, defence and national interests and for the preservation of shipping routes'.[102] Another cluster of states claiming

95 Article 24(1)(a), Convention on the Territorial Sea and the Contiguous Zone [hereafter, Territorial Sea Convention] (signed 29 April 1958, EIF 10 September 1964) 516 UNTS 205, 220; and article 33(1), UNCLOS, 409.

96 See the comments of the Swedish and Portuguese delegates: LN, *Conference for the Codification of International Law – vol. III*, pp. 129, 138.

97 M. L. Gwyer to UK Foreign Office (12 April 1930), p. 8: IOR L/E/9/471, IOR.

98 Ibid., p. 141.

99 H. K. Grey, 'Annex no. 2: claims of various states to limits beyond territorial waters for special purposes' (1 January 1937), pp. 56, 58 and 63: ADM 116/5709, TNA.

100 Ibid., pp. 68–69.

101 Ibid., p. 56.

102 Ibid., p. 68. (Earlier, in 1929, minister of court Abdolhossein Teymourtash handed the British representative a draft law proclaiming an eight-mile zone that would subject

security zones consisted of insecure European nations, including France (who had imposed peacetime restrictions in 1913 on warships within six miles and in 1928 on aircraft in the vicinity of naval ports),[103] Italy (who in 1912 declared a peacetime zone of ten miles)[104] and Poland (who in 1932 claimed a six-mile belt for coastal defence).[105] The delegates of Finland, Latvia and Romania were tempted to follow suit because they were troubled by Soviet warships conducting exercises just outside their territorial waters, thereby impeding access to navigable channels into their ports and rivers.[106]

An emerging trend among states was to claim a contiguous zone to regulate fishing and thereby conserve fish stocks. At the conference, Portugal and Denmark, supported by the Irish Free State, insisted on rights beyond their territorial waters to control trawling, which, they observed, had a particularly destructive effect on fish fry.[107] The Danish delegate V. L. Lorck, for example, wanted to insert the phrase 'or fry-protection,' into Basis 5, so that its purposes included 'customs, *or fry-protection*, or sanitary regulations or interference with its security by foreign ships'.[108] As the British noted, states were not directly claiming *exclusive* fishing rights, but rather couching their claims as the right to regulate the method and amount of fishing that took place in the contiguous zone in order to conserve fish stocks for all.[109] And when responding to these proposals, the British, keeping in mind their own large trawling industry, insisted that the question of conservation be shelved on the grounds that it was a fisheries question, and therefore beyond the remit of the committee.[110]

vessels to police supervision including quarantine checks, saying: 'There was no divine law . . . to prevent a microbe being carried on a warship': R. H. Clive to A. Chamberlain (25 February 1929), p. 1: FO 371/13773, TNA.)

103 Ibid., pp. 61, 62.

104 United Nations Law of the Sea Conference, 1960 [hereafter, UNLOSC II], vol. 1, A/Conf.19/4 (8 February 1960), p. 160.

105 H. K. Grey, 'Annex no. 2: claims of various states to limits beyond territorial waters for special purposes' (1 January 1937), p. 68: ADM 116/5709, TNA.

106 W. H. Hancock, 'Report on international conference' (u.d., c. May 1930), p. 13: FO 372/2639, TNA.

107 See comments by the Danish and Irish Free State delegates: LN, *Conference for the Codification of International Law – vol. III*, pp. 25, 26.

108 Ibid., p. 25. Emphasis added.

109 W. H. Hancock, 'Report on international conference' (u.d., c. May 1930), p. 13: FO 372/2639, TNA.

110 Ibid., pp. 13–14.

These claims to a fishing zone stretched the concept of a contiguous zone. Instead of using the zone to enforce laws pertaining to the sovereign domain, claimant states were now addressing issues arising from the contiguous zone itself. As Edwin Dickinson noted in 1926:

> Fishery regulations are unlike revenue legislation in that they are intended to conserve and protect an interest in the sea itself. Fishery zones are claimed for what they contain in resources and not primarily as a means of territorial security.[111]

Later, as will be seen, the contiguous zone and the fishing zone would be separated, with the fishing zone evolving into the exclusive economic zone.

When Gwyer delivered his speech on the contiguous zone, he stated in accordance with his instructions that his government opposed its universal application because it would entail too great an incursion into the high seas, although exceptions could be admitted by bilateral agreement in 'special and peculiar circumstances'.[112] The responses from other delegates showed how isolated Britain was on the issue, with almost all stating their support for some kind of contiguous zone. Even delegates from British dependencies such as India and South Africa wobbled on the issue.[113] Gwyer thus found himself stranded on the rock of British intransigence as new ideas swept past him, while Hancock, who observed the debate, reported to the Admiralty:

> It would in fact appear that we stand practically alone in declining to recognise any general right of control outside territorial waters . . . Other countries differ as to the extent of this control, the purpose for which it is to be exercised, and to what distance, but there is undoubtedly almost complete agreement that some such general right exists, and, more emphatically, that it is necessary.[114]

I'm Alone Again

The case of *I'm Alone*, which addressed the reach and rights exercised from within a contiguous zone, had been proceeding at a glacial pace.

111 E. D. Dickinson, 'Jurisdiction at the maritime frontier', *Harvard Law Review* 40 (1926), 1, 15.
112 LN, *Conference for the Codification of International Law – vol. III*, p. 126.
113 Ibid., pp. 25, 130.
114 W. H. Hancock to A. Flint (6 April 1930), p. 5: FO 372/2639, TNA.

In the early stages, the British had advised the Canadians to drag their heels because they feared that if the two commissioners found against the United States, Washington might renounce the Liquor Convention, which gave British shipping the special right to move alcohol through American waters.[115] Whether for this reason or others, the commissioners did not produce their interim report until 1933, and their final report until 1935, nearly six years after the schooner had gone down. By then, Prohibition had been lifted, which removed Britain's own rationale for adhering to the Liquor Convention: it no longer enjoyed any special rights, while the Americans retained the right to board its ships for suspected non-payment of duties.[116]

Interested parties paid close attention to the discussion of the right of hot pursuit at the codification conference. Although the case was *sub judice* between Canada and the United States, the issues it raised inevitably seeped into the discussion. Hancock reported:

> In view of the 'I'm Alone' case, special interest was aroused by a proposal by the Finland delegate, supported by the French, that the same right of pursuit should apply in an 'adjacent [contiguous] zone'. This was opposed by the British and Canadian delegations in emphatic terms. The United States did not take part in this discussion and the question was dropped on the understanding that the Finnish proposal would be merely recorded in the minutes and not in the Report. No other course was possible at that stage as it had not been agreed to insert any draft article which recognised the existence of an 'adjacent zone'.[117]

Clearly the delegates could not agree on whether a hot pursuit could be commenced from the contiguous zone. There was, however, consensus over some of the other conditions governing a pursuit. The Danish delegate V. L. Lorck put forward an amendment suggesting that before it commenced, the patrol vessel must establish by 'bearings, sextant angles, or other like means' that the suspect vessel was within territorial waters.[118] And the American delegate suggested adding a reference to boats associated with the suspect vessel[119] – an acknowledgement of the constructive presence of a mothership that remains on the high sea while dispatching its

115 G. Thompson minute (2 April 1929): FO 371/13513, TNA.

116 P. R., 'Memorandum: the future of the Liquor Convention' (14 November 1933), p. 2: FO 371/16602, TNA.

117 W. H. Hancock, 'Report on international conference' (u.d., c. May 1930), p. 33: FO 372/2639, TNA.

118 Ibid., pp. 32, 33.

119 Ibid., p. 33.

boats to operate inside another state's territorial waters. (A case in point was the *Tenyu Maru*, a Japanese schooner arrested when its boat was found taking seals within the United States' waters off Alaska in 1909.[120])

The Danish amendment also specified that the patrol vessel had to get close enough to give the suspect vessel an audible or visible signal to stop (wireless transmission not being sufficient),[121] and that the suspect vessel had to be within territorial waters when sighted and signalled to stop, whereas the patrol vessel did not.[122] Lorck explained why this was necessary when patrolling a coastal fishery:

> Inspection usually takes place along the line and outside the line [of territorial waters], because as soon as the trawler sees the inspection ship, he cuts his fishing-gear and goes outside the line. It nearly always happens, therefore, that they have to be taken outside the line.[123]

These Danish proposals would reappear in the 1958 high seas convention and the 1982 UN law of the sea convention.[124]

*

Returning to the *I'm Alone* case, the commissioners did not reach either 'agreement or disagreement' on the central question of whether American coastguard vessels had the right of hot pursuit outside territorial waters but inside treaty limits.[125] Instead, they worked on the assumption that the right existed, but agreed that the intentional sinking of the schooner was not justified either by the Liquor Convention or by any principle of international law.[126] They therefore ordered the United States to apologise and make a 'material amend' of US$25,000 to Canada, as well as paying compensation to crew members or their representatives, including the family of the deceased French national, Leon Mainguy.[127]

Another aspect of the case concerned the amount of force a state could use to apprehend a vessel subject to a hot pursuit. The Liquor

120 *The Tenyu Maru* (1910) 4 Alaska Reports 129.

121 W. H. Hancock, 'Report on international conference' (u.d., c. May 1930), pp. 32–33: FO 372/2639, TNA.

122 Ibid., p. 32.

123 LN, *Conference for the Codification of International Law – vol. III*, p. 100.

124 Article 23, Convention on the High Seas [hereafter, High Seas Convention] (signed 29 April 1958, EIF 30 September 1962) 450 UNTS 82, 94–96; and article 111, UNCLOS, 439–440.

125 *SS 'I'm Alone' (Canada/United States)* (1933) III RIAA 1609, 1614.

126 Ibid., 1617.

127 Ibid., 1618.

Convention had referred to 'improper or unreasonable' exercise of rights relating to the interception and seizure of suspect vessels, but instead of trying to reverse this formula, the commissioners (following *Church v Hubbart*[128]) instead decided that compulsion had to be '*necessary* and reasonable'. They considered the possibility that

> the United States might, consistently with the Convention, use necessary and reasonable force for the purpose of effecting the objects of boarding, searching, seizing and bringing into port the suspected vessel; and if sinking should occur *incidentally*, as a result of the exercise of necessary and reasonable force for such purpose, the pursuing vessel might be entirely blameless.[129]

They found, however, that in the case of *I'm Alone*, 'the admittedly intentional sinking of the suspected vessel was not justified by anything in the Convention'.[130]

Shortly afterwards, one of the British legal advisers, Gerald Fitzmaurice, protested that 'necessary' and 'reasonable' did not always coincide: 'The force which is necessary to achieve an object is not necessarily reasonable force, unless it be admitted that the object is one which the party trying to achieve it is entitled to achieve at all costs – the very conclusion which the Commissioners negatived.'[131] But the formula stuck. Seventy years after the sinking of *I'm Alone*, the International Tribunal for the Law of the Sea referred to 'reasonable and necessary' force when deciding the 1999 case of *M/V 'Saiga'*,[132] which involved Guinean patrol-boat officers firing indiscriminately as they boarded the St Vincent and the Grenadines-registered oil tanker, seriously injuring two crew members. The tribunal held that even if force was necessary as a last resort, 'appropriate warning must be issued to the ship and all efforts should be made to ensure that life is not endangered'.[133]

'A Capital Mistake'

In 1930, the territorial waters committee's negotiations stalled because the British could not compel other states to accept three-mile territorial waters,

128 *Church v Hubbart* (1804) 6 US 187, 235.
129 *SS 'I'm Alone' (Canada/United States)* (1933 and 1935) III RIAA 1609, 1615, 1617. Emphasis added.
130 Ibid.
131 G. G. Fitzmaurice, 'The case of the *I'm Alone*', *British Year Book of International Law* 17 (1936), 82, 99.
132 *M/V 'Saiga' (No. 2) (St Vincent and the Grenadines v Guinea)* (Judgment) [1999] ITLOS Rep 10 [155].
133 Ibid., [156].

and the other states could not compel the British to accept a contiguous zone. The American delegate David Hunter Miller eventually proposed that delegates abandon the idea of producing a convention and instead produce a final report summarising the committee's work.[134] This was agreed. The report, written by the Dutch rapporteur J. P. A. François, set out thirteen non-binding draft articles relating to some, but not all, of the issues discussed in the committee, as an invitation to further discussion.[135]

Upon his return to London from The Hague, Maurice Gwyer proved to be almost wilfully unreflective about the committee's failure to reach agreement. The problem, he wrote, was that there was not enough time for discussion. Had the conference been longer and had delegates spent less time on secondary issues, they would have eventually reached agreement, at least on baselines and some of the other 'technical' questions.[136] This claim sidestepped the essential problem: *Pax Britannica* was over. As a Foreign Office official would put it years later: 'The real force behind a legal system which kept maritime limits narrow was naval power'; and that if the law governing territorial waters was in flux, 'I think we must accept the fact that the ultimate cause is the relative decline of British naval power'.[137]

Four years after the conference broke up, Gilbert Gidel published a piece in *Recueil des cours* in which he argued that the British might have won endorsement for three-mile territorial waters in the proposed treaty if only they had been prepared to accept the contiguous zone as part of the package.[138] It must be said that this conclusion does not seem to be borne out by Gidel's tallies of the various states' positions, which put the number of states supporting the plain three-mile position even lower than Hancock's figures, at nine states.[139] Nevertheless, Gidel's message was absorbed, however reluctantly, and Whitehall eventually came around to the same view.[140]

[134] LN, *Conference for the Codification of International Law – vol. III*, p. 147.
[135] Ibid., annex V, appendix 1, pp. 212–217.
[136] Draft, 'Meeting of the Inter-departmental Committee on Territorial Waters' (u.d., c. May 1930), p. 1: FCO 372/2640, TNA.
[137] 'Attitude of Her Majesty's Government towards the I.L.C.'s deliberations' (u.d., c. May 1952), p. 1: LCO 2/5783, TNA.
[138] G. Gidel, 'La mer territoriale et la zone contiguë', *Recueil des cours de l'Académie de Droit International de la Haye* 48 (1934), 133, 190, 192.
[139] Ibid., 189.
[140] UK Foreign Office to UK Embassy Washington (19 May 1950), p. 2: CO 323/1926/1, TNA.

In 1950, with the wisdom of hindsight, the Foreign Office notified the British embassy in Washington of a shift in their position over the contiguous zone:

> It is now thought that at the Hague Conference in 1930, His Majesty's Government made a very bad error of tactics. There were, before the Conference, drafts which had a great deal of support, which (1) prescribed three miles breadth of territorial waters and (2) admitted a contiguous zone, outside the three mile limit in which the lit[t]oral State could exercise jurisdiction over foreign shipping to the extent necessary to protect its revenue and fiscal interests.[141]

They concluded that their predecessors had made 'a capital mistake' by not conceding a contiguous zone to protect their greater interest in three-mile territorial waters,[142] and no longer saw any objection to accepting claims to contiguous zones provided that they were limited in scope and jurisdiction.[143] This, they hoped, might enable them in the future to salvage the three-mile limit from the wreckage of the 1930 conference.

[141] Ibid.
[142] Ibid.
[143] Ibid.

2

Old Freedoms, New Rights

The Corfu Channel *and* Fisheries *Cases*

Two landmark cases heard before the International Court of Justice would move the debate forward after the Second World War and exert a strong influence over the law of the sea conventions that followed. The court's inaugural contentious case, *Corfu Channel* (1949), and a follow-up, *Fisheries* (1951), could be seen as two halves of a whole: one considering straits used for international navigation and the other, baselines marking the start of the territorial sea. Both cases were initiated by Britain, both were presided over by much the same bench, and both were prompted by a state's attempt to exclude foreign vessels from its coastal waters (warships in one case, trawlers in the other). Together, it is possible to discern from them the outlines of an approach to the law of the sea that attempted to preserve traditional freedoms of navigation while also recognising coastal states' expanded jurisdictional claims over resources.

The first case, *Corfu Channel*, addressed a series of incidents that took place just as the Cold War was escalating. On 22 October 1946, four British warships – the cruisers *Leander* and *Mauritius* and the destroyers *Saumarez* and *Volage* – sailed through the North Corfu channel, a narrow body of water between Albania and the Greek island of Corfu. When *Saumarez* struck a contact-mine, the explosion destroyed the starboard side of the ship, and threw up a large red flame and a plume of black smoke.[1] Dozens of crew members died from burns caused by fuel fires aboard the vessel and on the surface of the surrounding water.[2] When *Volage* went to the assistance of *Saumarez*, it too hit a contact-

[1] For an account of the incident see: Cruiser Squadron 1 to Commander-in-chief Mediterranean (22 October 1946): PREM 8/406, TNA; and Commander-in-chief Mediterranean to Admiralty (23 October 1946): ADM 116/5540, TNA.

[2] Surgeon Lt-Commander *et al.* to Commander-in-chief Mediterranean (8 November 1946), enclosure nos. 4, 5 and 6: ADM 116/5542, TNA.

mine: the explosion blew off its bows,[3] and more people were killed, this time by flying debris. After jettisoning topweight including two torpedoes,[4] *Volage* towed *Saumarez* back to Corfu. In all, forty-four crew members lost their lives.

This was just one of three sorties that British warships made through the North Corfu channel in 1946, and for connected reasons. On the first occasion, on 15 May, the British sent through two cruisers, *Orion* and *Superb*, whereupon they were fired on (but not hit) by Albanian shore batteries. On the second occasion, on 22 October, they sent the squadron of warships through the channel, when *Samaurez* and *Volage* hit the sea-mines. On the third occasion, on 12–13 November, the British dispatched minesweepers to clear the channel of mines and collect evidence for their forthcoming complaint against Albania.

The political context was highly significant. With the Cold War afoot, the Adriatic region was a tinderbox. Greece, straddling the fault-line between East and West, had from the March 1946 elections onwards been convulsed by a civil war between right-wing government forces backed by Britain and the United States, and Greek communist party insurgents backed by Albania, Bulgaria and Yugoslavia. This conflict radiated outwards beyond the nation's borders. As rear-admiral A. G. Talbot, the senior British naval officer in Greece, explained,

> The recent bandit [communist] operations in Western *Macedonia* have been mounted from bases in *Yugoslavia* and are now recognised as a prelude to the attempted seizure of that area. The pretext would be the restoration of law and order after the uprising of the *Greek* nation against its 'pro-*British* monarcho-fascist rulers' . . . In the case of such attack, the only *Slav* frontier open to prompt counter attack is the *Adriatic* Sea frontier. Neither *Yugoslavia* nor *Albania* have any naval units which could offer satisfactory resistance to the ships of the *Greek* navy [under de facto British command], nor are their air forces adequate to do so; so that in the event of war with *Greece* the whole of their *Adriatic* flank would be open to amphibious attack unless defended by guns and mines.[5]

The significance of the North Corfu channel was more political than commercial – almost all vessels moving between the Adriatic and Ionian seas passed through the Strait of Otranto on the other side of Corfu.

[3] Ibid., pp. 5, 8.
[4] Ibid., p. 5.
[5] A. G. Talbot, 'Mining of the North Corfu Channel' (27 January 1947), p. 2: ADM 116/5654, TNA. Original emphases.

Pierre Cot, the French counsel for Albania in the court case that followed, pointed out that during the war, the Germans had used the channel to avoid the larger straits, which were controlled by the Allies; then, after the Germans had departed the region in 1944, it was used by states interested in monitoring those on the opposite side of the East–West divide.[6] By 1946, the channel had acquired its greatest importance as part of the border between Albania and Greece, between whom, Cot said, there was high tension, with Greece declaring itself to be 'technically' at war with Albania.[7] The fact that the British – a far from disinterested party in the conflict – had on three occasions dispatched warships through the channel did little to reduce this friction.

Straight after the mining of *Saumarez*, the Porto Edda harbour master appeared close to *Volage*, before it too was mined, in a motor launch flying both an Albanian and a white flag.[8] He shouted out in Italian: 'What are you doing?'[9] The British naval officers on *Volage*, not understanding Italian, instructed a Maltese petty officer to answer that they could not reply because 'there is a ship sinking and we have got to help her'.[10] This same question – what were these warships doing in the channel? – would keep bubbling to the surface throughout the ensuing discussions.

Targeting Albania

When the British were considering raising their complaint against Albania in the Security Council, they thought they had a good case so long as they focussed exclusively on the damage and casualties caused by the mining of *Saumarez* and *Volage*. The problem, however, was that they did not know who had laid the mines. After eliciting strong denials from the Greeks, and ruling out Zionist organisations, they surmised that responsibility probably rested with Albania acting in concert with Yugoslavia, which possessed minelayers and stocks of German mines left over from the war. But although the British suspected both countries, they had a motive for singling out Albania. On legal grounds, they could argue that irrespective

6 *Corfu Channel (United Kingdom v Albania)* (Pleadings) [1950] ICJ Pleadings III 166, 346.

7 Ibid., 347.

8 Surgeon Lt-Commander *et al.* to Commander-in-chief Mediterranean (8 November 1946), p. 7: ADM 116/5542, TNA.

9 Ibid.

10 Ibid.

of who had laid the mines, the Albanians must have known of their presence along their shoreline and had therefore unlawfully failed to warn passing ships. And on political grounds, they hoped to use the 22 October incident – cast as a breach of the peace in violation of the UN Charter – as a reason for refusing Albania's application to join the United Nations.

After exchanges of diplomatic notes between London and Tirana, the British submitted to the UN secretary-general a formal complaint against Albania on 10 January 1947, citing article 35 of the Charter.[11] Rather than raising legal issues, they concentrated instead on the threat the Albanians' unfriendly conduct posed to international peace. (Foreign secretary Ernest Bevin insisted that the British not get 'bogged down' in legal discussions about innocent passage in case Soviet deputy foreign minister Andrei Vyshinsky presented the Royal Navy's actions as justifying Albania's countermeasures.)[12]

But when the British UN mission in New York were preparing the presentation to the Security Council, they were troubled by a now familiar question: what *were* the four British warships doing in the North Corfu Channel? Admiralty officials explained that the real reason for the squadron's passage was 'to test Albanian reactions' after the first incident on 15 May involving *Orion* and *Superb*, but suggested that they should avoid mention of this; rather, they should say that it was just passing through to 'rendezvous later on with rest of the Fleet at Argostoli for the Fleet regatta'.[13] This was not a convincing explanation: as one official acknowledged, 'Our weakest point is to explain why the ships from Corfu bound for Argostoli [to the south] went [north] through the North Corfu channel at all'[14] – but it would have to do.

On 25 March 1947, the British followed up their complaint against Albania with a resolution stating that the Security Council:

> (1) Considers that the laying of mines in peace time without notification is unjustified and an offence against humanity:-
> (2) Finds that an unnotified minefield was laid in the Corfu Straits ... which cannot have been laid *without the knowledge of the Albanian government*:-[15]

[11] A. Cadogan to UN secretary-general (10 February 1947): FO 961/2, TNA.
[12] G. G. Fitzmaurice, 'Corfu incident' (24 November 1946), p. 1: ADM 116/5542, TNA.
[13] Admiralty via UK Foreign Office to UK Mission to the UN (10 January 1947): ADM 116/5654, TNA.
[14] A. J. Le Maitre (10 January 1947): ADM 116/5654, TNA.
[15] 'The Corfu Channel dispute' (u.d., c. May 1947), p. 5: FO 961/2, TNA. Original emphasis.

This motion was vetoed by the USSR. After that, as Foreign Office permanent undersecretary Orme Sargent noted, 'there was really no other course open to us than to propose that the case should go to the International Court, unless we were prepared to accept a stalemate resulting from the Russian veto'.[16] They were not, so they tabled another resolution on 3 April proposing that the dispute be referred to the International Court of Justice.[17] This carried and the case went to The Hague.

*

As a prelude, the two parties concluded a special agreement to submit their dispute to the court, requesting its decision on two questions:

> (1) Is Albania responsible under international law for the explosions which occurred on the 22nd October 1946 in Albanian waters and for the damage and loss of human life which resulted from them and is there any duty to pay compensation?
> (2) Has the United Kingdom under international law violated the sovereignty of the Albanian People's Republic by reason of the acts of the Royal Navy in Albanian waters on the 22nd October and on the 12th and 13th November 1946 and is there any duty to give satisfaction?[18]

The second question, proposed by Albania, expanded the scope of the case beyond the mining of *Saumarez* and *Volage* by calling for a decision about the lawfulness of the British passage through the channel on two occasions in 1946 – one involving the squadron of warships, discussed here, and the other involving the minesweepers. These were precisely the issues that Ernest Bevin and Admiralty officials had not wanted raised but, having got the tiger by the tail, they could not let go.

In particular, the reference to 'the Royal Navy in Albanian waters' raised questions about the status of all warships' passage through other states' territorial seas. In law, warships had (and have) distinctive features, neatly summarised in the 2012 *ARA Libertad* decision: 'a warship is an expression of the sovereignty of the State whose flag it flies', and 'a warship enjoys immunity, including in internal waters'.[19] For a powerful state with an

[16] O. G. Sargent to C. R. A. Attlee (9 November 1948), p. 2: PREM 8/1312, TNA.
[17] Security Council Res. 22, S/324 (9 April 1947).
[18] Special Agreement, *Corfu Channel (United Kingdom v Albania)* (Pleadings) [1948] ICJ Pleadings 29, 29.
[19] *ARA Libertad (Argentina v Ghana)* (Provisional Measures) ITLOS (2012) ITLOS Rep 21, [94]–[95].

international reach, naval vessels, as mobile splinters of sovereignty, are especially useful as the instruments of coercive diplomacy in circumstances short of war, when the state might not wish to commit to the outright use of force. As a US Navy manual indicated in 1987,

> The international character of the high seas and the sovereign rights associated with men-of-war provide such overseas deployed naval forces with a unique ability to make U.S. military presence overseas known in crises short of conflict. This presence can be modulated to exert the degree and kind of influence best suited to resolve the situation in a manner compatible with U.S. interests.[20]

This capacity to exert influence through 'presence' sets warships apart from ground and air forces, whose actions during periods of tension are often legally restrained in accordance with the existence or otherwise of access agreements and landing rights. The manual again:

> Naval forces may be positioned near potential trouble spots without the political entanglement associated with the employment of land-based forces. Naval forces, unlike land-based forces, do not have to rely on prior international agreements before taking a position in an area of potential crisis. By loitering in the proximity of a potential or real trouble spot, naval forces communicate a capability for action which ground or air forces can duplicate only by landing or entering the sovereign air space of another nation.[21]

In court, as a prelude to the discussion about the specific events in the North Corfu channel, Pierre Cot argued that warships should not enjoy automatic passage rights through another state's territorial waters because, unlike merchant ships, they represented a threat to the state concerned. In this context, he referred to American counsel Elihu Root's argument during the 1910 *North Atlantic Coast Fisheries* arbitration that:[22]

> War-ships may not pass without consent into this zone [of territorial waters], because they threaten. Merchant-ships may pass and repass, because they do not threaten.[23]

[20] United States Department of the Navy, *Strategic concepts of the U.S. Navy*, NWP 1 (A) (Washington, DC: Naval Warfare Publications Library, 1987).

[21] Ibid.

[22] *Corfu Channel (United Kingdom v Albania)* (Pleadings) [1950] ICJ Pleadings III 166, 377.

[23] *North Atlantic Coast Fisheries (Great Britain/United States)* (Proceedings) (1910) PCA XI 1593, [1214]–[1215].

Because warships threatened, Cot argued, their presence in other states' territorial waters was on sufferance only. In periods of stability, a state might extend the privilege of innocent passage as a concession to other states, but if threatened by war or unrest, this concession could be withdrawn because 'the coastal State has the perfect right – one could even say the duty' – to restrict the movement of foreign warships through its territorial waters.[24]

The opposing argument, presented by the British agent and counsel Eric Beckett, was that warships should be treated no differently than merchant ships because navigational exigencies affected both equally, 'and it is a definite fact that for upwards of a century warships have enjoyed freedom of navigation through territorial waters on their lawful occasions in precisely the same way as merchant ships'.[25] As for their character, Beckett countered 'Mr. Root's dictum' with T. J. Lawrence's aphorism that the word 'innocent' relates to 'the character of the passage and not the quality of the ship'.[26] Finally, contrary to Cot's presentation of warships, Beckett emphasised their 'useful and humanitarian' functions during peacetime, such as suppressing slavery and piracy, safeguarding fishing zones, and acting as goodwill ambassadors.[27]

Rights and Privileges

Turning to the specific issue of the Royal Navy squadron's passage through the North Corfu Channel, the Albanian team argued on two grounds: first, that the channel was not an 'international strait' (the term used at the time) allowing warships' unrestricted innocent passage; and second, that the British warships' passage through it was not innocent.

On the channel's legal status, Cot rejected the British argument that this body of water, while overlapped by Albania's territorial waters, was an international strait through which warships lawfully exercised the right of innocent passage. While he did not deny that the channel was a strait, he contested the idea that it was an *international* strait. It was, he said, merely a 'secondary strait' that had not been legally affirmed as having international status (as had, say, the Turkish straits, governed by

[24] *Corfu Channel (United Kingdom v Albania)* (Pleadings) [1950] ICJ Pleadings III 166, 381.
[25] Ibid., 272.
[26] *Corfu Channel (United Kingdom v Albania)* (Pleadings) [1950] ICJ Pleadings IV 9, 543.
[27] Ibid.

the 1936 Montreux Convention[28]), and was not important enough to justify 'a departure from ordinary law in the matter of innocent passage of warships'.[29] Continuing the argument about its secondary status, he pointed to a map of the Adriatic, comparing the North Corfu Channel, measuring a mile across at its narrowest, to the neighbouring Strait of Otranto, measuring at least thirty-nine miles across:

> You can see ... a large maritime communication route which connects two parts of the open sea: this is the Strait of Otranto ... And then, gentlemen, if you take a close look, you will see, against the coast, the small island of Corfu and a very small dot: this is the Straight of Corfu. This [according to the British] is the great international communication channel! Voilà *l'international highway!*[30]

Having dismissed the idea that the channel was an international strait, Cot stated that during the 1946 crisis between Albania and Greece, passage through Albania's overlapping territorial waters without the required authorisation from Tirana was a violation of international law.[31] States, he said, demanded authorisation because it enabled them to discriminate between vessels based on their nationality (whether friendly states or not) and their function (whether merchant ships or warships).[32] If Britain decided to override this requirement by unilaterally asserting the 'so-called right of passage',[33] it was challenging Albania's sovereignty and thereby breaching international law. He explained:

> Let us suppose that a State makes known, through diplomatic channels or other means, to another State that, for security reasons of which it is the sole judge, it will not allow its warships to pass. Its expression of sovereign will is very clear ... The State which has been informed therefore knows exactly, as if there were regulations, the position taken by the coastal State, and it is quite obvious that if this State nevertheless dispatches its ships to the territorial waters of whoever has so warned him, it will violate the rules of international law.[34]

[28] Convention regarding the Régime of Straits [hereafter, Montreux Convention] (signed 20 July 1936, EIF provisionally on 15 August 1936 and definitively on 9 November 1936, in accordance with article 26) 173 LNTS 213.

[29] *Corfu Channel (United Kingdom v Albania)* (Pleadings) [1950] ICJ Pleadings III 166, 383.

[30] Ibid., 384.

[31] Counter-memorial of Albania, *Corfu Channel (United Kingdom v Albania)* (Pleadings) [1948] ICJ Pleadings [1], [145].

[32] *Corfu Channel (United Kingdom v Albania)* (Pleadings) [1950] ICJ Pleadings III 166, 382.

[33] Ibid., 381.

[34] Ibid.

Turning to innocence, Cot's second charge was that once the British squadron of warships had entered Albania's waters, its passage was not innocent. He proposed a simple test: if a ship did not appear threatening – if it were simply moving from one part of the high sea to another by the quickest route – then its innocence could be assumed; but if it did appear threatening, either in itself or because accompanied by other warships, its innocence could not.[35] He was thus moving beyond Root's objective position – that all warships, as the embodiments of lethal force, represented a threat – to a different and more subjective position. In Cot's view, it was the state's perception of a warship's intent, whether threatening or otherwise, that determined its innocence. A state, he continued, might deduce offensive intent from several factors: was there a whole flotilla of warships in their territorial waters; were they in combat order; did they look ready to intervene?[36] The fact that the British warships had appeared in a group of four, apparently in combat formation, with crews at action stations, suggested that their intent was not innocent. The British aim, he said, 'was not to make a passage from one point to another by the shortest route, but . . . to go to see if the Albanian government had learned to behave itself'.[37]

So, then, to the British team's position. They argued that the North Corfu channel *was* an international strait; that all vessels, including warships, enjoyed the right of innocent passage through both international straits and territorial waters; and that Albania's laying of the minefield in an international strait without notification was a violation of this right.[38] They concluded that the squadron's movement through the channel on 22 October was thus 'a normal passage through an international highway and, as such, innocent according to the law and practice of civilised nations'.[39]

When arguing that the North Corfu channel was an international strait, Eric Beckett pointed to its geographic configuration – as a route between two parts of the high seas – and to the shipping traffic that had passed through it during the interwar years. Yet when preparing the case, the British found the second claim unexpectedly difficult to substantiate. The

[35] Ibid., 387.
[36] Ibid., 388.
[37] Ibid., 395.
[38] Memorial of the United Kingdom, *Corfu Channel (United Kingdom v Albania)* [1947] ICJ Pleadings 19, [96].
[39] Ibid., [87].

Greeks, when pressed for information about the movement of vessels from Corfu, could not help much: most of their shipping records had been destroyed during the war, and they produced only a 'scrappy' list of ferry companies that had transported tourists and cargos through the channel a few times each week.[40] States further afield were even less able to assist: the French, for example, had sent just two vessels through the channel in the previous decades, in 1924 and 1932, respectively.[41] In court, Beckett made the best he could of these slim pickings by arguing that the channel was important 'both for the local traffic and for coastal traffic', and had in the past 'served an appreciable volume of general trade moving between the Eastern Mediterranean or Ægean, and ports in the North Adriatic'.[42] (He artfully left the date unspecified; he might have meant the movement of freight in the 1930s, or he might have meant Venetian trade with Butrint in 700 AD.) Furthermore, to get around the problem that traffic tended to be local, he argued that for a strait to be international 'it is enough to show that it is a route serving a particular region'.[43]

The British also argued that when traversing the North Corfu Channel, the Royal Navy squadron was simply exercising its right of innocent passage in straits – a right, Beckett said, derived from the needs of navigation.[44] In this context, he made a careful distinction between 'territorial waters forming part of a strait' and 'ordinary territorial waters'.[45] He argued that warships had 'an unqualified right of innocent passage' in the former, whereas in the latter 'the right of passage is qualified by a right of the coastal state to suspend the passage in emergency'.[46]

Having made this distinction, he conceded that in 'ordinary territorial waters' states could during a crisis impose temporary restrictions over parts of them, but not permanent restrictions over all of them, as Albania had attempted to do in 1946.[47] He also conceded that in these waters a coastal state could discriminate between warships according to their nationality, provided that any restrictions were directed only towards

[40] UK Embassy Athens to UK Foreign Office (3 January 1949) and enclosed list: FO 371/78229, TNA.
[41] UK Embassy Paris to UK Foreign Office (28 January 1949): FO 371/78229, TNA.
[42] *Corfu Channel (United Kingdom v Albania)* (Pleadings) [1950] ICJ Pleadings III 166, 279.
[43] *Corfu Channel (United Kingdom v Albania)* (Pleadings) [1950] ICJ Pleadings IV 9, 548.
[44] Ibid., 544.
[45] Ibid., 542.
[46] Ibid., 546.
[47] Ibid., 542–543.

the other state causing the anxiety about security.[48] But, he added, 'the grounds for withholding its customary right from any State must, we submit, be solid grounds: and by solid grounds I mean something more than caprice or morbid suspicion'[49] – his implication being that the Albanians were prone to these unwarranted sentiments whenever British warships moved through the waters off their coast.

Aside from situations such as these, the essence of the British arguments about the right of innocent passage in 'ordinary territorial waters' was that it was exactly that – a *right* – applying, with a few minor caveats, to all vessels and in all zones beyond internal waters. This was not just an expedient legal argument; it was also an expression of entrenched British policy. Since the nineteenth century they had championed innocent passage to minimise foreign interference with their fleets' movements in distant coastal waters – a reflection of the imperatives of free trade, and their steamships' ability to hew close to coastlines, being less affected than ships under sail by tides and currents. But even the British, among themselves, conceded that the asserted 'absolute right' of innocent passage for warships was, as Foreign Office legal adviser Cecil Hurst admitted, more 'a matter of international comity'.[50] Furthermore, it was strongly contested by other states: as J. H. Phillips noted fifteen years before *Corfu Channel*: 'Obviously, it is of advantage to a strong maritime country to maintain the right, and equally obviously, it is the policy of the smaller powers ... to maintain that it does not exist.'[51]

British 'Coat Trailing'

At this point, however, another issue arose that put the British on the back foot over the innocence of their warships' passage through the channel: the content of the 'XCU' operation orders. The British had earlier submitted to the court two reports, by *Saumarez* captain W. H. Selby and *Volage* commander R. T. Paul, written the day after the sea-mining incident, which had referred to these orders.[52] But when these references were

[48] Ibid., 546.
[49] Ibid.
[50] Cited by H. K. Grey, 'The passage of foreign warships through territorial waters (including straits)' (6 December 1946), p. 11: ADM 116/5542, TNA.
[51] J. H. Phillips to R. L. Craigie (31 July 1934), p. 1: FO 371/17619, TNA.
[52] Selby report at *Corfu Channel (United Kingdom v Albania)* (Pleadings) [1950] ICJ Pleadings V:III 9, 48; and Paul report quoted in *Corfu Channel (United Kingdom v Albania)* (Merits) [1949] ICJ Rep 4, 32.

picked up by the court and the Albanian team, the British refused to release them. Beckett explained that this was because the XCU orders addressed what *might* have happened if the Albanians had fired on British ships, not to what *did* happen; and because they contained references to 'certain technical matters which navies at all times keep secret'.[53] This rebuff did not have the hoped-for deterrent effect. When R. T. Paul took the witness stand on 30 November, the President asked him: 'What do you mean by the words "with reference to XCU"?'[54] Paul answered that he had been instructed not to discuss the matter.[55] The next day, Cot asked P. K. Lankester, the *Mauritius'* navigating officer, about 'the famous orders referred to as XCU', and received the same reply.[56]

Eventually, on 14 December, the President requested the production of the XCU orders 'for the use of the Court'.[57] The British had seen this coming, because as British counsel Frank Soskice noted, 'a great deal has been made by the other side of our failure to produce the document'.[58] He also explained that the term 'for the use of the Court', meant that the British were only obliged to disclose it to judges, not to the other side, but that 'as the Slav members will deliver no doubt dissenting judgments, the contents of XCU will thus probably become wholly or partly public property'.[59]

Why were the British so reluctant to release the orders? Both XCU and its follow-up XCU1 revealed that the squadron's movement through the North Corfu channel was not as innocent as portrayed. Order XCU, dated 5 October 1946, from rear-admiral H. R. G. Kinahan, stated in a crucial paragraph:

> It has been decided to test the Albanian reactions to the above diplomatic notes by making use of the North Channel, Corfu, on 22nd October 1946 for the passage of H.M. Ships *Mauritius*, *Leander*, *Saumarez* and *Volage* from Corfu to Argostoli. H.M.S. *Ocean* will be in the offing so that air spotting will be available if required. The Commander-in-Chief Mediterranean will adjust the programmes of H.M. Ships *Leander*, *Ocean* and *Raider* accordingly.[60]

53 *Corfu Channel (United Kingdom v Albania)* (Pleadings) [1950] ICJ Pleadings III 166, 291.
54 *Corfu Channel (United Kingdom v Albania)* (Pleadings) [1950] ICJ Pleadings IV 9, 27–28.
55 Ibid., 28.
56 Ibid., 77.
57 Ibid., 428.
58 F. Soskice, 'Corfu Channel case' (u.d., c. 7 January 1949), p. 1: FO 371/78229, TNA.
59 Ibid.
60 H. R. G. Kinahan, 'The use of the North Channel, Corfu (short title XCU)' (5 October 1946), p. 1: LCO 2/4515, TNA.

> ...
>
> No [Albanian] guns or gun flashes could be seen on 15th May ... Subsequently air photographs of the whole area were obtained.[61]

Order XCU1, dated 13 October 1946, also from Kinahan, stated that if Albanian shore batteries opened fire on the British ships:

> Cruisers are to open fire on the gun positions as soon as they can be located, using air spotting ... Destroyers are to be prepared to carry out direct bombardment if ordered to do so.[62]
>
> ...
>
> Should the Albanian guns open fire it is hoped that retaliatory action will be completed within an hour.[63]

In sum, the XCU orders showed that the squadron's passage was not a normal peacetime cruise through a strait. Instead, the Admiralty had mounted a naval operation to 'test' the Albanians, which had involved deploying the four warships through the North Corfu Channel, backed up by the aircraft carrier *Ocean* (with a combat air patrol in its vicinity), the destroyer *Raider*, and two airborne spotting aircraft. Aside from the Cold War consequences, the nature of this operation raised legal questions about the innocence of the British passage: moving through a strait from one part of the high sea to another was one thing, provoking the straits state by dispatching a powerful naval force readied to take retaliatory action was quite another.

British ministers, officials, and the three senior counsel involved with the case – attorney-general Hartley Shawcross, solicitor-general Frank Soskice and Eric Beckett – met to discuss the problem on 4 January 1949. Their take on it was revealing. First, they thought the orders, if released, would be damaging to Britain's public image because they brought to light plans for retaliatory firing on Albania lasting for up to an hour, which suggested that the warships had been engaged in a 'punitive expedition'.[64] Second, they revealed that Britain had carried out aerial reconnaissance over Albania after the firing on *Orion* and *Superb* on

[61] Ibid., p. 2.

[62] H. R. G. Kinahan, 'XCU One – plan of operations' (13 October 1946), p. 1: LCO 2/4515, TNA.

[63] Ibid., p. 2.

[64] P. N. N. Synnott, 'Corfu case: notes of a meeting' (4 January 1949 [misdated 1948]), p. 1: ADM 116/5758, TNA.

15 May 1946, which was 'by implication inconsistent with what was said at the Security Council and previously before this Court'.[65] Finally, and most damagingly of all, the documents made clear that the operation was 'a special test or coat trailing expedition' – a calculated provocation – involving not only the four warships but also *Ocean* and *Raider* and supporting aircraft, which 'might lead to the conclusion that this was not an innocent passage'.[66] Shawcross in particular stressed that the reasons for the passage, and possibly also its conduct, were 'quite inconsistent with "innocent passage"'.[67] They faced a choice: either divulging the orders to the court, which would likely be fatal to their case,[68] or suppressing the evidence, which, if it later came to light, might be seen, Soskice said, as perpetrating 'virtually a fraud [o]n the Court'.[69]

The British found themselves in this situation because of an interdepartmental foul-up, compounded by the legal team's carelessness. But wherever the blame lay, they were now compelled to respond to the court's request on terms not of their own making.[70] In the ensuring debate about how to respond, Viscount Hall, the First Lord of the Admiralty, made two decisive points: first, if they disclosed the orders, the court would find out about the aerial reconnaissance and proposed retaliatory action – facts that could not be derived with certainty from the other documents submitted;[71] and second, the court would not be obliged to derive adverse inference from the orders being withheld; it could instead simply deduce nothing from it.[72] At any rate, the debate was soon settled. Clement Attlee stepped in and ruled that the XCU orders should not be produced in court, and that was that.[73]

65 Ibid.
66 Ibid.
67 H. W. Shawcross to C. R. A. Attlee (3 November 1948), p. 2: PREM 8/1312, TNA.
68 H. W. Shawcross to C. R. A. Attlee (29 October 1948), p. 2: LCO 2/4515, TNA.
69 F. Soskice, 'Corfu Channel case' (u.d., c. 7 January 1948), p. 2: FO 371/78229, TNA.
70 On the interdepartmental controversy, see A. Carty, 'The Corfu Channel case – and the missing Admiralty orders', *Law and Practice of International Courts and Tribunals* 3 (2004), 1–35; and on the evidentiary issues, see K. J. Keith, '"Naval secrets", public interest immunity and open justice', in K. Bannelier *et al.* (eds.), *The ICJ and the evolution of international law: the enduring impact of the* Corfu Channel *case* (London: Routledge, 2011), pp. 124–146; and W. M. Riesman and C. P. Skinner, *Fraudulent evidence before public international tribunals* (Cambridge: Cambridge University Press, 2014), pp. 54–77.
71 Viscount Hall to C. R. A. Attlee (12 January 1949), p. 1: FO 371/78229, TNA.
72 Ibid.
73 C. R. A. Attlee to Viscount Hall (12 January 1949): FO 371/78229, TNA.

The Question of Straits

The judgment was handed down on 9 April 1949, and, read as a whole, it conveyed the strong message that navigational rights should not be impeded. On the mining of *Saumarez* and *Volage* on 22 October 1946, it held by eleven votes to five that Albania was responsible for the damage and loss of life, on the grounds that the minefield could not have been laid without Albania's knowledge.[74] This vindicated the British. On Britain's minesweeping operation of 12–13 November 1946, the court unanimously decided that this was a violation of Albanian sovereignty (although not a display of force designed to exert pressure on the nation).[75] This partly vindicated the Albanians.

Then came the crucial issue of the passage – innocent or otherwise – of the four warships, raised in the first part of the second question in the special agreement. The court rejected by fourteen votes to two the Albanian claim that the squadron's actions on 22 October 1946 violated Albanian sovereignty,[76] stating:

> It is, in the opinion of the Court, generally recognized and in accordance with international custom that States in time of peace have a right to send their warships through straits used for international navigation between two parts of the high seas without the previous authorization of a coastal State, provided that the passage is *innocent*. Unless otherwise prescribed in an international convention, there is no right for a coastal State to prohibit such passage through straits in time of peace.[77]

The court thus confirmed that under international law, foreign warships enjoyed the unsuspendable right of innocent passage through straits used for international navigation in peacetime.

As previously discussed, the Albanians had challenged the British claim that the North Corfu Channel was an international strait. It was, they had said, merely a secondary route carrying mostly local traffic; consequently, foreign vessels did not enjoy the same rights as they would in a recognised international strait. Responding, the court proposed a two-part test for international straits for the purposes of passage: 'its geographical situation as connecting two parts of the high seas and the fact of its being used for international navigation'.[78] This test, as was later

[74] *Corfu Channel (United Kingdom v Albania)* (Merits) [1949] ICJ Rep 4, 36, 22.
[75] Ibid., 36, 35.
[76] Ibid., 36.
[77] Ibid., 28. Original emphasis.
[78] Ibid.

observed, rendered Cot's arguments about the channel's insignificance 'irrelevant' as far as passage rights were concerned.[79] It also put paid to the opinions of the jurists who had inspired Cot, some claiming that international straits should be of major importance to commerce, and others that they should be an indispensable – not alternative – route connecting two parts of the high seas.[80] The court did not address these arguments, but had it done so, it might well have rejected them for being either too broad (the 'importance' of a strait being open to different interpretations) or too narrow (the categories of 'indispensable' and 'alternative' apply to some straits, but not all).

The 'decisive criterion' for international straits having been set out, equivocation crept in regarding the volume of traffic passing through the channel. The court introduced this issue by quoting from Beckett on the vessels that put into Corfu's port from the channel between 1 April 1936 and 31 December 1937, which, the court stated, showed that the channel was 'a useful route for international maritime traffic' and 'of special importance to Greece by reason of the traffic to and from the port of Corfu'.[81] The passage from Beckett reads:

> The following is the total number of ships putting in at the Port of Corfu after passing through or just before passing through the Channel. During the period of one year nine months, the total number of ships was 2,884. The flags of the ships are Greek, Italian, Roumanian, Yugoslav, French, Albanian and British. Clearly, very small vessels are included, as the entries for Albanian vessels are high, and of course one vessel may make several journeys, but 2,884 ships for a period of one year nine months is quite a large figure. These figures relate to vessels visited by the Customs at Corfu and so do not include the large number of vessels which went through the Strait without calling at Corfu at all.[82]

The court's use of this passage is notable for tacitly readmitting volume of traffic as a supplementary factor, even though it had been deemed irrelevant by the two-step test. If it had simply wished to confirm the fact of traffic of an international nature, they could have quoted Beckett's third sentence only: 'The flags of the ships are Greek, Italian, Roumanian, Yugoslav, French, Albanian and British.' By the same token, if it had

[79] R. R. Churchill and A. V. Lowe, *The law of the sea*, 3rd ed. (Manchester: Manchester University Press, 1999), p. 103.

[80] W. E. Beckett, 'Report by the agent on the Corfu case' (19 May 1949), p. 8: FO 371/78231, TNA.

[81] *Corfu Channel (United Kingdom v Albania)* (Merits) [1949] ICJ Rep 4, 28, 29.

[82] Ibid., 29.

wanted to exclude any argument about the volume of traffic, positing the idea that mere usage of a strait was sufficient, it would not have quoted the rest of the passage. That said, Beckett's figures suggest that any proposed minimal standard would have to be set so low as to be virtually meaningless: although he tried to talk up 2,884 vessels over the twenty-one-month period as 'quite a large figure', the traffic into the Corfu port thus averaged four and a half vessels a day, some of them repeat visitors and some vessels 'very small'. Unless this trickle of traffic was significant for other reasons, the figures suggest that the court greatly exaggerated the channel's 'special importance to Greece by reason of the traffic to and from the port of Corfu'.[83]

*

Next, on the question of innocent passage, the court held that Britain's naval operation of 22 October 1946 was not unlawful because it 'was designed to affirm a right which had been unjustly denied'.[84] In other words, a passage designed to uphold the right of innocent passage was itself innocent. But what about the *way* the British had asserted this right? The Albanians had stated that the squadron of warships had passed through the channel with their crews at action stations, but the court held that this precaution was not unreasonable given that the Albanians had earlier fired on *Superb* and *Orion*.[85] The Albanians also claimed that the positions of the ships' guns demonstrated hostile intent, but the court rejected this argument, dismissing the criteria of motive, and citing evidence that the guns were unloaded and in normal positions fore and aft.[86] As these decisions indicated, a coastal state's perception of ill-intent does not necessarily render a passage non-innocent.

Having found in Britain's favour on these issues, the court did not wholly accept the British contention that they were merely gauging the Albanians' response by exercising their right of innocent passage through the channel. Instead, it decided that the squadron's purpose was not only to 'test' the Albanians but also make a show of force, yet that these actions *did not constitute a violation of Albania's rights*. Noting that the four warships had passed close to Albania's coast during a period of political tension, it stated that:

[83] Ibid.
[84] Ibid., 30.
[85] Ibid., 31.
[86] Ibid.

> The intention must have been, not only to test Albania's attitude, but at the same time to demonstrate such force that she would abstain from firing again on passing ships. Having regard, however, to all the circumstances of the case, as described above, the Court is unable to characterize these measures taken by the United Kingdom authorities as a violation of Albania's sovereignty.[87]

The dissonance between the first sentence, which acknowledged that the British action was both a test and a show of force, and the second, which absolved them of violating Albania's sovereignty, indicates that the court was prepared to accept provocation as a valid action so long as it did not violate international law. As it stated:

> The legality of this measure taken by the Government of the United Kingdom cannot be disputed, provided that it was carried out in a manner consistent with the requirements of international law.[88]

Of course, the court's decisions relating to innocent passage were based only on the known facts: it did not have access to the XCU orders, and had decided to draw no adverse inference from the British refusal to disclose them.[89] On the evidence available, however, the court was prepared to accept 'coat trailing', perhaps in recognition of the very thing that the British sought to play down: warships *are* inherently threatening. As ocean-going splinters of sovereignty, immune from foreign interference, they are consummate provocateurs, conveniently offering, as Rob McLaughlin observed, 'a lesser form of "provocation" than crossing a land border'.[90] Their mere presence in another state's territorial waters is both a demonstration of latent violence and in some cases, a calculated affront. In short, McLaughlin says, they embody 'gunboat diplomacy – a concept that was well recognised, and endorsed, in the *Corfu Channel* case'.[91]

The court's decision suited the British, with Beckett declaring the outcome to be 'pretty satisfactory', especially on the issue of innocent

[87] Ibid.

[88] Ibid., 30.

[89] Ibid., 32.

[90] R. McLaughlin, 'Dangerous waters and international law: the *Corfu Channel* case, warships, and sovereignty irritants' in K. Bannelier *et al.* (eds.), *The ICJ and the evolution of international law: the enduring impact of the* Corfu Channel *case* (London: Routledge, 2011), p. 167.

[91] Ibid., p. 168.

passage.[92] Even so, he was surprised that the majority judgment was so short, and that it had paid so little attention to the works of legal authorities, writing: 'this Court on a most important point of law simply says what it considers the rule to be and there is no discussion of authorities at all'.[93] Beckett also offered an appraisal of the judges, describing the Chilean, Mexican and Brazilian judges, respectively, as 'useless', 'useless' and 'of little use'; while lauding the British, Belgian, Canadian, French and Norwegian judges as being 'first-rate'.[94] He further noted that the Polish judge, Bohdan Winiarski and the Czech judge ad hoc for Albania, Bohuslav Ečer, had voted with the majority on innocent passage, which he saw as an unexpected vindication of the independence and impartiality of the court.[95] When all was said and done, the decision about innocent passage in international straits would be of general application, and this, he wrote, 'should be particularly welcome to us as a naval Power'.[96]

In all, the *Corfu Channel* judgment upheld the status quo, safeguarding navigation rights through straits for the foreseeable future. This, as Beckett pointed out, benefited the powers, whose command of the oceans depended on the uninterrupted flow of navies, commerce and cables between seas as well as through them. It also marked the last gasp of the old British-dominated maritime order as custom and judicial decisions began to respond to the claims of coastal states over fisheries, and as the newly constituted International Law Commission began work on a commentary to guide the next treaty-making conference. The law of the sea, once minimal and elastic, was about to enter a new phase.

Baseline Controversies

In April 1949, Beckett filed his internal report on the *Corfu Channel* case and consigned the related documents to the departmental archives – including copies of the XCU orders, which would be withheld from public inspection for the next fifty years. Within a few months though, British ministers, flushed with victory, decided to bring a new case, this

92 W. E. Beckett to C. H. M. Waldock (11 April 1949), p. 1: FO 371/78230, TNA.
93 Ibid., p. 2.
94 W. E. Beckett, 'Report by the Agent on the Corfu case' (19 May 1949), pp. 2–3: FO 371/78231, TNA.
95 Ibid., p. 2.
96 Ibid., p. 1.

time against Norway for stepping up its enforcement of a 1935 royal decree that excluded foreign trawlers from its northern coastal waters. The *Fisheries* case, like *Corfu Channel*, would strike a balance between the freedom of the seas and the rights of coastal states, but for the British, the outcome would be very different.

Before examining the case, a note about trawling. This method of fishing, which involves vessels dragging a trawl-net along the seabed, had been used for centuries, but the nineteenth-century combination of steam power and the beam trawl (which kept nets open) revolutionised the industry.[97] For a fishing state such as Britain, size of catches, and financial returns for investors, grew dramatically. But as the industry expanded, so did concerns about overfishing.[98] Fish populations began to dwindle, not just because more were being caught, but also because the trawls destroyed sea floor eco-systems, including spawning grounds and the organisms on which fish fed. Faced with diminishing returns, British trawlers moved further afield. As Thomas Fulton wrote in 1911:

> As the North Sea became, comparatively speaking, more and more exhausted, the vessels were compelled to go farther and farther away in order to maintain the supply. The grounds at Iceland, now so important not only to the British trawlers but to the Germans and the French, were first visited in 1891, and those in the neighbourhood of the Faröe Islands a little later ... Then the grounds in the Bay of Biscay and those on the coasts of Spain and Portugal began to be frequented, mostly from about the year 1902; and in the next year the operations of the trawlers were extended farther south to the coast of Morocco, as far at least as Agadir.[99]

A similar process was unfolding in other parts of the world, with demand driving the technology, and technology increasing the catches: the Japanese first appeared with sail-powered beam trawlers in Manila Bay in the Philippines in 1900, then with diesel-powered trawlers in the late 1920s.[100] These developments had knock-on economic and social effects. Because trawling was an investment-heavy, technology-driven method of

[97] B. Fagin, *Fishing: how the sea fed civilization* (New Haven, CT: Yale University Press, 2017), p. 240.

[98] R. Thurstan *et al.*, 'Origins of the bottom trawling controversy in the British Isles: nineteenth century witness testimonies reveal evidence of early fishery declines', *Fish and Fisheries* 15 (2014), 506–522.

[99] T. W. Fulton, *The sovereignty of the sea* (Edinburgh: William Blackwood & Sons, 1911), pp. 711–713.

[100] G. R. Morgan and D. J. Staples, *The history of industrial marine fisheries in Southeast Asia* (Bangkok: Food and Agriculture Organisation: RAP Publication 2006/12, 2006), 7.

fishing, vessels had to land large catches to turn a profit. The sheer scale and reach of these operations had a damaging effect on more traditional fishing communities reliant on lines, pots or nets, first in the trawlers' country of origin and then further abroad – the trawling industry competing with them first for fish, and then for a share of their market. Fulton again:

> The influx of alien vessels, the most powerful and efficient fishing machines in existence, along these foreign coasts is not, as was naturally to be expected, viewed with satisfaction by the native fishermen. They see the fishing-grounds which they had so long been accustomed to consider as their own – in many cases lying within the territorial waters preserved to them by the laws of their own country, though possibly outside 'the ordinary three-mile limit' – invaded and exploited by foreigners, and their own livelihood threatened. They fear that what has occurred in the North Sea will happen along their own coasts; that the fishing-grounds, often of limited extent, will be impoverished and exhausted for the sole benefit of the foreigners, and their efforts to maintain themselves and their families rendered difficult or impossible.[101]

Concerns about overfishing and its incremental economic effects thus advanced hand-in-hand, and states with important offshore fishing grounds, especially those in the North Atlantic and Southeast Pacific, started to impose more rigorous restrictions on domestic and foreign trawlers working the waters adjacent to their coasts. Norway was among them, and in September 1948 it began to strictly enforce the royal decree, promulgated on 12 July 1935, which declared an exclusive 'Norwegian fisheries zone' extending outwards from straight baselines connecting forty-eight extremities 'on the mainland, on islands or rocks' along the northern Norwegian coast.[102]

Thereafter, most of the West European states whose vessels had previously fished off Norway's coast kept outside the waters covered by the decree, but the British did not, with the result that some of their trawlers were seized, their catches confiscated and their masters fined. At this point, the British decided to take Norway to court, alleging that it had extended its sea domain further than it was entitled to by reckoning the start of its territorial sea from straight baselines rather than the low-water line, and thereby illegally excluding British trawlers

[101] Fulton, *The sovereignty of the sea*, pp. 713–714.
[102] Annex, 'Application instituting proceedings', *Fisheries (United Kingdom v Norway)* (Pleadings) [1949] ICJ Pleadings 8, 14–16.

from fishing grounds that were in fact high seas. On 28 September 1949, Britain filed an application requesting that the court 'declare the principles of international law' governing baselines by reference to 'the lines of delimitation of the Norwegian fisheries zone laid down by the Royal Decree of 1935', and, based on this decision, award damages for any British fishing vessels arrested outside the waters to which Norway was legally entitled.[103]

The Low-Water Line

From the outset, all parties understood that although the 1935 decree claimed exclusive rights over a 'fisheries zone', this was 'none other than the sea area which Norway considers to be her territorial sea'.[104] It was also understood that the case concerned the straight baselines marking the start of the territorial sea, not the declared *breadth* of Norway's territorial sea – the British having already conceded Oslo's claim to four miles as an historic right.[105] The central question was: should the territorial sea be measured from the low-water line following every undulation of the coast, which the British claimed was the rule applicable to all, or from baselines that cut across indentations in the general direction of the coast, as was Norway's practice?

In court, the British team – led by *Corfu Channel* veterans Eric Beckett and Frank Soskice – argued that under customary international law,[106] the proper way to reckon the starting point of the territorial sea was by tracing the low-water line along the coastline, following all its twists and turns.[107] This, Beckett said, was the most precise method because it marked 'the actual line of the land where it meets the sea'.[108] There were

[103] Ibid., 11–12, 10.

[104] *Fisheries (United Kingdom v Norway)* (Judgment) [1951] ICJ Rep 116, 125. From this point onwards, following the judgment, we will use the newer term 'territorial sea' (which distinguishes waters seaward of the baseline from internal waters landward of it), rather than the older term 'territorial waters' (which often did not). For the contemporaneous debate in the International Law Commission about which term to use, see: *Yearbook of the International Law Commission* (1952), vol. 1, 147–150.

[105] This concession was somewhat reluctant, as the Norwegians noted: *Fisheries (United Kingdom v Norway)* (Pleadings) [1951] ICJ Pleadings IV, 8, 242.

[106] Ibid., 63.

[107] Ibid., 60.

[108] Ibid., 61.

exceptions to this system, however: where a baseline skirted uncontested historic waters claimed by the coastal state; and where it crossed the mouth of a bay as a straight 'closing line' of no more than ten miles long.[109]

Norway's baselines, they observed, did not follow the mainland and islands' low-water line, but instead skipped across water between headlands and other features, and skirted the outer edges of the '*skjærgaard*' – the 120,000-odd islands, rocks and reefs fringing Norway's northern coastline. The effect of this was to push Norway's territorial sea outwards beyond four miles from the mainland shoreline.[110] Not only that, but because Norway claimed the waters landward of its baselines as internal waters, foreign vessels moving through these would be denied the right of innocent passage.[111] In the British view, the Norwegians were making unwarranted jurisdictional encroachments into waters on either side of its four-mile territorial sea, transforming high seas into territorial sea, and territorial sea into internal waters. It was, as Foreign Office legal adviser Gerald Fitzmaurice wrote, 'simply a disguised method of claiming additional waters'.[112]

When making their case that the low-water line rule was generally recognised, the British cast their eyes back to the 1930 codification conference. Discussion basis 6 seemed to serve their case well, stating that, 'Subject to the provisions regarding bays and islands, the breadth of territorial waters is measured from the line of the low-water mark along the entire coast.'[113] The difficulty was that the negotiations did little to confirm this conclusion. As W. H. Hancock reported at the time, it had given rise of a great deal of discussion, 'mainly due to the special claims of Norway and Sweden to measure the belt from baselines drawn between the outermost rocks (a method which found supporters in Spain and Yugoslavia) and to the difficulty of agreeing as to which low

[109] Ibid. Maurice Bourquin, the Belgian counsel for Norway, retorted that if in Beckett's view bays were an exception to the rule, the whole north coast of Norway, indented with fjords from Traena up to the Soviet border, was an 'uninterrupted procession of . . . exceptions' (ibid., 494).

[110] Annex, 'Application instituting proceedings', *Fisheries (United Kingdom v Norway)* (Pleadings) [1949] ICJ Pleadings 8, 11.

[111] 'Draft' annexed to joint memorandum, 'Territorial waters' (17 June 1952), p. 1: MT 59/2976, TNA.

[112] G. G. Fitzmaurice, 'The law and procedure of the International Court of Justice, 1951–54: points of substantive law I', *British Year Book of International Law* 31 (1954), 371, 421.

[113] LN, *Conference for the Codification of International Law – vol. III*, p. 179.

water mark should be taken'.[114] As a sop to Norway and Sweden, the Americans had tabled a proposal admitting four-mile baselines in certain circumstances, and the British submitted a revision of it, reducing the length to two miles.[115] But the subcommittee did not review either proposal;[116] the committee did not reconsider the issue; and the final committee report made no reference at all to baselines.[117]

Norwegian Principles

Putting Norway's side of the case, agent and counsel Sven Arntzen and counsel Maurice Bourquin argued on two grounds. First, there was no customary international law enforceable against Norway for demarcating their fishing zone under the terms of the decree, and even if there was, Norway's exceptional geographic and economic situation meant it would not be bound by it.[118] Second, the 1935 decree was not unlawful because Norway enjoyed historic title over the fisheries zone it had enclosed with baselines.[119] As Arntzen stated, 'the geographical situation, the nature of the resources, the configuration of the coasts and the economic and social singularities which result from it... means that our country has had, over the centuries, evolved autonomously in this legal domain'.[120] Furthermore, the 1935 decree and the previous decrees on which it was based were validated by the general absence of objections from other states – Britain being unusual in raising an objection.[121] The Norwegian team therefore requested that the court 'adjudge and declare that the delimitation of the fishing area, fixed by the Royal Decree of 12 July 1935, is not contrary to international law'.[122]

Arntzen and Bourquin explained that the baselines set out in the decree were not drawn arbitrarily, as the British had suggested, but were governed by essential principles. The first of these was that they should

114 W. H. Hancock, 'Report on international conference' (u.d., c. May 1930), p. 14: FO 372/2639, TNA.
115 Ibid., pp. 14–16.
116 Ibid., p. 16.
117 For example, *Fisheries (United Kingdom v Norway)* (Pleadings) [1951] ICJ Pleadings IV, 8, 404.
118 Ibid., 174, 166.
119 Ibid., 174, 221.
120 Ibid., 166.
121 Ibid., 218, 234.
122 Ibid., 461.

follow the general direction of the coast, anchored by basepoints located either on the mainland or along the outer edge of the skjærgaard.[123] They stressed that the baseline system incorporated restrictions: baselines should be drawn within sight of land,[124] and basepoints should 'not be covered by the sea'.[125] (The British expressed their scepticism about these constraints. Counsel Humphrey Waldock suggested that if the only requirement for basepoints was that they were located on soil or rocks 'occasionally peeping above the water',[126] it meant that baselines could be drawn from low-tide elevations as well as from dry land – an idea that was later accepted, but which Beckett dismissed as 'completely unreal'.[127] Beckett also noted that Norway's longer baselines were only within sight of land because its coastline was so mountainous; if Norway were a low-lying country like the Netherlands, they would be out of sight. This meant that some countries could claim more sea 'because the land which it possesses is mountainous rather than flat!'[128])

The second essential feature of baselines, according to the Norwegians, was that they should be *reasonable*, 'based on considerations drawn either from the configuration of the coast, from fishing conditions, or from other objective realities'.[129] Following the criteria set out in the 1935 decree, the first consideration governing the choice of baselines was the exceptional character of the Norwegian coastline.[130] Their point was that it was so heavily indented with fjords and so densely fringed with islands, rocks and reefs that it resisted the application of the low-water mark method; the straight baseline method of drawing lines between prominent points around the outer circumference was the more rational approach. Even if there had been a *rule* on baselines, excluding all others – a contention the Norwegians did not accept – the British application of it was too rigid and mechanical.[131] International law, Bourquin argued, was 'more flexible and more realistic than that', and

[123] Ibid., 165.
[124] Ibid., 165, 243.
[125] Ibid., 243.
[126] Ibid., 400.
[127] Ibid., 93.
[128] Ibid., 392.
[129] Ibid., 223.
[130] Annex, 'Application instituting proceedings', *Fisheries (United Kingdom v Norway)* (Pleadings) [1949] ICJ Pleadings 8, 14.
[131] *Fisheries (United Kingdom v Norway)* (Pleadings) [1951] ICJ Pleadings IV, 8, 243.

was able to take diverse situations into account.[132] With 'a coast with an exceptional character, like the Norwegian coast, it is the exceptional rules which must be applied'.[133]

Another consideration for the Norwegians when determining baselines, again based on reasonableness, was the economic wellbeing of the coastal population. In hindsight, this argument may appear unremarkable, with 'economic and social advancement' being *sine qua non* of the UN law of the sea convention.[134] But at the time in certain West European legal circles, arguments based on economic wellbeing would have been seen as a radical, and for some even a preposterous, justification for the demarcation of maritime zones.

Bourquin began by arguing that the impetus behind the decree was the expansion of British fishing operations in Norwegian waters, with its trawlers first appearing off the coast of Eastern Finnmark in 1906, and then later along the coasts of western Finnmark, Troms and Nordland.[135] These were the northern counties covered by the decree, which stated that its aim was to 'safeguard . . . the vital interests of the inhabitants of the northernmost parts of the country'.[136] It was clear how this argument would develop – trawling diminished fish stocks and destroyed local people's livelihoods – and Soskice tried to pre-empt it by stating that it was 'quite irrelevant for the measurement of territorial waters whether the best fishing grounds are inside or outside the dividing line; whether the population of the State concerned are fishermen dependent on fishing or whether they are not; whether trawling is or is not damaging to stocks of fish'.[137] Counsel Richard Wilberforce followed, stating that there were enough fishing grounds off the coast of Norway for all parties, and that the damage caused by trawling was overstated because 'the trawl fertilizes the ground rather like a plough and releases more and better food for the fish'.[138]

Bourquin pressed on, explaining that the drawing of baselines was influenced by the fact that in the northern counties, all within the Arctic circle, fishing was the mainstay of the economy, with the local communities

132 Ibid.
133 Ibid., 495.
134 Preamble, UNCLOS, 398.
135 *Fisheries (United Kingdom v Norway)* (Pleadings) [1951] ICJ Pleadings IV, 8, 224.
136 Annex, 'Application instituting proceedings', *Fisheries (United Kingdom v Norway)* (Pleadings) [1949] ICJ Pleadings 8, 14.
137 *Fisheries (United Kingdom v Norway)* (Pleadings) [1951] ICJ Pleadings IV, 8, 30.
138 Ibid., 159.

depending on the sea just as farmers in more temperate regions depended on their fields.[139] Yet their livelihoods were under threat not just because foreign trawlers had been fishing off the coast in ever-increasing numbers,[140] but also because their trawls fouled the nets and lines of the local fishermen,[141] with the result (according to expert Gunnar Rollefsen) that 'the Norwegians were being driven out of their former fishing grounds and now have to be content to a large extent with the poorest fishing grounds'.[142] It was argued that unless foreign trawlers were kept out, the consequences would be ruinous: Norwegian fishing communities' means of subsistence would be removed completely, and the northern part of the country would become depopulated.[143] 'To fish or to starve,' Bourquin said, 'this is the alternative.'[144]

Winners and Losers

After the hearings had concluded, Beckett thought the British team had made a good showing in court, claiming that 'they had clearly the best of the legal argument' and 'had disproved Norway's case in favour of her historical and prescriptive claim on the facts'.[145] He also thought the odds in their favour had been shortened by the absence of three judges likely to have opposed their position[146] – the Brazilian judge Philadelpho Azevedo (who died before the oral pleadings began), and two ill judges, the Mexican Isidro Fabela and the Soviet Sergei Krylov. But Britain lost the case. In its judgment of 18 December 1951, the court held by ten votes to two 'that the method employed for the delimitation of the fisheries zone by the Royal Norwegian Decree of July 12th, 1935, is not contrary to international law'; and by eight votes to four 'that the base-lines fixed by the said Decree in application of this method are not contrary to international law'.[147] Responding in *The Times*, Hersch Lauterpacht, choosing his words carefully, wrote that even if some saw

[139] Ibid., 178–179.
[140] Ibid., 233.
[141] Ibid., 230.
[142] Ibid.
[143] Ibid., 179.
[144] Ibid., 325.
[145] W. E. Beckett, 'Anglo-Norwegian fisheries case' (14 February 1952), p. 2: LCO 2/5783, TNA.
[146] Ibid.
[147] *Fisheries (United Kingdom v Norway)* (Judgment) [1951] ICJ Rep 116, 143.

the judgment as 'a daring piece of judicial legislation' it would likely rank 'among the most significant pronouncements' of the court.[148]

Meanwhile, at the Foreign Office, Beckett produced reports for departmental consumption that included assessments of the enunciated principles that offered clearer insights into the British response than did some of his colleagues' more guarded appraisals published in the law journals.[149] Generally speaking, he ascribed the decision against Britain to the shifting tides of opinion on law of the sea, writing:

> [I]t must be admitted that the international law on which the United Kingdom founded its case is, speaking broadly, unpopular at the present time with the majority of States, and the current of opinion has been rising against it. Still, a law does not cease to be a law because it is unpopular.[150]

The court did, however, enunciate important principles, to which Beckett and other Foreign Office legal advisers now turned their attention. On the question of baselines, the court disagreed with the British argument that the low-water-mark method was the only lawful method for determining the start of the territorial sea. In one respect, it closely followed the Norwegian argument that the 'very distinctive' nature of Norway's northern coastline called for a different method of demarcation:[151]

> Where a coast is deeply indented and cut into, as is that of Eastern Finnmark, or where it is bordered by an archipelago such as the 'skjærgaard' along the western sector of the coast here in question, the base-line becomes independent of the low-water mark, and can only be determined by means of a geometrical construction. In such circumstances the line of the low-water mark can no longer be put forward as a rule requiring the coastline to be followed in all its sinuosities.[152]

148 H. Lauterpacht, 'Freedom of the seas', *The Times* (8 January 1952).

149 See, for example, G. G. Fitzmaurice, 'The law and procedure of the International Court of Justice, 1951–1954: general principles and sources of law', *British Year Book of International Law* 30 (1953), 1–70; Fitzmaurice, 'The law and procedure . . . points of substantive law', 371–429; D. H. N. Johnson, 'The Anglo-Norwegian fisheries case', *International and Comparative Law Quarterly* 1 (1952), 145–180; R. O. Wilberforce, 'Some aspects of the Anglo-Norwegian fisheries case', *Transactions of the Grotius Society* 38 (1952), 151–168; and C. H. M. Waldock, 'The Anglo-Norwegian fisheries case', *British Year Book of International Law* 28 (1951), 114–171.

150 W. E. Beckett, 'Anglo-Norwegian fisheries case' (14 February 1952), p. 2: LCO 2/5783, TNA.

151 Ibid., 127, 129.

152 *Fisheries (United Kingdom v Norway)* (Judgment) [1951] ICJ Rep 116, 128–129.

But in another respect, the court rejected Norway's argument that the baseline system was an *exception* to the low-water mark system, arguing instead that it was 'the application of general international law to a specific case'.[153] In other words, the straight baseline method, and by implication the low- water-line method, were both variants of the same principle: that the belt of territorial sea, anchored by the baseline, 'must follow the general direction of the coast'.[154] Or, as Gerard Fitzmaurice put it more critically, 'the Court endeavoured to transcend, as it were, the supposed diversities of international practice by propounding an overriding rule which would comprehend within itself and resolve all the various exceptions and special cases'.[155] (Maurice Bourquin, looking back at the case, stated: 'Exceptional situations call for exceptional rules. The Court shared this view.'[156] In fact, as just discussed, the court did not.)

Having set down the general approach to the different methods of establishing the starting point of the territorial sea, the court set out three principles governing the application of straight baselines, here addressed in turn: that they should follow the general direction of the coast; that they should be reasonable; and that the landward waters they enclose should have the character of internal waters.

On the first principle – that baselines should follow the general direction of the coast – the court, following Norway's lead, stated that 'while ... a State must be allowed the latitude necessary in order to be able to adapt its delimitation to practical needs and local requirements, the drawing of base-lines must not depart to any appreciable extent from the general direction of the coast'.[157] The rationale behind this principle was that the land bestows on the coastal state its right to coastal waters.[158] Beckett, unsurprisingly, regretted that the court had sacrificed

[153] Ibid., 131.

[154] Ibid., 129. As Fitzmaurice argued, 'There is ... some ground for thinking that the Court regarded the low-water-mark rule as being itself only a special application of a more general rule, of which the Norwegian base-line method was another application.' ('The law and procedure ... general principles and sources of law', 1, 20.)

[155] Fitzmaurice, 'The law and procedure ... general principles and sources of law', 1, 22.

[156] M. Bourquin, 'La portée général de l'arrêt rendu le 18 Décembre 1951 par le Cour Internationale de Justice dans l'affaire Anglo-Novégienne des pêcheries', *Nordisk Tidsskrift and International Ret og Jus Gentium* 22 (1952), 101, 110.

[157] *Fisheries (United Kingdom v Norway)* (Judgment) [1951] ICJ Rep 116, 133.

[158] Ibid.

the precision of the low-water line by recognising the less precise 'general direction of the coast' idea.[159]

On the second principle – that straight baselines should be reasonable – the court agreed with Norway that straight baselines could depart from 'the physical line of the coast' as long as the departure was 'within reasonable limits'.[160] What, though, would be considered reasonable, given that the court did not impose enumerated limits on baseline length or degree of deviation? As an indication, the majority stated that one of Norway's demarcations – the Lopphavet baseline – was 'within the bounds of what is moderate and reasonable'.[161] The Chinese judge Hsu Mo, while agreeing that the straight baseline method was not contrary to international law, imposed more exacting standards, however, taking issue with the Lopphavet baseline's 'excessive deviation' from the direction of the coast (as well as with the 'excessively long' baseline over Sværholthavet).[162] On the British side, Beckett thought there should be *some* enumerated limits imposed on baselines,[163] and that the court's application of reasonableness in the Lopphavet area suggested that the test did not operate 'as a serious limitation'.[164] Developing the point, Humphrey Waldock said that reasonableness was a subjective concept, dependent on the standards used and the weight accorded to other states' interests,[165] while Gerald Fitzmaurice observed that any decision on the 'general direction of the coast' would depend on the size of map being used.[166]

Bays, Curvatures, Archipelagos

Last but by no means least, the court turned to the third principle governing baselines – that the landward waters they enclosed should have the status of internal waters – when it stated that the question governing

159 W. E. Beckett, 'Anglo-Norwegian fisheries case' (14 February 1952), p. 7: LCO 2/5783, TNA.
160 *Fisheries (United Kingdom v Norway)* (Judgment) [1951] ICJ Rep 116, 129.
161 Ibid., 142.
162 *Fisheries (United Kingdom v Norway)* Separate Opinion of Judge Hsu Mo [1951] ICJ Rep 154, 156.
163 W. E. Beckett, 'Copy of note handed by Sir Eric Beckett to Professor Lauterpacht' (4 June 1952), p. 3: LCO 2/5783, TNA.
164 W. E. Beckett, 'Anglo-Norwegian fisheries case' (14 February 1952), p. 7: LCO 2/5783, TNA.
165 Waldock, 'The Anglo-Norwegian fisheries case', 149.
166 Fitzmaurice, 'The law and procedure ... points of substantive law', 1, 389, fn. 1.

the choice of straight baselines was 'whether certain sea areas lying within these lines are sufficiently closely linked to the land domain to be subject to the regime of internal waters'.[167] The court offered no objective test for 'sufficiently closely linked' but set out three categories of waters that could be considered as internal waters in Norway's case: bays; waters within minor curvatures of the coast; and the waters of the *skjærgaard*.

Starting with bays, Norway's enclosure with baselines of its fjords as internal waters was not an issue between the parties. As noted by the Canadian judge John Read (earlier involved with the *I'm Alone* case), states had from the nineteenth century declared bays, which sometimes penetrated far into land territory, to be internal waters on security grounds.[168] At the start of the case at hand, Beckett stated that to qualify as a bay, and hence internal waters, their mouths should be no more than ten miles wide, but that this was 'not a question which we think the Court has to decide'.[169] Towards the end, he conceded that Norway could on historic grounds claim as internal waters 'all fjords and sunds which fall within the conception of a bay . . . whether the proper closing line of the indentation is *more* or less than 10 sea miles long'.[170] From the British perspective, then, closing lines for Norwegian bays, fjords and sunds were off the table. But despite their denials that a decision was being sought, the court *did* pronounce on the issue, noting that the ten-mile rule was not universally practiced and therefore had 'not acquired the authority of a general rule of international law'.[171]

On this, Maurice Bourquin later wrote: 'It was once said that the three-mile rule was the "great loser" of the 1930 codification conference. It can be said with equal certainty that the ten-mile rule is the great loser in the Anglo-Norwegian fisheries case.'[172] Norwegian team member Jens Evensen added that it was 'probably one of the most important findings' because henceforth a ten-mile limit could not be imposed on closing lines for bays, or – in an analogy proposed by the British – to baselines

167 *Fisheries (United Kingdom v Norway)* (Judgment) [1951] ICJ Rep 116, 133.

168 *Fisheries (United Kingdom v Norway)* Dissenting Opinion of Judge J. E. Read [1951] ICJ Rep 186, 188.

169 *Fisheries (United Kingdom v Norway)* (Pleadings) [1951] ICJ Pleadings IV, 8, 86.

170 Ibid., 457. Emphasis added.

171 *Fisheries (United Kingdom v Norway)* (Judgment) [1951] ICJ Rep 116, 131. The court added that in any event, 'the ten-mile rule would appear to be inapplicable as against Norway inasmuch as she has always opposed any attempt to apply it to the Norwegian coast', giving impetus to the 'persistent objector' principle (ibid.).

172 Bourquin, 'La portée général de l'arrêt rendu', 101, 113.

connecting archipelagic islands to each other and to the mainland.[173] All over the world, states with bays and archipelagos sat up and took note.

The next category of internal waters enclosed by straight baselines were those within minor curvatures of the coast. The court observed that 'several States' had already applied the straight baseline method without objections from other states to 'minor curvatures of the coast line where it was solely a question of giving a simpler form to the belt of territorial waters'.[174] Beckett feared that the court's decision on minor curvatures would have two effects. For one, it would deal a blow to the idea of a bay as a distinct legal entity, different from curvatures in the coast.[175] And for another, unless the phrase 'minor curvatures' was taken to mean 'small' and 'gradual' curvatures, it would prompt states to make excessive maritime claims for larger curvatures: he warned that France, for example, could in theory draw a straight baseline some 297 miles long from Pointe de Penmarch in Brittany to Henday in Haute Pyrénées in the French portion of the Bay of Biscay, claiming everything within as internal waters.[176]

The final category of internal waters enclosed by straight baselines were those within the skjærgaard – the archipelagos, islands, rocks and reefs fringing the northern part of Norway's coast. The court decided: 'Since the mainland is bordered in its western sector by the "skjærgaard", which constitutes a whole with the mainland, it is the outer line of the "skjærgaard" which must be taken into account in delimiting the belt of Norwegian territorial waters.'[177] The emphasis here was on the unity of

[173] J. Evensen, 'The Anglo-Norwegian fisheries case and its legal consequences', *American Journal of International Law* 46 (1952), 609, 622.

[174] Fitzmaurice, who made some of his sharpest comments about the judgment in his footnotes, responded that:

> One of the striking features of the *Fisheries* case was the elevation of minority practices into general rules of law ... Conclusions were based on the practice of 'several States' ... yet when it came to the practice of the *overwhelming* majority of States in favour of the tide-mark rule, or of a maximum ten- or twelve-mile closing-line for bays, this was apparently regarded as having no weight because *not all* States adopted this practice.

('The law and procedure ... points of substantive law', 1, 389, fn. 1. Original emphases.)

[175] W. E. Beckett, 'Anglo-Norwegian fisheries case' (14 February 1952), p. 8: LCO 2/5783, TNA.

[176] Ibid.

[177] *Fisheries (United Kingdom v Norway)* (Judgment) [1951] ICJ Rep 116, 128.

the skjærgaard with the mainland. Noting that the British had recommended a ten-mile limit on straight baselines around this outer perimeter by drawing an analogy with closing lines for bays, the court held instead that because there was no general rule to draw on, 'the coastal State would seem to be in the best position to appraise the local conditions dictating the selection'.[178] 'This is not good enough,' Beckett wrote: 'The local State's discretion is not unqualified but must be regulated by international law.'[179] Even so, he conceded that although the British government had previously opposed the outer coastline theory, 'it must be admitted that a considerable body of State practice can be pointed to as substantiating the validity of this theory in international law'.[180]

Finally on baselines, the court gave credence to Norway's arguments that economic criteria could shape the demarcation of the territorial sea, stating that one consideration that extended beyond geographical factors should not be overlooked, namely: 'certain economic interests peculiar to a region, the reality and importance of which are clearly evidenced by a long usage'.[181] Likewise, traditional rights over certain fishing grounds 'founded on the vital needs of the population and attested by very ancient and peaceful usage' could be 'taken into account'.[182] The court seems to have considered these economic-historic criteria as having a subsidiary rather than a determinative role, especially when applied to a whole baseline system; the phrase 'taken into account' suggests that economic issues should be considered alongside geographic factors, not as the only criterion. Even so, the court's recognition of economic factors was a significant departure. The British judge Arnold McNair alluded to this in his dissent, noting that one of the fundamental issues that had divided the parties was 'the difference between the subjective and the objective views of the delimitation of territorial waters', his own view being that 'the manipulation of the limits of territorial waters for the purpose of protecting economic and other social interests has no justification in law'.[183] Later, commentator

178 Ibid., 131.

179 W. E. Beckett, 'Copy of note handed by Sir Eric Beckett to Professor Lauterpacht' (4 June 1952), p. 3: LCO 2/5783, TNA.

180 W. E. Beckett, 'Anglo-Norwegian fisheries case' (14 February 1952), p. 9: LCO 2/5783, TNA.

181 *Fisheries (United Kingdom v Norway)* (Judgment) [1951] ICJ Rep 116, 133.

182 Ibid., 142.

183 *Fisheries (United Kingdom v Norway)* Dissenting Opinion of Sir Arnold McNair [1951] ICJ Rep 158, 169.

Leslie Green stated that the 'economic interests peculiar to a region' formula was 'a subjective test which, if generally applied, could lead to the negation of most principles of law'.[184] Be that as it may, states' determination to protect coastal fisheries and the livelihoods of those depending on them would play a central role in future law of the sea negotiations.

Overall on baselines, Beckett thought the principles governing their application were so general that they robbed the law of its precision and predictability. Legal advisers would be hard put 'to advise with any confidence what is permissible and what is not', he wrote, and states would exploit them to extend sovereign claims:

> [M]any foreign States, which have hitherto followed more or less the strict principles enunciated by the United Kingdom, will now make use of the greater latitude allowed by the principles of the Court's judgment, with the result that great portions of the sea which have hitherto been regarded as open sea under the sovereignty of no State will now be claimed to be under national sovereignty.[185]

He added that even Britain, as the exemplar of these strict principles, would, acting in accordance with the judgment, now be perfectly within its rights to girdle the whole west coast of Scotland with straight baselines running from Cape Wrath in the north to the Butt of Lewis in the west and down the outer coast of the West Hebrides, enclosing the Minches as internal waters.[186]

The Tide Turns

After the *Fisheries* decision was handed down, the British drew a few crumbs of comfort from the court's enunciation of the 'international aspect' of maritime claims:

> The delimitation of sea areas has always an international aspect; it cannot be dependent merely upon the will of the coastal State as expressed in its municipal law. Although it is true that the act of delimitation is necessarily a unilateral act, because only the coastal State is competent to

[184] L. C. Green, 'The Anglo-Norwegian fisheries case, 1951', *Modern Law Review* 15 (1952), 373, 376.

[185] W. E. Beckett, 'Anglo-Norwegian fisheries case' (14 February 1952), p. 2: LCO 2/5783, TNA.

[186] Ibid.

> undertake it, the validity of the delimitation with regard to other States depends upon international law.[187]

The British interpreted this as a rebuke to Norway and made something of an issue of it. In his dissent, McNair wrote that while the demarcation of territorial waters fell to the coastal state 'the principles followed in carrying out this delimitation are within the domain of law and not within the discretion of each State'.[188] Fitzmaurice followed, arguing that 'there is in fact no reason why the sovereign right of any one State should prevail over that of another *except* by reference to an overriding legal system from which sovereign rights themselves spring'.[189]

Beckett, however, was dismayed not only with the decision, but also with the quality of the reasoning informing it. If it represented the best view of the law, he wrote, it 'completely failed to demonstrate why this is so', being little more than 'a series of *ex cathedra* legal pronouncements with virtually no reference to any supporting authority'.[190] And where it did rely on authorities, such as in its decision on Norway's claim of having title based on prescription, he claimed that the court erred in Norway's favour by, for example, citing the Norwegian supreme court's *St. Just* case of 1934, which supported Norway's position, while ignoring the same court's *Deutschland* case six years earlier, which supported Britain's position.[191] (He did not mention that *St. Just* overruled *Deutschland*.)

All these developments, he said, were very disquieting,[192] and reflected the turn of the political tide against the maritime powers. 'Running through the entire judgment is a concern for the interests of the coastal State almost exclusively, and one is inclined to think that the coastal State will now get away with almost anything, except possibly something absolutely gross, such as the 200 mile claims of some of the Latin American States.'[193] The court had, in his view,

187 *Fisheries (United Kingdom v Norway)* (Judgment) [1951] ICJ Rep 116, 132.
188 *Fisheries (United Kingdom v Norway)* Dissenting Opinion of Sir Arnold McNair [1951] ICJ Rep 158, 160.
189 Fitzmaurice, 'The law and procedure ... general principles and sources of law', 1, 12. Original emphasis.
190 W. E. Beckett, 'Anglo-Norwegian fisheries case' (14 February 1952), p. 3: LCO 2/5783, TNA.
191 Ibid.
192 Ibid.
193 W. E. Beckett to A. S. Fisher, 'Territorial waters: I.C.J. judgment in the Anglo-Norwegian fisheries dispute' (u.d., c. January–February 1952), p. 2: POWE 33/1972, TNA.

unwisely capitulated to the coastal states' special pleading based on geographic happenstance and economic hardship, and this would have an adverse effect on the development of international law. 'A Court which considers itself free to indulge in judicial legislation,' he wrote, 'is a Court whose decisions cannot be predicted and which is shaking itself free to a considerable extent of the shackles of the law which are the protection against decisions given on the basis of national or personal prejudice.'[194]

Beckett ascribed this tendency to the non-Western judges in the majority – these being the Latin Americans, the East Europeans and the Egyptian judge Abdul Hamid Badawi.[195] He had a particularly low opinion of the Chilean judge Alejandro Álvarez, having already dismissed him after *Corfu Channel* as 'senile and perfectly useless', and for advancing 'peculiar views about the new international law'.[196]

These apparently 'peculiar' views reappeared in Álvarez's individual opinion in *Fisheries*, consonant with those held by many coastal states of the global South. He argued that the old law of nations had to adapt to meet the new conditions of international life rather than merely restating the law 'advocated by Anglo-Saxon jurists as a means of ending the crisis in international law'.[197] He set out two principles governing claims to the territorial sea. First, because states operated under different geographic and economic circumstances, 'it is not possible to lay down uniform rules, applicable to all'[198] – a view challenging the powers' claim that territorial seas had to be uniform in breadth and universal in application. And second, because states' claims to a territorial sea had to meet certain conditions, such as being reasonable, not infringing the rights of other states or the general interest, and not constituting *abus de droit*.[199] When declaring the breadth of its territorial sea, Álvarez wrote, 'the State must indicate the reasons, geographic, economic, etc., which provide the justification therefor', thereby doing away with the need to discuss

194 W. E. Beckett, 'Anglo-Norwegian fisheries case' (14 February 1952), p. 3: LCO 2/5783, TNA.
195 Ibid., p. 2.
196 W. E. Beckett, 'Report by the Agent on the Corfu case' (19 May 1949), p. 2: FO 371/78231, TNA.
197 *Fisheries (United Kingdom v Norway)* Individual Opinion of Judge Alvarez [1951] ICJ Rep 145, 146.
198 Ibid., 150.
199 Ibid.

baselines and closing lines.[200] These views, of course, reflected a modernising approach to the law of the sea.

While the British had expected the non-Western judges to express views favouring Norway, they had not banked on Western judges doing so as well. Beckett criticised the 'very weak' American judge Green Hackworth for not elaborating on his single-sentence concurrence with the majority.[201] He also speculated that the French president Jules Basdevant and the Belgian Charles de Visscher had voted tactically with the majority to prevent an even split over the lawfulness of straight baselines.[202] Finally, he argued that the Norwegian Helge Klæstad, whom he considered to be otherwise 'reliable', could on this occasion 'hardly be expected to be against Norway'.[203] That left the two dissenters, Arnold McNair and the Canadian John Read, to hold the line for the British position.

*

At the start of the proceedings, Frank Soskice had proclaimed that the court's decision on the law governing coastal waters 'will be of the very greatest importance … as a precedent'.[204] Once the judgment was handed down, the British back-pedalled, insisting that the court's decision should *not* be seen as a precedent. Invoking article 59 of the ICJ statute stating that decisions have 'no binding force except between the parties and in respect of that particular case',[205] they argued that even if the court had endorsed Norway's straight baselines, it did not mean that they would be applicable elsewhere.[206]

Privately, though, the British knew that this argument would not wash. In the year following the decision, *Fisheries* seemed to accelerate the trend towards states' extension of their jurisdiction over coastal waters.

[200] Ibid.
[201] W. E. Beckett, 'Anglo-Norwegian fisheries case' (14 February 1952), p. 4: LCO 2/5783, TNA. (Hackworth's declaration is at: *Fisheries (United Kingdom v Norway)* (Judgment) [1951] ICJ Rep 116, 144.)
[202] Ibid.
[203] Ibid., p. 5.
[204] *Fisheries (United Kingdom v Norway)* (Pleadings) [1951] ICJ Pleadings IV, 8, 23.
[205] Statute of the International Court of Justice (signed 26 June 1945, EIF 24 October 1945), *Documents of the United Nations Conference on International Organization* (New York: United Nations Information Organizations, 1945–1955), vol. 15, p. 355, 362.
[206] S. Lloyd, UK House of Commons, *Hansard* (14 December 1953), vol. 522, cols. 36–37.

Norway decided to enclose its whole coast (not just the northern part) with straight baselines; Iceland issued new regulations for a four-mile exclusive fishing zone measured from straight baselines; the USSR denounced the 1930 fishing agreement allowing British vessels to fish within three miles of the USSR's northern coast; Romania and Bulgaria declared twelve-mile territorial seas; Israel declared a six-mile territorial sea; Ecuador declared a twelve-mile territorial sea measured from straight baselines; Chile, Ecuador and Peru declared the enforcement of fishing and whaling regulations extending out to 200 miles; and the Philippines declared its sovereignty over waters extending out to the limits set by the 1898 Treaty of Paris.[207]

In response to this evolving practice, jurists' interpretation of the law also started to shift. A Foreign Office briefing paper observed:

> (a) The International Court of Justice has delivered a judgment [o]n the Anglo-Norwegian Fisheries Dispute which not only approves the principle of baselines but also upsets so much of the existing law of the sea as to make it very possible that, if the issue of the breadth of territorial waters were put to the Court, it would rule against the three mile limit.
> (b) The International Law Commission has shown in its discussions that its approach is similar to that of the Court. It also favours base lines for indented coasts and may well recommend a six-mile, or even a twelve-mile, limit for territorial waters.[208]

Seven years after the *Fisheries* decision, the court's holding on straight baselines was incorporated into article 4 of the 1958 territorial sea convention, which stated that they could be deployed where the coastline was 'deeply indented and cut into, or if there is a fringe of islands along the coast in its immediate vicinity'.[209] These baselines were made conditional on the by now familiar criteria: they 'must not depart to any appreciable extent from the general direction of the coast'; the landward sea areas behind them 'must be sufficiently closely linked to the land domain to be subject to the regime of internal waters'; and account 'may be taken, in determining particular baselines, of economic interests peculiar to the region concerned, the reality and the importance of

[207] 'Draft brief for talks with the State Department' (u.d, c. late 1952–early 1953), pp. 3–4: MT 59/2976, TNA.
[208] Ibid., pp. 2–3.
[209] Article 4(1), Territorial Sea Convention, 208.

which are clearly evidenced by a long usage'.[210] (No reference was made to baselines' 'reasonable' departure from the line of the coast, however.)

Two weeks after the convention was ratified in 1964, the British declared a series of straight baselines that enclosed most of the west of Scotland, starting from Cape Wrath in the north, skirting westwards around the Western Hebrides and finishing 282 miles to the south at the Mull of Kintyre[211] – almost exactly as Beckett had prophesied.

[210] Article 4(2) and 4(4), ibid.
[211] Territorial Waters Order in Council 1964 (25 September 1964): FO 371/176333, TNA.

3

North, South, East and West

New Ideas and New Actors at the 1958 Conference

When Ferdinand Kruegel of Aristotle Onassis's staff announced in Hamburg that the Onassis fleet would continue its whaling operations off the coast of Peru despite the nation's recently declared 200-mile fishing exclusion zone, Lima decided to act. On 15 November 1954, the Peruvian destroyer *Aguirre* seized *Olympic Challenger*, the mothership of Onassis's whaling fleet, 364 miles from Peru's coast. Over the next twenty-four hours, Peruvian destroyers intercepted four more ships – *Olympic Victor*, *Olympic Lightning*, *Olympic Fighter* and *Olympic Conqueror* – between 160 and 280 miles from the coast.[1] The ships and their crews were taken into the port of Paíta in northern Peru, where they were detained until Onassis's underwriters Lloyds paid the US$3 million fine. Shortly afterwards, Onassis appeared in a London hotel, where he told the press that the arrest of his whalers was 'unbelievable', and that had they been armed, 'we would have blown something up'.[2]

Whaling was an international business, and this was an international case involving companies owned by an Argentine citizen, headquartered in Monaco, managed from Hamburg, running whalers registered in Panama, crewed by Germans, Canadians and Norwegians, and insured in London. Panama, as the flag state, and the United States, whose tuna clippers also fished inside Peru's exclusion zone, protested that the intervention contravened international law. But what, exactly, *was* the international law?

Peru pointed to the tripartite Santiago Declaration, signed by Chile, Ecuador and Peru in 1952, which asserted 'exclusive sovereignty and jurisdiction' over a maritime zone encompassing both the sea and seabed

[1] Distances taken from 'Translation of report by the Panamanian foreign minister Mr. Guizado to the National Assembly on November 22, 1954', p. 1: FO 371/110656, TNA.
[2] 'Action of Peru ridiculed', *The Times* (27 November 1954).

'to a minimum distance of 200 nautical miles from these coasts',[3] thereby justifying the arrest of whalers outside the 200-mile limit. Further explanations followed. The newspaper *El Comerico* ran a long interview with Carlos Balarezo Delta, a prominent adviser on fishing matters, who presented four legal arguments for the confiscations. First, Peru's response to the Onassis fleet's incursion was 'rooted in her imperative need to defend her national sovereignty'.[4] Second, it was asserting its economic rights, validated by the ICJ's 1951 *Fisheries* judgment, which recognised the 'economic factor in the delimitation of territorial waters'.[5] Third, it was acting in accordance with customary law 'that permits a sea-coast State to reject by force illicit acts such as excessive or clandestine fishing'.[6] And fourth, it was following the new direction of international law that conferred 'authority and jurisdiction' on coastal states to conserve and exploit their maritime resources.[7] This last claim unsettled the Americans and the British because it pointed to their own precedent-setting maritime claims over the preceding decade.

In September 1945, a month after the end of the war, Harry Truman had proclaimed the United States' regulation of coastal fisheries within designated conservation zones, [8] and its jurisdiction over the natural resources of the contiguous continental shelf.[9]

These two proclamations were designed to assert American control over the *resources* of the conservation zones and the continental shelf – not over these zones themselves. Although neither specified the parameters of jurisdictional control, the press release accompanying the continental shelf proclamation defined the area concerned as 'submerged land which is contiguous to the continent and which is covered by no

[3] Article 3(2), Declaration on the Maritime Zone (signed and EIF 18 August 1952) 1006 UNTS 323, 326.

[4] Translation of the *El Comercio* interview, 'Peru has exercised an indisputable right in capturing vessels of the Onassis fleet' (20 November 1954), p. 1: FO 371/110657, TNA.

[5] Ibid.

[6] Ibid.

[7] Ibid.

[8] 'Presidential proclamation no. 2668, concerning the policy of the United States with respect to coastal fisheries in certain areas of the high seas' (28 September 1945), reprinted in United Nations Legislative Series, *Laws and regulations on the regime in the high seas*, vol. 1 (New York: United Nations, 1951), pp. 112–113.

[9] 'Presidential proclamation no. 2667, concerning the policy of the United States with respect to the natural resources of the subsoil and sea bed of the continental shelf' (28 September 1945), reprinted in UN Legislative Series, *Laws and regulations ... high seas*, pp. 38–40.

more than 100 fathoms (600 feet) of water'.[10] These proclamations would provide the touchstone for subsequent claims to continental shelves and fishing zones.

Meanwhile, the British had made their own substantial contribution to state practice by claiming continental shelves off nine Gulf region protectorates and four Caribbean colonies between 1945 and 1949. Of these, the nine Gulf claims, all made in June 1949, each confirmed the importance of Truman's shelf proclamation, by stating that 'the right of any littoral state to exercise its control over the natural resources of the seabed and subsoil adjacent to its coasts has been established in international practice by the action of other states'.[11] In reality, though, the British claims went beyond Truman's proclamation by asserting exclusive jurisdiction and control over not only resources but also the seabed and subsoil itself.[12] A dozen or so other states also followed Truman's lead, extending jurisdiction over the continental shelf, offshore fishing, or both, with the Latin American states prominent among them. By the time Peru intercepted *Olympic Challenger* in 1954, every independent mainland coastal state in the region, from Mexico to Chile, claimed wider jurisdictions off their coasts than they had done before the United States' initiatives.

By then, the Americans and British, having made their own maritime claims, decided to apply the brakes. In 1949, the International Law Commission (ILC) was vested with responsibility for producing a set of draft articles to guide negotiations over a single law of the sea convention, which, it was hoped, would rein in future claims. In 1956, this body produced a guideline text – grouped under the headings of the territorial sea, contiguous zone, continental shelf, high seas and the conservation of the living resources of the sea – consisting of seventy-three articles.

Of all these issues, the essential question, preceding all the others, was still the breadth of the territorial sea, described by the Saudi UN delegate Ahmad Shukairy as 'the base of the pyramid' on which all other claims stood.[13] Should its breadth be three miles for all, or could states legitimately extend it according to local circumstances as a buffer against foreign

[10] Ibid., p. 39.

[11] 'Proclamation with respect to the sea bed' (concerning respectively Abu Dhabi, Ajman, Bahrain, Dubai, Kuwait, Qatar, Ras al Khaimah, Sharjah and Umm al Qaiwain), reprinted in UN Legislative Series, *Laws and regulations . . . high seas*, pp. 23–30.

[12] Ibid.

[13] J. R. Freeland to G. G. Fitzmaurice (24 October 1958), summarising Shukairy's speech at the General Assembly on 1 October 1958: FO 371/133748, TNA.

navies and fishing fleets? The ILC draft declined to break the deadlock, stating in article 3(2) and (4) only that it considered 'that international law does not permit an extension of the territorial sea beyond twelve miles' and recommending that its breadth 'be fixed by an international conference'.[14] The General Assembly adopted the ILC's draft,[15] and the conference was duly convened the following year, opening on 24 February 1958. The United States and Britain, having earlier released the genie of expanded jurisdictions from its bottle, would now attempt to stuff it back in again. But it was too late.

Not the Cold War

The conference in Geneva was attended by eighty-six delegations, with the list of invitees being weighted, where the Western powers could contrive it, towards Western interests. All UN members were eligible to attend, and invitations were also extended to countries and entities that although not UN members were likely to support their position, namely, the Holy See, Monaco, South Korea, San Marino, Switzerland and West Germany. (By the same token, no invitations were issued to non-UN members unlikely to be supportive, such as North Korea, Mongolia and the People's Republic of China.) Meanwhile, these same powers strongly encouraged smaller potentially sympathetic UN members disinclined to send a delegation to send one anyway: when considering how to induce landlocked Luxembourg to put on an appearance, the British Foreign Office legal adviser Gerald Fitzmaurice wrote, 'I know that sort of thing does not look very good, but we do not need to be over-scrupulous.'[16]

The date of the conference suggests that it was a Cold War affair; indeed, this was the impression conveyed by some participants' accounts published at the time.[17] Yet the major disputes were not between East and West but, as will be seen, between the Western powers themselves and between North and South.

[14] International Law Commission, 'Articles concerning the law of the sea with commentaries' [hereafter, ILC, 'Articles ... with commentaries'], *Yearbook of the International Law Commission* (1956), vol. 2, 264, 265.

[15] UNGA Res. 1105(XI) (21 February 1957).

[16] G. G. Fitzmaurice to W. V. J. Evans (30 January 1958), p. 1: FO 371/133261, TNA.

[17] Not least those by the American delegation head, Arthur Dean: 'Freedom of the seas', *Foreign Affairs* 37 (1958), 86, 88; and 'Achievements at the law of the sea conference', *Proceedings of the American Society of International Law* 53 (1959), 186, 196.

By contrast, relations at the conference between the Western powers and the Soviets, while not exactly cordial, were less volatile. The USSR was an aspiring maritime power with an ambitious shipbuilding programme in progress, which meant it had interests in common with the United States and Britain over navigational rights. Because both sides were so acutely aware of security *vis-à-vis* each other, they wished to prevent any other states' maritime claims from impeding their manoeuvrability in the oceans. The main difference between the two sides concerned the maximum breadth of territorial sea that each could tolerate, with the Western powers eventually stopping at six miles, and the USSR stopping at twelve – the breadth of the customs zone they had declared in 1909, as well as the limit recommended by the ILC.

During the conference, the Soviet delegation leader Grigori Tunkin emphasised to the American deputy delegation leader William Sanders that Soviet and American interests 'were quite similar if not identical in preventing broad extensions of the territorial sea'.[18] Tunkin (as Sanders reported) continued:

> In view of the interest of the great majority of the countries represented at the Conference in a broad extension of the territorial sea and of their fisheries jurisdiction, it was important from the point of view of both the Soviet Union and the United States that some check be put on their ambitions. The Soviet Union considers that this could only be done by working for and accepting a reasonable extension of the territorial sea. I [Sanders] said I assumed he meant the twelve miles. He said yes.[19]

In sum, the Soviet and Western powers' policies converged, with each wishing to rein in incursions into the high seas. When they clashed during the conference –and it was not very often – it was over the West's closure of large tracts of the high seas to carry out naval exercises and conduct nuclear tests.

These two issues arose in the conference committee on the high seas when delegates began discussing article 27 of the ILC draft. This stated: 'The high seas being open to all nations, no State may validly purport to

[18] W. Sanders, 'Memorandum of conversation' (12 April 1958): box 136, RG 43, Records of international conferences, commissions and expositions, Bureau of International Organization Affairs, Office of International Conferences, administrative files 1928–1967, National Archives and Records Administration, Maryland, US [hereafter, NARA].

[19] Ibid.

subject any part of them to its sovereignty.'[20] The ILC's accompanying commentary added that, 'States are bound to refrain from any acts which might adversely affect the use of the high seas by nationals of other States.'[21]

On the issue of naval exercises, Tunkin, clearly concerned about the activities of the Americans' Seventh Fleet in Asian and West Pacific waters, stated that the United States had closed off zones for naval manoeuvres in the North Pacific, the Yellow Sea, the Caribbean and the Sea of Japan.[22] Furthermore, the British had months earlier declared submarine exercise zones in 'extensive sea areas south west of Portsmouth and south of Plymouth located on international routes in the English Channel'.[23] Albania, Bulgaria and the USSR therefore proposed adding to the end of article 27: 'No naval or air ranges or other combat training areas limiting freedom of navigation may be designated on the high seas near foreign coasts or on international sea routes.'[24]

This proposal was voted down. The British and Americans argued that naval exercises on the high seas were generally accepted, and that the USSR had itself closed off areas of the Barents Sea and Kara Sea for manoeuvres in 1957.[25] Moreover, the British said, the closure of high seas for naval exercises did not greatly impede navigation, and 'merchant ships frequently sail through areas in which manoeuvres are being carried out'.[26] Recalling that high seas activities had to meet the test of reasonableness, they proposed inserting a clause at the end of the article stating that high seas freedoms 'shall be exercised by all States with reasonable regard to the interests of other States'.[27]

The issue of nuclear tests proved less easy to dismiss. Czechoslovakia, Poland, the USSR and Yugoslavia proposed inserting after article 27 a new article stating: 'States are bound to refrain from testing nuclear

20 ILC, 'Articles . . . with commentaries', 278.

21 Ibid.

22 Canadian delegation to External Affairs Ottawa (6 March 1958), p. 1: vol. 7182, 9456-RW-2-40, pt. 1, RG 25, LAC.

23 Ibid.

24 United Nations Law of the Sea Conference, 1958 [hereafter, UNLOSC I], vol. 4, A/Conf.13/C.2/L.32 (21 March 1958), p. 124.

25 UK delegation to UK Foreign Office (10 March 1958), p. 1: MAF 209/1643, TNA; and 'Freedom of the high seas – another international lost cause?', *Manchester Guardian* (4 February 1958).

26 UK delegation to UK Foreign Office (10 March 1958): FO 371/133264, TNA.

27 UNLOSC I, vol. 4, A/Conf.13/C.2/L.68 (26 March 1958), p. 134.

weapons on the high seas.'[28] This, Tunkin explained, was because the tests adversely affected other states' use of the oceans,[29] by diverting ships from their routes, compelling fishing vessels to find new fishing grounds, and contaminating the ocean with radioactive waste. (The Americans' announcement the previous month of a test at Eniwetok atoll in the Marshall Islands entailing the closure of a 390,000-square-mile zone illustrated the point.[30]) This was a fruitful subject for the USSR to pursue: detonating nuclear weapons was not illegal but, under custom, curtailing high seas freedoms was. In 1957, for example, the British had temporarily suspended their acceptance of the ICJ's jurisdiction because they feared being taken to court by Japan for impeding high seas rights with their Christmas Island (now Kiritimati) nuclear tests in the Gilbert and Ellice Islands.[31] For the Soviets, another advantage of focussing on the testing of nuclear weapons at sea was that it selectively targeted the Americans and the British, who carried out their tests in the Pacific, while exempting themselves, who carried out nuclear tests on land. As Ghana's external affairs' permanent secretary Amishadai Adu noted, the 'prohibition of tests over the seas would leave the Russians free to have as many tests as they liked in Siberia'.[32]

The British and Americans, caught on the back foot by the Soviet proposal, countered on two grounds. First, they argued that the conference did not have the competence to discuss the issue, and that the matter should be left to the General Assembly and its Disarmament Commission because the issues of nuclear tests and nuclear disarmament were inseparable.[33] Second, the British delegation leader Reginald Manningham-Buller insisted that tests were carried out with the 'most scrupulous regard for the interests of all users of the high seas', based on research revealing 'no harmful effects from them to human, animal and marine life'.[34] And the American delegation leader Arthur Dean claimed that 'nuclear explosions produced a minimal radio-active fall-out' and

[28] UNLOSC I, vol. 4, A/Conf.13/C.2/L.30 (21 March 1958), p. 124.

[29] Canadian delegation to External Affairs Ottawa (6 March 1958), p. 1: vol. 7182, 9456-RW-2-40, pt. 1, RG 25, LAC.

[30] 'Nuclear test area set', *New York Times* (15 February 1958).

[31] One British legal adviser stated, 'Japan could have made out a pretty respectable legal case': F. A. Vallat (27 September 1958): FO 371/135535, TNA.

[32] L. J. D. Wakeley to M. E. Allan (21 March 1958): FO 371/135535, TNA.

[33] 'Speech delivered ... in the plenary meeting by Sir Reginald Manningham-Buller' (23 April 1958), pp. 1, 2: FO 371/135535, TNA.

[34] Ibid., p. 1.

that nuclear research, including detonations, 'would be of benefit to agriculture and industry'.[35] These tendentious claims were more difficult to disprove at a conference than in a courtroom: by what measure might 'scrupulous regard' or 'harmful effects' or 'minimal ... fall-out' be appraised?

Even so, the powers found themselves trapped in a pincer between the Soviet bloc's opposition to nuclear tests at sea and most other states' opposition to nuclear tests altogether. As Gerald Fitzmaurice reported, even New Zealand's delegates told him they would be 'embarrassed' if asked to vote against the Soviet proposal.[36] The British tabled a long-shot resolution proposing to transfer the nuclear tests issue out of the conference and into the General Assembly.[37] Then the Indian delegation leader Ashoke Sen threw the British a lifeline by suggesting an amendment that supported the transfer of the issue to the General Assembly while also offering a sop to the states opposed to nuclear tests. This clause read: '*Recognizing* that there is a serious and genuine apprehension on the part of many States that nuclear tests constitute an infringement of the freedom of the seas.'[38] The British and Americans supported it because it referred only to states' apprehension about tests without passing judgment on the tests themselves. A revised version of the Indian resolution[39] passed by a substantial majority, with only Japan voting against it for not opposing nuclear tests vigorously enough.[40] Having disposed of this issue, Sen then proposed that the Soviet motion not be put to the vote, and this carried.[41] The Indian delegation had thus rescued the United States and Britain by disposing of the Soviet proposal and prompting other delegates to collectively abdicate responsibility for taking a firmer stand on the issue.

Divisions in the Western Camp

These issues aside, the 1958 conference was characterised more by the divisions between the Western states than by East–West tensions. On the

35 UNLOSC I, vol. 4, '18th meeting', A/Conf.13/C.4/SR.16–20 (27 March 1958), p. 47.

36 G. G. Fitzmaurice, 'Geneva law of the sea conference, 1958' (July 1958), p. 8: FO 371/133746, TNA.

37 UNLOSC I, vol. 4, A/Conf.13/C.2/L.64 (25 March 1958), p. 132.

38 UNLOSC I, vol. 4, A/Conf.13/C.2/L.71 (26 March 1958), p. 134.

39 UNLOSC I, vol. 4, A/Conf.13/C.2/L.71/Rev.1 (27 March 1958), p. 134.

40 A. Randall to H. C. Hainworth (1 April 1958), p. 2: FO 371/135535, TNA.

41 UNLOSC I, vol. 4, '20th meeting', A/Conf.13/C.4/SR.16–20 (28 March 1958), p. 52.

essential issue of the breadth of the territorial sea and fishing limits, a chasm would open up between the defensive maritime powers, led by Britain and the United States, who insisted on the retention of narrow territorial seas, and the disaffected and increasingly assertive coastal states, including Western states such as Canada and Iceland, who wished to extend their territorial seas, or claim jurisdiction over an exclusive fishing zone, or both.

Before the conference opened, ministers in Canada had considered declaring a twelve-mile territorial sea[42] to prevent long-distance American, Portuguese, Spanish and Soviet fleets from fishing in the high seas within the Gulf of St Lawrence and close to the coasts of Nova Scotia and British Columbia. Then the Americans and British intervened, insisting that it was essential for Canada, as a NATO member, to support the three-mile territorial sea for geo-strategic reasons.[43] The American and British delegation leaders Arthur Dean and Reginald Manningham-Buller also impressed on their Canadian colleague George Drew that they would *never* endorse an extension of the territorial sea beyond three miles.[44] As Dean explained, the security of the whole Mediterranean area was at stake: if the territorial sea were extended to twelve miles, the US Sixth Fleet would be prevented from deploying through the Strait of Gibraltar and within the Aegean Sea.[45]

This placed the Canadians in a quandary. As the northern affairs minister Alvin Hamilton later told parliament, their dilemma was how to 'reconcile the defence interests, freedom of the seas and the freedom of the air, which really required a very narrow territorial sea, and the needs of our people on our coasts for some priority in harvesting the fish off their shores'.[46] The Canadian solution, put forward at the conference, accommodated both concerns. States could claim a territorial sea extending three miles from the baseline, thereby meeting NATO requirements, plus a twelve-mile exclusive fishing zone (i.e. one extending nine miles beyond the territorial sea), thereby protecting Canadian fisheries

42 Canadian delegation to External Affairs Ottawa (27 February 1958), pp. 1, 2: vol. 7182, 9456-RW-2-40, pt. 1, RG 25, LAC.
43 Ibid., p. 1.
44 'Summary of the Geneva conference' (u.d., c. July 1958), p. 12: vol. 7183, 9456-RW-4-40, pt. 3, RG 25, LAC.
45 Canadian delegation to External Affairs Ottawa (27 February 1958), p. 1: vol. 7182, 9456-RW-2-40, pt. 1, RG 25, LAC.
46 'Report on law of sea conference – statement by Mr. Alvin Hamilton' (25 July 1958), p. 6: vol. 7183, 9456-RW-4-40, pt. 3, RG 25, LAC.

out to twelve miles.[47] This was dubbed the '3+9' plan, and attracted different responses from its two powerful allies: the Americans supporting it because it retained the three-mile territorial sea; and the British opposing it because of its proposed exclusive fishing zone.

The Americans were prepared to accept the 3+9 plan with its exclusive fishing zone as the price to be paid for delegates' acceptance of a narrow territorial sea.[48] The US Navy, in particular, hoped that the plan would secure enough support to see off claims to wider territorial seas which, if endorsed, might impede its ability to 'show the flag', track enemy submarines and disperse its fleet in the Mediterranean and other confined areas as a precaution against nuclear threat.[49]

The British baulked at the Canadian plan, however. They argued on legal grounds that unlike the contiguous zone, which preserved high seas rights, the proposed exclusive fishing zone overturned them, enabling the coastal state to prevent foreign vessels from fishing off its coasts.[50] (Britain's limpet-like adherence to this argument was connected to their anticipated ICJ case regarding their fishing dispute with Iceland.) They also argued on material grounds that if the zone were instituted, Britain's long-distance trawling fleets would be shut out of fishing areas off the Faroes and Norway as well as Iceland, thus sharply reducing its landed catch, damaging fishing communities in Aberdeen, Fleetwood, Grimsby and Hull, and depriving the country of a cheap source of food.[51] As the president of the British Trawlers Association put it, 'a six-penny piece of fried fish would become a thing of the past' and 'cod would be as expensive as smoked salmon'.[52]

*

[47] This plan was proposed as an amendment to ILC articles 3 and 66 on the breadth of the territorial sea and the scope of the contiguous zone: UNLOSC I, vol. 3, A/C.13/C.1/L.77/Rev.1 (29 March 1958), p. 232.

[48] G. G. Fitzmaurice, 'Statement of the American position' (1 March 1958), p. 1: LO 2/646, TNA.

[49] J. E. Chadwick to A. MacDonald (26 March 1958), p. 2: LO 2/646, TNA.

[50] G. G. Fitzmaurice, 'Statement of the American position' (1 March 1958), p. 2: LO 2/646, TNA.

[51] 'United Kingdom policy on the breadth of the territorial sea' (15 January 1958), p. 7: MAF 209/1643, TNA; and Canadian delegation to External Affairs Ottawa (26 February 1958), p. 2: vol. 7182, 9456-RW-2-40, pt. 1, RG 25, LAC.

[52] 'Fleetwood concerned about fishing limits', *West Lancashire Evening Gazette* (21 February 1958).

Once the conference began, the first committee was convened to consider the territorial sea and the contiguous zone. The breadth of the territorial sea was bound to be controversial, so discussion of it was left until last, some five weeks into the conference, by which time many delegates had already denounced the three-mile limit as an outmoded relic of imperialism.

When the discussion finally opened on 31 March 1958, the first to speak was the Canadian delegation head George Drew, proposing the 3 +9 plan. Turning a deaf ear to the criticisms, he claimed that he had not heard any convincing argument for wider territorial seas, and that coastal states would be 'anxious to agree upon a limit of 3 miles for the territorial sea' if offered a fishing zone as well.[53] Within days he would come to rue these words, because as well as misreading the mood of the conference, he was about to be ambushed by a presumed ally.

The British, noting the opposition to the three-mile territorial sea, and faced with Drew's unsupportable fishing zone, decided to break ranks with Canada and the United States. Two days after Drew's speech, the British delegation launched their proposal for a six-mile territorial sea, with the caveat that in peacetime, foreign vessels and aircraft would enjoy high seas navigation rights – but not fishing rights – in the outer three miles.[54] As well as serving their own interests, the British hoped that this would win the support of states pushing for a wider territorial sea. But despite the labelling as a six-mile territorial sea, it was in reality a 3+3 plan, with the coastal state enjoying sovereignty over the inner three miles, and rights pertaining to non-navigational issues in the outer three miles (turning the latter into a de facto exclusive fishing zone, although the British could not call it that for reasons related to Iceland). The upshot was that the area affecting fishing would shrink from twelve miles, as per Canada's plan, to six miles, as per Britain's plan, which would have a less damaging effect on Britain's long-distance fishing industry. Moreover, it introduced the hitherto unrecognised right of innocent passage of foreign aircraft flying over a territorial sea, reflecting Whitehall's concern about overflying the Strait of Gibraltar if the territorial sea were to be extended on either side.[55] In sum, the British hoped

[53] UK delegation to UK Foreign Office (10 April 1958), p. 2: FO 371/133265, TNA, recounting Drew's speech, delivered on 31 March 1958.
[54] Article 3(1), UNLOSC I, vol. 3, A/Conf.13/C.1/L.134 (1 April 1958), p. 248.
[55] Ibid.

to silence the critics of the three-mile territorial sea by seemingly offering six miles, while also scuttling Canada's proposal.

When launching it, the British delegation head Reginald Manningham-Buller did nothing to spare the Canadians. His government, he said, had to oppose their 3+9 plan because the exclusive fishing zone idea was 'wrong in principle, incompatible with the status of the high seas and undesirable in practice'.[56] This rocked the Canadians, who had earlier modified their own plans in light of British and American claims that a three-mile territorial sea was essential for NATO security, and who were now faced with a rival British plan dressed up as a six-mile territorial sea. In the committee, George Drew responded to this with the frostiness usually reserved for the Soviets:

> Sir Reginald Manningham-Buller had contended that there was no juridical authority for the Canadian proposal. It might be pertinent to ask what juridical basis there was for the novel concept of a territorial sea which Sir Reginald himself had put forward.[57]

The Americans were not happy about Britain's new position either, and came down on the side of the Canadians. Arthur Dean announced that he had listened to Manningham-Buller's speech with the greatest regret because his delegation believed that any departure from the three-mile limit 'would deal a disastrous blow to the accepted legal order'[58] – a repudiation that effectively killed off the British proposal.

New Legal Concepts

While some of the powers were at loggerheads with each other, states from the South were pursuing different priorities. Although these nations constituted a numerical majority at the conference, they could hardly be described as a unified bloc – their maritime interests were simply too diverse. As the Ghanaian delegate Geoffrey Bing noted, the emerging Afro-Asian group, by now consisting of twenty-nine states, 'never acts as a group except for the purpose of agreeing on nominees for various positions'.[59] On the one hand, he wrote, some states from Asia and

56 UNLOSC I, vol. 3, '35th meeting', A/CONF.13/C.1/SR.31–35 (2 April 1958), p. 104.
57 UNLOSC I, vol. 3, '36th meeting' A/CONF.13/C.1/SR.36–40 (3 April 1958), p. 108.
58 UNLOSC I, vol. 3, '35th meeting', A/CONF.13/C.1/SR.31–35 (2 April 1958), p. 105.
59 'Note by attorney-general on political trends at the conference' (u.d. c. 23 May 1958), p. 1: RG 17/1/121, Public Records and Archives Administration Department, Accra [hereafter, PRAAD].

Africa always followed the American line: namely, Laos, Liberia, Pakistan, South Korea, South Vietnam and Taiwan.[60] On the other, there was a 'hard core' of states pursuing a more independent course: the African states of Libya, Morocco, Tunisia and the United Arab Republic; and the Asian states of Afghanistan, Burma, Ceylon, India, Indonesia, Malaya and Nepal.[61] This latter group, despite their diverse maritime interests, were, along with some of the Latin American states, drawn towards each other by their shared suspicion of the motives of the powers, and their desire to bend the law of the sea to meet their own needs.

Some delegates from the South pronounced – earlier than is often assumed – that the sea was 'the common heritage of mankind' (the Thai conference president, Wan Waithayakon[62]), and that its resources should be appropriated for 'the use of mankind for the benefit of all' (the Indian delegate, Ashoke Sen[63]). But although the idea of common heritage would assume great prominence in law of the sea debates a decade later, many delegates in 1958 were much more interested in agitating for greater control over their coastal waters. The states from the Asia-Pacific region – ranging from the Indian subcontinent in the west to the Pacific seaboard Latin American states in the east – were particularly active in this campaign, proposing several innovative ideas designed to extend coastal state jurisdiction over adjacent waters while restricting the maritime powers' claims to navigational freedoms and resource exploitation. These states were joined by the Arab nations, whose claims to twelve-mile territorial seas were designed to cut sea-borne access to Israel through the Gulf of Aqaba. As Bing noted, the African states' attitude to the territorial sea was dominated by the United Arab Republic, whose approach was 'purely political; a 12 mile limit being considered a good weapon against Israel'.[64]

The campaign for these objectives was spearheaded by India and Mexico, who put forward a single-sentence conference proposal that began, 'Every State is entitled to fix the breadth of its territorial sea up to a limit of twelve nautical miles.'[65] This plan allowed states to choose

[60] Ibid.
[61] Ibid.
[62] UNLOSC I, vol. 2, '1st plenary meeting' (24 February 1958), p. 3.
[63] UNLOSC I, vol. 3, '7th meeting', A/Conf.13/C.1/SR.6–10 (7 March 1958), p. 15.
[64] 'Note by attorney-general on political trends at the conference' (u.d. c. 23 May 1958), p. 1: RG 17/1/121, PRAAD.
[65] UNLOSC I, vol. 3, A/Conf.13/C.1/L.79 (29 March 1958), p. 233.

any breadth between the accepted minimum of three miles and the ILC-endorsed maximum of twelve miles. It had a bumpy ride: it was formally launched on 29 March 1958, then temporarily withdrawn on 16 April, then relaunched before being put to the vote on 19 April. Despite this, it presented the most significant threat to the maritime powers' campaign to retain a narrow territorial sea. The powers denounced it as being an invitation to states to claim twelve-mile territorial seas, but they could not deny its attractions, as were itemised by Arthur Dean: 'its apparent reasonableness, the blessing ILC has given it, the happy freedom of choice . . . and the idea that flexibility is progressive'.[66] For these reasons, he wrote, he could foresee 'a bandwagon movement bringing it dangerously close to [the required] two-thirds of the vote'.[67]

The powers, hitherto preoccupied with their own internecine squabbles, finally faced up to the threat posed by the India-Mexico plan towards the end of the conference. After the disagreement between Canada and Britain, Dean hosted a dinner at a restaurant to which he invited Reginald Manningham-Buller and Gerald Fitzmaurice of Britain, George Drew of Canada and Kenneth Bailey of Australia to discuss the tactics for dealing with this latest threat. According to Manningham-Buller, the assembled party thought it was likely that the India-Mexico plan would win a simple majority in committee, and might even scrape together a two-thirds majority in plenary.[68] They also agreed that a win in committee would be almost as bad as a win in plenary because all states who wished to claim twelve miles could point to the vote and say the majority supported them.[69]

Dean then introduced his guests to an American solution. He had, he said, been in contact with Dwight Eisenhower about the India-Mexico plan. The President, taking a narrow Cold War view, was worried about the political consequences of it succeeding in committee because this would be presented as 'another triumph for the Soviet bloc and as an example of what might be secured by Afro-Asian and Soviet cooperation'.[70] Dean also revealed that 'though the American Chiefs of

[66] 'Telegram from the delegation to the conference on the law of the sea to the Department of State' (14 March 1958): *FRUS, United Nations and general international matters*, 1958–1960, vol. 2, doc. 344.

[67] Ibid.

[68] UK delegation to UK Foreign Office (14 April 1958), p. 1: CO 936/588, TNA.

[69] Ibid.

[70] Ibid.

Staff remained adamant in their adherence to the 3-mile limit, the President might be prepared to override them to avoid a breakdown or acceptance of the 12-mile plan'.[71] Eisenhower's intervention would enable the American delegation to put forward a more palatable alternative to three miles: a six-mile territorial sea plus a six-mile non-exclusive fishing zone that allowed foreign states who had fished there regularly over the previous ten years to retain fishing rights in perpetuity.[72] This was dubbed the '6+6+historic fishing rights' plan.

The new plan, the Americans hoped, would be capable of attracting three groups: states considering a moderate extension of their territorial sea who might otherwise vote for the India-Mexico proposal; states wanting to protect their off-shore fishing resources who might be tempted by the promise of a fishing zone; and West European states anxious to retain their long-distance fishing grounds who had been alienated by the '9' part of the 3+9 plan. The Americans tabled this new proposal two days later.

The British, tempted by the idea of historic fishing rights in perpetuity, decided to back the American idea. But the Canadians opposed it. The Americans' *volte face* over the territorial sea – first claiming they would *never* support territorial seas of more than three miles[73] and then shifting their position to six – did not play well in Ottawa. Not only that, but the Americans' new 6+6+historic rights plan was a bad deal for Canada. While the 3+9 proposal had allowed for exclusive fishing rights over twelve miles, the latest plan removed that exclusivity for the outer six miles by introducing the idea of historic fishing rights. This provision would allow long-distance fishing states – including the United States – to fish forever off Canada's shores because it had already done so over the previous ten years, while at the same time excluding any newcomers.[74] Drew protested when Dean proposed the idea at the dinner party, and he protested again when the Americans launched their proposal in the committee. 'The Canadian Government,' he said, 'could never agree to

[71] Ibid.

[72] UNLOSC I, vol. 3, A/Conf.13/C.1/L.159 (15 April 1958), p. 253. Two days later, the Americans reduced the ten years to five years: A/Conf.13/C.1/L.159/Rev.1 (17 April 1958), p. 253.

[73] Australian High Commission Ottawa to External Affairs Canberra (18 April 1958), p. 1: A1838/392 1592/10, pt. 4, National Archives of Australia [hereafter, NAA].

[74] 'Memorandum: conference on the law of the sea' (10 July 1958), p. 2: vol. 7182, 9456-RW-3-40, pt. 3-FP, RG 25, LAC.

a proposal which would authorize certain foreign nationals to exploit a State's reserved fishing zone in perpetuity'.[75]

The Canadians consequently withdrew their 3+9 plan, launched an ill-starred motion along with India and Mexico that survived a day,[76] and then launched a 6+6 plan without the accompanying historic fishing rights.[77] None of these motions attracted the level of support hoped for, which was embarrassing for the Canadians, who 'reacted vigorously by heaping scorn on the United States and the British'.[78] According to American observers, this was 'not a very pretty spectacle'[79] and, they added, did little to enhance the prestige of the West.[80] Meanwhile, Arthur Dean, having abandoned the Canadian plan, tried to claim the moral high ground, suggesting that Washington tell Ottawa that they were shocked by:

> first, Canadian action in moving its proposal without any prior consultation with us even though we had consulted most closely with them on our own developing strategy; [and] second, by repeated, thinly veiled gibes at United States by Drew, though on our part we carefully refrained from any such innuendo or denunciation and constantly maintained friendly and constructive attitude.[81]

The Canadian delegation's relations with the British were even worse. There had already been 'lively exchanges' between Drew and Manningham-Buller in a meeting of British Commonwealth delegates, when Manningham-Buller had explained the British position, and then, exploiting his position as chair, had tried to stop Drew presenting the Canadian view.[82] Things escalated after the dinner party with Dean when the two men had

75 UNLOSC I, vol. 3, '50th meeting', A/Conf/13/C.1/SR.46–50 (16 April 1958), p. 154.
76 UNLOSC I, vol. 3, A/Conf.13/C.1/L.77/Rev.2 (16 April 1958), p. 232.
77 UNLOSC I, vol. 3, A/Conf.13/C.1/L.77/Rev.3 (17 April 1958), p. 232.
78 W. M. Chapman to 'Harold' (30 April 1958), p. 5: box 1, RG 370, Records concerning international groups and organizations, Records concerning the United Nations conference on law of the sea, 1957–1958, NARA.
79 Ibid.
80 W. C. Herrington, 'Comments on Mr Becker's memorandum' (30 June 1958), p. 2: box 137, RG 43, Records of international conferences, commissions and expositions, Bureau of International Organization Affairs, Office of International Conferences, administrative files 1928–1967, NARA.
81 'Telegram from the delegation to the conference on the law of the sea to the Department of State' (26 April 1958): *FRUS, United Nations and general international matters*, 1958–1960, vol. 2, doc. 371.
82 G. A. Drew, 'Report of the Canadian delegation' (c. 10 July 1958), p. 17: vol. 7182, 9456-RW-3-40, pt. 3-FP, RG 25, LAC.

a public shouting match, with Drew accusing Manningham-Buller of misrepresenting his views, and then subjecting him to language that Manningham-Buller claimed was 'of a character to which I am not accustomed'.[83] A week later, Manningham-Buller wrote to Drew, demanding an apology for 'observations which I cannot but regard both as highly offensive and wholly unwarranted'.[84]

News of this altercation made its way back to London, where some thought must have been given to smoothing the Canadians' ruffled feathers. In cases like this, proximity to the Queen was seen as a suitable emollient, and an invitation was dispatched to Drew and his wife to stay the night at Windsor Castle, which he was delighted to accept.[85]

The West's Pet Projects

While the less powerful coastal states were demanding wider territorial seas and exclusive fishing zones, the powers had their own priorities. These were reflected in four of the five themes addressed by the conference committees. The first committee on the territorial sea and contiguous zone addressed issues of concern to all the coastal states, including the powers. But the second, third and fourth committees – considering, respectively, the high seas, high seas fishing and the conservation of living resources, and the continental shelf – tended to be dominated by the states with the longest global reach. (The fifth committee, addressing the access rights of landlocked states to the sea, was short-sightedly regarded as a minority concern.)

In the second to fourth committees, the powers addressed, among other things, three issues: the nationality of ships, the conservation of high seas fisheries and the delineation of the continental shelf. Each of these reflected trends that had ripened in the period following the war. The debate about the nationality of ships was propelled by the emergence of the open registry states, and the ramifications for the major shipping states of the rise of 'flag of convenience' fleets. The discussion of fisheries conservation, while not new, was given impetus by the rocketing demand for fish coupled with more efficient fishing vessels, which had led to overfishing around the world. And the debate about the continental shelf

83 R. Manningham-Buller to G. A. Drew (17 April 1958), p. 2: LO 2/646, TNA.
84 Ibid., p. 1.
85 G. A. Drew to R. Manningham-Buller (19 April 1958): LO 2/646, TNA.

was driven forward by discoveries of new off-shore oil fields and advances in underwater drilling technology.

It is not surprising that the Western states devoted so much energy to these themes, given that they possessed the world's largest merchant shipping fleets, ran the most efficient fishing operations, and deployed the most advanced oil and gas extraction technologies. There were serious disagreements between them, however. These centred on one fundamental question: should unfettered free-market competition prevail or should states be allowed to manage their own segment of the market? This theme ran through all three debates: the Americans and Greeks clashed with the West Europeans over the flagging of ships; the Americans and Canadians with the British and the Japanese over high seas fisheries; and the Japanese with the Australians over the harvesting of living resources on the continental shelf. These differences also explain why their delegates were so ineffective in clarifying the ambiguities of the ILC's draft – ambiguities which were designed to paper over the cracks of earlier differences of opinion.

*

The relationship between ship and state became an issue in the second committee, where the articles on the high seas were being drafted. The West European shipping nations put forward a proposal indicating that states should exert effective control over ships sailing under their flag, which, Soviet adviser A. K. Zhudro recalled, 'evoked stormy debates … with the U.S. delegates being most vehemently opposed to it'.[86] This was because American and Greek merchant shipowners had over the previous decade been moving away from costly closed national registries, bound by national tax, labour and safety regimes, towards registration with open-registry states abroad, whose control over vessels operating under their flag tended to be lax. As Zhudro wrote, 'the rate of taxation is comparatively low, social legislation is not stringent enough, and labour is much cheaper'.[87]

In the years since the war, Liberia and Panama had led the field among the open-registry states,[88] followed by Costa Rica and Honduras.

86 A. Zhudro, 'The law of the open sea', *Nedelya* 42 (18 December 1962), p. 3: A1838 1592/10, pt. 11, NAA.

87 Ibid.

88 Organisation for European Economic Co-operation, 'Study on the expansion of the flags of convenience fleets and on various aspects thereof' (31 January 1958), pp. 2, 3: vol. 7182, 9456-RW-2-40, pt. 1, RG 25, LAC.

A British shipping inquiry set out their common features: as small states, they had no foreseeable national requirement for the merchant vessels under their flag; they permitted non-citizens to own, control and crew these vessels; they made foreign access to the registry easy; taxes were low or not levied locally; and they lacked the power to impose government or international regulations or control the shipping companies.[89] Eighty per cent of the tonnage flagged by these four open registry states was owned by American or Greek born or domiciled shipowners, who, according to an Organisation for European Economic Co-operation report, were seeking 'opportunities for avoiding taxation on earnings of ships … and in some cases relief from high crew standards and consequent high operating costs'.[90] These shipowners could then use higher profit-margins to invest in the expansion of their fleets, with Aristotle Onassis's Panama- and Honduras-flagged whaling and oil fleets being well-known examples.

The debate in the committee was played out between 'pros' and 'antis' on open registries, with the United States, Greece and the open registry states on one side, and their Western European shipping competitors on the other. The starting point for the debate was the ILC's article 29(1) on the nationality of ships, which read:

> Each State shall fix the conditions for the grant of its nationality to ships, for the registration of ships in its territory, and for the right to fly its flag. Ships have the nationality of the State whose flag they are entitled to fly. Nevertheless, for purposes of recognition of the national character of the ship by other States, there must exist a genuine link between the State and the ship.[91]

The controversy arose over the tension between the opening sentence's assertion that each state 'shall fix the conditions for the grant of its nationality to ships' and the last sentence's recognition, based on genuine link, 'of the national character of the ship by other States'. Who, then, determined a ship's nationality – the flag state or other states? El Salvador, Liberia, Panama and the United States argued that the reference to 'other States' usurped a state's exclusive right to decide

[89] 'OECD study on flags of convenience', *Journal of Maritime Law and Commerce* 4 (1973), 231, 232.

[90] Organisation for European Economic Co-operation, 'Study on the expansion of the flags of convenience fleets and on various aspects thereof' (31 January 1958), p. 4: vol. 7182, 9456-RW-2-40, pt. 1, RG 25, LAC.

[91] ILC, 'Articles … with commentaries', 278.

whether a vessel should fly its flag.[92] Liberia and Panama tried to delete the first clause of the final sentence but failed; then El Salvador, 'evidently acting on instruction from the United States',[93] secured its deletion in the plenary.[94] As a result, it did not appear in the forthcoming high seas convention.

Disagreement also arose over the second clause of the final sentence, 'there must exist a genuine link between the State and the ship' – the phrase 'genuine link' being the ILC's. The United States and Greece[95] argued that the concept of a genuine link between a state and the vessel bearing its flag was an unwelcome innovation in international law. For one thing, the Greeks stated, it was too vague to satisfy legal requirements.[96] For another, the Americans said, the absence of a genuine link might lead to the non-recognition of the nationality of ships, raising issues related to marine insurance, the ownership of cargoes and the validity of contracts.[97] Uncertainty would abound: could the flag state offer diplomatic protection to an unlinked vessel or would it be deemed to be stateless?[98] As American delegate Oswald Colclough said, these ships 'might be described – to use a picturesque expression from the great State of Texas – as mavericks, motherless, unbranded calves which can be claimed by the first one able to brand them'.[99]

On the other side of the debate, the Western European states strongly supported the idea of a genuine link because their shipping industries, operating through closed national registries, were bound by stricter regulatory regimes. Although European practice was far from uniform, the state would often impose fees and taxes, issue certifications and licences, and set standards for seaworthiness, while seafarers' unions would negotiate contracts over wages, pensions and working conditions.

[92] See Salvadorean delegate F. R. Lima's comments: UNLOSC I, vol. 2, '10th plenary meeting' (23 April 1958), p. 20.
[93] B. E. Bellamy to T. F. Bird (25 April 1958), p. 1: MT 59/3154, TNA.
[94] UNLOSC I, vol. 2, '10th plenary meeting' (23 April 1958), p. 20.
[95] An Australian official noted that the Greek government would be unlikely to obstruct Onassis' interests because doing so 'could only lead to a still greater tonnage of the Onassis fleet to adopt Panamanian instead of Greek registration': 'United Nations conference on the law of the sea: comments on the memorandum of the Greek legation' (u.d., c. December 1957), p. 3: A1838 1592/10, pt. 1, NAA.
[96] Royal Greek Legation Canberra, 'Memorandum' (5 December 1957), p. 2: A1838 1592/10, pt. 1, NAA.
[97] UNLOSC I, vol. 4, '24th meeting' A/CONF.13/C.2/SR.21–25 (2 April 1958), p. 64.
[98] Ibid.
[99] 'U.S. fights curb on ships' flags', *New York Times* (3 April 1958).

By contrast, the open registry states' connection with the ships bearing their flags was subject to less oversight and control. The West European states, backed by shipowners and trades' unions, seized on the lack of an apparent genuine link beyond registration to turn the screw on their less regulated competitors.

While the West Europeans were arguing with the Americans and the Greeks, the open registry states under discussion presented another dimension to the problem – their desire, as impoverished countries, to develop and diversify their economies. The sale of small tokens of sovereignty – flags – served the larger objective of economic progress. The Panamanian delegate Renato Ozores said he

> could not understand why other countries were worried about the growth of the flags of convenience. It was essential for countries with a low level of economic activity to develop their resources, and Panama's case as an emergent country with low standards of living was entirely different from that of the fully developed countries.[100]

Ozores went on to argue that it was surprising how shipping powers who declared themselves as being in favour of the freedom of the high seas 'wanted that freedom to be limited by making it impossible for shipping companies to register their ships where they wished'.[101] He also suggested that the authors of the ILC draft had avoided defining the concept of genuine link because 'like everybody else' they had no idea what it was.[102]

In the end, the genuine link concept survived. The authors of what would become article 5(1) of the high seas convention, recognising that a mere 'link' such as registration was insufficient, and doubtless aware that 'genuine' was a matter of interpretation, tethered the concept to effective control. The relevant sentence thus stated: 'There must exist a genuine link between the State and the ship; in particular, the State must effectively exercise its jurisdiction and control in administrative, technical and social matters over ships flying its flag.'[103] This approach, based on a proposal advanced by Angelo Franchi of Italy ('effectively exercise its jurisdiction and control') and added to by Gilbert Gidel of France

[100] UK delegation to UK Foreign Office (22 March 1958), p. 3: FO 371/133265, TNA.

[101] W. A. Wynes, 'Second committee: general debate continued' (29 March 1958), p. 2: A1838 1592/10, pt. 3, NAA.

[102] UNLOSC I, vol. 4, '23rd meeting' A/CONF.13/C.2/SR.21–25 (1 April 1958), p. 62.

[103] Article 5(1), High Seas Convention, 84.

('in administrative, technical and social matters'),[104] sets out a standard, but not necessarily *the* standard by which a state might demonstrate a genuine link. (The words 'in particular' suggest that other unparticularised standards, including of course, registration itself, might also apply.) As it was, the absence of enforcement measures derived from this standard failed to satisfy some commentators, producing what one described as 'an extremely soft treaty norm'.[105]

Conserving Fish Stocks

The next point of disagreement between the Western states was over the conservation of fish stocks in the high seas, discussed in the third committee. Under customary law, no state could impose its will over nationals of another state in the high seas except by agreement, which meant that many areas were being overfished. Not only were mechanised fleets casting their nets further afield than before, but as George Drew explained, the ships themselves were 'no longer fishing craft in the accepted sense, but mobile canning factories and commercial carriers combined'.[106] As a consequence of their devastating efficiency, some species were unable to reproduce themselves season to season, leading to stock collapses – Kamchatka salmon being one example. All states could agree what the problem was: as the Peruvian delegate Luis Edgardo Llosa observed, the industrial fishing concerns, in search of constant profits, were contributing to overfishing 'by extending the range of their fleets' and 'taking over, wherever they were, fishing bank after fishing bank'.[107] The American delegate William Herrington, too, acknowledged that this problem was 'not adequately met by the classical principles of *mare liberum*', and that unless fishing operations were controlled, fish stocks would decline drastically 'to the detriment of mankind'.[108]

[104] UNLOSC I, vol. 4, A/CONF.13/C.2/L.28 (21 March 1958), p. 123; amended by L.93 (2 April 1958), p. 141.

[105] J. E. Noyes, 'Treaty interpretation and definitions of the law of the sea convention: comments on "Defining terms in the 1982 Law of the Sea Convention"', *California Western International Law Journal* 32 (2002), 367, 380.

[106] UNLOSC I, vol. 3, '50th meeting' A/Conf/13/C.1/SR.46–50 (16 April 1958), p. 154.

[107] 'Intervencion del delegado del Peru … en la tercera comision' (10 March 1958), p. 11: 7-7-A Delegados y Conferencias (entradas) 1958, Archivo Central, Ministerio de Relaciones Exteriores [hereafter, MRE del Perú].

[108] W. C. Herrington, 'U.S. policy on fisheries and territorial waters' (u.d, c. April 1956), p. 1: vol. 4286, 10600-S-40, pt. 1, RG 25, LAC.

Solutions differed. While the coastal states were preoccupied with conserving fish-stocks by excluding or controlling the activities of the major fishing states in their own coastal waters, the major fishing states focussed on conserving the fish stocks in their preferred distant fishing grounds by keeping out their most powerful competitors – each other. This tendency was most clearly expressed during the debate over an American proposal, co-sponsored by Canada, to add a new article to the proposed convention promoting 'abstention'.[109]

The 'abstention' idea was that if a state or states had invested in a conservation programme to maintain or increase the yield of a particular species of fish, and were exploiting this stock to the full, they should have the exclusive right to continue to exploit that species on the high seas. Or, as the Americans put it: 'the U.S., by itself, or in conjunction with some other qualifying nation (such as Canada or the USSR) would have the exclusive right to take certain stocks of fish (such as salmon, halibut) regardless of where found'.[110] By the same token, other states who had not invested in the fishery would have to 'abstain' from taking these fish.

The Americans presented this policy as an alternative to the international expansion of territorial seas and fishing zones by ringfencing specific species of fish instead of carving out exclusive fishing zones. But this international-sounding policy was driven almost entirely by domestic fishing concerns. Its champions in the Department of the Interior argued that if it were put into place, the American industries that harvested salmon, halibut and fur seals in the Pacific Northwest would no longer have to compete with long-distance fishing and sealing fleets from elsewhere (especially Japan); and would consequently have less reason to push for a wider territorial sea, which, if generally recognised, would hurt the Americans' long-distance fishing industries.[111] Their enthusiasm for abstention was not shared by everyone, however. The Defense Department was highly sceptical,[112] as was the State Department's

[109] UNLOSC I, vol. 5, A/Conf.13/C.3/L.69 (8 April 1958), p. 155.

[110] 'Paper prepared in the Office of the Legal Adviser for special functional problems' (20 February 1958): *FRUS, United Nations and general international matters*, 1958–1960, vol. 2, doc. 333.

[111] 'Conference of plenipotentiaries . . . procedure of abstention' (21 October 1957), pp. 1–2: box 1, RG 370, Records of the Oceanic and Atmospheric Administration, Records concerning the United Nations conference on the law of the sea, 1957–1958, NARA.

[112] 'Conference of plenipotentiaries' (28 October 1957), p. 2: box 1, RG 370, Records of the Oceanic and Atmospheric Administration, Records concerning the United Nations conference on the law of the sea, 1957–1958. NARA.

legal adviser Loftus Becker, who thought it represented a derogation from the freedom of the seas, and was 'so patently discriminatory in favour of the US that it is naive to expect other states to accept it as a principle of international law'.[113]

The Americans and Canadians raised abstention at the conference nonetheless, whereupon it ran into a blizzard of criticism, just as Becker had predicted. Most of this criticism came from other developed long-distance fishing states – namely, Japan and the West Europeans – who feared that if abstention became globally established, their fleets would be prevented from harvesting certain fish on the high seas because they had been earmarked as 'American' Pacific halibut, or 'Icelandic' cod, or 'Canadian' sockeye salmon. The Japanese delegate Tsuruoka Senjin, against whose nation the abstention policy was primarily directed, decried it for being monopolistic and inequitable and therefore 'at variance with the principles of equality of States before the law and the freedom of the high seas'.[114] Why, he asked, should states who had hitherto been guilty of overfishing now be allowed to use abstention against other states?[115] The West Europeans, too, denounced abstention: for being discriminatory (Norway, Sweden, Portugal, Spain); contrary to the principle of the freedom of the seas (Netherlands, West Germany); and superfluous because conservation was already well provided for by other articles (France, Portugal, Spain).[116]

The British were also hostile to the idea. While they supported programmes to conserve high seas fish stocks so long as all states sought permission for conservation measures, and could participate equally in their application, they opposed any assertion of 'special interest' as a justification for unilateral action[117] – especially the abstention concept. They opposed it out of self-interest, because Britain might be excluded from engaging in new fishing activities just as it was being ejected from its old fishing grounds around Iceland. And they opposed it in principle

113 'Conference of plenipotentiaries ... procedure of abstention' (21 October 1957), p. 2: box 1, RG 370, Records of the Oceanic and Atmospheric Administration, Records concerning the United Nations conference on the law of the sea, 1957–1958, NARA.

114 UNLOSC I, vol. 5, '36th meeting', A/Conf.13/C.3/SR.36–43 (16 April 1958), p. 105.

115 UK delegation to UK Foreign Office (26 April 1958), p. 2: FO 371/133268, TNA.

116 UNLOSC I, vol. 5, '36th meeting', A/Conf.13/C.3/SR.36–43 (16 April 1958), pp. 106–107; and UK delegation to UK Foreign Office (22 April 1958), p. 2: FO 371/133268, TNA.

117 UK Ministry of Agriculture, Fisheries and Food, 'United Nations conference ... report on fishery aspects' (13 April 1958), p. 1: FO 371/133745, TNA.

because it transgressed the freedom of the seas by instituting the 'principle of monopoly' over high seas fisheries.[118] On this issue at least, the British much preferred the cut-and-thrust of the free market: as long as conservation was practised, 'fisheries are a matter for proper economic competition', wrote British delegate R. G. R. Wall.[119] *Pace* John Locke, if you catch them, they are yours.

What the Western critics of the abstention idea failed to mention was that it was a variation of the historic fishing rights idea, which they all supported. The text says: 'States whose nationals are not fishing the stock regularly or which have not theretofore done so within a reasonable period of time, shall abstain from fishing such stock'[120]). Whether the policy applied to zones or to fish, the net effect was the same, with the rights of existing claimants upheld, and newcomers shut out. But abstention never gained sufficient support, and so the Americans and Canadians were forced to withdraw their proposal in committee. When they proposed a watered-down declaration in plenary, it failed to win enough votes. The British, having orchestrated the campaign against abstention, tactfully abstained, because, they said, they would therefore not have to suffer 'the odium of having killed the American proposal'.[121]

Exploiting the Continental Shelf

Another innovation perfectly illustrated the difficulties the Western states had in agreeing the parameters of their own creations. The concept of the continental shelf, which had made just a few fleeting appearances at the 1930 conference,[122] rapidly gained traction after Truman made his proclamation in 1945. The idea that states should ring-fence their continental shelf for future exploitation advanced hand in hand with the commercial development of offshore oil platforms. (One of the first of these operated in Vermilion Bay, Louisiana, where *I'm Alone* had earlier

118 New Zealand High Commission London to External Affairs Wellington (24 January 1958), p. 2: A432 1957/3145 Attachment 16, NAA.

119 Australian High Commission London to External Affairs Canberra (17 January 1958), p. 1: A432 1957/3145 Attachment 16, NAA.

120 UNLOSC I, vol. 5, A/Conf.13/C.3/L.69 (8 April 1958), p. 155.

121 UK Ministry of Agriculture, Fisheries and Food, 'United Nations conference . . . report on fishery aspects' (13 April 1958), p. 4: FO 371/133745, TNA.

122 There, Portugal had alluded to its then unusual 1910 'Decree Regulating Fishing by Steam Vessels' over its continental shelf, reprinted in: UN Legislative Series, *Laws and regulations . . . high seas*, pp. 19–21.

been intercepted.) At the 1958 conference, the fourth committee faced the task of transforming what was still *lex ferenda* into a set of workable rules governing the shelf. But although this process had been initiated by Western states, and discussed on largely Western terms, their efforts produced very mixed results.

The first problem was how to characterise the continental shelf itself. The ILC's article 67 set out a tripartite definition based on adjacency, depth and exploitability:

> For the purposes of these articles, the term 'continental shelf' is used as referring to the seabed and subsoil of the submarine areas adjacent to the coast but outside the area of the territorial sea, to a depth of 200 metres (approximately 100 fathoms), or, beyond that limit, to where the depth of the superjacent waters admits of the exploitation of the natural resources of the said areas.[123]

Separately and together, these criteria thus represented a departure from the usual Western view that maritime zones should extend a certain uniform and universally applied distance from the baseline.

Articles 68 and 69 meanwhile set out the qualifications: states would exercise only 'sovereign rights', not sovereignty, over the continental shelf for the purposes of exploring and exploiting natural resources (leaving military uses of the shelf unimpeded);[124] and the rights enjoyed by the coastal state on the shelf would not affect the legal status of the high seas and the airspace above it.[125]

The Americans had ensured that article 67 adhered closely to Truman's proclamation on the continental shelf. This specified that the shelf would begin outside the territorial sea, not from the baseline, in accordance with the proclamation's characterisation of the shelf as being under the high seas. It also emphasised the shelf's adjacency to the coast, in line with the proclamation's stress on 'contiguity', and set out a depth criterion of '200 metres (approximately 100 fathoms)', thus mirroring the 100 fathoms specified by the press release accompanying the proclamation. In addition, it proposed a moveable limit based on the capacity to exploit the seabed – the exploitability criterion – which had been broached by the US delegate to the ILC, then dropped, then restored after its

[123] ILC, 'Articles . . . with commentaries', 296.
[124] Ibid., 297, 298.
[125] Ibid.

endorsement by the 1956 inter-American conservation conference at Ciudad Trujillo.[126]

In the article, the continental shelf as a legal construct departed from the continental shelf as a geological form. The adjacency criterion gave no indication of where adjacency might shade into non-adjacency; the exploitability criterion placed no limit on exploitation beyond the shelf; and the depth criterion was only a round figure (because, as the United Arab Republic delegate pointed out, 'the depth of the edge . . . might vary from less than 100 metres to more than 300 metres').[127] William Terry of the US Fish and Wildlife Service explained that the ILC had departed from the geological conception of the shelf deliberately and 'after much soul searching' for two reasons:

> 1. The Commission recognized that the 200-meter limit would meet current needs, but thought it desirable to anticipate technological developments which would permit exploitation of the seabed beyond this depth. . .
>
> 2. The Commission did not wish to differentiate between the continental shelf, as understood in the geological sense, and other submarine areas where the depth would permit exploitation in the same way as if there were a shelf.[128]

The latter would allow for exploitation in deeper depressions, channels and trenches in the shelf area, as well as exploitation, at least in theory, of the deep seabed beyond the continental margin.

This approach suited the Americans because it provided a justification for the expansion of exploitative activities based on the capacity to develop underwater extractive technologies without impinging on the high seas. It also suited American oil companies, who were already sizing up concessions further out towards the edge of the shelf. At the conference, the US delegate Marjorie Whiteman denied that exploitation could 'continue indefinitely towards the middle of the ocean' because it would not be a viable economic proposition.[129] (She also emphasised that the

[126] Ibid., 296.

[127] A. F. Gohar, UNLOSC I, vol. 6, '12th meeting', A/CONF.13/C.4/SR.11–15 (19 March 1954), p. 27.

[128] 'The United Nations conference . . . and its effect on the interests of the United States petroleum industry' (u.d., c. 1957), p. 4 (misnumbered 3): box 1, RG 370, Records of the Oceanic and Atmospheric Administration, Records concerning the United Nations conference on the law of the sea, 1957–1958, NARA.

[129] UNLOSC I, vol. 6, '16th meeting', A/CONF.13/C.4/SR.16–20 (21 March 1958), p. 40.

article was a package, with adjacency restraining exploitability.[130]) But the question still arose: if the technology and the finance *were* to exist, how far could exploitation advance beyond the shelf and down into the deep seabed? The British delegate Joyce Gutteridge thought that it was 'not . . . entirely impossible for a coastal State to claim that the sea bed and subsoil of oceanic areas was exploitable, thus opening the door to a division of oceanic areas between coastal States'.[131] Another British delegate, Cyril Lucas, envisaged a time when 'quite genuine claims of exploitation or exploitability might easily provide grounds in which the sea bed of much, or all, of the oceans would become "exclusive"'.[132]

The exploitability clause won the backing of Latin American states such as Chile, El Salvador, Panama and Venezuela, plus Ghana and South Korea. These countries possessed narrow continental shelves and would gain little from the 200-metre isobath. As Manouchehr Fartash, the Iranian delegate to the first committee at the UN, would later explain:

> A major difficulty with a limit based on depth alone – whether 200 metres or more – is that States would be allotted submarine regions of varying sizes, some gaining huge areas and others relatively small areas. That approach, which in our view is highly discriminatory, leads to extremely unequal treatment . . . [T]he exploitability clause was added principally at the behest of countries that had no geological shelf and whose coast dropped into deep waters. Since the definition using the 200-metre isobath would give them nothing, the exploitability clause was added to give them equal treatment in principle.[133]

In other words, the narrow-shelf states, seeking parity with states with wider shelves, sought compensation in the form of sovereign rights over the potentially exploitable seabed beyond the geological continental shelf. A decade later, this would bring these states into conflict with the proponents of an internationalised deep seabed.

On the other side, the European states whose coasts did not face open sea and who were compelled to share their continental shelves with others in confined waters, raised different objections to article 67. Friedrich Münch speaking for shelf-locked West Germany and Paul de La Pradelle representing shelf-locked Monaco both proposed internationalising the continental shelf. This idea sank almost without

[130] UK delegation to UK Foreign Office (27 March 1958), p. 2: FO 371/133265, TNA.
[131] J. A. C. Gutteridge (5 April 1958), p. 1: MAF 209/1580, TNA.
[132] C. E. Lucas (19 April 1959): MAF 209/1580, TNA.
[133] GAOR, A/C.1/PV.1782 (3 December 1970), p. 8.

trace – by now, many states were wedded to their shelf claims.[134] Jacques Patey of France, meanwhile, proposed deleting the exploitability clause, stating that the concept was imprecise and variable:

> It would be imprecise, because it would not be clear whether all the seabed, and the subsoil below it, off the coast of a given State which could be exploited by mankind as a whole should be taken into account, or only that part which the coastal State itself was able to exploit. It would be variable, because the areas concerned would doubtless increase in extent with further technical progress, and it was plain that such progress would materialise. It was a dangerous practice to lay down rules which would soon stand in need of modification.[135]

Other states from around the crowded Mediterranean, such as Greece, Italy and Lebanon, were also critical. But the French proposal was rejected by a significant majority, and the ILC's original article, with all its uncertainties, was transferred almost wholesale into the 1958 continental shelf convention.

Stickers and Swimmers

For all their divisions over the continental shelf, the Western states could agree on one thing: the importance of keeping the shelf regime separate from the high seas regime. Article 69 – beginning with the words, 'The rights of the coastal State over the continental shelf do not affect the legal status of the superjacent waters as high seas' – was designed to halt claims such as those of Chile, Ecuador and Peru to integrated maritime zones encompassing both the seabed and the water column.[136] That agreed, the delegates turned to article 68: 'The coastal State exercises over the continental shelf sovereign rights for the purpose of exploring and exploiting its natural resources.'[137] Delegates had to decide first what these 'natural resources' were, and second how to distinguish the shelf's natural resources from high seas natural resources.

Addressing the first issue, Japan and some European states wished to restrict the definition of resources on the shelf to non-living resources, so

[134] The Peruvian delegate Edwin Letts described de la Pradelle's approach as 'extreme': 'Memorándum: votacion del articulo 68' (29 March 1958), p. 1: 7-7-A Delegados y Conferencias (entradas) 1958, Archivo Central, MRE del Perú.

[135] UNLOSC I, vol. 6, '13th meeting', A/CONF.13/C.4/SR.11–15 (20 March 1958), pp. 31–32.

[136] ILC, 'Articles … with commentaries', 298.

[137] Ibid., 297.

that they could continue plucking living resources – from molluscs to bivalves – from distant shelves around the world. As the Japanese delegate Tsuruoka Senjin asserted, 'The creatures living at the bottom of the sea on the continental shelf were not an integral part of the seabed; the cases of both the so-called sedentary fisheries and bottom fish had been governed for centuries by traditional rules of the international law of the sea.'[138] The coastal states on the receiving end, however, wanted to claim all natural resources on their shelves, both living and non-living. The dispute between Japan and Australia over Japan's harvesting of pearlshell from Australia's proclaimed continental shelf, or between Italy and its former colony Libya over Italy's harvesting of sponges from Libya's (as yet unclaimed) shelf, were typical cases.

The problem for nations with exploitable living resources on their continental shelves was where to draw the line between shelf-dwelling organisms, over which they hoped to claim jurisdiction, and high-seas-swimmers, to which any state could help themselves. This distinction was bound to be arbitrary because many creatures failed to behave in accordance with these neat categories: valuable catches such as halibut and langoustine, for example, spent most of their lives in contact with the shelf while also being capable of moving about in the waters above. This problem was posed starkly in 1963, when Brazil threatened to seize French vessels harvesting langoustine from Brazil's decreed continental shelf. Brazil claimed they were part of their shelf's resources, and France claimed they were a high seas resource. The continental shelf convention was not yet in force, and both dispatched warships. Some commentators regretted that the case was not brought before the ICJ: 'There is something rather appealing about the thought of 15 learned judges … addressing their erudition to the question of whether a lobster, from the larval stage to the stage when it appears on a Parisian menu' was shelf-based or free-swimming.[139]

In the conference committee, the plan put forward by Australia, Britain, Ceylon, India, Malaya and Norway (and later joined by France) gained the greatest traction. It proposed that a definition be added to article 68, which included both non-living and living resources but restricted the latter to organisms that were in constant contact with the shelf:

[138] UNLOSC I, vol. 6, '9th meeting', A/CONF.13/C.4/SR.6–10 (13 March 1954), p. 14.

[139] C. Fincham and W. van Rensberg, *Bread upon the waters: the developing law of the sea* (Jerusalem: Turtledove Publishing, 1980), pp. 89–90.

> The natural resources referred to in these articles consist of mineral and other non-living resources of the seabed and the subsoil together with living organisms belonging to sedentary species, that is to say, organisms which, at the harvestable stage, either are immobile on or under the seabed or are unable to move except in constant physical contact with the seabed or the subsoil; but Crustacea and swimming species are not included.[140]

This six-power formula was designed, among other things, to see off claims to swimming fish that stayed close to the shelf (i.e. bottom fish), while at the same time meeting the needs of its sponsors, with Australia focussing on pearlshell, which at the specified 'harvestable stage' sat immobile on the seabed, and with India and Ceylon concentrating on the chank mollusc, which was unable to move except in contact with the shelf.[141]

The Americans, meanwhile, were fretting over shrimp. The United States and Mexico disagreed sharply over the harvesting of warm-water shrimp from the continental shelf skirting the Gulf of Mexico, and this had led to bloody encounters between American and Mexican shrimpers off Mexico's coast. The US Department of the Interior and the shrimping industry suspected that the words 'sedentary species' in the ILC's article 68 might be a slippery slope to 'swimming species' in other states' continental shelf claims, and thus the basis for excluding American fishing vessels. As the fisheries scientist Elton Sette put it, 'it is but a short step in semantics from the one-footed snails to the multi-footed crustacea' – shrimp, of course, being multi-footed crustacea.[142] The Americans therefore decided to draw the line between organisms that were attached to the shelf at harvestable stage, and those that were not; their fall-back position being to distinguish between those organisms that were immobile on the shelf at harvestable stage, and those that were not.[143] Shrimp, needless to say, were neither attached to nor immobile upon the shelf.

[140] UNLOSC I, vol. 6, A/Conf.13/C.4/L.36 (24 March 1958), p. 136.

[141] External Affairs Canberra, 'Aide-memoire' (12 February 1958), p. 5: A1838/383 1592/10, pt. 1, NAA; and 'International Conference on the Law of the Sea – continental shelf' (u.d, c. May 1958), p. 3: A1209 1958/5106, pt. 3, NAA.

[142] O. E. Sette, 'Miscellaneous comments on what living resources should go with the shelf' (16 July 1957), p. 2: box 1, RG 370, Records concerning international groups and organizations, Records concerning the United Nations conference on law of the sea, 1957–1958, NARA.

[143] Draft paper, 'United Nations conference ... United States position on meaning of term "natural resources"' (u.d., c. August 1957), p. 4; and 'Geneva conference of

When the Australians and the others raised the six-power formula at the conference, the American delegation approached it with caution because it did not refer to their own preferred option, attachment, but only to the fall-back, immobility. Rather than oppose it, they devised a tactical approach designed to protect their position (to which the Australian delegate Kenneth Bailey was partly privy): first, they would propose a more restrictive formula than the one on offer, and then, so long as the vital immobility provision survived intact, they would support the six-power proposal.[144] This plan was set in motion in the committee. First, the American delegate Marjorie Whiteman stated that, 'The most satisfactory criterion for defining those marine organisms . . . appeared to be that of *attachment* to the seabed during the harvestable stages of life'[145] – a proposal that would have excluded, among other things, pearlshell, which, as the Australians were acutely aware, was not attached to the shelf in maturity.[146] Then the Americans changed tack, with another delegate, William Herrington, finally giving American support to the six-power proposal.[147]

All these attempts to restrict the definition of natural resources on the shelf rankled with the Mexican delegate, Antonio Gómez Robledo, who pushed for the deletion of the words 'crustacea and' in the six-power proposal.[148] He cannily made no direct reference to the obvious crustacean, shrimp, but he regretted that another exploitable crustacean – the percebes barnacle – would not be considered a shelf-dweller, even though it clung to the shelf at the harvestable stage.[149] The British delegate R. G. R. Wall was unsympathetic, arguing that this barnacle was only harvested in territorial waters, and few people liked eating it, so 'it was scarcely

plenipotentiaries' (7 May 1958), p. 3: box 1, RG 370, Records concerning international groups and organizations, Records concerning the United Nations conference on law of the sea, 1957–1958, NARA.

144 Australian Consulate-general Geneva to External Affairs Canberra (10 March 1958): A1209 1958/5106, pt. 1, NAA.

145 UNLOSC I, vol. 6, '10th meeting', A/Conf.13/C.4/SR.6–10 (14 March 1958), p. 20. Emphasis added.

146 External Affairs Canberra, 'Aide-memoire' (12 February 1958), p. 5: A1838/383 1592/10, pt. 1, NAA. After Whiteman's speech, Australian officials cabled Bailey for reassurance that the Americans would come around to the six-power view. Bailey cabled back saying that: 'Dean has promised that our pearling position . . . will be taken care of': Australian Consulate-general Geneva to External Affairs Canberra (20 April 1958), p. 2: A1838 681/14/1, pt. 1, NAA.

147 UNLOSC I, vol. 6, '22nd meeting', A/Conf.13/C.4/SR.21–25 (27 March 1958), p. 62.

148 UNLOSC I, vol. 6, '24th meeting', A/Conf.13/C.4/SR.21–25 (28 March 1958), p. 68.

149 UNLOSC I, vol. 6, '22nd meeting', A/Conf.13/C.4/SR.21–25 (27 March 1958), p. 62.

likely that it would be the subject of an international dispute, whatever the wording of the article'.[150] As it turned out, delegates decided to delete the whole phrase 'but Crustacea and swimming species are not included' on the basis that it was superfluous, thereby restoring the delectable (and highly sought-after) percebes barnacle to its rightful place on the continental shelf.

*

While the negotiations were taking place, officials in Eisenhower's administration were giving careful thought to the US Senate's view of the text emerging from the conference, and concluded that ratification was more likely if it was broken up into its constituent themes. The word went out, and more than three weeks before the end of the conference, Kenneth Bailey reported to Canberra:

> The State Department apparently believes that these articles [on the continental shelf] might be treated as a separate convention thus simplifying ratification problems. He also said that the same techniques could be used for other parts of the International Law Commission Articles on the Law of the Sea.[151]

A few weeks later, Canadian adviser George Carty formally proposed that the fourth committee recommend to the conference that its work should be contained in a standalone instrument on the continental shelf.[152] This was agreed. A few days later, Indian representative N. Kesava Panikkar formally proposed that the third committee recommend to the conference that its work be contained in a stand-alone instrument on the conservation of high seas fisheries.[153] This was also accepted. This set in train the division of the single ILC draft into four substantive conventions, dealing respectively with the territorial sea and contiguous zone, the high seas, conservation of high seas fisheries, and the continental shelf. Two of these conventions expressly accepted reservations, two did not; two made provision for dispute settlement, two did not. (The high seas fishing convention was then unusual among multilateral treaties for

150 UNLOSC I, vol. 6, '24th meeting', A/Conf.13/C.4/SR.21–25 (28 March 1958), p. 69.
151 Australian Consulate-general Geneva to External Affairs Canberra (2 April 1958), p. 2: A1838/283 852/15/10/3, pt. 2, NAA.
152 UNLOSC I, vol. 6, '38th meeting', A/CONF.13/C.4/SR.36–42 (16 April 1958), p. 109.
153 UNLOSC I, vol. 5, '41st meeting', A/CONF.13/C.3/36–43 (21 April 1958), p. 125.

providing for compulsory arbitration in the event of a dispute.[154]) A fifth and final convention gave states the option of signing up for compulsory settlement of disputes arising from the interpretation or application of any of the four conventions – except on the parts of the high seas fishing convention for which settlement was already provided.[155]

The creation of single-theme conventions may have solved the American government's immediate difficulties with Congress, but it created a new problem: states could sign up to just one or two conventions if they were reluctant to accept the whole package, which would diminish the prospect of creating a comprehensive and integrated law of the sea regime.

Votes, Votes, Votes

When the issue of the territorial sea came up for the vote in the first committee on 19 April 1958, ten plans were on the table, starting in order of submission with the plan from Sweden, then from Canada, India-Mexico, the USSR, Colombia, Peru, Britain, Greece, Italy and the United States. (The Americans had contrived to be last in the queue by submitting a slightly revised version of their plan just before the deadline.) Votes were taken in the same order, with a simple majority required to pass in committee. Five of these plans were withdrawn. This left the plans of Canada, India-Mexico, the USSR, Colombia and the United States to be voted on. The session, chaired by the Australian Kenneth Bailey, could not have been more dramatic, with most attention focussed on the battle for votes between the India-Mexico plan, backed by most of the states from the South, and the American plan, backed by most of the states from the West.

First up was the revised Canadian plan, calling for 6+6,[156] which at the instigation of Ghana was voted on in two parts. Paragraph one ('A State

[154] Articles 9–12, Convention on Fishing and Conservation of the Living Resources of the High Seas (signed 29 April 1958, EIF 20 March 1966) 559 UNTS 285, 292–296. Arthur Dean later explained, 'Not only is this Convention the only one of the four Conventions which provides its own mechanism for the settlement of disputes, but it is one of the very few multilateral treaties in recent times to make such provision.': 'Statement by the Honorable Arthur H. Dean before the Senate foreign relations committee' (20 January 1960), p. 13: vol. 5307, 9456-RW-4-40, pt. 6-FP, RG 25, LAC.

[155] Articles I and II, Optional Protocol of Signature concerning the Compulsory Settlement of Disputes [hereafter, Optional Protocol] (signed 29 April 1958, EIF 30 September 1962) 450 UNTS 169, 170.

[156] UNLOSC I, vol. 3, A/Conf.13/C.1/L.77/Rev.3 (17 April 1958), p. 232.

is entitled to fix the breadth of its territorial sea up to a limit of six nautical miles measured from the baseline...') was rejected, but paragraph two ('A State has a fishing zone contiguous to its territorial sea extending to a limit twelve nautical miles from the baseline...') was adopted – the only proposal on the exclusive fishing zone to survive the committee stage.

Then came the India-Mexico plan, which, in a cliff-hanging result, secured thirty-five votes for, thirty-five against, and twelve abstentions.[157] Under the rules of procedure, a split vote would not carry. In the hubbub after the recording of the vote, but before the chair's announcement of the result, the Ecuadoran Enrique Ponce y Carbo put up his hand to declare that he wanted to change his vote from abstention to support, which would mean a win for the proposal – the very thing the Western states most wanted to avoid. A British liaison officer, William Sullivan, took up the story:

> It was noticed that just before the Ecuadoran delegate intervened on this point Dr. García Robles of Mexico had approached [Ponce y Carbo's] seat and entered into a brief whispered conversation with him. It is difficult to avoid the conclusion that Dr. García Robles was engineering a thoroughly unscrupulous attempt ... to reverse the decision of the Committee. That this conclusion had been reached by other delegates and the public in the galleries was evident by the ironic or hostile laughter with which Sr. García's frequent interventions on the point were greeted. The whole performance reached an even lower level than the General Assembly at its worst.[158]

An American delegate, legal adviser Loftus Becker, gave an even more colourful account of this incident, with García Robles running to Ponce y Carbo, and coercing him to change his vote by 'not only shouting at him but also by lifting his arm' to attract Bailey's attention.[159]

Whatever took place between the two delegates, Bailey ruled Ponce y Carbo's attempt to change his vote as out of order. The Soviet appeal against Bailey's decision was then put to the vote and defeated. A Soviet motion protesting the decision was also defeated. The USSR and Colombian plans both fell. Canadian and Mexican attempts to split

[157] UNLOSC I, vol. 3, '56th meeting', A/CONF.13/C.1/SR.56–60 (19 April 1958), p. 177.

[158] W. J. Sullivan, 'Report on the Latin American delegations' (c. May 1958), p. 7: FO 371/133269, TNA.

[159] US State Department press release, 'Address by the Honorable Loftus Becker' (26 April 1958), p. 5: LO 2/646, TNA.

the American plan, removing the provision for historic fishing rights, failed. And then the American plan was put to the vote, and rejected by 36–39–7.[160] The upshot of 'this Gilbertian process', as Sullivan put it, was that the committee declined to pass any proposal on the territorial sea: it did, however, accept the second paragraph of the Canadian proposal, relating to the exclusive economic zone.[161] What the votes showed with great clarity was that the two proposals most likely to succeed in plenary were running almost neck and neck, with the American plan (with thirty-six votes in favour) a fraction ahead of the India-Mexico plan (with thirty-five).

Four days later, the Americans tried to bounce the delegates into a decision in their favour. With the voting apparently out of the way in the first committee, and members of smaller delegations away at another session, Arthur Dean, calculating his plan might win a majority among the depleted number of delegates present in the room, proposed a reconsideration – that is, another vote on their already rejected motion. A 'most acrimonious' debate ensued.[162] George Drew condemned what he saw as underhand American tactics: 'The manoeuvre which had taken place should be deplored by every representative present who hoped to see recognition in the future of the dignity and responsibility of the United Nations.'[163] Two other delegates – García Robles of Mexico and Sinaceur Ben Larbi of Morocco – proposed the immediate adjournment of the meeting but their motion was rejected. Others still, including Ahmed Shukairy of Saudi Arabia and Omar Loutfi of the United Arab Republic, filibustered until the end of the meeting, so a vote on reconsideration could not be taken at that session.[164] Bailey in the chair proposed holding the vote at the next meeting, but this was not pursued, presumably because Dean knew that all the delegates who had previously voted against the American plan would return en masse to vote against its resurrection.

Meanwhile, Dean's move made it into the Canadian newspapers, with the *Toronto Globe and Mail* reporting:

> When the U.S. proposal was defeated in committee – at which time [part of] the Canadian proposal carried – a subsequent attempt to have the

160 UNLOSC I, vol. 3, '57th meeting', A/CONF.13/C.1/SR.56–60 (19 April 1958), p. 180.
161 W. J. Sullivan, 'Report on the Latin American delegations' (c. May 1958), p. 8: FO 371/133269, TNA.
162 UK delegation to UK Foreign Office (26 April 1959), p. 3: FO 371/133268, TNA.
163 UNLOSC I, vol. 3, '62nd meeting', A/CONF.13/C.1/SR.61–66 (23 April 1958), p. 196.
164 Ibid.

> committee's decision reconsidered was sprung by the United States at a time when a conflicting meeting made it reasonable to expect some delegates would be absent. This bit of what was looked upon as trickery annoyed more than the Canadian delegation.[165]

At this stage, an adviser to the American delegation wrote that after all the conflicts between Britain, Canada and the United States, 'nobody but the Russians and the Arabs were getting much fun out of the conference'.[166] Not quite. A few years later, a Canadian diplomat in Warsaw reported having met the Polish delegate Miroslaw Gasiorowski, who 'recalled with some pleasure, as I seemed to detect, what he described as a heated debate between the United States and Canadian delegates'.[167]

Threats and Pleas

The final reckoning took place in the conference plenary two days later, on 25 April. The Americans resubmitted their 6+6+historic rights plan, but the sponsors of the India-Mexico plan did not resubmit theirs. India had pulled out, leaving Mexico to table a new motion along with co-sponsors Burma, Colombia, Indonesia, Morocco, Saudi Arabia, the United Arab Republic and Venezuela.[168] Even so, the eight-power proposal was very similar to the original India-Mexico plan, with its first paragraph exactly duplicating the earlier proposal.

So why did India abandon its own plan? In the days between the committee vote and the plenary vote, the Americans and British exerted pressure on Indian ministers to instruct the delegation to vote in favour of the American plan. This pressure took two different forms: pleading and threatening. Harold Macmillan tried the personal touch, appealing directly to Jawaharlal Nehru to use his leadership to support the United States and so 'avoid a collapse of the conference'.[169] The Americans pursued a more aggressive line. George Drew reported to Ottawa that,

165 G. Bain, 'Fight for 12-mile fishing limit', *Toronto Globe and Mail* (7 May 1958).

166 W. M. Chapman to 'Harold' (30 April 1958), p. 5: box 1, RG 370, Records concerning international groups and organizations, Records concerning the United Nations conference on law of the sea, 1957–1958, NARA.

167 G. H. Southam to External Affairs Ottawa (8 March 1960), p. 2: vol. 5308, 9456-RW-4-40, pt. 16, RG 25, LAC.

168 UNLOSC I, vol. 2, A/Conf.13/L.34 (25 April 1958), p. 128.

169 'Personal message for Mr. Nehru from Mr. Macmillan' (22 April 1958): J.N. (S.G.), f. no. 610, pt. 1, Jawaharlal Nehru papers, Nehru Memorial Museum and Library [hereafter, NMML].

'Once it became evident [to the Americans] that the voting trend in favour of their proposal was insufficient, it is understood they adopted tactics – particularly among beneficiaries of United States foreign aid programs – that were extreme.'[170] These tactics 'split off many Asian and African States from their earlier position', and helped to break down the cohesion of the Afro-Asian group, but of all these efforts, 'direct pressure on India' produced the best result.[171] The Indians caved in, backed away from their plan, abstained on the eight-power replacement, and voted for the American position.[172]

But it was all for nought. Towards the end of the conference, on 25 April, all eighty-six delegations except Yemen attended the plenary to wrap up the outstanding issues of the breadth of the territorial sea and the limits of the fishing zone. The session was characterised by 'tremendous tension, fervid drama and emotional excitement', wrote the US delegation adviser Wilbur Chapman.[173] Two-thirds of the vote was required for the inclusion of one of the remaining proposals within the draft text of the convention on the territorial sea and the contiguous zone. The result was that no plan was accepted. First, the paragraph of the Canadian plan on the exclusive fishing zone was defeated 35–30–20; then the Americans' 6+6+historic rights plan was rejected 45–33–7; then the eight-power proposal based on the India-Mexico plan was defeated 39–38–8; and then the Soviet proposal was rejected 21–47–17.[174] Over the remaining two days of the conference, while the delegates were adopting each of the law of the sea treaties, the American delegation, wrote Chapman, 'trembled in its boots, and so did I, until the final gavel fell . . . lest the [the eight-power] proposal be brought up again and win or at least beat the favourable vote the U.S. proposal had got'.[175]

170 G. A. Drew, 'Report of the Canadian delegation' (u.d., c. April–May 1958), p. 13: vol. 7182, 9456-RW-3-40, pt. 3-FP, RG 25, LAC.

171 Ibid., p. 15.

172 UNLOSC I, vol. 2, '14th plenary meeting' (25 April 1958), pp. 40, 39.

173 W. M. Chapman to 'Harold' (30 April 1958), p. 13: box 1, RG 370, Records concerning international groups and organizations, Records concerning the United Nations conference on law of the sea, 1957–1958, NARA.

174 UNLOSC I, vol. 2, '14th plenary meeting' (25 April 1958), pp. 39–40.

175 W. M. Chapman to 'Harold' (30 April 1958), p. 12: box 1, RG 370, Records concerning international groups and organizations, Records concerning the United Nations conference on law of the sea, 1957–1958, NARA.

Once the conference was over, the dissection of the votes on the breadth of the territorial sea and the extent of the fishing zone began. The result showed that the balance of forces between the six-mile and the twelve-mile advocates was about even, with the American plan gaining six more votes than the eight-power plan (the six votes from non-UN members such as Monaco and the Holy See for the former contributing to the difference[176]). Support for the United States plan had proved to be soft around the edges, however, and half a dozen of the delegates expected to vote for or abstain ended up voting against it. According to State Department records, the Argentinian delegate Isidore Ruiz Moreno voted against, contrary to government instructions (which the Argentines later claimed was 'unauthorised and embarrassing').[177] The Burmese delegate Ba Han voted against allegedly 'as result failure of Delegation Head to decode his instructions in time'.[178] The Chilean delegate Luis Melo Lecaros 'personally opposed GOC [government of Chile] instructions to support US and disobeyed them in Committee'.[179] The Guatemalan delegate Luis Aycinena Salazar voted against the plan, apparently contrary to his government's instructions.[180] The Jordanian delegate Shukri Muhtadi voted against it seemingly because instructions to support it 'arrived after the voting had occurred'.[181] Finally, the South Korean delegate Kim Yong Woo ignored his instructions to vote for it, was dismissed and called home by the Rhee government, and later 'abjectly' apologised to the Americans for 'failing to understand the issues'.[182]

There was more to it than just votes, however. The powers made concession after concession over the territorial sea, extending it from three to six miles and adding the inducement of fishing zones, whereas

[176] Some non-UN-members were more willing to vote with the United States than others: West Germany voted for the American plan 'with considerable reluctance' and the Holy See had required 'strenuous persuasion' (because of countervailing pressure from the Catholic Latin American states): 'Germany' (u.d., c. early 1960), p. 1; and 'Holy See' (u.d., c. early 1960): box 136, RG 43, Records of international conferences, commissions and expositions, Bureau of International Organization Affairs, Office of International Conferences, administrative files 1928–1967, NARA.

[177] Ibid., 'Argentina' (u.d., c. early 1960), p. 1.

[178] Ibid., 'Burma' (u.d., c. early 1960), p. 1.

[179] Ibid., 'Chile' (u.d., c. early 1960), p. 2.

[180] Ibid., 'Guatemala' (u.d., c. early 1960), p. 1.

[181] Ibid., 'Jordan' (u.d., c. early 1960), p. 1.

[182] Ibid., 'Korea' (u.d., c. early 1960), p. 1.

the advocates of twelve miles, according to one senior British official, 'made no concessions whatever'.[183] In the meantime, the absence of a decision about the breadth of the territorial sea meant, in Chapman's words, 'we don't quite yet know where the high seas is'.[184] This lack of clarity better suited the states who wished to extend their territorial seas than those who wished to restrict them. India's defence minister Krishna Menon took the view that in the absence of agreement, states wanting a twelve-mile territorial sea could 'go ahead and claim it'.[185] Where the Western states foretold chaos, Menon and others saw opportunities.

The West German delegate Peter Pfieffer ascribed the failure of the conference on this score to the lack of unity within the Western camp:

> The Western powers had failed to agree on a common line, at least on the main issues, and they did not maintain sufficient contact with each other in Geneva to compensate for this failure. There was no sign at all at the conference that NATO existed. It should never have happened that the United States and Canada, after initial cooperation, had heated debates on the floor in front of 86 nations that came close to personal vilification. The United Kingdom showed an astonishing willingness to compromise, and on several occasions backed away from a position that it had briefly declared to be irreversible.[186]

The Ghanaian delegate Richard Abusua-Yedom Quarshie was just as blunt, attributing the conference's outcome to Iceland, Manningham-Buller's manner, and 'the fact that UK and CDA could not ... get together'.[187]

The day after the final vote, Arthur Dean sent a cable to Washington that argued that the American proposal had been thwarted by the actions of three blocs: the Soviet bloc, the Afro-Asian bloc, and the Latin

183 K. J. Pritchard, 'Conference on the Law of the Sea: first committee' (29 April 1958), p. 1: LO 2/646, TNA.

184 W. M. Chapman to 'Harold' (30 April 1958), p. 16: box 1, RG 370, Records concerning international groups and organizations, Records concerning the United Nations Conference on Law of the Sea, 1957–1958, NARA.

185 'Draft report on preparatory talks...' (3 June 1959), p. 2: DO 35/9047, TNA.

186 P. H. Pfieffer, 'Die internationale seerechtskonferenz ... abschlussbericht der Deutschen delegation' (23 May 1958), pp. 19–20: Bundesministerium der Justiz B-Arch B141/ 22024, Bundesarchiv Koblenz. Thanks to Alex G. Oude Elferink for the relevant pages and the reference.

187 Canadian High Commission Accra to External Affairs Ottawa (8 December 1959): vol. 7185, 9456-RW-4-40 pt. 12.1, RG 25, LAC.

American bloc.[188] At the State Department, Ruth Bacon offered a more nuanced appraisal of the forces at work at the conference. This was not a typical bloc *versus* bloc situation, she wrote.[189]

> As Mr. Dean notes, our position with regard to the Gulf of Aqaba [supporting the Israeli position] removed the possibility of Middle Eastern support; our efforts to meet Western European views on fisheries weakened Asian support for our proposal; early in the Conference when we announced support for a Canadian-type proposal, the UK countered with its six mile proposal; later, when we moved away from a Canadian-type proposal, the Canadians worked actively against us.[190]

Bacon concluded that 'the Conference brought together two mutually abrasive topics – territorial waters and fisheries – and our positions on either one all too often served to reduce our prospects for support on the other'.[191]

As a result, the 1958 conference drafted conventions on the territorial sea and contiguous zone, the high seas, high seas fishing, and the continental shelf, plus a protocol on dispute settlement. But it failed to settle the most important issue – the breadth of the territorial sea. The pyramid still lacked its base.

[188] Referred to in R. Bacon, 'Ambassador Dean's comments on bloc voting and international conferences' (30 April 1958), p. 1: box 6, RG 59, Records of the Bureau of Far Eastern Affairs, 1956–1958, Conferences, meetings and visits, 1958, NARA.

[189] Ibid.

[190] Ibid.

[191] Ibid.

4

A Conference Collapses

No Settlement on the Territorial Sea or Fishing Limits in 1960

The UN secretary-general's legal adviser Constantin Stavropoulos was dismayed by the 1958 Law of the Sea Conference's inability to decide the territorial sea's breadth and perturbed by states' slowness in ratifying the resultant conventions. Just before the start of the follow-up conference in 1960, he buttonholed the Canadian delegate to point out that the international conference on statelessness had not reached agreement at its 1959 session, and that it was important from the UN's perspective to make a success of the next law of the sea proceedings. As the British official John Simpson noted, 'the number of conventions negotiated under United Nations auspices that have actually entered into force must be very small', and this time around, the organisation could not afford another failure.[1]

The 1958 and 1960 conferences were of a piece, with the second carrying on the work of the first. At the earlier conference, the Western powers had been so preoccupied with their own internal disputes that they were slow to recognise the growing challenge posed by coastal states hailing from the global South. At the second conference, the latter's interests and influence would prove decisive, with Asian and African states making common cause with Latin American nations. Although these constellations of interest were partly a product of the Cold War, with many smaller states defining themselves as 'non-aligned', their campaign for greater control over their coastal waters would present the Western powers with problems quite distinct from those arising directly from the East-West conflict.

The Western states' apprehension about the growing assertiveness, commitment and organisation of these less powerful coastal states become apparent in the run-up to the 1960 conference. At the US State

[1] J. L. Simpson to G. G. Fitzmaurice (29 January 1960): FO 371/150831, TNA.

Department, Ruth Bacon observed that there was not yet a completely solid bloc of African and Asian states – as evidenced by their lack of unity over Cyprus and West Irian – but that the United States and its allies would have only themselves to blame if such a bloc were to emerge.[2] 'We and the West Europeans can . . . help to *create* such a bloc', she wrote, if the United States 'deserts its principles in order to give support to its NATO friends on colonial and related matters' and if the West Europeans 'assert positions which seem to fail to take account of the Twentieth Century developments in political relations'.[3] The debates at the conference would demonstrate the prescience of her warning.

*

The UN's second Law of the Sea Conference was held in Geneva over five weeks from 17 March to 26 April 1960, and it would consider just two issues: the breadth of the territorial sea, and fishery limits.[4] It was attended by delegations from almost all the nations represented at the 1958 conference, plus Ethiopia, Sudan and newly independent Cameroun and Guinea, bringing the total to eighty-eight.

The proceedings opened on predictable lines. It began with a protest from Soviet delegate Grigori Tunkin that the communist states, including the People's Republic of China and the German Democratic Republic, had not been invited.[5] The American Arthur Dean replied that Tunkin's point was out of order because the matter had already been decided by the General Assembly.[6] Then the Taiwanese and Polish delegates belaboured each other over the legitimacy of the governments in Beijing and Taipei, and the West German and Polish delegates exchanged words over the standing of the two Germanys, with the former describing the GDR as a Soviet zone 'governed . . . in defiance of the principle of self-determination', and the latter denying his right to lecture others about the law because its sitting judges had earlier dispensed 'the law of the jungle'.[7] But although this debate had all the hallmarks of a Cold War

[2] R. Bacon, 'Ambassador Dean's comments on bloc voting' (30 April 1958), p. 2: box 6, RG 59, Records of the Bureau of Far Eastern Affairs 1956–1958, Conferences, meetings and visits – 1958, NARA.
[3] Ibid. Original emphasis.
[4] UNGA Res. 1307(XIII) (10 December 1958).
[5] UNLOSC II, vol. 1, '1st plenary meeting', A/Conf.19/SR.1 (17 March 1960), p. 2.
[6] Ibid.
[7] Ibid.

confrontation, the delegates were just going through the motions. Having raised the issue, Tunkin let the matter go. No formal resolution was raised, and the conference proceeded as if nothing had happened.

The following day, the Mexican delegate Alfonso García Robles made a more telling intervention, this time reflecting the interests of the South. During pre-conference debates in the UN's sixth committee, he had suggested inviting only states that were either members of the UN or members of more than half of the UN agencies, which would have excluded three previously pro-American voters – the Holy See, San Marino and Monaco.[8] Once the conference was up and running, he turned to the rules of procedure, which he thought had been manipulated by the powers at the previous conference. To prevent this from recurring, he proposed adding to rule 20 the words: 'The Secretariat shall be in charge of drawing up a list of ... speakers'.[9] This was because the speakers' order had hitherto been subject to 'tampering', and those responsible, the Mexicans thought, 'had not been scrupulously fair in handling the list at the last Conference'.[10] (One suspect was Wan Waithayakon of Thailand, who presided over both conferences and was reportedly 'in the pocket of the Americans'.[11]) Further to that, García Robles proposed adding to rule 49 the requirement for a two-thirds majority vote for a reconsideration of proposals or amendments in committee.[12] This, he explained, would prevent a repeat of that 'unfortunate' incident in 1958 when the Americans had tried to force a re-examination of their own plan by a simple majority although it had already been voted down in committee, thereby setting off 'acrimonious and needless discussions'.[13] Despite opposition from the United States and Britain, García Robles's proposed rule changes carried.[14]

On the substantive issues, the motions put forward in 1960 were similar to those submitted towards the end of the previous conference, with the Western powers advocating plans based on a six-mile territorial

[8] 'Question of convening a second United Nations conference' (6 January 1959), p. 35: vol. 7183, 9456-RW-4-40, pt. 1, RG 25, LAC.

[9] UNLOSC II, vol. 1, A/Conf.19/L.1 (16 March 1960), p. 3.

[10] 'Final report of the Canadian delegation' (u.d., c. May 1960), p. 6: vol. 5309, 9456-RW-8-40, pt. 1.1, file 2, RG 25, LAC.

[11] M. Cadieux, 'Conversation with the Norwegian ambassador' (18 December 1959), p. 1: vol. 5308, 9456-RW-4-40, pt. 16, RG 25, LAC.

[12] UNLOSC II, vol. 1, A/Conf.19/L.1 (16 March 1960), pp. 3, 4.

[13] Ibid., p. 4.

[14] UNLOSC II, vol. 1, '2nd plenary meeting', A/Conf.19/SR.2 (18 March 1960), p. 4.

sea, and the smaller coastal states and the Soviet bloc pushing for a flexible limit out to twelve miles. The Americans and Canadians, having patched up their earlier differences, proposed a US-Canada plan that emerged as a front-runner. This called for a six-mile territorial sea plus a six-mile fishing zone, with a ten-year phase-out of fishing rights for states that had fished in another state's waters over the previous five years (or in the conference shorthand, '6+6+phased-out historic rights').[15] This won the support of the conservative West European fishing states, the Western states within the British Commonwealth, and moderates elsewhere. But could it gain the two-thirds of the vote required for the proposed treaty?

Showing the Flag

The powers had three reasons for campaigning for a six-mile territorial sea, which, they estimated, was the narrowest that other states would accept. First, they hoped to stop the momentum towards twelve-mile territorial seas, which would, among other things, reduce their navies' room to manoeuvre, especially in enclosed seas such as the Mediterranean. Second, an extension to twelve miles would place most international straits – the great arteries through which naval traffic, trade and communications flowed – under the jurisdiction of the straits-adjacent states. (The Americans estimated that of the 116 most important international straits, 52 would be subject to state sovereignty if the territorial sea was extended universally to six miles, and all would be subject to it if the territorial sea was extended to twelve miles.[16]) Finally, an extension to twelve miles would prevent the powers from getting close to other states' coastlines for the purposes of coercion short of war and the gathering of intelligence. While the powers had no difficulty stressing the importance of unrestricted navigation across the high seas and through straits for all states, they obviously could not make public reference to these other objectives.

As an illustration of this difficulty, the State Department sent out an instruction to American diplomatic posts just before the start of the 1960 conference setting out points they could make in favour of narrow

[15] UNLOSC II, vol. 1, A/Conf.19/C.1/L.10 (8 April 1960), p. 169; and A/Conf.19/L.11 (22 April 1960), p. 173.

[16] 'Statement by the Honorable Arthur H. Dean before the Senate Foreign Relations Committee' (20 January 1960), p. 18: vol. 5307, 9456-RW-4-40, pt. 6-FP, RG 25, LAC.

territorial seas. One argument – that broader territorial seas would allow states to close off straits – could be made to just about any government except unfriendly straits states. Another argument of a more explicitly Cold War character – that wider territorial seas would offer shelter to undetected Soviet submarines and pose a 'grave threat to the free world defensive capability'[17] – could be made to most nations outside the Soviet bloc. But the remaining arguments were of a far more delicate nature and could only be aired with the Americans' closest allies.

One of the most sensitive of these related to what the State Department instruction called 'showing the flag' (and what others might have called, with pejorative intent, 'gunboat diplomacy'). It stated:

> A timely display of force has not infrequently served as an effective means to secure important foreign policy objectives. In recent years the United States has used effectively a display of naval and air force a number of times to deter aggression or bring stability to disturbed situations ... Though the impact is one of mass psychology (of which the outcome is not always predictable) the effect that ships and aircraft can have which are *clearly visible* from the shore, though outside the territorial sea, is generally far more pronounced than mere reports ... that such forces are near. Because this tool of diplomacy can be used before irrevocable commitment and with a minimum risk [to] life, it is politically feasible to use it early in a developing crisis. The ability of the US to calm troubled situations in this indirect but efficacious fashion would be substantially reduced by a wide extension of the territorial sea.[18]

In other words, a show of strength was more visible, and hence more effective, at three to six miles than at twelve. But this line could not be used with states fearful of possible American intervention in their affairs, which is why the instruction added a caveat: 'this argument should be employed cautiously in Latin America and in other areas potentially sensitive to displays of force'.[19]

Another reason that the maritime powers wanted the narrowest possible territorial sea was to gather intelligence about others. If the target state had a three- to six-mile territorial sea, the targeting state could get their submarines, ships and aircraft up close to its coastline without having to enter its territorial waters or airspace, whereas if it had a

[17] 'Law of the Sea: basic security reasons why US supports the retention of a narrow territorial sea' (1 March 1960), p. 4: box 136, RG 43, Records of international conferences, commissions and expositions, Bureau of International Organization Affairs, NARA.

[18] Ibid. Original emphasis.

[19] Ibid.

twelve-mile territorial sea, the collection of intelligence would require more powerful and sophisticated technology. The State Department instruction noted, for example:

> Adequate visual and photographic intelligence is vital to the success of such military operations as amphibious landings, bombing missions, mine laying and sweeping, and to missile guidance. As the distance from a coastal object increases, a sharp drop occurs in the value of the intelligence collectible from the sea or the air.[20]

Not only that, but the then discrepancy between those states still claiming three miles – such as Canada, Britain and the United States – and those claiming twelve miles – such as the People's Republic of China – worked to the advantage of the latter because the twelve-mile states 'could come close to our shores; but we could not go close to theirs'.[21] Furthermore, many states thought the maritime powers' intelligence gathering activities were a reason *for*, not against, widening their territorial sea, and consequently this argument, the State Department instruction stated, was '*not* recommended for general use'.[22]

Sen on Warships

The trajectory of India at the conference signalled the deepening differences between the powers and the less powerful coastal states over the issue of the territorial sea. India's accommodation to Western interests in 1958, when it had bailed out the nuclear powers and had abandoned its own plan in favour of the Americans', had created problems for New Delhi by exacerbating the disputes between Congress Party ministers, tarnishing its reputation among its non-aligned allies, and diminishing its stature at the UN General Assembly.[23] Arthur Lall, India's permanent representative at the UN, told a Canadian official that India's vote for the

20 Ibid.

21 'Interdepartmental sub-committee on territorial waters' (23 January 1959), p. 3: vol. 7183, 9456-RW-4-40, pt. 2, RG 25, LAC.

22 'Law of the sea: basic security reasons why US supports the retention of a narrow territorial sea' (1 March 1960), p. 4: box 136, RG 43, Records of international conferences, commissions and expositions, Bureau of International Organization Affairs, NARA. Original emphasis.

23 See Ashoke Sen's comments: UK High Commission New Delhi to UK Commonwealth Relations Office (1 February 1960), p. 1: DO 35/9048, TNA.

United States in 1958 had been a mistake, not to be repeated.[24] And Biswanath Sen, the secretary-general of the Asian Legal Consultative Committee, told the Australian delegate Kenneth Bailey that 'U.A.R. Indonesian and other members of the Legal Consultative Committee at recent Cairo meeting had been very critical of Indian delegation at Geneva for having as they said let down the 12-mile group and given pride of place to membership of Commonwealth rather than of Afro-Asian group'.[25]

So in 1960 the question arose: should the Indian delegation, led once again by Ashoke Sen, attempt to recover lost ground by relaunching their plan for a flexible territorial sea out to twelve miles, or could they be persuaded to support the '6+6+phased-out historic rights' plan being touted by the United States and Canada? While Krishna Menon came down firmly in favour of a twelve-mile limit to maintain security and show solidarity with the 'have-nots',[26] Sen was inclined to back the US-Canada plan on tactical grounds, because a twelve-mile plan could not win enough votes.[27] Menon, Sen and the other Indian Cabinet ministers all agreed on one thing, however: warships and submarines should not be given the automatic right of innocent passage through the territorial sea. Instead, their passage would require the permission of the coastal state. Menon explained:

> The maritime powers insist on the inclusion of the right that warships can treat the seas beyond the 6-miles as the High Sea. This does not suit us or any of the Asian-African countries. (It was not long ago the United States Fleet showed the flag around the Lebanon).
>
> . . .
>
> Indonesia [which claimed archipelagic status in 1957 in response to the movement of American, British and Dutch warships through the archipelago] may be crude and extreme in her demands but her future is in jeopardy and her skin comes in for a close shave.[28]

[24] 'Question of convening a second United Nations conference' (6 January 1959), p. 27: vol. 7183, 9456-RW-4-40, pt. 1, RG 25, LAC.

[25] Australian High Commission Karachi to External Affairs Canberra (30 October 1958), p. 2: A1838/2 852/15/10/3, pt. 6, NAA.

[26] K. Menon to J. Nehru, 'Defence minister's letter' (18 February 1960), p. 1: MEA 1960 Southern Division 3102 (1) – SD/60, National Archives of India [hereafter, NAI].

[27] A. K. Sen, 'Law minister's note' (1 February 1960), p. 1: MEA 1960 Southern Division 3102 (1) – SD/60, NAI.

[28] K. Menon to J. Nehru, 'Defence minister's letter' (18 February 1960), p. 2: MEA 1960 Southern Division 3102 (1) – SD/60, NAI.

The Americans and British were therefore somewhat alarmed when, at the conference, Sen privately sounded out Kenneth Bailey about whether the US-Canada plan 'might contain also a provision requiring prior authorisation for passage of warships through territorial sea and contiguous zone'.[29] He argued that the plan would not gain the required two-thirds of the vote unless the powers made provision for the authorisation of warships in both zones, because the small African and Asian states 'feel very strong reaction against past and possible future demonstrations by Western Navies'.[30] In short, Sen was offering support for the US-Canada plan on the condition that provision was made for the authorisation of the passage of warships in both zones, out to twelve miles.

As well as vesting the coastal state with the power to control the movement of foreign warships, Sen's proposal had a number of political advantages. For one thing, it met Menon's insistence on a twelve-mile zone in which foreign warships could be controlled or excluded, while also satisfying other ministers' desire for a six-mile territorial sea, which would give India's merchant marine sufficient freedom of movement off foreign coasts. For another thing, the proposal met the concerns of other states in the developing world who faced similar security and trade dilemmas, while also posing a significant threat to the US-Canada plan, whose main purpose was to protect the powers' naval mobility, including in the territorial sea. Consequently, as the British delegate Denis Cleary wrote, Sen's proposal was 'a very dangerous idea from our point of view'.[31]

A few days after his approach to Bailey, Sen publicly addressed delegates in the committee of the whole. He did not refer directly to the authorisation of warships but he alluded to it when he took up the West's argument that narrow territorial seas were essential for the deployment of their navies during periods of crisis: 'it is difficult to carry conviction that the outer six miles of a twelve miles sea are not necessary for the security of the Coastal State but are important for the security of a non-Coastal State though it may be situated thousands of miles away'.[32] Rather,

[29] Australian Consulate-general Geneva to External Affairs Canberra (28 March 1960), p. 1: A1209/100 1960/190, pt. 1, NAA.

[30] Ibid.

[31] W. Peters (quoting Cleary) to J. M. D. Ward (31 March 1960): DO 35/9048, TNA.

[32] 'Speech delivered by Shri A. K. Sen' (31 March 1960), p. 9: vol. 7306, 10600-BA-40, pt. 1.1, RG 25, LAC.

> It seems to us that the interests of Coastal States in peace time must take precedence over the interests of non-Coastal States [i.e. the powers] in times of war. The domination of smaller countries by the big powers is still a vivid reality. A small country is fearful of any encroachments by land or by air, particularly of foreign war ships coming into its adjacent seas and remaining there for long periods ... It will not help the cause of codification of international law if we ignore this genuine apprehension on the part of the smaller countries.[33]

The Canadian delegation leader George Drew reported that Sen's statement was 'delivered with polished conviction' and 'held the close attention of all delegates'.[34]

About Innocent Passage

Faced with Sen's proposal, the powers were compelled to consider the law governing the innocent passage of warships through the territorial sea. Publicly, they claimed that the issue had been settled once and for all at the 1958 conference, when states had voted *for* article 14(1) of the territorial sea convention stating that 'ships of all States, whether coastal or not, shall enjoy the right of innocent passage through the territorial sea',[35] and had voted *against* the ILC's article 24 referring to notification and authorisation for warships. The British, in particular, suggested that because only a few states required notification or authorisation, this was evidence of the absence of customary law supporting restrictions – *ergo*, a coastal state had no right to impose conditions on warships' passage.[36]

Privately, though, other Western states were either uncertain about the status of warships in other states' territorial seas, or thought the ILC when originally proposing 'notification or authorization' had got it about right. The Americans were among them. At the 1930 codification conference they had supported the requirement for the authorisation of warships. Three decades later they had abandoned this position but were still doubtful about whether the law prevented authorisation, as the British were claiming. In the run-up to the 1960 conference, the State Department indicated that American officials should not let on to other

[33] Ibid., pp. 9–10.
[34] 'Final report of the Canadian delegation' (u.d., c. May 1960), annex 6, p. 1: vol. 5309, 9456-RW-8-40, pt. 1.1, file 2, RG 25, LAC.
[35] Territorial Sea Convention, 214.
[36] Australian Consulate-general Geneva to External Affairs Canberra (1 May 1960), p. 1: A1209/80 1958/5106, pt. 2, NAA.

states' officials 'the uncertainty in international law regarding the innocent passage rights of warships'.[37] It continued: 'If called upon to discuss this question, posts should state that the US is confident existing international law supports the US view that warships and merchant vessels enjoy identical, or nearly identical, rights of passage, but that it must be recognized some nations assert that different rules should apply.'[38] The use of the phrase 'nearly identical' and the acknowledgement of 'different rules' indicated that the Americans were saying one thing and thinking another.

This was confirmed by Kenneth Bailey, who noted that the State Department's legal advisers 'still think the I.L.C. text of Article 24 correctly represents customary law viz. that warships have no legal right of passage through the territorial sea without authorisation though in practice, passage should normally be granted as a matter of courtesy'.[39] As for the Canadians, Lt. Commander E. M. Jones stated:

> The right of innocent passage for warships is not firmly established in law. The 'innocence' of a warship in getting as quickly as possible to a potential trouble spot is debatable and could give cause for dispute.[40]

When considering this debate, it is as well to consider the context in which it took place. The influential Dutch observer, J. P. A. François, took issue with the belief among smaller states that the powers were calling for innocent passage for warships, not subject to authorisation, so they could 'exert pressure, for political reasons, on weaker powers by displaying their naval might off the coasts of the latter'.[41] He observed that this sort of pressure would contravene the aims and principles of the United Nations, and that those holding this view 'sometimes appeared to be hypnotizing themselves over the possibility of naval demonstrations'.[42]

This final comment might have seemed less gratuitous had it not coincided with a series of naval sorties and exercises carried out in

[37] 'Law of the Sea: basic security reasons why US supports the retention of a narrow territorial sea' (1 March 1960), p. 1: box 136, RG 43, Records of international conferences, commissions and expositions, Bureau of International Organization Affairs, NARA.

[38] Ibid.

[39] Australian Consulate-general Geneva to External Affairs Canberra (1 May 1960), p. 1: A1209/80 1958/5106, pt. 2, NAA.

[40] E. M. Jones to M. Cadieux, 'Re: territorial sea' (19 May 1959), p. 2: vol. 7184, 9456-RW-4-40, pt. 6, RG 25, LAC.

[41] J. P. A. François, 'Second international conference on the Law of the Sea', *United Nations Review* 6 (1960), 12, 14.

[42] Ibid.

Indonesia's vicinity in 1958–1960 at a particularly sensitive stage of the dispute between the Dutch and Indonesians over West Irian, and at the high point of the conflict between Jakarta and rightist rebels in Padang. After December 1957, when Indonesia proclaimed its archipelagic status (and shut down Dutch businesses including the island shipping line KPM), the powers and their Australasian allies tested the Sukarno government's resolve to exert greater control over the claimed archipelagic waters. Without notifying Jakarta, they dispatched both individual warships and flotillas of naval vessels through the Indonesian straits – usually bound for the annual Southeast Asia Treaty Organization (SEATO) exercises in the South China Sea.

One incident preceding SEATO's *Sea Demon* exercise in 1959 aroused great controversy in Indonesia. In April that year, a large Western naval flotilla, made up of the Australian and British aircraft carriers *HMAS Melbourne* and *HMS Albion*, the New Zealand cruiser *HMNZS Royalist*, as well as destroyers, a frigate and fleet auxiliaries, sailed north through Indonesia's Sunda Strait towards Singapore. The flotilla passed within three miles of the Kepulauan Seribu island group,[43] and carried out 'replenishment exercises' in the area,[44] whereupon they were buzzed by two Indonesian MIG aircraft.[45] (The Australian navy minister John Gorton tried to pass off the buzzing as a 'a friendly waggle of their wings' before the Indonesians confirmed that it was anything but.[46])

While the Indonesian foreign minister Subandrio did not make a formal complaint, he told the Australian ambassador Lawrence MacIntyre that 'the Indonesian Government would like to be informed, as a matter of courtesy, when foreign warships were to pass close to Indonesian territory'.[47] Later, he explained to the British ambassador Leslie Fry that he did not want to make an issue of the incident, but the approach of this fleet 'not unnaturally caused some consternation in the area'.[48] In the ensuing months, the Western states involved agreed

[43] UK Embassy Jakarta to Commissioner-general's Office Singapore (24 April 1959): ADM 2/27057, TNA.

[44] H. D. Anderson, 'Passage of H.M.A. ships through Indonesian waters' (15 May 1959): A1838/269 TS688/25/10, NAA.

[45] 'Buzzing of ships confirmed by Indonesian', *Canberra Times* (15 April 1959).

[46] Ibid., and 'Seato naval force' (14 April 1959): A1838/269 TS688/25/10, NAA.

[47] L. McIntyre, 'Passage of naval ships through Indonesian waters' (2 April 1959): A1838/269 TS688/25/10, NAA.

[48] UK Embassy Jakarta to Commissioner-general's Office Singapore (24 April 1959): ADM 2/27057, TNA.

between themselves that notification should be given to Indonesia as a courtesy (not as a right) if the route, exercise or number of warships involved was unusual.[49] This suggests that far from states 'hypnotizing themselves over the possibility of naval demonstrations', as François had suggested, the Indonesians had experienced the reality of them and had responded with restraint.

India Turns Up the Heat

A few weeks after sounding out Bailey, Sen made a formal approach to the delegation heads leading the campaign for the US-Canada plan to push his proposal for the authorisation of warships in the territorial sea and contiguous zone. He stressed that he was under strict instructions from Jawaharlal Nehru to extract concessions on this issue, and that if these were forthcoming, the US-Canada plan would likely secure the votes of India, Ceylon, Ghana and possibly Iran.[50] He also specified that the provision for authorisation should take the form of an article – not a resolution, which would be seen as 'eyewash' by the Asian and African states.[51]

Four senior legal experts from the states backing the US-Canada plan – Raymond Yingling (United States), Marcel Cadieux (Canada), Gerald Fitzmaurice (Britain) and Bailey (Australia) – met to work out a formula to satisfy India without conceding more than they had to. They recognised two major obstacles to agreement. First, the Indians could not accept just notification, as distinct from authorisation, over both six-mile zones, because their African and Asian allies were insisting on authorisation out to twelve miles.[52] Second, the United States and Britain could not accept authorisation, as distinct from notification, over the two six-mile zones, because doing so would amount to 'the granting to the coastal states of a 12 mile territorial sea'.[53] Finding common ground would be a challenge.

This group eventually produced a proposal allowing for notification (not authorisation) of warships in the outer-six-mile contiguous zone,

[49] J. G. Butcher and R. E. Elson, *Sovereignty and the sea: how Indonesia became an archipelagic state* (Singapore: National University of Singapore Press, 2017), pp. 109–110.

[50] Canadian delegation to External Affairs Ottawa (13 April 1960), p. 1: vol. 7306, 10600-BA-40, pt. 1.2, RG 25, LAC.

[51] Ibid., p. 2.

[52] Ibid., pp. 1–2.

[53] Ibid., p. 1.

while omitting to propose anything about warships in the inner-six-mile territorial sea. This read:

> Without prejudice to the respective views entertained by States as to the rules of international law applicable to the passage of warships through the territorial sea, a State will give prior notification to the coastal State concerned of any intended passage of warships through the contiguous zone provided for in article 24 of the convention on the territorial sea and the contiguous zone adopted at Geneva on April 27, 1958.[54]

The Western delegates were rather pleased with this effort, which they felt spiked the guns of the Indians under the guise of offering concessions. Bailey cabled Canberra to say:

> The merit of the text . . . is that it leaves entirely open the conflicting views of (e.g.) United Kingdom and (e.g.) India as to the present position of warships in the territorial sea and concedes a new and explicit right to notification in the outer six miles. Nothing is said as to not[i]fication in territorial sea but of course in most cases a ship cannot enter the territorial sea except through contiguous zone.[55]

When Sen sent the proposal to New Delhi, the Cabinet turned it down and instructed Sen to abstain on the US-Canada plan in the committee of the whole. 'This is very bad news indeed,' George Drew wrote, because the Indians' abstention might influence the other Asian countries to do likewise.[56] He added that Krishna Menon was taking advantage of the situation to 'compel retrospective acceptance of pet ideas' on authorisation that the previous conference had not resolved to his liking.[57]

The Last Card

After the instruction to Sen to abstain, everyone beat a path to the doors of the ministries in New Delhi. The first to arrive at the external affairs department was the Soviet ambassador Ivan A. Benedictov, who encouraged secretary-general Raghavan Pillai to push hard for a twelve-mile territorial sea. As Pillai recounted to another visitor,

[54] UK delegation to UK Foreign Office (13 April 1960): DO 35/9048, TNA.

[55] Australian Consulate-general Geneva to External Affairs Canberra (13 April 1960), p. 2: A1209/100 1960/190, pt. 2, NAA.

[56] Canadian delegation to External Affairs Ottawa (16 April 1960), p. 1: vol. 5309, 9456-RW-8-40, pt. 2, RG 25, LAC.

[57] Ibid.

> the Soviet Ambassador . . . had annoyed him for over an hour trying to pressure him to wreck the conference rather than yield on the demand for a twelve-mile territorial sea. This, said the Ambassador, should be the minimum demand by all nations which had been oppressed by 'the great imperial and colonial powers'. Coming from the great power controlling a host of satellites, this made Pillai furious.[58]

The Canadian ambassador Chester Ronning was next, and he did not arrive empty handed. With the US-Canada plan at stake, he first tried to persuade Pillai to get word to the Indian delegation to find grounds for agreement with the Americans and the British – by asking them, for example, to prohibit manoeuvres, demonstrations and formation sailing in the contiguous zone (to which the powers could agree) rather than pushing for authorisation.[59] Then, as the Indian foreign secretary Subimal Dutt would later explain to Sen, Ronning indicated that the Americans and Canadians would be willing to budge over warships in the territorial sea:

> We are informed by Canadian High Commissioner that Canada and U.S.A. are now prepared to amend their resolution so that prior notification to coastal State will be given of any intended passage of warships through territorial sea and contiguous zone, that is, through twelve miles from the coast.[60]

In short, the sponsors of the US-Canada plan were prepared to accept *notification* of warships in the territorial sea, not just the contiguous zone. But would this induce India to back down over authorisation? Dutt indicated to Sen that it would not:

> We would suggest to you that you might move an amendment to U.S.-Canadian proposal providing for prior authorisation by coastal State in regard to warships. This would make clear our reason for not supporting American-Canadian proposal as it stands. If amendment is not accepted, you should vote against the U.S.-Canadian proposal.[61]

The Indian response to the US-Canada plan had thus hardened from authorisation or India would abstain, to authorisation or India would oppose.

58 Canadian High Commission New Delhi to External Affairs Ottawa (no. 218, 19 April 1960), p. 1: vol. 7306, 10600-BA-40, pt. 1.2, RG 25, LAC.

59 Ibid.

60 'For law minister' (19 April 1960), p. 1: J.N. (S.G.), f. no. 703, Jawaharlal Nehru papers, NMML.

61 Ibid.

In Washington, meanwhile, State Department official Gordon Arneson met the Canadian ambassador Arnold Heeney to discuss India's decision to hold out for authorisation. Arneson, Heeney reported, was 'much concerned at this news and wondered out loud whether it might be necessary to bring strong pressure to bear on India, "which had worked at the last conference"'.[62] Heeney responded that 'strong-arm tactics' would probably induce Nehru's government to become less flexible, not more.[63]

By then, a note of desperation had crept into the telegraphic traffic between the powers and their missions in New Delhi: surely *something* could be done to move the Indians? As the conference entered its final week, the Americans, Canadians and the British decided it was time to make one last push to bring them onside. Dwight Eisenhower and prime ministers John Diefenbaker and Harold Macmillan all sent personal messages to Nehru to persuade him to drop authorisation and support the US-Canada plan. Macmillan told Nehru that India's attitude would be 'highly important for the success or failure of the Conference', and that its breakdown would prompt unilateral action that 'could give rise to dangerous friction'.[64] Yet he offered nothing more than had already been rejected by Nehru's Cabinet – to wit, that 'we would be prepared to agree to a requirement for prior notification of the passage of warships through the outer six miles' but 'could not, however, accept a requirement for prior authorisation by the coastal states'.[65]

A few days later, and just two days before the end of the conference, Nehru sent an equally unyielding reply to Macmillan:

> As you know, there is conflict of opinion between some of the great maritime powers and the smaller countries who, from past experience, are rather apprehensive of any interference with their freedom and independence. In regard to one matter particularly there has been strong feeling among these countries which, I feel, is justified. This is in regard to foreign warships coming within coastal waters without prior authorisation. We have given a great deal of thought to this matter and we feel that the proper course would be for such authority or permission

[62] Canadian Embassy Washington to External Affairs Ottawa (20 April 1960): vol. 5388, 10600-S-40, pt. 3, RG 25, LAC.
[63] Ibid.
[64] UK Commonwealth Relations Office to UK High Commission New Delhi (22 April 1960), p. 1: DO 35/9048, TNA.
[65] Ibid.

> to be obtained from the coastal State. Even normal courtesy would demand this.[66]

The British had played their last card, and in return, they had received nothing from Nehru except a rebuke. The correspondence showed that there was no middle ground on authorisation of warships: one side or another would have to give way, or the conference would likely break down.

Against Historic Rights

While India was holding out against the powers over warships, other states were chipping away at the historic fishing rights component of the US-Canada plan, which proposed a six-mile territorial sea plus a six-mile fishing zone, with a ten-year phase-out period for foreign states who had fished the zone for the previous five years.

Peru led the resistance. Over the course of the two conferences, the Peruvian delegation had constructed a justification for terrestrial claims to a maritime zone based on analogy with terrestrial claims to the continental shelf. Just as the shelf was a physical extension of the land, so the maritime zone was an ecological extension of it, with riverine silt feeding plankton, which fed anchovies, which fed birds, whose guano could be used to fertilise the land. Now, they argued, this relationship between land and sea was being usurped by other states' unjustified proclamations of their historic fishing rights in Peru's waters. The Peruvian delegation head, Alberto Ulloa, asked what these historic rights were, and concluded that the attempt to claim them did not involve the application or transposition of a well-known idea in relation to fisheries; instead, it was 'the attempt to supplant concepts and realities; to alter the essence of things'.[67] He recalled:

> At the first Geneva conference on the law of the sea I asked the United States delegation ... what criterion had led it to fix a measure, then said to be ten years [of previous fishing], to fishing rights up to six miles from the coast? The question remained without an answer ... indeed, it was evaded, and wrapped up in vague words ... That the United States

[66] 'From prime minister ... to prime minister MacMillan' (24 April 1960), p. 1: J.N. (S.G.), 703, Jawaharlal Nehru papers, NMML.

[67] 'Discurso del Doctor Alberto Ulloa, presidente de la delegacion del Peru' (29 March 1960), p. 7: 7-7-A Delegados y Conferencias (entradas) 1960, Archivo Central, MRE del Perú.

> persists at this second sea conference in its extravagant claim, clothing the fishing companies' greed for profit in the garb of 'historic rights', gives us some assurance about the true origin of this claim . . . The United States would like to make certain fisheries 'historic' in order to back up their flagged tuna clippers' abusive incursions into Peruvian waters.[68]

Peru was not alone. Milan Bartoš of Yugoslavia stated that,

> The Yugoslav delegation, without distinguishing between the kind of fishing carried out since time immemorial and that practised during the five years preceding 1958, regarded the affirmation of so-called historic rights as an effort to uphold the theory of acquired rights. It was evident from the circumstances in which those rights had come into being that in most cases they represented vestiges of colonialism or an abuse of power by politically or economically stronger States. It would be contrary to the spirit of the Charter to deprive States of their national resources on the pretext that they had had to give them up when they had been unable to exploit them themselves.[69]

Examples of powerful states exploiting others' offshore fisheries were legion, and some coastal states pushed back: in the fifties, while the Peruvians were impounding Onassis's whalers and the Mexicans were chasing off American shrimpers, the South Koreans were arresting (and sometimes sinking) Japanese trollers and trawlers that ventured behind the 'Rhee Line'. While most states resisting incursions were from the South, some were from the North, with Norway (viz. the *Fisheries* case) and Iceland prominent among them.

Iceland had only recently gained its independence from Denmark, in 1944. Like many newly independent states, it possessed a single-commodity economy (fish), though unlike many it was far from impoverished, having as it did one of the higher standards of living in Europe.[70] Even so, vestiges of the past lingered: the United States, after its wartime occupation of Iceland, maintained a 'forward location' military base at Kleflavik, now directed at the USSR rather than Germany; and many West European states continued to trawl for halibut and cod in the surrounding high seas without much concern about the long-term viability of these fisheries.

Herein lay the problem: if Iceland were to sustain itself, it had to protect these fishing grounds from being overexploited. Icelandic delegates

68 Ibid., pp. 7–8.
69 UNLOSC II, vol. 1, 8th meeting of committee of the whole (30 March 1960), p. 70.
70 R. G. R. Wall to G. G. Fitzmaurice (4 February 1960), p. 1: FO 371/150829, TNA.

cited evidence of overfishing by foreign fleets, pointing out that when they fished off its coasts either side of the war, fish stocks fell, but when they stayed away during the conflict, they recovered.[71] Their policy, then, was to push foreign trawlers away from the coast and bring the exploitation and conservation of fish stocks under control. In March 1952, Reykjavik unilaterally declared the extension of the nation's territorial sea from three to four miles, and in June 1958, it issued a regulation extending an exclusive fishing zone out to twelve miles. Even though many Western European countries protested, most of them respected the new twelve-mile limit. One country did not, however: Britain, whose fishing catch off Iceland was roughly half of Iceland's own.[72] When the new regulation entered into force on 1 September 1958, British trawlers, escorted by Royal Navy warships, entered the twelve-mile zone and dropped their trawls up to the four-mile line, as they had done previously. This display of muscle convulsed relations between Iceland and Britain and reverberated around the world.

This dispute gave rise to the question of its settlement. As will be recalled, fishery limits had not been decided at the 1958 conference. The British foreign secretary John Selwyn Lloyd stated his wish to submit the dispute to the ICJ, but Iceland had not accepted its compulsory jurisdiction and declined the offer. Some interested observers, including the Canadian legal adviser Marcel Cadieux, doubted the appropriateness of using the Court. For one thing, proceedings were slow and would hold up the conference, tempting more states to make unilateral declarations. For another, it was a law-declaring, not a law-making, body, and, in the absence of agreement by either the ILC or the conference on the issues, 'the International Court could not settle this dispute without in effect legislating or making law'.[73]

As it turned out, Iceland aired its complaint in the UN General Assembly instead. The Icelandic representative Thor Thors claimed that decade after decade, British trawlers had 'scraped the bottom of the sea almost up to the doors of our poor fishermen's humble homes'.[74] His words resonated with other states because American, French, Japanese,

[71] Extracts from Gudmundur i Gudmundsson's speech before the General Assembly (25 September 1958), p. 1: FO 371/133749, TNA.

[72] 'Iceland' (u.d, c. March 1960), p. 1: box 136, RG 43, Records of international conferences, commissions and expositions, Bureau of International Organization Affairs, NARA.

[73] M. Cadieux, 'Memorandum for the minister: Icelandic fisheries dispute' (4 September 1958), p. 2: vol. 7183, 9456-RW-3-40, pt. 4, RG 25, LAC.

[74] 'Icelandic attack on "gunboat diplomacy"', *Daily Telegraph* (6 October 1959).

Portuguese, Spanish and Soviet trawlers were scraping the sea up to doorsteps the world over. Not only that, but as Thors reminded them, powerful states like Britain were selective about who they targeted: in September 1958, two countries had extended their maritime limits to twelve miles – Iceland with its fishing zone, and China with its territorial sea – but Britain had only intervened against the former. 'What is the reason for this double standard?', Thors asked, 'Is it because we are a small nation and the Government of Peking rules over 640 million people?'[75]

Outside Britain, the news stories about Royal Navy warships materialising in the Icelandic fog to prevent Iceland's coastguard vessels from arresting British trawlers sent out many messages, none of them positive. For the West, they appeared to herald the break-up of NATO and the prospect of Iceland being drawn into the orbit of the USSR. For the South, they presented the essence of historic fishing rights – the powers' self-proclaimed right to exploit fisheries in other states' waters, backed up by the threat of violence.

Special Circumstances

The coastal states' opposition to historic rights took two forms. Some states claimed or wished to claim exclusive fishing rights in their fishing zone, thereby cancelling out long-distance fishing states' claims to historic rights. Other states claimed or wished to claim preferential fishing rights in the adjacent high seas, thereby clawing back the loss of exclusive fishing rights in the fishing zone by making exclusionary claims to fishing rights outside it. The target of both groups was paragraph 3 of the US-Canada plan, which read:

> Any State whose vessels have made a practice of fishing in the outer six miles of the fishing zone established by the coastal State . . . for the period of five years immediately preceding 1 January 1958, may continue to do so for a period of ten years from 31 October 1960.[76]

The Icelandic delegation challenged paragraph 3 head-on with an amendment stating that, 'The provisions of this paragraph shall not

[75] Ibid.

[76] This paragraph appears in both versions of the US-Canada plan (UNLOSC II, vol. 1, A/Conf.19/C.1/L.10 (8 April 1960), p. 169; and A/Conf.19/L.11 (22 April 1960), p. 173) as well as being adopted by the committee of the whole (A/Conf.19/L.4 (14 April 1960), p. 171).

apply to the situation where a people is overwhelmingly dependent upon its coastal fisheries for its livelihood or economic development'.[77] Gudmundur i Gudmundsson explained that for Iceland, control over its coastal fisheries was 'a matter of life or death' because fishing was the mainstay of its economy, with 97 per cent of its export income being derived from fish products.[78] Contrast that to Britain, he said, whose delegates bemoaned the sacrifices they had to make under the proposed US-Canada plan, even though fishing accounted for less than 1 per cent of its national income (with an even smaller percentage derived from the catch off Iceland).[79] Gudmundsson's point was that Britain's special dispensation to fish – for that is what a claim to historic rights amounted to – should be overridden by Iceland's special circumstances, given that its economy depended almost entirely on fishing.

While Iceland sought to deny historic rights in the fishing zone on exceptional grounds, Argentina attempted to impose stricter conditions on the exercise of these rights across the board. Paragraph 3 required a state to have fished another state's coastal waters 'for the period of five years' to enjoy historic rights, whereas an Argentinian amendment proposed instead 'for an uninterrupted period of thirty years'.[80] This set the bar high. Given that most distant fishing had been suspended during the Second World War, the word 'uninterrupted' would have prohibited many long-distance fishing states from operating in other states' zones, thereby endowing the latter with exclusive fishing rights. When introducing this, Luis María de Pablo Pardo *verbally* assured fellow delegates that the interruption of war (but not interruptions brought about by the weather, or by currents, or by better fishing elsewhere, or by peacetime extensions of jurisdiction) would be allowed for when calculating the thirty years.[81] But the written amendment made no mention of war as an exemption, and it aroused deep suspicions among the Western delegations, with the New Zealand delegate reporting that, 'this is plainly

77 UNLOSC II, vol. 1, A/Conf.19/L.13 (22 April 1960), p. 174.

78 UNLOSC II, vol. 2, '11th meeting' (31 March 1960), p. 206.

79 Canadian delegation to External Affairs Ottawa (12 April 1960), p. 4: vol. 8353, 10600-J-40, pt. 1, RG 25, LAC.

80 UNLOSC II, vol. 1, A/Conf.19/C.1/L.11 (11 April 1960).

81 UNLOSC II, vol. 1, 25th meeting of the committee of the whole, A/Conf.19/C.1/SR.25 (12 April 1960), p. 134.

a wrecking amendment inspired by twelve milers to prevent vote on compromise proposal'.[82]

The coastal states' second line of attack on historic fishing rights was to try to make up for their loss of exclusive fishing rights in the fishing zone by acquiring exclusionary fishing rights in the high seas beyond it – again, on grounds of special circumstances. Argentina, Cuba, Iceland and Peru each submitted motions designed to give fishing-dependent coastal states preferential rights to exploit fish stocks in adjacent high seas, these rights prevailing over outsiders' fishing rights.

Peru suggested in a detailed proposal that in special circumstances given by the interrelation between the sea, fisheries, livelihoods and the national economy, a state could impose conservation measures and enjoy preferential rights to exploit fisheries if it provided scientific grounds for the circumstances, did not discriminate between foreign fishermen, and did not impede navigation.[83] Other proposals were simpler and more far-reaching. Cuba suggested that when it was necessary to limit the catch of fish, 'preferential consideration should be given to the special requirements and interests of the coastal State'.[84] Argentina proposed that in the adjacent high seas, a coastal state 'shall have a preferential right of fishing, especially if its economic development or the feeding of its population depends on that activity'.[85] And Iceland contended that if a people was overwhelmingly dependent on fisheries, and the catch had to be limited, 'the coastal State shall have preferential rights . . . to the extent rendered necessary by its dependence on the fishery'.[86] The common feature of all these proposals, Gerald Fitzmaurice noted, was that 'they would more or less allow the coastal State to decide when it should exercise such preferential rights and to what extent'.[87]

Although the claim to historic fishing rights was giving rise to various forms of opposition from the coastal states, the Americans were not prepared to abandon the position because they had to placate their domestic fishing industries while keeping on board Japan and the West European fishing states. That said, they were quite prepared to strike

[82] New Zealand delegation to External Affairs Wellington (12 April 1960), p. 1: A1838/2 852/13/10/3, pt. 11, NAA.
[83] UNLOSC II, vol. 1, A/Conf.19/C.1/L.8 (8 April 1960), p. 2.
[84] UNLOSC II, vol. 1, A/Conf.19/C.1/L.9 (8 April 1960), p. 1.
[85] UNLOSC II, vol. 1, A/Conf.19/C.1/L.11 (11 April 1960), p. 1.
[86] UNLOSC II, vol. 1, A/Conf.19/C.1/L.7 (6 April 1960), p. 168.
[87] G. G. Fitzmaurice, 'Law of the Sea Conference... Report to the secretary of state' (29 June 1960), p. 3: FO 371/150827, TNA.

bilateral deals with the more insistent advocates of preferential rights to secure the most important part of the US-Canada plan: the six-mile territorial sea. So, in exchange for votes supporting (or at least abstaining on) the plan, the Americans offered some Latin American states one-on-one deals that would cancel future claims to historic rights in their coastal waters. As George Drew reported to Ottawa:

> The USA del has now been authorized to make a unilateral commitment to Argentina, Chile, Guatemala Ecuador and El Salvador that the USA will not claim historical fishing rights in the outer zone off their coasts during the phasing-out period, and to make a public statement in the conference to that effect.[88]

These offers had two functions: to win votes; and, by making offers to Chile and Ecuador but not to Peru, to drive a wedge between the signatories of the 1952 Santiago Declaration (which, as will be recalled, established the 200-mile maritime zone). In the meantime, Arthur Dean hastened to assure officials in Washington that their effect would be minimal: the fisheries advisers attached to the US delegation had told him that 'there were no such historical rights in most areas, and that where there were any, they were of little value to the industry'.[89] In return, he said, Argentina, Chile, Ecuador, El Salvador and Guatemala would either vote for or abstain on the US-Canada plan.[90]

Still more was in the offing. Dean said that to arrest further support for the more expansive Latin American proposals, it was also necessary to offer states preferential fishing rights on the adjacent high seas.[91] The British took a similar view. Indeed, having suspended its fishing in Iceland's twelve-mile zone for the duration of the conference, they privately offered the Icelanders both a shorter phase-out period for historic rights and a promise that Britain and other West European states would refrain from fishing designated areas of the adjacent high seas[92] in exchange for Iceland withdrawing its preferential rights motion – an offer that Iceland refused.

[88] Canadian delegation to External Affairs Ottawa (22 April 1960), p. 1: vol. 5309, 9456-RW-8-40, pt. 2, RG 25, LAC.

[89] 'Memorandum of conversations, Department of State' (21 April 1960): *FRUS, United Nations and general international matters*, 1958–1960, vol. 2, doc. 424.

[90] Ibid.

[91] Ibid.

[92] Canadian delegation to External Affairs Ottawa (4 April 1960), p. 3: vol. 5388, 10600-S-40, pt. 2, RG 25, LAC.

These developments did not please American long-distance fishing interests. Congressman Thomas Pelly and Senator Warren Magnuson dispatched a strongly worded letter to Secretary of State Christian Herter:

> [W]e are reliably informed that the American delegation has been attempting to 'buy' votes of nations heretofore abstaining from voting, as well as the votes of those in opposition, with additional concessions and further compromises involving extension of additional rights beyond the twelve-mile limit. In short, we believe that Chairman Dean and the United States delegation propose a policy of settlement at any price ... If the United States delegation is successful in implementing such a sell-out agreement, which would in effect abrogate the historic rights of its own citizens, it will force us to initiate legislative measures for the protection of the United States fishing industry and the fishermen who depend on it for their livelihood.[93]

Other equally critical observers dispensed with the quotation marks around the word 'buy'.

The American delegation pressed ahead nonetheless. They believed that a proposal for preferential rights acceptable to themselves would have greater appeal if it were presented to the conference as a Latin American rather than North American motion. The Americans and Canadians therefore drafted a proposal recognising preferential rights in special circumstances[94] (with a clause that recognised the bilateral deals cancelling historic rights[95]), which they then gave to delegations from Brazil, Cuba and Uruguay to co-sponsor as an amendment to the US-Canada plan. Or, to put it another way, the Americans and Canadians amended their own plan using these three Latin American states as intermediaries. The main difference between this proposal – henceforth, the Brazil-Cuba-Uruguay amendment[96] – and the earlier ones on preferential rights was that this one was hedged with restrictions. These rights were subject to strict conditions on special circumstances and conservation, and to compulsory third-party settlement based on the

[93] 'Letter from representative Thomas M. Pelly and senator Warren G. Magnuson' (19 April 1960): *FRUS, United Nations and general international matters*, 1958–1960, vol. 2, doc. 418.

[94] Drew complained that the Canadians had to rewrite the Americans' 'barely intelligible' draft: 'Final report of the Canadian delegation' (u.d., c. May 1960), p. 30: vol. 5309, 9456-RW-8-40, pt. 1.1, file 2, RG 25, LAC.

[95] The relevant words are: 'The provisions of paragraph 3 shall not apply or may be varied as between States which enter into bilateral, multilateral or regional agreements to that effect': UNLOSC II, vol. 1, A/Conf.19/L.12 (22 April 1960), p. 173.

[96] UNLOSC II, vol. 1, A/Conf.19/L.12 (22 April 1960), p. 173.

arbitration procedure set out in the as yet unratified 1958 high seas fishing convention.

Having made these agreements with some of the Latin American states, the Americans and Canadians also had to keep their West European allies on side, which entailed more deals, including with Britain. The British delegation leader John Hare reported that he had reluctantly supported the Americans over preferential rights not just because it was the necessary price for securing Latin American support of the US-Canada plan but also, more to the point from Britain's point of view, 'for ensuring the rejection of the Icelandic proposal adopted by the Committee of the Whole'.[97] In return for British support, Dean told the Icelandic delegation that the United States would support only one preferential rights proposal in plenary – the Brazil-Cuba-Uruguay amendment – and would actively oppose any others, including Iceland's.[98]

The stage was set: if the Brazil-Cuba-Uruguay amendment passed, the deal was that Argentina, Chile and Guatemala would vote for the US-Canada proposal while Ecuador and El Salvador would abstain instead of voting against. These votes, the Americans and Canadians calculated, would be enough to ensure that their plan would win the two-thirds majority required for it to be transformed into a draft treaty. But there's many a slip 'twixt cup and lip, and slip things did.

Winning and Losing

During the final days, the Americans used all means at their disposal to pressure other countries to vote for the US-Canada plan. In Brussels, for example, Dean reported that 'our [diplomatic] representative and others had put so much pressure on the Foreign Minister [Pierre Wigny] that he had left town for three days'.[99] In Geneva, conference delegates had fewer places to hide, and evidence of behind-the-scenes arm-twisting occasionally seeped into the public debate. The day before the final votes, the Iranian delegate Ahmad Matine-Daftary, who had earlier supported a twelve-mile territorial sea, made a speech announcing Iran's abstention on the US-Canada plan. He offered no justification for the change,

[97] UK delegation to UK Foreign Office (22 April 1960): FO 371/150825, TNA.
[98] Ibid.
[99] 'Memorandum of conversations, Department of State' (21 April 1960): *FRUS, United Nations and general international matters*, 1958–1960, vol. 2, doc. 424.

remarking that a mere vote 'did not necessarily create law' and that states would only be bound if they signed and ratified a treaty arising from the negotiations.[100] Observers concluded that the Americans had compelled the Iranians to abstain rather than vote against: George Drew, for example, noted that Matine-Daftary's statement about abstention seemed to have been 'delivered reluctantly and only under pressure from USA'.[101] Arthur Dean had few qualms, however, reporting that the plan's opponents were equally capable of applying pressure: some, he wrote, were using 'third degree methods' such as threatening delegates with violence or ostracism if they voted in favour of the US-Canada plan.[102]

The same day, Dean delivered a speech of his own which seemed to have been expressly designed to annoy the less powerful states. British liaison officer B. H. Ashford-Russell reported that he had come across as 'aggressive and bullying' with his message that 'this was the United States position ... and it must be accepted without question by the smaller nations in his audience'.[103] Even so, most governments had already issued voting instructions to their delegations based on the deals that had been struck earlier at the conference. The Americans and Canadians had done the sums and were cautiously predicting that they had just enough support for their proposal to carry. But in the hours preceding the vote on 26 April 1960, things started to unravel.

This process began on the morning, when the Chilean delegation, who had earlier agreed to vote in favour of the US-Canada position, received instructions from Santiago to vote against it. Observers speculated that Peru had decided to hold the Chilean government to the terms of the 1952 Santiago Declaration, and that this had proved to be decisive.[104] The Chilean delegate Luis Melo-Lecaros showed Ashford-Russell the telegram changing his instructions, stating (as the latter later recalled):

> At meeting today attended by President [Jorge Alessandri], Parliamentary Commission, Deputies and the Peruvian Ambassador ... it was decided you will vote against repeat against Canadian/U.S. proposal. There will be

[100] UNLOSC II, vol. 1, '10th plenary meeting', A/Conf.19/SR.10 (25 April 1960), p. 13.

[101] Canadian delegation to External Affairs Ottawa (26 April 1960), p. 3: vol. 7305, 10600-AK-40, pt. 1, RG 25, LAC.

[102] 'Telegram from the delegation to the conference on the law of the sea' (28 April 1960): *FRUS, United Nations and general international matters*, 1958–1960, vol. 2, doc. 429.

[103] B. H. Ashford-Russell, 'Report on the Latin-American delegations' (2 May 1960), p. 2: FO 371/150826, TNA.

[104] Ibid.

> no repeat no reservation on this vote. Until Peruvian position is determined we shall adhere strictly to the agreement of 1952.[105]

Chile's change of position, Drew reported, came as a 'complete surprise'.[106]

The Americans and Canadians were in for another shock. Up to this point, Ecuador had been expected to abstain on the US-Canada plan. Dean reported that he had agreed earlier with the Ecuadoran delegates José Antonio Correa and Enrique Ponce y Carbo that the historic rights provision in paragraph 3 would not apply between the United States and Ecuador, and they 'shook hands on basis Ecuador would abstain'.[107] But on the evening before the vote, the Ecuadoran delegates had seemingly raised their price. Referring to United States' claims for compensation for Ecuador's seizure of American fishing boats in their 200-mile maritime zone, Dean reported that,

> Ponce Carbo (Ecuador) demanded I waive, release and quit claim to Ecuador all claims U.S. Government and American nationals against Ecuador ... [I e]xplained Congress alone could do this and had no authority sign such an agreement and would be fraudulent if I did. Then delegated Wainhouse to work this matter out finally and up to 1 a.m. Tuesday, April 26, Ecuadorans were still contending for this clause. At 1:15 a.m. politely but firmly told them we could not grant.[108]

In the morning the Ecuadorans tried one last time to persuade Dean to waive the claims for compensation. He recalled:

> At 10:30 a.m. while in Assembly Hall after plenary voting session called to order by Prince Wan, Correa (Ecuador) sent me note 'must see in corridor,' where he and Ambassador Trujillo and Ponce Carbo insisted I sign document with abovementioned release in it immediately or Ecuador would vote 'no.' As I was explaining why this could not be done received message from Prince Wan he was holding up voting because I was not in my seat. Thereupon left to re-enter Assembly Hall.[109]

Luis María de Pablo Pardo of Argentina gave a different account of these exchanges. After mentioning that Dean behaved like 'a schoolmaster

[105] Ibid.

[106] 'Final report of the Canadian delegation' (u.d., c. May 1960), appendix 1, p. 6: vol. 5309, 9456-RW-8-40, pt. 1.1, file 2, RG 25, LAC.

[107] 'Telegram from the delegation to the Conference on the Law of the Sea' (28 April 1960): *FRUS, United Nations and general international matters*, 1958–1960, vol. 2, doc. 429.

[108] Ibid.

[109] Ibid.

addressing school boys' whenever he dealt with the Latin American delegates, he explained to the Canadians that 'the US delegation had promised to give Ecuador guarantees in a bilateral agreement concerning preferential fishing rights before the vote in plenary session but that the Americans had refused to do so at the last moment and this had prompted Ecuador to vote against the Canadian-US proposal instead of abstaining'.[110]

Chile and Ecuador had defected, but would this be enough to sink the US-Canada plan? After Dean had rushed to join the morning plenary, the Brazil-Cuba-Uruguay amendment sailed through with a comfortable two-thirds majority.[111] The Americans and Canadians hoped that this result would induce all the remaining Latin American states with whom deals had been struck to vote as had been agreed. But there was one more surprise to come, and from another quarter entirely. Opposition to the amendment had been brewing in Japan – home to one of the world's largest long-distance fishing industries – on grounds of both preferential rights and compulsory dispute settlement. As a result, Tokyo had instructed its delegation head Okumura Katsuzo to abstain rather than vote for the US-Canada plan if it was amended by the Brazil-Cuba-Uruguay proposal. Okumura divulged this instruction to Dean in the minutes before the US-Canada plan was put to the vote, explaining that Japan's fishing lobbies already 'strongly objected to commission created Paragraph 9 Fishing Convention 1958 having jurisdiction to grant preferential rights coastal state beyond twelve miles'.[112] The question for all the vote-counters on the American and Canadian teams was whether, all things considered, Japan's switch to abstention would prove to be fatal.

The Reckoning

Of all the proposals on the territorial sea and fishing zone advanced over both UN law of the sea conferences, this US-Canada plan won the most support. Yet it was not enough, securing fifty-four votes for, twenty-eight

[110] Canadian Embassy Buenos Aires to External Affairs Ottawa (5 August 1960): vol. 5388, 10600-S-40, pt. 3, RG 25, LAC.
[111] UNLOS II, vol. 1, '13th plenary meeting', A/Conf.19/SR.13 (26 April 1960), pp. 29–30.
[112] 'Telegram from the delegation to the Conference on the Law of the Sea' (28 April 1960): *FRUS, United Nations and general international matters*, 1958–1960, vol. 2, doc. 429.

against, and five abstentions (Lebanon was absent).[113] It failed by a single vote to win a two-thirds majority, and the conference collapsed.

In the days that followed, the Western delegation leaders dispatched dispirited telegrams back to their capitals, laying most of the blame for the outcome on three states: India, Chile and Ecuador. In his conference report, the British deputy delegation leader Gerald Fitzmaurice singled out India, which, he wrote, 'must bear greater responsibility for the ultimate negative result than any other single State'.[114] He continued:

> [B]ecause of a private quarrel with Pakistan, and for other ulterior reasons probably personal to Mr. Krishna Menon, India preferred to wreck the Conference by insistence on an issue – prior authorization for the passage of foreign warships within 12 miles – that was outside the strict terms of reference of the Conference, had only a peripheral connexion with it, and was supposed to have been settled at the first Geneva Law of the Sea Conference by means of the articles on innocent passage then adopted ... India's responsibility is thus a very heavy one.[115]

The Canadians wrote in similar vein. But the New Zealand delegation leader Robert Quentin-Baxter best captured the various reasons for the failure of the conference. India, he said, was the biggest contributor because its opposition to the US-Canada plan 'gave heart to the twelve-milers', encouraging some to shift their positions, and emboldening others to hold out for better deals.[116] Meanwhile, the US deals offering preferential fishing rights rebounded badly against the plan's sponsors. Not only did these fail to move Iceland away from opposition, but they could not prevent Chile's move from support to opposition, nor Ecuador from pressing 'new private demands against United States to which latter could not agree', prompting it to switch from abstention to opposition.[117] Furthermore, the Japanese, who were reacting against the offer of preferential fishing rights, changed their vote from support to abstention.[118] All told, Quentin-Baxter concluded, these shifts were enough to deny the powers the two-thirds majority.

113 UNLOSC II, vol. 1, '13th plenary meeting', A/Conf.19/SR.13 (26 April 1960), p. 30.
114 G. G. Fitzmaurice, cover letter, 'Law of the Sea Conference... Report to the Secretary of State' (29 June 1960), p. 2: FO 371/150827, TNA.
115 Ibid.
116 New Zealand High Commission London to External Affairs Wellington (26 April 1960): vol. 8354, 10600-Y-40, pt. 1, RG 25, LAC.
117 Ibid.
118 Ibid.

Surveying the landscape beyond the conference, Kenneth Bailey concluded that the failure of the US-Canada plan 'has created widespread conviction here that United Nations is not an appropriate milieu for further attempts to stabilise Law of Territorial Sea'.[119] This would have given Constantin Stavropoulos at the UN secretariat much to be concerned about.

*

The powers, wishing to create treaties to curtail the emergence of custom likely to undermine their navigational freedoms, had been instrumental in inaugurating the two treaty-making conferences of 1958 and 1960. These negotiations had shown that the law of the sea was defined less by East–West conflict than by intra-Western and North-South tensions. The USSR, as an emerging maritime power, had little incentive to dispute the other powers' claims to navigational rights, which it would itself benefit from in time. This Soviet acquiescence meant that the Western states did not rally together against their Cold War foe, but instead fell out among themselves. Their disagreements at the conferences over coastal fishing rights, flags of convenience and the continental shelf, and their willingness to pursue their own national interests at the expense of the others, demonstrated the rifts behind the façade of NATO unity. The 1958 conventions glossed over these differences, which did not bode well for their future efficacy. Before long they would be overtaken by new technological developments and emerging customary law, and a decade or so later, overhauled by a new convention.

Another distinctive feature of the negotiations in the post-war decades was the challenge presented to traditional conceptions of law of the sea by the states of the South. Many of these countries portrayed the powers as defenders of a discredited imperialist status quo and sought to transform the law to deter unwanted naval incursions into their coastal waters and protect their marine resources from foreign exploitation. While only a few of them carried much weight individually in international affairs – many were even more vulnerable than Iceland to external pressure –

119 Australian Consulate-general Geneva to Australian High Commission London (28 April 1960), p. 1: A1209/100 1960/190, pt. 2, NAA.

their coordinated action to safeguard their national interests played a crucial role in the powers' failure to secure agreement to a narrow territorial sea. In 1960, they had put the powers on notice that their interests could no longer be ignored, but it remained to be seen whether, by attempting to recalibrate the Law of the Sea, they could realise their aspirations.

5

Internationalising the Seabed

Common Heritage and the UN Seabed Committee

In 1974, Philip Manhard, the American representative in Mauritius, cited a study that found that all the treaties signed 'in perpetuity' since 1815 had lasted on average only twenty-five years, and that the average was decreasing.[1] The 1958 law of the sea conventions seemed to testify to this. Less than a decade after they were opened for signature, states were declaring them to be, in whole or in part, virtually obsolete. Some regretted their failure to address salient issues; others condemned them as imperialist holdovers. One factor in their perceived obsolescence was political, with critical newly independent states joining the debate; another was economic, with an expanding and asymmetric global economy; and another still was technological, with leaps forward in military and extractive technologies. The negotiators at the 1958 conference either could not or did not factor in the impact of OPEC, oilspills, bobbin trawlers, the 'group of five', flash-frozen fish, Polaris missiles, containerisation, satellite surveillance, polymetallic nodules, the 'group of seventy-seven', ultra-large crude carriers and the new international economic order. But over the next decade, these factors helped to render parts of these treaties irrelevant, if not actually unhelpful.

All the conventions were affected. The territorial sea convention failed to specify the breadth of the territorial sea; the high seas convention, while codifying custom on the high seas, scarcely touched on the deep seabed; the conventions on the territorial sea and high seas fisheries did not engage with coastal states' claims to exclusive fishing zones; the continental shelf convention did not delineate the outer edge of the continental shelf; and the optional protocol on compulsory dispute settlement did not attract enough adherents to create a viable regime. Ultimately, they were unable to answer the questions that preoccupied

[1] US Embassy Port Louis to US State Department (29 October 1974), p. 2: 1974PORTL00904, US National Archives and Records Administration – Access to Archival Databases [hereafter, AAD].

states throughout the sixties arising from claims to wider territorial seas, the search for oil and gas on the continental shelf, the prospect of seabed mining and the campaign for an exclusive economic zone.

In 1967, two separate initiatives were launched to counter the coastal states' unilateral claims to the oceans. In July, the USSR launched one of these, soliciting the active support of the Americans and British in their campaign to preserve navigational rights by reining in the extension of territorial seas, and thereby safeguarding passage through straits used for international navigation. The following month, Arvid Pardo, Malta's ambassador to the UN, launched the other initiative with his proposal to internationalise the seabed beyond national jurisdiction, aiming to preserve it for the peaceful use and benefit of all. These two approaches were markedly different in target and approach, with the USSR mounting a conservative endorsement of the status quo, and Pardo appealing to the natural law idea of the 'common heritage of mankind'. Both, however, were expressly designed to inhibit the coastal states' expanding claims to the seabed.

The Common Heritage Initiative

Pardo's proposal would set the tone for the future debate on the law of the sea. In August 1967, the Maltese mission submitted a *note verbale* to the UN secretary-general proposing that the General Assembly agree a declaration and treaty 'concerning the reservation exclusively for peaceful purposes of the sea-bed and of the ocean floor, underlying the seas beyond the limits of present national jurisdiction, and the use of their resources in the interests of mankind'.[2] Its central premise was that the seabed was the 'common heritage of mankind'.[3] The concept was not new, but the Maltese note was useful for separating out the four strands of the concept.[4] First, it set out a negative duty: the seabed should not be subject to national appropriation. Second, it proposed a positive obligation: the international community should exercise stewardship over the seabed. Third, it specified that the use and exploitation of the seabed should be founded on the idea of *sharing* the benefits, especially with the most impoverished states. Finally, it stated that the seabed should be used exclusively for peaceful purposes. Pardo's aim was to 'counter the

[2] GAOR, A/6695 (18 August 1967), p. 1.
[3] Ibid., p. 2.
[4] Ibid., pp. 2–3.

excessive expansion of coastal state jurisdiction in ocean space',[5] by expelling from the seabed both the territory-centred concept of sovereignty and manifestations of its militarisation and exploitation by sovereign states.

The common heritage concept was distinctive because it moved beyond the existing subjects of international law – states and individuals – and towards a new subject: 'mankind'. Moreover, in Pardo's conception, it transcended the idea of ownership embodied in the dual ideas of *res nullius* (owned by none) and *res communis* (owned by all) by insisting that humankind did not own but could only *use* the seabed and its resources. As he said in 1970:

> we did not think it advisable to use the word *property* . . . Property is a form of power. Property as we have it from ancient Romans implies the *jus utendi et abutendi* (right to use and misuse).[6]

This theme was taken up by others, who argued that the concepts of *res nullius* or *res communis* were not applicable to the deep seabed: it should instead have a 'special legal status as the common heritage of mankind'.[7] Following on from this, rights would attach not to property or territory, but only to access;[8] they would apply equally to the use and exploitation of the seabed; and they would be exercised on behalf of generations present and future.

One commentator, Jean Buttigieg, suggests that Pardo's approach was inspired by Catholic natural law, with its emphasis on the common good, stewardship, and concern for the disadvantaged as dimensions of the moral order created by God. Buttigieg thus stresses the lineage between Pope John XXIII's 1963 encyclical, *Pacem in terris*, and Pardo's common heritage proposal.[9] But elements of this idea had also been circulating in the largely secular debates about the law of the sea. The phrase 'common heritage' was used during the 1958 and 1960 conferences, sometimes to describe the high seas and sometimes all ocean space. As for the four

[5] A. Pardo, 'Law of the Sea Conference – what went wrong', in R. L. Friedheim (ed.), *Managing ocean resources: a primer* (Boulder, CO: Westview Press, 1979), p. 140.
[6] Quoted in J. Buttigieg, 'The common heritage of mankind: from the law of the sea to the human genome and cyberspace', *Symposia Melitensia* 8 (2012), 81, 82.
[7] GOAR, A/7230 (1968), p. 44.
[8] C. C. Joyner, 'Legal implications of the concept of the common heritage of mankind', *International and Comparative Law Quarterly* 35 (1986), 190, 194.
[9] J. Buttigieg, 'Arvid Pardo – a diplomat with a mission', *Symposia Melitensia* 12 (2016), 13, 14; citing John XXIII, *Pacem in terris* (11 April 1963) at: www.vatican.va.

criteria, the first strand – ocean spaces should not be subject to appropriation – was an old idea, dating back to the birth of the modern era and enshrined in the concept of the high seas. The second strand – global stewardship of resources – had been growing since the nineteenth century, when overfishing presented itself as an international problem. The third strand – economic hardship being grounds for preferential claims to marine resources – had been gaining ground since the *Fisheries* case in 1951.

Even the fourth strand – the seabed should be reserved for peaceful purposes – was already part of the international dialogue, with references to 'peaceful purposes' appearing in the 1959 Antarctic treaty and 1967 UN Outer Space treaty, and proposed with respect to the seabed by the US-based Commission to Study the Organization of the Peace.[10] But Pardo recognised that his insistence on an explicit reference to peaceful purposes would inevitably jar with the powers most likely to engage in naval activities on the seabed. At a lunch held in his honour at the Maltese High Commission in London a few months after he dispatched the *note verbale*, he told Lord Dunrossil that while he thought the idea of peaceful purposes was 'the most vital aspect' of the work on the seabed, he also recognised that 'powerful influences were going to work to delay progress'.[11] After the lunch, US defence attaché Louis Kirn told others that this comment was 'the understatement of the day'.[12]

Pardo therefore proceeded cautiously on peaceful purposes, not only keeping the Western powers closely informed about his campaign's progress, but also accepting their guidance on what was acceptable to them. Before he sent his proposal to the secretary-general, for example, he showed it to an American desk officer at the UN, who advised him to remove references to 'military activity' and to the seabed being 'demilitarised in perpetuity'.[13] Pardo seemed to have accepted this advice, stating in the dispatched note that the seabed and ocean floor beyond the limits of existing national jurisdiction 'shall be reserved exclusively for peaceful

[10] The Antarctic Treaty (signed 1 December 1959, EIF 23 June 1961) 402 UNTS 71; Treaty on Principles Governing the Activities of States in the Exploration and Use of Outer Space, including the Moon and Other Celestial Bodies (signed 27 January 1967, EIF 10 November 1967) 610 UNTS 205; C. M. Eichelberger (ed.) (report for the Commission to Study the Organization of the Peace), *New dimensions for the United Nations: the problems of the next decade* (Dobbs Ferry, NY: Oceana, 1966), p. 41.

[11] Lord Dunrossil, 'The Maltese item' (24 January 1968), p. 2: FCO 10/235, TNA.

[12] Ibid.

[13] UK Mission to the UN to UK FCO (22 August 1967), p. 1: FCO 10/232, TNA.

purposes [not demilitarised] in perpetuity'.[14] This new phrasing softened the injunction against militarisation, leaving the door open to military activities on the seabed provided that they served 'peaceful' (i.e. defensive) purposes.

Pardo might have thought that peaceful purposes was 'the most vital aspect', but for many states, the prospect of exploiting the seabed aroused even greater interest – driven, it should be emphasised, more by fear than by optimism. The 'developing' countries were afraid of being left behind by the 'industrial' states (to use the words of the time) in an unregulated race to the bottom of the oceans and wanted to find a mechanism to control the process and share the benefits.

The industrial states, on the other hand, had seen rising prices for copper and nickel,[15] foreign nationalisations of oil and other mineral operations, and moves towards OPEC-style cartels in other industries. They thus began to look seawards. If seabed polymetallic nodules could be extracted in commercial quantities – and it was a big if – then these states could reduce their exposure to foreign shortages and the need for stockpiling. A handful of US-based mining and energy companies expressed an early interest: Kennecott because it wanted to diversify beyond land-based copper operations;[16] International Nickel because it predicted greater demand for stainless steel, and hence for nickel;[17] Tenneco Inc. because it wished to diversify beyond energy, forming the subsidiary Deepsea Ventures;[18] and United States Steel because it wanted to cut back on foreign manganese, and to create income for its subsidiary, Newport News Shipbuilding.[19] Before long these companies, wishing to attract capital and spread the risk of their proposed ventures, formed consortia with other Western-based companies from countries such as Canada, Japan and West Germany.[20] In short, the US government and

14 GAOR, A/6695 (18 August 1967), p. 3.

15 World Bank, *Price prospects for major primary commodities*, vol. 4 (Washington, DC: World Bank, 1984), pp. 36, 85.

16 'Group of 77 position on law of the sea' (c. August 1976), p. 5: CIA-RDP82S00697R-000400160021-6, Central Intelligence Agency Historical Collections [hereafter, CIAHC].

17 Ibid.

18 Ibid.

19 Ibid.

20 Deepsea Ventures, for example, transformed itself into a multinational joint venture made up of the International Nickel Company of Canada, Ltd; the Japanese group Deep Ocean Mining Co. Ltd; the German group Arbeitsgemeinschaft Meerestechnisch Gewinnbare Rohstoffe, plus SEDCO, an offshore drilling operation based in Dallas, Texas (ibid.).

corporations had both the motive and means to explore the possibilities of seabed mining. What Elizabeth Mann Borgese dubbed the 'industrial revolution in the oceans' seemed to be about to crank into action.[21]

*

Arvid Pardo gave a much fuller presentation of his ideas in the first committee of the General Assembly on 1 November 1967. Seeking to pre-empt a scramble for the seabed, he proposed a motion to convene a UN committee to examine the question of its reservation for peaceful purposes, and the use of its resources for the benefit of all. He opened his speech by dismissing speculation about his motives for raising the issue, stating that contrary to suspicions aired in the US House of Representatives that he was a 'sounding board for the British', he had not been put up to it by any other state.[22] The available British correspondence seems to confirm this: Whitehall officials privately expressed their surprise that the Maltese had launched the initiative,[23] and struggled to identify its author (never mind spell his name).[24]

Having asserted his independence from the powers, Pardo then turned to the substance of his submission, presenting an impressive but ominous account of potential developments at the bottom of the ocean. The seabed, he said, was covered by incredible concentrations of nodules bearing manganese, copper, cobalt and nickel, that would provide the world's needs for thousands, if not hundreds of thousands, of years.[25] Calcareous marine oozes could be transformed into aggregates for concrete and insulation bricks.[26] Oceanic plants would replace land-grown plants as a major source of food.[27] Farmed fish would be protected by bubble-curtains and dolphins would be used like sheepdogs.[28] Colonies of aquanauts would be living 500 metres underwater and exploring the deep in glass-hulled submersibles.[29]

[21] E. Mann Borgese, 'The complexities of a sea change', *New York Times* (1 October 1976).
[22] GAOR, A/C.1/PV.1515 (1 November 1967), p. 1.
[23] UK Mission to the UN to UK FCO (22 August 1967), p. 1: FCO 10/232, TNA.
[24] One British official contributed a potted biography of 'Avrid' Pardo: M. F. Cullis (5 December 1967): FCO 10/233, TNA.
[25] GAOR, A/C.1/PV.1515 (1 November 1967), p. 4.
[26] Ibid.
[27] Ibid.
[28] Ibid., pp. 4–5.
[29] Ibid., p. 6.

Yet danger loomed. While the ocean could be harnessed to *serve* the land, he warned, it might also be used by forces occupying the seabed to *dominate* the land. In the missile age, states might choose to transfer their capabilities to the more conducive environment of the oceans because, he said, the oceans unlike the atmosphere above were 'highly resistant to the over-pressures of nuclear attack'.[30] If this happened, an arms race on the seabed would likely ensue. Naval forces would occupy strategic oceanic areas, living in undersea barracks oxygenated by 'electrolysis of seawater' and sustaining themselves on oceanic nutrients.[31] While there, they would likely block off and insonify defensive areas above their underwater redoubts to prevent detection of their movements, thereby curtailing other states' non-military navigation through the oceans.[32]

Some of Pardo's predictions may have seemed overblown at the time, but he was merely synthesising material already in circulation, mostly of American origin. John Mero's book *The mineral resources of the sea* predicted a bonanza of exploitable nodules (and helped to kickstart the seabed mining industry).[33] The President's Science Advisory Committee's report on oceanography gave credence to the idea of the militarisation of the seabed.[34] Researchers considered the prospects of using deep-sea submersibles, establishing underwater communities, and developing 'marine protein concentrate' to feed the hungry.[35] And the press reported

[30] Ibid., pp. 6, 7.

[31] Ibid., p. 7.

[32] Ibid.

[33] J. L. Mero, *The mineral resources of the sea* (Amsterdam: Elsevier Oceanography Series, 1965).

[34] Report of the Panel of Oceanography, President's Science Advisory Committee, *Effective use of the sea* (Washington, DC: US Government Printing Office, 1966), p. 33 (indicating that underwater missile systems, if realised, 'can involve much larger missiles, might require underwater maintenance by personnel also located underwater, . . . might necessitate new kinds of detection and survival equipment to prevent attacks on the implacements'). See also, 'Next: an arsenal of new weapons for U.S.', *US News & World Report* (16 October 1967), p. 39 (on sinking remote-controlled missiles into the seabed off the coasts of hostile states); and W. Andrews, 'DOD delays decision on advanced ICBM', *Aerospace Technology* (11 September 1967), p. 16 (referring to a US study covering sea-based submerged systems possessing ICBM second-strike capability).

[35] For example, J. P. Craven, 'Sea power and the sea bed', *United States Naval Institute Proceedings* 92 (April 1966), 36–51, 43, 44–45 (on bottom-crawlers and the potential use of glass-hulled vessels); C. F. Austin, 'Rock site – a way into the sea', *Sea Frontiers* 13 (1957), 342, 348, 350 (on the electrolysis of sea water to produce oxygen, and the prospect of underwater communities with 'full family living'); and E. Miles, 'Some socio-cultural problems involved in expanding use of marine protein concentrate for human consumption', in Mershon Center for Education in National Security/Carnegie Endowment for

on Tuffy the porpoise, fish farms, bottom-crawlers, aquanauts and Sealab.[36] (The legal observers caught up the next decade, creating an interesting sub-genre on seabed regimes that pointed, among other things, to the gaps in the arms control treaties governing the use of military technology on the seabed.[37]) Of course, many commentaries were bound to be speculative because so many underwater programmes were wreathed in commercial or naval secrecy. But by 1967, when Pardo made his speech, it was clear that the seabed was already being used for military purposes – as a resting spot for surveillance systems, submarines, mines and cables[38] – and that it would be commercially exploited in the foreseeable future, possibly using technologies derived from those used to exploit off-shore oil, gas, tin and coal deposits.

The Trusteeship Plan

The powers paid close attention to Pardo's proposal. The Soviets were initially opposed to the common heritage idea, arguing that only states – not 'mankind' – were the proper subjects of public international law; and that while superficially attractive, it might be a front for 'monopoly capitalism'.[39] The Americans and their Western allies came around to the idea sooner, taking the view that the proposed internationalisation of the seabed might achieve what they would have had to propose anyway to hold back other states' nationalisation of the sea floor. That common heritage also had the pleasing ring of anti-hegemonic universalism added to its cachet.

International Peace (eds.), *Second conference on law, organization and security in the use of the ocean* (Columbus, OH: Ohio State University, 1967), pp. 3–33 (on using 'marine protein concentrate' to alleviate hunger).

36 For example, 'Oceanology: journey to inner space', *Time* (17 September 1965); and 'Environment: squeezing more out of the seas', *Time* (29 July 1975), at: time.com.

37 For example, J. Evensen, 'Present military uses of the seabed and foreseeable developments', *Cornell International Law Journal* 3 (1970), 121–132; R. J. Zedalis, 'Peaceful purposes and other relevant provisions of the revised composite negotiating text: a comparative analysis of the existing and the proposed military regime of the high seas', *Syracuse Journal of International Law and Commerce* 7 (1979), 1–36; and T. Treves, 'Military installations, structures, and devices on the seabed', *American Journal of International Law* 74 (1980), 808–857.

38 H. G. Darwin, 'Maltese motion on the ocean bed' (18 September 1967), p. 2: FCO 10/232, TNA.

39 For example, V. L. Issraelyan, GAOR, A/C.1/PV.1777 (30 November 1970), p. 9.

The powers' concern about other states' expanding jurisdictions were twofold. First, they thought that the partitioning of the deep seabed between states would be inimical to their own strategic interests. This was because they needed a sovereignty-free seabed as a stopping point for their submarines, as a repository for their communications systems, and as a site for their military experiments. (They also wanted to be able to retrieve their sunken submarines and misplaced nuclear weapons without too much interference from inquisitive coastal states – the latter issue coming to the fore in 1966 when a ditched US Airforce B-52 Stratofortress lost a hydrogen bomb down a sea trench off Spain.) The second issue of concern to the powers was that a nationally partitioned seabed would not provide the best conditions for their commercial activities, because each state around the world would impose its own leasing and operating conditions. The Americans in particular wanted a uniform and regulated international regime covering the whole seabed, with guaranteed access and investment protection, so that US-led consortia would not encounter foreign impediments. As Robert Osgoode at the National Security Council wrote:

> In the existing areas of foreign sovereign rights U.S. companies are under a growing threat of expropriation, tax discrimination, and other harassments ... An international regime beyond the 200-meter isobath provides the best assurance of U.S. access in the future.[40]

From this perspective, a regime presided over by an international seabed authority would have several advantages. For one thing, the United States would ensure that Americans would exercise commanding influence over this body's decision-making processes.[41] For another, the international authority would need American technology to exploit the seabed more than the United States needed the international authority. Osgood again:

> U.S. deep-sea extraction industries are far ahead of any others in technology. They will dominate extraction for years to come, no matter who does the leasing. An international authority that would distribute royalties from extraction to an international community fund would have a direct interest in inducing U.S. companies to exploit the continental margin.[42]

[40] 'Memorandum from Robert Osgood of the National Security Council staff' (7 April 1970): *FRUS*, 1969–1976, vol. E-1, *Documents on global issues*, 1969–1972, doc. 371.

[41] Ibid.

[42] Ibid.

The remaining issue was how to persuade other states, especially in the developing world, to subscribe to this international regime. This is where the common heritage idea, with its promise of distributing the proceeds to the most impoverished, came into play. Some in Washington thought that the United States should as a matter of principle promote the common good – seabed resources should be used for the benefit of all, 'including the poorer countries', instead of just for the benefit of the few able to exploit them.[43] Others, more openly self-serving, thought that unless the United States baited the hook with the distribution of common heritage proceeds from the seabed's exploitation, it would not be able to win enough adherents to a seabed treaty.[44] As Osgood wrote,

> some argue that unless we formulate and conduct our oceans policies with attention to the sensitivities and interests of the LDCs [less developed countries], we are in danger of getting into a rich-poor contest . . .; and that, in any case, we cannot induce enough LDCs to accept the restrictions of national exploitation rights that are necessary for the orderly use of the oceans unless we can show them that such a legal regime is attentive to their interests (i.e., go along with their desire to be bribed).[45]

In sum, the Americans, for their own military and commercial reasons, were seeking to hold back others' national claims, and, as State Department official Samuel De Palma put it, Pardo's plan consequently 'ties in with our concern to obtain agreement on a moratorium on national claims to . . . the deep sea bottom'.[46] They thus aimed to establish on the seabed a regulated regime distinct from both sovereign rights and high seas freedoms, and Pardo's proposed internationalisation of this area – couched in the enticing language of common heritage – offered a way to win support for the idea.

This meant that the Americans, far from resisting Pardo, instead tried to steal some of his thunder. In 1970, they incorporated the common heritage approach into their own 'trusteeship' plan, conceived by attorney-general

43 'Memorandum from Robert Osgood of the National Security Council staff' (20 January 1970), *FRUS*, 1969–1976, vol. E-1, *Documents on global issues*, 1969–1972, doc. 363.

44 'Memorandum from the President's assistant for national security affairs (Kissinger)' (8 May 1970), *FRUS*, 1969–1976, vol. E-1, *Documents on global issues*, 1969–1972, doc. 373.

45 'Memorandum from Robert Osgood of the National Security Council staff' (20 January 1970), *FRUS*, 1969–1976, vol. E-1, *Documents on global issues*, 1969–1972, doc. 363.

46 'Memorandum from the Assistant Secretary of State for International Organization Affairs (de Palma)' (2 April 1969): *FRUS*, 1969–1976, vol. E-1, *Documents on global issues*, 1969–1972, doc. 335.

Elliot Richardson and launched by Richard Nixon in May that year.[47] This suggested the creation of three zones – national, trusteeship and international – covering the whole sea floor from the coastline to the deep seabed. In the national zone, coastal states would possess sovereign rights to the seabed out to a depth of 200 metres. In the trusteeship zone beyond, extending out to the continental margin, states would be expected to renounce their sovereign rights and act instead as 'trustees' of seabed resources. Here, they would be permitted to license exploration and exploitation and collect international royalties, retaining a share for themselves and contributing the rest to assist the 'economic advancement of developing countries' and 'the safe, efficient and economic exploitation of the mineral resources'.[48] Finally, in the seabed zone beyond the continental margin, an international authority would licence exploration and exploitation and collect international royalties, based on the same principles.[49]

The trusteeship plan, packaged as an endorsement of common heritage and the exercise of international responsibilities, served markedly American ends. First and most importantly, it would corral states' claims within the designated national zone – an arrangement expressly conceived to halt 'jurisdiction creep' (a newly minted American phrase). Second, the 200-metre depth marking the end of the national zone, while purportedly inherited from the 1958 continental shelf convention, met US Defence Department needs: their 'sound surveillance system' (SOSUS) submarine detection devices placed on other states' continental shelves operated best at depths of between 200 and 550 metres.[50] Finally, the provisions governing the exploration and exploitation of the continental shelf within the trusteeship zone assuaged the concerns of the US Department of the Interior by assisting American oil companies, who would be able to exploit not only their own but also other states'

[47] Nixon did not use the phrase 'common heritage' when he launched the idea, but an accompanying decision memorandum stated that, 'The entire area of the seabed and its natural resources seaward from the 200-meter depth . . . shall be regarded as the common heritage of mankind' ('National security decision memorandum 62' (22 May 1970): *FRUS*, 1969–1976, vol. E-1, *Documents on global issues*, 1969–1972, doc. 375).

[48] 'Memorandum from the legal adviser of the Department of State (Stevenson)' (29 July 1970): *FRUS*, 1969–1976, vol. E-1, *Documents on global issues*, 1969–1972, doc. 379).

[49] 'National security decision memorandum 62' (22 May 1970): *FRUS*, 1969–1976, vol. E-1, *Documents on global issues*, 1969–1972, doc. 375.

[50] 'Memorandum from Robert Osgood of the National Security Council staff' (20 January 1970): *FRUS*, 1969–1976, vol. E-1, *Documents on global issues*, 1969–1972, doc. 363.

continental shelves, subject only to the trustee's licencing and royalty arrangements.

But would other nations support the trusteeship idea? When the Americans broached the plan, it was not at all well received. The British reported that the developing countries 'seemed suspicious of the very word "trusteeship"' and 'expressed fears of neo-colonialism and welfare imperialism'.[51] Some delegates, such as the Iranian Manouchehr Fartash, pointed out that the 200-metre depth limit marking the end of the national zone would discriminate against Latin American and African states with narrow continental shelves[52] – while also, it might be added, favouring states with broad and shallow continental shelves, such as the United States. Others delegates, such as the Peruvian Alfonso Arias Schreiber, calculated that once all the production, research, environmental and survey costs had been paid off, states in the developing world would receive a pittance.[53] And others still argued that the plan was contrary to both the principle of common heritage and to the private law concept of trusteeship because it served the trustees better than the purported beneficiaries.[54] This opposition, as well as the notable lack of support from Western allies (other than the British, with whom the Americans shared SOSUS intelligence) spelt the eventual demise of Nixon's initiative.

Sidelining Peaceful Purposes

Keeping their options open, the powers also set to work kneading Pardo's proposal into a form more acceptable to themselves. They began by letting it be known that his proposal in the *note verbale* for a declaration and a treaty was premature, and that it should be downgraded to an 'examination' of the question. It was left to another Maltese delegate, Y. F. Gauci, to backpedal in the UN, explaining that although the general committee had unanimously accepted a declaration and treaty, his amendment to 'examination' was necessary because some delegations had 'doubts ... about the legal aspects'.[55] This examination would be

51 'Seabed: limits' (22 December 1971), p. 2: FCO 76/332, TNA.
52 GAOR, A/C.1/PV.1782 (3 December 1970), p. 8.
53 GAOR, A/C.1/PV.1777 (30 November 1970), p. 4.
54 Asian-African Legal Consultative Committee, 'Report of the sub-committee on the law of the sea' (18–27 January 1971), p. 4: FCO 76/329, TNA.
55 GAOR, A/PV.1583 (6 October 1967), p. 19.

carried out by a specially formed 'Ad hoc Committee to Study the Peaceful Uses of the Sea-bed and the Ocean Floor beyond the Limits of National Jurisdiction',[56] which met on several occasions in 1968, and the succeeding standing 'Committee on the Peaceful Uses of the Sea-bed and the Ocean Floor beyond the Limits of National Jurisdiction' that succeeded it,[57] meeting from 1969 to 1973.

Once the project was moving, the powers then proceeded to break down Pardo's proposal into its constituent parts, with the aim of sidelining its peaceful purposes element and controlling its seabed exploitation element. This began with the framing of the committee's terms of reference, during which, the British reported, peaceful purposes had been 'satisfactorily buried away'.[58] Meanwhile, the Americans adopted a two-pronged approach to ensure that their military activities on the seabed would not be unduly constrained by the peaceful purposes provision. First, they indicated that delegates should consider not just the seabed but 'all marine questions which come before the General Assembly',[59] with the aim, among other things, of diffusing the attention being paid to military activities. Second, they sought to draw the sting out of peaceful purposes by using the same tactics they had employed during the negotiations over the Outer Space treaty, when they had argued that military activities not specifically prohibited by treaty were permitted.[60]

Even so, the onus rested on the maritime powers to make the case, if pressed, that their activities on the seabed really did serve peaceful purposes. Much would depend on the interpretation of the phrase itself, with the powers arguing that 'peaceful' meant 'non-aggressive', while less powerful states contended that 'peaceful' meant 'non-military'.[61] As the summary of the debates in 1968 recorded:

[56] Convened by UNGA Res. 2340(XXII), 18 December 1967.

[57] Convened by UNGA Res. 2467(XXIII)A, 21 December 1968.

[58] D. L. Benest, 'Maltese initiative on the sea bed' (20 December 1967), p. 1: FCO 10/232, TNA.

[59] UK Embassy Washington to UK FCO (17 October 1967), p. 1: FCO 10/232, TNA. The Maltese, discerning the Americans' attempt to water down the seabed proposal, expressed their disappointment: A. White to D. L. Benest (4 November 1967): FCO 10/232, TNA.

[60] 'Memorandum from the assistant secretary of state for International Organization Affairs (De Palma)' (2 April 1969): *FRUS*, 1969–1976, vol. E-1, *Documents on global issues, 1969–1972*, doc. 335.

[61] H. G. Darwin, 'Maltese motion on the ocean bed' (18 September 1967), p. 3: FCO 10/232, TNA.

> Two views were expressed ... on the concept of exclusive reservation of the area for peaceful purposes. One was that peaceful use completely excluded all military use. The other was that a positive approach required the affirmation and acceptance of the principle that the area be used exclusively for peaceful purposes and that military activities in pursuit of peaceful aims or in fulfilment of peaceful intents, consistent with the United Nations Charter and the obligations of international law, should not be banned.[62]

The Americans' third tactic, executed in tandem with the USSR, was to break the peaceful purposes element of common heritage away from the resources exploitation element by asserting that the proper forum for the discussion of arms control issues was the UN's eighteen-nation Conference of the Committee on Disarmament, which was about to embark on negotiations over the Seabed Arms Control treaty, signed in February 1971.[63] Other delegates argued that the debate about peaceful purposes was not primarily about disarmament but about the prevention of military activities on the seabed.[64] The powers' view prevailed, however. The seabed committee's original remit was therefore halved: it was left to preside over the exploitation of seabed resources, while the disarmament committee was tasked with presiding over the *denuclearisation* (and prohibition of other weapons of mass destruction) but not the complete demilitarisation of the seabed beyond the territorial sea.

*

While the powers were sidelining proposals to demilitarise the seabed, they were also trying to shape the debate about the exploitation of seabed resources. The industrial states were the world's largest mineral consumers. Many were heavily reliant on certain mineral imports: the European Economic Community countries and Japan, for example, were largely dependent on copper from elsewhere, essential for their electric and electronic industries; and all bar Australia, South Africa and the USSR were dependent on manganese from abroad, essential for making

62 GOAR, A/7230 (1968), p. 10.

63 Treaty on the Prohibition of the Emplacement of Nuclear Weapons and Other Weapons of Mass Destruction on the Sea-bed and the Ocean Floor and in the Subsoil thereof (signed 11 February 1971, EIF 18 May 1971) 955 UNTS 115. The two superpowers' unanimity on this issue aroused comment from, among others, L. Benites of Ecuador: GAOR, A/C.1/PV.1676 (4 November 1969), p. 9.

64 GOAR, A/7230 (1968), p. 12.

impact- and wear-resistant steel alloys.[65] The powers, as the leading consumers, recognised that they had a great deal to gain from the seabed's regulated internationalisation, irrespective of whether they had to share the proceeds with the developing states. By their calculation, the extraction of minerals from polymetallic nodules would have the likely effect of driving down the global prices of the commodities for which they constituted by far the largest market, while at the same time reducing their exposure to the risk of shortages of minerals currently imported from potentially hostile or politically unstable producers.

Yet even before the 1973 OPEC oil crisis – which offered the developing countries a model for controlling the global supply of other raw materials – there were gaping unknowns for the industrial states. Early ventures on the seabed were bound to be risky and expensive; the distribution of costs and benefits had yet to be negotiated; and the major land-based mineral exporters among them might be adversely affected by seabed mining. On balance, however, it seemed that they had everything to play for, especially under a stable treaty-governed international regime. In 1975, for example, the UN secretary-general produced a report indicating that the main beneficiaries would be 'the world community at large and the advanced countries possessing nodule technology in particular'.[66] It continued:

> The latter countries would benefit from a redistribution of revenues among mineral producers, and would tend to become the dynamic centres of future mineral production. They would gain from: *(a)* the spill-over effect of technology into other activities; *(b)* the income effect of producing equipment and supplies for nodule miners (backward linkages), incomes and employment from nodule mining, transporting and processing, and the establishment of new industries for further processing the metals (forward linkages); and *(c)* lesser dependence on foreign suppliers of raw materials – in fact, they would become net exporters of cobalt, and perhaps of manganese and nickel.[67]

These advantages notwithstanding, when making their tactical calculations about the seabed negotiations the industrial states had to proceed on the basis of two as yet untested assumptions: first, that they would soon be able to overcome the physical barriers to extracting nodules from the seabed; and second, that they could secure agreement to a regime

[65] UNLOSC III, vol. 16, A/Conf.62/L.84 and Add.1 (1982), pp. 186, 189.
[66] UNLOSC III, vol. 4, A/Conf.62/37 (18 February 1975), p. 124.
[67] Ibid.

guaranteeing access to mining sites and the protection of investments. As it turned out, only one of these assumptions proved to be correct.

Alternative Routes to Self-Sufficiency

The developing countries were preoccupied with a different set of problems. Most of them agreed that the powers should be prevented from partitioning and unilaterally appropriating the seabed and its resources. But not all of them endorsed Pardo's proposal, as some commentators have assumed. Instead, the debate exposed the differences within the 'group of seventy-seven': between the land-based mineral producers and the non-mining consumers; and between the coastal countries and the landlocked and geographically disadvantaged states.

The most enthusiastic supporters of Pardo's plan were the landlocked and geographically disadvantaged states without land-based mineral industries, for whom any share in the benefits derived from common heritage would be a boon. The least enthusiastic group were land-based mineral producers, who feared competition from seabed mining, whether internationalised or not. Yet the most effective and coordinated opposition to Pardo's initiative came from the Pacific seaboard Latin American mining states who already claimed extensive maritime jurisdictions, and who feared that their claims might be rolled back by an international regime. The first indication that he had not won their endorsement came as soon as he launched his plan, when some Latin American delegations tried to steer his motion towards the General Assembly's sixth (legal) committee – where, as one jaded observer noted, the discussion would have dragged on for a 'very long time'[68] – rather than to Pardo's preferred forum, the Assembly's first (disarmament and international security) committee.

In the event, in November 1967, the proposal was discussed in the latter committee, where the same Latin American opponents voiced their concerns about the reversal of their national claims. Chilean delegate Hugo Ballesteros Reyes, while appreciating Pardo's 'comprehensive' and 'well-documented' statement, did not go so far as supporting it.[69] Instead, he emphasised that his own and fellow delegations were 'particularly anxious to establish quite clearly that the Maltese proposal covered an area of the sea-bed or ocean floor and sub-soil beyond national

[68] UK Mission to the UN to UK FCO (8 February 1968), p. 5: FCO 10/235, TNA.
[69] GAOR, A/C.1/PV.1526 (13 November 1967), p. 4.

jurisdictions, and therefore [would] not directly or indirectly affect[ ] those jurisdictions, whatever their nature'.[70] Both he and the Peruvian delegate Alberto Ulloa reminded the committee that Chile, Ecuador and Peru had signed the Santiago Declaration in 1952 extending their jurisdictions outwards, which, Reyes explained, was designed to 'provide their peoples with the necessary conditions for a decent livelihood and the means of achieving economic development'.[71] Their point was that while the proposed internationalisation of the seabed and distribution of the benefits of seabed mining offered developing countries one route towards economic self-sufficiency, the expansion of national jurisdiction over adjacent waters offered another route – the latter, moreover, being under the direct control of the coastal state.

Yet despite these divisions within the G77, the common heritage idea gained momentum because it held out the promise of providing the material basis for the proposed new international economic order. Its champions argued that the inequalities created by untrammelled global capitalism served neither rich nor poor nations. While the wealthy could maintain their growth only by out-competing others in the global market, the developing countries, who were at the mercy of fluctuating commodity prices and fickle aid-donors, were unable to move forward at all. All nations thus had an interest in creating a stable environment for economic expansion. The fortuitous convergence of two factors – the discovery of seemingly vast mineral resources on the seabed, and the apparent technological capacity to exploit them – offered a unique opportunity to make this a reality. Because seabed mineral wealth was untapped and outside national jurisdiction, no state would be obliged to give up anything; it was new value that could be used to underwrite a more balanced and equitable global economy. The relationship between North and South could therefore progress beyond the demeaning inequality between donor and recipient countries, and towards an association based on greater equality, derived from the common responsibility for stewarding and exploiting the riches of the deep.

In the meantime, though, there was the danger that the powers' mining consortia would steal a march on the negotiators and begin exploiting the seabed before a new regime upholding common heritage had been instituted. This encouraged Mexico (led by Alfonso García Robles, who reprised his earlier role as a scourge of the powers), along

[70] Ibid.

[71] Ibid.; and A/C.1/PV.1529 (15 November 1967), p. 11.

with Ceylon, Ecuador, Guatemala, Kuwait and Mauritania, to table the 'moratorium resolution' in the General Assembly in December 1969. This declared that until a regime was in place, 'States and persons, physical or juridical, are bound to refrain from all activities of exploitation of the resources of the area'.[72] The resolution was passed by a vote of sixty-two for, twenty-eight against, twenty-eight abstaining and eight absent.[73]

The 'ayes' were a mixed bag: the Latin American states wanted to postpone seabed exploitation until after the regimes governing the economic zone and the continental shelf had been decided; the land-based mineral producers aimed to hold off rival seabed operations until production controls and compensation schemes had been put in place; and the landlocked and geographically disadvantaged states wanted to lock in common heritage resources earmarked for developing countries before the seabed mining consortia got to them. This latter group included Afghanistan, whose delegate, Abdul Samad Ghaus, explained:

> As international law governing the activities of the States with respect to the exploitation of the sea-bed and the subsoil thereof is, to say the least, rudimentary, it would be in the interests of the developing countries that no commercial exploitation of the resources should take place before an international legal regime and machinery governing the provisions of this legal regime are established. Pending the adoption of a generally accepted status concerning the ocean floor and its subsoil and procedures for its exploitation, all claims to the land beneath the high seas and its subsoil beyond the limits of present national jurisdiction should in our view be frozen.[74]

As for the 'nays' to the moratorium, all hailed from the West and the Soviet bloc except for Ghana.[75] The American delegate Christopher Phillips condemned the resolution for being 'unsound and self-defeating' because it retarded the development of seabed exploitation and technological capacity, which would serve precisely no-one 'developed or developing, coastal or landlocked, east or west, north or south'.[76] The Italian delegate Piero Vinci, noting that the resolution did not cover

[72] UNGA Res. 2574(XXIV)D (15 December 1969).

[73] GAOR, A/PV.1833 (15 December 1969), p. 3.

[74] GAOR, A/C.1/PV.1681 (7 November 1969), p. 7.

[75] Ghana's vote may have been influenced by the recent commencement by foreign companies of oil prospecting off its coast: *Petroleum Commission, Ghana*, at: www.petrocom.gov.gh/exploration-history.

[76] GAOR, A/PV.1833 (15 December 1969), pp. 1, 2.

seabed already subject to national claims, argued that this would create a counter-productive inducement to states to nationalise even greater areas of sea floor to avoid the prohibition – thereby hastening the very effect that the common heritage idea was designed to combat.[77] The French delegate Claude Chayet said it was paradoxical that a committee formed to encourage seabed exploitation should want to freeze this activity,[78] and the Maltese delegate, Pardo himself, stated that the resolution was 'meaningless' as long as the seabed's limits remained undefined.[79]

Over the year that followed the moratorium resolution, the developing countries, acting on India's suggestion,[80] and aiming to entrench the common heritage idea in customary international law, pushed the seabed committee to agree a 'declaration of principles' on the seabed. This new resolution stated in its opening paragraph that, 'The seabed . . . as well as the resources of the area, *are* the common heritage of mankind',[81] the present tense indicating that the concept was the enunciation of natural law and not reliant on the formulation of a future treaty. It also stated that the exploration and exploitation of the seabed and its resources 'shall be carried out for the benefit of mankind as a whole, irrespective of the geographical location of States, whether land-locked or coastal, and taking into particular consideration the interests and needs of the developing countries'.[82]

The declaration was characterised by many omissions and ambiguities, signalling the disagreements that dogged its creation. One major omission concerned the boundary between the continental shelf and the international seabed area. Some committee delegates proposed setting the limit at either a fixed depth, or a fixed distance from the baseline: Pardo, for example, suggested that negotiations start with 200 miles from the baseline.[83] Others, including some Latin American and Caribbean states, strongly resisted drawing a line marking the edge of the seabed area, lest it be used to reverse their own jurisdictional claims. They argued that it was perfectly possible to recognise the seabed as a legal

77 Ibid., p. 2; and GAOR, A/C.1/PV.1779 (1 December 1970), p. 11.
78 GAOR, A/C.1/PV.1680 (7 November 1969), p. 10.
79 GAOR, A/PV.1833 (15 December 1969), p. 5.
80 GAOR, A/C.1/PV.1673 (31 October 1969), p. 7; and the Indian resolution reproduced in: GOAR, A/7230 (1968), pp. 52–53.
81 UNGA Res. 2749(XXV) (17 December 1970), para. 1. Emphasis added.
82 Ibid., para. 7.
83 'Memorandum from F. Allen Harris, special assistant to the legal adviser' (2 December 1969): *FRUS*, 1969–1976, vol. E-1, *Documents on global issues*, 1969–1972, doc. 359.

subject and posit a regime for it without needing to know where the boundary lay; indeed, this was precisely how the 1958 conventions dealt with the territorial sea and the continental shelf.[84] They also suggested that the demarcation of the edge of the continental shelf was not part of the seabed committee's remit.[85] As a consequence, the declaration stated in the preamble that the seabed's limit was 'yet to be determined'.[86]

Other omissions from the declaration showed that the maritime powers had managed to keep out or avoid clarification of ideas that might prejudice their future negotiating positions. There was no mention of a moratorium. The terms 'common heritage' and 'peaceful purposes' were not defined. There was no indication of what the 'particular consideration' given to the developing countries entailed in practice.[87] There was no reference to the structure of the international authority, or to the transfer of technology from the industrial countries to the developing world, or to national initiatives to conduct scientific research on the seabed. There *was* mention of minimising price fluctuations – a particular concern of land-based mining states – but it was buried in the preamble.

As for the ambiguities, the question of what common heritage applied to was answered in three different ways. Some paragraphs referred to 'activities in the area' (suggesting it applied to the seabed only),[88] another paragraph referred to 'activities regarding the exploration and exploitation of the resources of the area' (suggesting it referred to resources only),[89] and others referred to 'activities in the area, including those relating to its resources' (suggesting that it applied to both the seabed and resources).[90]

Before the draft declaration was put before the General Assembly, delegates to the UN's first committee agreed that it was an ugly piece of work, disfigured by all the compromises. Even the Salvadorean delegate Reynaldo Galindo Pohl, who had steered the draft through the seabed committee, conceded: 'It is not the best of declarations, but it is

84 See comments by P. V. J. Solomon (Trinadad and Tobago) and F. Zegers (Chile): GAOR, A/C.1/PV.1677 (5 November 1969), p. 4; and GOAR, A/C.1/PV.1679 (6 November 1969), p. 6.
85 See comment by F. Zegers (Chile): GAOR, A/C.1/PV.1682 (10 November 1969), p. 17.
86 UNGA Res. 2749(XXV) (17 December 1970).
87 Ibid., para. 7.
88 Ibid., paras. 11, 13.
89 Ibid., para. 4.
90 Ibid., paras. 12, 14.

the only declaration acceptable to a goodly number of delegations.'[91] Even so, the Ecuadoran delegate Leopoldo Benites declared it to be the necessary expression of a new legal idea, because 'we cannot apply the old legal rules nor the rules of Roman law'; and the Canadian delegate Robert Kaplan heralded it as being 'a bold new approach . . . and a turning away from traditional land-oriented concepts of jurisdiction and sovereignty'.[92] Pushing and pulling over custom, the Guyanese delegate Paterson Thompson claimed that common heritage was already a peremptory norm, permitting no derogation (which was going too far), while Galindo Pohl asserted that the declaration embodying the idea was merely a political pronouncement (which was not going far enough).[93] In December 1970, the General Assembly passed the declaration 108-0-14, with most of the abstentions coming from the Soviet bloc.

The Tanzanian Draft

After the debates about the declaration, the delegates on the seabed committee moved on to the discussion about the international seabed authority – the body that would preside over the deep seabed and its resources. Many developing countries wanted to vest this authority with the power to exercise exclusive control over resource-related activities on the seabed, covering not only exploitation (to be carried out by its mining arm, the Enterprise), but also the regulation of scientific research and the prevention of seabed pollution. By contrast, the Western states, and the Soviet bloc countries (after some initial hesitation about establishing a new international body), envisaged an authority with limited powers, operating as a registry able to issue mining licences to states and companies, but little more than that. The British, for example, insisted that the authority should not have sole operating rights in the seabed, stating:

> We oppose the creation of an International Authority with the monopoly power of exploitation, as most unlikely to prove viable. It would inevitably be cumbersome and expensive. How would this Authority acquire the

[91] GAOR, A/C.l/PV.l781 (2 December 1970), p. 1.

[92] GAOR, A/C.l/PV.1782 (3 December 1970), p. 5; and GAOR, A/C.l/PV.1779 (1 December 1970), p. 2.

[93] GAOR, A/C.l/PV.l788 (8 December 1970), p. 10; and GAOR, A/C.l/PV.l781 (2 December 1970), p. 3.

requisite capital and technology? If it failed to function effectively it would produce no revenues.[94]

This approach brought the industrial states up against one of the major players in the decade-long debate about the seabed – Tanzania – whose delegation in 1971, led by E. E. Seaton, tabled the first comprehensive draft statute for the proposed authority. This encapsulated many of the tenets of the new international economic order and plugged some of the holes in the declaration of principles. It set out a broad conception of sharing (including transfers of technology, knowledge and data, as well as revenues), a broad conception of participation (including states' involvement in administration, management and development), proposals for distributing the benefits of common heritage to the countries that most needed it, and measures for ameliorating the negative effects of seabed exploitation on land-based mineral producers.

The Tanzanian draft thus gave the international authority a wide and exclusive mandate covering, 'All activities regarding exploration and exploitation of the resources of the International Sea-bed Area, and other related activities.'[95] It was thus empowered to explore and exploit the seabed; license other parties to do the same; distribute income and scientific information; take measures to minimise mineral price fluctuations; provide for scientific research and development; foster the exchange of information and training; provide technical assistance; institute safeguards against its activities being used for military purposes; set safety and environmental standards; acquire or establish facilities, plant and equipment; and take measures to effect treaty provisions.[96] On the distribution side, the authority would concern itself not only with the sharing of the proceeds of mining but also the sharing of the technology required for it, having the right 'to acquire or establish any facilities, plant and equipment useful in the carrying out of its authorized functions'.[97]

The industrial states thought the Tanzanian draft statute vested the international authority with far too much power. The British, for example, noted:

Its fundamental approach is to protect the interests of developing countries by creating an extremely powerful International Sea Bed Authority

[94] UK FCO to UK missions, 'Law of the Sea' (28 March 1973), p. 5: FCO 76/758, TNA.
[95] UN Seabed Committee, article 8, A/AC.138/33 in GAOR, A/8421 (1971), p. 53.
[96] Article 16, ibid., pp. 55–56.
[97] Article 16(13), ibid., p. 56.

> which will be dominated by developing country voting strength ... It would give the international authority supra-national powers. It would be extremely costly. It contains elaborate provisions for price stabilisation for commodities. All these features are unacceptable.[98]

One sticking point was how the proceeds of exploitation would be distributed to states. The Tanzanian draft proposed a distribution agency to recommend an equitable apportionment of income, with UN members receiving it in inverse ratio to their contribution to the UN budget, and non-UN members receiving it according to their stage of development.[99] This same body would also supervise the actual distribution of income,[100] the assumption being that the proceeds would be paid directly to the recipient states with no conditions attached. But the industrial powers apparently had other ideas. As a correspondent for the Tanzanian news agency *Maeleza* reported:

> The United States and to an extent Britain and France propose that the income should be allocated to U.N.'s specialised agencies which would then use it for development purposes in developing nations. This proposal has caused suspicion among the developing countries which see it as an attempt to shift from the developed countries the obligation they owe to the developing nations. Another disadvantage is that once the specialised agencies are allowed to use the money, developing countries would not have the power to determine the allocation of such funds.[101]

The developing countries' growing concern was not only with the control of distribution but also with the control of production, their aim being to shield land-based mineral producers against potentially damaging competition from seabed mining operations.[102] The Tanzanian draft addressed this by proposing a price stabilisation board under the authority's control, which would appraise the conditions of supply and demand, fix the prices of minerals obtained by seabed mining, determine the

98 'Brief 4: Tanzanian draft convention' (15 July 1971), p. 1: FCO 76/346, TNA.

99 UN Seabed Committee, article 34(2), A/AC.138/33 in GAOR, A/8421 (1971), p. 61.

100 Ibid.

101 S. Mulokazi, 'The scramble for the seabed', *Maelezo Feature Service, Information Services Division* (4 June 1971), p. 4: FCO 76/346, TNA.

102 This preoccupation with the potential damage of seabed mining to land-based mineral producers would shortly after be informed by a series of UN reports commissioned by G77 members about the potential impact of seabed mining on the international economy, including one published in 1972 that concluded that seabed operations would likely lead to lower mineral prices, which in turn would hurt some developing producer states: UN Seabed Committee, A/AC.138/73 in GAOR, A/8421 (1972), p. 124.

quantities to be released onto the market,[103] and take measures 'to minimize and eliminate fluctuation of prices of land minerals and raw materials that may result from the exploitation of the resources of the International Sea-bed Area, and any adverse economic effects caused thereby'.[104]

The British, among others, resisted what they perceived to be the manipulation of the market. Although they were prepared to accept the equitable distribution of the proceeds of mining, they were not prepared to accept measures designed to protect existing mineral producers from competition from future seabed producers.[105] They also thought that if price stabilisation had to be embarked upon, it should be a feature of a multilateral commodities agreement rather than being implemented by the international authority.[106] The Fijian delegate Satya Nandan thus reported that the industrial states gave 'a quiet warning' to the developing countries that any attempt to set up a system of production and price controls 'could only have an adverse effect on the achievement of our objectives'.[107]

A final area of disagreement concerned the representation of states on the decision-making bodies within the proposed authority. Most countries expected that decision-making powers would reside in both its plenary wing, the Assembly, on which all parties to the treaty would have a vote, and its executive wing, the Council, which would be open to a smaller number of states. So began a tussle between the developing countries and the industrial states over which body would be dominant, with the former pushing for the Assembly's supremacy and the latter pushing for the Council's.[108] Moreover, while all states accepted 'one nation, one vote' in the Assembly, the industrial states' approach to voting arrangements on the Council was a different matter. They contended that because they would have to provide all the investment and technology and shoulder all the financial risks, they should enjoy commensurate voting privileges. As the British argued in 1971:

[103] UN Seabed Committee, article 35(2), A/AC.138/33 in GOAR, A/8421 (1971), p. 62.
[104] Article 16(4), ibid., p. 55.
[105] 'Brief 4: Tanzanian draft convention' (15 July 1971), p. 3: FCO 76/346, TNA.
[106] Ibid.
[107] S. N. Nandan, 'Summer session 1973' (u.d., c. mid-1973), p. 5: folder 1, box 69, Mss82–6, Satya Nandan papers, University of Virginia Law School Library UNLOSC III collection [hereafter, UVLSL].
[108] 'Sea bed – regime and institutions' (u.d., c. November 1971), p. 2: FCO 76/337, TNA.

> [J]ust as it would be appropriate to give developing States a special position on any institutions of the Authority which might be set up for the purpose of distributing sea bed benefits, so it would be necessary to make special provision on the Council for those States with an established sea bed technology, who have a special contribution to make in organising sea bed activity and without whose support no international regime in this field would be viable.[109]

The powers thus proposed that on the Council they should enjoy either permanent membership and the power of veto (as they did on the Security Council) or weighted voting (as they did in the International Monetary Fund and International Bank for Reconstruction and Development). In 1970, the Americans proposed Council membership for the 'six most industrially advanced Contracting Parties'.[110] Other states suspected that this would amount to permanent membership because changes to the arrangement could only be brought about by the Council itself.[111] (These suspicions were entirely justified: the Americans privately assured the British that their two countries 'would always be members of the Council'.[112]) In 1971, the British addressed the issue from another angle, suggesting that industrial states possessing both seabed technology and expertise in transferring technical skills to developing countries should acquire 'designation' – by which they really meant permanent designation – to Council membership.[113] The same year, the Soviets, supported by the Bulgarians, proposed that Council decisions should be made 'by agreement', which meant that a state's dissenting opinion would possess the power of veto.[114] And in 1972, the Americans proposed that Council decisions would require not just a majority but also a majority of the six industrial states, meaning that if three industrial states dissented, they would have a veto.[115]

[109] UN Seabed Committee, A/AC.138/46 in GOAR, A/8421 (1971), p. 88.

[110] 'Memorandum from the legal adviser of the Department of State (Stevenson)' (29 July 1970): *FRUS*, 1969–1976, vol. E-1, *Documents on global issues*, 1969–1972, doc. 379.

[111] 'Sea bed – regime and institutions' (u.d., c. November 1971), p. 3: FCO 76/337, TNA.

[112] Ibid.

[113] UN Seabed Committee, A/AC.138/46 in GOAR, A/8421 (1971), p. 88.

[114] UN Seabed Committee, article 23(1), A/AC.138/43 in GAOR, A/8421 (1971), p. 74.

[115] 'Memorandum from Helmut Sonnenfeldt and Denis Clift of the National Security Council staff' (9 June 1972), *FRUS*, 1969–1976, vol. E-1, *Documents on global issues*, 1969–1972, doc. 432.

The developing countries argued instead for decision-making based on either a simple majority or a two-thirds majority vote. The British reported after one of the sessions in 1972:

> It was again clear that the American proposals for 'permanent' membership of the Council of the International Authority and for weighted voting in the Council were totally unacceptable to the vast majority . . . The Soviet Union, on the other hand, made a lengthy defence – characteristically out of tune with the Committee – of their proposal for a veto in the Council.[116]

The Tanzanian correspondent for *Maeleza* rebuked the powers for advancing the veto idea, directing criticisms both eastwards and westwards towards the 'unscrupulous' and the 'imperialist' powers:

> Tanzania does not endorse the view that the veto power should be invested only in the hands of 'industrially advanced' nations which are members of the Seabed Council. It is imperative that developing nations should be on the lookout lest their democratic rights and sovereignty are t[a]mpered with by unscrupulous and imperialist powers who are bent on a second scramble. This time the target won't be Africa alone. It will be all the unfortunate developing maritime nations with rich, untapped natural resources under the sea.[117]

*

The mood darkened as the seabed negotiations progressed. Some G77 members thought the industrial powers were manipulating the common heritage idea for their own ends. A few Latin American countries suspected them of deliberately exaggerating the prospects of a seabed bonanza to drive a wedge between mineral producers and mineral consumers, and thereby undermine the solidarity of the G77.[118] And some 'underdeveloped countries', wrote the Algerian jurist Mohammed Bedjaoui, thought the industrial states were embracing the common heritage principle 'merely so that they can share in the resources of the Third World countries, not so that they can share their own prosperity with the countries which are lagging behind'.[119]

[116] 'First 1972 session of United Nations' (22 June 1972), p. 5: CAB 148/126, TNA.
[117] S. Mulokazi, 'The scramble for the seabed', *Maelezo Feature Service, Information Services Division* (4 June 1971), p. 4: FCO 76/346, TNA.
[118] 'Session of the seabed committee . . . Report by the United Kingdom delegation' (u.d., c. March 1971), p. 6: FCO 76/329, TNA.
[119] Bedjaoui, *Towards a new international economic order*, p. 229.

But even though the industrial states upheld common heritage in principle, they were also chipping away at the scope of rights that could be invoked in its name. In 1972, for example, the Americans proposed that the only beneficiaries of seabed exploitation should be the states parties to the future treaty – not all of 'mankind', and especially not the liberation movements of which they and their allies disapproved.[120] They also led the move away from the 'uses and exploitation' of the seabed to 'exploitation' only; away from the exploitation of all seabed resources to non-living mineral resources only; and away from common heritage over resources to common heritage over revenues only. Regarding the last, the Soviets claimed that although the benefits of resources were common heritage, the resources themselves were not (or, as the Fijian delegate Satya Nandan tartly summarised it, 'mankind shares only in the profits').[121]

The powers' whittling down of common heritage, and the year-on-year shrinkage of the seabed due to the unilateral expansion of national jurisdictions, disillusioned those most invested in the concept. They included Arvid Pardo himself, whose attitude according to the British 'grew increasingly querulous as he came to recognise that the general trend, including that of his own Government, was in favour of broad limits which would reduce the amount of exploitable resources subject to an international regime'.[122]

On that note, we turn now to the other plan – this time conceived by the Soviets and launched at much the same time as Pardo's proposal – to deal with the coastal states' unilateral claims to the oceans.

120 'Statement by the Honorable John R. Stevenson, United States representative' (10 August 1972), p. 3: FCO 76/452, TNA.

121 S. N. Nandan, 'Summer session 1973' (u.d., c. mid-1973), p. 2: folder 1, box 69, Mss82–6, Satya Nandan papers, UVLSL.

122 'Report on the session of the United Nations committee on the peaceful uses of the seabed' (u.d., c April 1969), p. 8: CAB 148/114, TNA.

6

Passage through Straits

From Innocent Passage to Transit Passage at the 1973–1982 Conference

While Pardo proposed the idea of internationalising the seabed, the maritime powers mounted a campaign against the coastal states' expanding claims to coastal waters. This was initiated not by the Americans and British, who had led the way in the fifties, but by a new member of the powers' club: the USSR.

In the decade following the 1960 conference, the Soviets had embarked on a significant shipbuilding programme to enlarge their conventional naval and submarine fleets,[1] and to expand their merchant marine, with the latter's vessel numbers quadrupling and deadweight tonnage more than doubling between 1965 and 1975.[2] They thus transformed themselves from a very large coastal state into a fully-fledged maritime power, with an attendant and very pronounced interest in upholding the oceanic status quo. Abroad, they sought to defend the rights of their long-distance fishing fleets, and to catch up on the collection of the hydrographic data needed to sustain their global reach before states precluded this by expanding their territorial seas (hence the frequent appearance of well-equipped Soviet trawlers-cum-research-vessels in far-flung waters during the sixties and seventies). Meanwhile closer to home, they were keen to avoid the perennial problem of their fleets being bottled up in port by campaigning for passage rights on the routes to and through the Atlantic, the Baltic, the Mediterranean and the Pacific.

The Soviets therefore agitated for an international conference to agree a treaty that would restrict maritime claims to a twelve-mile maximum

[1] 'Soviet policy on law of the sea' (15 February 1979), p. 2: CIA-RDP08C01297R000500010007-1, CIAHC.

[2] D. M. Long, *The Soviet merchant fleet – its growth, strategy, strength, and weaknesses* (London: Lloyd's of London Press, 1986), p. 3.

for territorial seas and fishing zones.[3] In 1967, they instructed their diplomatic missions to sound out sixty-two states about convening another conference to complete the work of the previous two, and once they had received positive responses from fifty-two,[4] they solicited the support of the Americans and British for their initiative.[5]

The two Western powers were both initially taken aback by the Soviets' overture, but they recognised that the time for collaboration was ripe. After the collapse of the 1960 conference, British legal adviser Gerald Fitzmaurice had advised his successors to 'seize any opportunity afforded by an improvement in East-West relations ... which might enable us to agree to a twelve-mile territorial sea, since this appears now to be the only basis on which a really worldwide and universally accepted rule could be framed'.[6] This opportunity had now arisen, and with *détente* on the cards, the timing was propitious. The Americans and British conferred about the prospects of working with the Soviets – could they be kept in line?[7] – and decided that the benefits would probably outweigh the risks. The Soviets would be less likely than the Western powers to arouse the suspicions of the developing countries,[8] and they would bring the East European satellites and other allies into the fold.

The Soviets initiated a series of bilateral talks with the British and with the Americans in June–July 1968.[9] These meetings, and later meetings between the powers making up the 'group of five', though rarely discussed in the commentaries, were particularly important because they set the parameters for a collaborative approach to navigational issues over the next eight years – a coincidence of interest between East and West that would not break down until they had succeeded in creating a regime acceptable to themselves.

The Soviets set the ball rolling on 26 June 1968, when the foreign ministry official Y. A. Ostrovsky met British officials in London. He argued that the struggles in 1958 and 1960 between three-milers and twelve-milers over the territorial sea had been counterproductive

3 'Record of first meeting between Soviet and British officials' (26 June 1968), pp. 2, 5: FCO 14/484, TNA.
4 Ibid., p. 2.
5 'Soviet proposal on the law of the sea' (8 July 1968), pp. 1–2: FCO 14/484, TNA.
6 Quoted in G. G. Brown, 'Annex C: Soviet proposal for a conference' (8 December 1967), p. 3: FCO 14/484, TNA.
7 'Record of a meeting held in Sir F. Vallet's room' (10 June 1968), p. 5: FCO 14/484, TNA.
8 S. Darling to J. T. Masefield (20 September 1967), p. 2: FCO 14/373, TNA.
9 'Soviet proposal on the law of the sea' (8 July 1968), pp. 1–2: FCO 14/484, TNA.

because the failure to set a limit had given rise to the idea that unilateral expansion was acceptable: in 1958, just fourteen states claimed twelve-mile territorial seas; a decade later it was thirty-six, and the figure rose to seventy if fishing zones were added to the tally.[10] If this trend continued, Ostrovsky warned, the high seas would simply disappear.[11] A twelve-mile maximum should therefore be instituted to prevent this from happening, and, he said,

> The earlier this was done the better, since the process of the extension of territorial waters was continuing. The Soviet Union was not the only interested state. Regardless of ideology and other views they [the USSR and the Western powers] should work together.[12]

The British demurred, unsure whether another codification conference would succeed where the previous ones had failed. If they decided to go ahead, could the powers limit the focus to territorial seas and fishing zones without reopening other issues, such as the limits of the continental shelf?[13] No-one could say, but a month later, on 5 July, the Soviet ambassador Mikhail N. Smirnovsky nudged the British again. 'The time had come for something to be done', he said: the longer claims were left unchecked the harder it would become to impose limits.[14] The British took these points seriously; they shared the same concerns. But they also noted, with more than a trace of satisfaction, that the Soviets were now embracing the powers' maritime priorities. The USSR's endorsement of the twelve-mile maximum limit, in line with the ILC's recommendation, had not changed, but their packaging of it had, with apparent nonconformism being replaced by outright conservativism.

The Soviets followed up with a meeting with the Americans in Washington in July 1968, where they again proposed a campaign for a treaty to set a twelve-mile maximum for both territorial seas and fishing zones. The Americans accepted the Soviet proposal and added elements of their own, the most important concerning straits used for international

[10] 'Record of first meeting between Soviet and British officials' (26 June 1968), p. 1: FCO 14/484, TNA.

[11] 'Second meeting between Soviet and British officials' (26 June 1968), p. 6: FCO 14/484, TNA.

[12] 'Record of first meeting between Soviet and British officials' (26 June 1968), p. 4: FCO 14/484, TNA.

[13] 'Fourth meeting between Soviet and British officials' (27 June 1968), p. 5: FCO 14/484, TNA.

[14] 'Record of a meeting between the Rt. Hon. Fred Mulley and the Soviet Ambassador' (25 July 1967), p. 1: FCO 50/12, TNA.

navigation. They argued that the knock-on effect of the universal extension of territorial seas to twelve miles would be the 'closing' by overlapping territorial seas of around 116 straits of less than twenty-four miles' width.[15] This would bring about a change: as it stood, vessels could transit straits wider than six miles through a ribbon of high seas, but in the future, if territorial seas extended to overlap more straits, vessels would be subject instead to the *Corfu Channel*-inspired regime of unsuspendable innocent passage. The Americans, who disliked this idea, proposed campaigning for a new regime in straits, analogous to high seas freedoms, that would guarantee unrestricted passage to vessels and aircraft. To this the Soviets, whose fleets' movements between ports and oceans depended on straits, readily agreed.

Dissatisfaction with the Old Regime

After a brief diplomatic hiatus caused by the USSR's invasion of Czechoslovakia, the Soviets and Americans met again on 16–18 December 1968. This meeting was again at the Soviets' instigation, and involved some arm-twisting; they threatened to start canvassing for a conference by themselves if the Americans turned down the invitation.[16] Eventually, the two settled down to work on a collaborative strategy inspired by the USSR's original proposal and based on an American draft, which aimed to limit the territorial sea to twelve miles, claim 'free transit' through international straits, and, as a sop to the coastal states, institute preferential fishing rights beyond twelve miles.[17]

Of these three issues, the superpowers' greatest concern was not with the twelve-mile limit, which they both now deemed acceptable; nor with fisheries, which while important took second place to strategic issues; but with the effect that the extension of territorial seas would have on passage through straits used for international navigation. The Soviets were primarily

[15] The Americans cited the figure of 116 straits throughout the sixties and early seventies: for an early example, see, 'Statement by the Honorable Arthur H. Dean before the Senate Foreign Relations Committee' (20 January 1960), p. 18: vol. 5307, 9456-RW-4-40, pt. 6-FP, RG 25, LAC. When arriving at this figure, they worked on the assumption that all states had hitherto claimed a three-mile territorial sea, whereas in fact some claimed more than that. Had this been factored in, the number of straits *newly* overlapped by twelve-mile territorial seas would have been fewer than the 116 claimed.

[16] 'Circular airgram CA-406 from the Department of State' (23 January 1969): *FRUS*, 1969–1976, vol. E-1, *Documents on global issues*, 1969–1972, doc. 333.

[17] Ibid.

concerned about their own fleets' movement to and from home ports through straits not yet governed by treaties, especially in the Aegean and Mediterranean,[18] and – in anticipation of future wars – through the Indian Ocean via the Malacca-Singapore straits should they need access to an exposed flank of the USSR. The Americans, by contrast, did not have to rely on straits to move in and out of their home waters, but were preoccupied with international policing, especially through the Strait of Gibraltar to defend Israel and supervise the Arab world, and the Strait of Hormuz, to keep oil moving. As these examples show, neither of the superpower's priorities necessarily involved rivalry between them; rather, their common fear was about straits states restricting their freedom of action. As Kenneth Booth, referring to the Strait of Gibraltar, put it: 'It would be a bad day for Israel . . . if Morocco's disapproval of U.S. support were to be decisive in determining whether or not the U.S. dispatched warships.'[19]

To safeguard the movement of their fleets through straits, the two powers considered three possibilities. The best option, so far as they were concerned, would be to create a multilateral treaty that provided for the uninhibited passage of submarines, surface vessels and aircraft through all straits not already covered by treaties. If this option was not available, the fall-back would be for each to conclude bilateral treaties with all straits states bordering the most important straits – a somewhat harder task for the Soviets than for the Americans, and risky for both, as bilateral agreements might not necessarily be renewed. The worst option, available only to the Americans, would be to refuse to recognise any unilateral extension of the territorial sea beyond three miles in the hope of blocking the emergence of new custom.[20] A policy of non-recognition, pursued to its logical conclusion, might entail their having to make a 'show or use of force' if naval or air mobility was impeded in a strait[21] – up to and including, the British thought, the US Navy shooting its way through.[22]

[18] The exception being the Turkish straits, covered by the 1936 Montreux Convention.

[19] K. Booth, 'Military implications of the changing law of the sea', in J. K. Gamble (ed.), *Law of the sea: neglected issues* (Honolulu: University of Hawaii Law of the Sea Institute, 1979), p. 348.

[20] 'Memorandum from Robert Osgood of the National Security Council staff' (12 June 1969): *FRUS*, 1969–1976, vol. E-1, *Documents on global issues*, 1969–1972, doc. 341.

[21] Ibid.

[22] M. Elliott, 'Law of the Sea: article 2' (20 April 1971), p. 1: FCO 76/258, TNA.

In the meantime, both the Soviets and the Americans were concerned about what might happen between the two of them if straits states allied to the Americans began to interfere with Soviet vessels in straits with newly overlapping territorial seas. As State Department legal adviser Bernard Oxman explained later:

> For the Soviets, this was a relatively obvious problem: they feared direct harassment. For the U.S., the problem was more subtle. The U.S. did not want to be forced into a position of either backing a coastal state right to interfere with navigation and overflight in principle or allowing a Western ally to suffer a political defeat at the hands of the Soviets.[23]

When contemplating the best option of a multilateral treaty covering navigation through straits, neither liked the provisions in the 1958 territorial sea convention, to which they were both parties. They especially disliked article 16(4)'s opening words: 'There shall be no suspension of the innocent passage of foreign ships through straits.'[24] The problem was that the emphasis on innocence gave the straits states leeway to proclaim either that a vessel's passage was not innocent because it was prejudicial to security at the time,[25] or that certain types of vessels (such as warships), certain cargoes (such as nuclear waste) and certain destinations (such as, some claimed, Israel) were inherently non-innocent. That said, the powers were notably reluctant to publicly cite any examples of innocent passage having been impeded thus far by straits states: when the Peruvian delegate in the seabed committee asked his Soviet colleague to identify any states that had threatened to suspend passage through straits, the latter batted the question away, saying it was 'too general to reply to in concrete terms'.[26] (The Peruvian likely had in mind the Soviets' denial of transit to two American coastguard icebreakers through the Vilkitsky Strait within the Northeast Passage in 1967.)

The next problem with the 1958 territorial sea convention so far as the powers were concerned was that it failed to address the requirements

[23] B. Oxman, *From cooperation to conflict: the Soviet Union and the United States at the third U.N. Conference on the Law of the Sea* (Seattle, WA: Washington Sea Grant/Institute for Marine Studies, University of Washington, 1985), p. 20.

[24] Territorial Sea Convention, 216.

[25] Article 14(4) states that: 'Passage is innocent so long as it is not prejudicial to the peace, good order or security of the coastal State' (ibid., 214).

[26] US Mission Geneva to US State Department (27 July 1973), p. 5: 1973GENEVA03965, AAD.

of nuclear submarines. As the Soviet Navy stated in a manual on international law in 1966,

> under present-day conditions, with the appearance of nuclear submarines armed with missiles, as well as new ASW [anti-submarine warfare] equipment (sonobuoys, sonar, ASW carriers etc.), international law rules now in effect have become quite obsolete.[27]

Thereafter, the requirements of submarines, particularly nuclear submarines, would pervade the law of the sea negotiations, despite there being only fleeting references to them in the transcripts. With respect to straits, it is almost impossible to overstate their importance within the debate.

The particular concern for both the Soviets and the Americans was article 14(6) of the convention, applicable both to territorial seas and to straits used for international navigation, which stated that, 'Submarines are required to navigate on the surface and to show their flag.'[28] When this article was drafted in 1958, the powers envisaged it as applying only to straits of widths of up to twelve miles - i.e. overlapped by narrow territorial seas - and deep enough for submerged submarines to move through. (It was welcomed by straits states such as Greece and Italy, who wished to compel Soviet submarines to surface as they passed between the Aegean islands and through the Strait of Messina.) Later, with the expansion of territorial seas, the powers worried that article 14(6) would also apply to the transit of submarines through far broader straits than they had earlier intended, of widths of up to twenty-four miles.

Another factor was the submarines themselves. Throughout the Second World War and the years following, the tactical deployment of diesel-electric submarines was restricted. These submarines were heavily dependent on the surface environment: they had to surface frequently or snorkel at periscope depth to replenish their batteries and crew with oxygen, to emit exhaust, and to pick up communications. Consequently, they were at their most useful as attack vessels, tracking and engaging with the target. An archetypical example was the U-boat, on which some post-war submarines were modelled, which used hit-and-run tactics to minimise its time submerged – stalking a vessel at snorkel depth, releasing its torpedoes, then making its escape

[27] Quoted in: D. P. O'Connell, 'International law and contemporary naval operations', *British Year Book of International Law* 44 (1970), 19, 51–52.

[28] Territorial Sea Convention, 214.

underwater. As a result, article 14(6)'s requirement for submarines to surface in straits did not make a great deal of difference to their tactical effectiveness: for one thing, there were then not that many straits of strategic importance that lacked a ribbon of high seas down the centre, and for another, while they divulged their presence by having to surface in straits, they in any case risked detection everywhere because they had to surface so frequently.

This situation changed in the sixties. Many more states were claiming twelve-mile territorial seas that would overlap in straits of up to twenty-four miles wide. And the United States, followed a few years later by the USSR, launched a new generation of nuclear-powered submarines, starting with the world's first, *USS Nautilus*, commissioned in 1955. These boats were far less surface-dependent, being able to remain submerged – and, their operators hoped, undetected – for months, perhaps even years, at a time.[29] Submarine-mounted nuclear missiles evolved in tandem: the US Navy's submarine-mounted Polaris missile, introduced in 1961, and the more powerful Poseidon missile, introduced in 1972, each had a range of 2,500 miles.

These developments transformed strategy. The missile-bearing submarines' ability to sink into the depths of the ocean for long periods of time within missile range of a target enabled them to play a central role in deterrence: if one state was contemplating launching a nuclear attack against another, it had to factor in the risk of submarine counterattack. Unlike attack submarines, these nuclear submarines' modus operandi was to *avoid* contact with the enemy until summoned to launch their missiles, their effectiveness until that point being predicated on their concealment. Article 14(6), which obliged them to surface when transiting a strait, was the legal fly in the ointment because it compelled them to reveal their whereabouts, thereby temporarily stripping away their usefulness as the bearer of a second strike.

Another problem with the 1958 convention as far as the powers were concerned was that it lacked any provision permitting military aircraft to overfly straits used for international navigation. Without an explicit

[29] According to one report, 'Despite the unending technical and mechanical complications, Polaris subs are built to stay at sea up to three years. They are untethered by the standard submarine's fuel and oxygen limitations. They can manufacture their own atmosphere without surfacing': 'Defense: Polaris goes to work', *Time* (28 November 1960), at: time .com.

endorsement, they feared that straits states would challenge the lawfulness of airborne transit: the Spanish, for example, raised concerns about US Air Force aircraft overflying the Strait of Gibraltar during the 1973 Yom Kippur war.[30] The powers' concerns about this were heavily influenced, once again, by submarines. When they wanted to defend a high-value target – such as an aircraft carrier – as it moved towards and through a strait, they would typically create a mobile safety zone around it using helicopters and fixed-wing aircraft, the aerial workhouses of anti-submarine operations, to detect the presence of foreign submarines. Yet the issue of overflight was politically contentious, especially at the tail-end of the Americans' war in Indochina. In 1973, for example, the Soviets expressed their doubts about whether it was worth even trying to sell the idea to the G77[31] – especially after revelations about the USAF's intensive aerial bombing of neutral Cambodia.

The 'Free Transit' Concept

The fruits of the superpowers' discussions about straits were first publicly discernible during debates in the seabed committee in 1971–1972, when the Americans and Soviets presented different but complementary proposals advocating what would be dubbed 'free transit' through straits used for international navigation. The premise of their arguments for free transit was that a fundamental change in circumstances – the prospect of twelve-mile territorial seas overlapping within straits – required a fundamental change in passage rights.

The Americans led off in July 1971 with a proposal that attempted to transform the existing straits regime into one in which 'all ships and aircraft in transit shall enjoy the same freedom of navigation and overflight, for the purpose of transit through and over such straits, as they have on the high seas'.[32] This differed from the 1958 territorial sea convention by allowing all vessels, including submarines and aircraft, to traverse a strait while submerged or airborne as well as on the surface. Their delegates emphasised that vessels would be subject to more restrictions than they would be on the high seas, as they would have no right to

[30] US State Department to US Embassy Madrid (12 August 1974), p. 3: 1974STATE176311, AAD.

[31] US memo, 'Group of 5 straits meeting' (u.d., c. May 1973), p. 3: FCO 76/725, TNA.

[32] UN Seabed Committee, A/AC.138/SC.II/L.4 (30 July 1971), p. 241.

fish or conduct marine scientific research, and if they threatened the straits state's security, they would risk triggering the UN Charter's article 51 on self-defence.

The proposal was not greeted with approval. The Americans reported that almost all the other straits states on the seabed committee opposed the motion,[33] including NATO straits states – Greece, Italy and Denmark – who claimed exemptions for their own straits,[34] and straits states in the Asia-Pacific region, including Japan.[35] The British reported that a number of delegates argued that the existing right of innocent passage in straits was sufficient for everyone except for 'militarists and polluters'.[36]

After the Americans' attempt to drum up support for free transit, the USSR followed suit in July 1972 with a draft that opened with the words: 'In straits . . . all ships in transit shall enjoy the same freedom of navigation, for the purpose of transit though such straits as they have on the high seas.'[37] But unlike the American proposal, and in contrast to the 1958 convention, it dropped any reference to transit through straits connecting the high seas and a territorial sea, thereby excluding the straits leading to the 'closed' Sea of Okhotsk off their own coast, and the Strait of Tiran leading to the 'closed' Gulf of Aqaba, which pleased the Arab states. And while the American proposal asserted free transit for all vessels without specifically mentioning warships and military aircraft, the USSR singled them out and listed what they could not do in straits used for international navigation – warships, for example, would be prohibited from conducting exercises, using weapons, launching aircraft, carrying out hydrographic (but not other) surveys, and engaging in other acts unconnected to transit.[38]

[33] 'Analytical summary prepared by John Negroponte of the National Security Council staff' (u.d., c. late 1971): *FRUS*, 1969–1976, vol. E-1, *Documents on global issues*, 1969–1972, doc. 400.

[34] 'Memorandum prepared by the Chairman of the Inter-agency Task Force on the Law of the Sea (Stevenson)' (u.d., c. August 1971): *FRUS*, 1969–1976, vol. E-1, *Documents on global issues*, 1969–1972, doc. 412.

[35] 'Analytical summary prepared by John Negroponte of the National Security Council staff' (u.d., c. mid- to late 1971): *FRUS*, 1969–1976, vol. E-1, *Documents on global issues*, 1969–1972, doc. 400.

[36] 'Free transit through straits' (u.d., c. June 1973), p. 2: FCO 76/725, TNA.

[37] UN Seabed Committee, A/AC.138/SC.II/L.7 (25 July 1972), p. 1.

[38] Ibid.

Despite these caveats, the Soviet proposal did no better than the American one.[39] It drew an especially hostile response from the Chinese delegate, Shen Wei-liang, who observed that the USSR exhorted other states to keep their straits open while keeping its own straits closed (one example, though not mentioned by him, being the Soviets' denial of passage through the Vilkitsky Strait in 1967). Shen added: 'This is acting like the magistrates in an ancient fable, who allow themselves to burn down houses while forbidding the common folk to light lamps.'[40]

The following year, in March 1973, eight straits states and their allies – led by Spain, and backed by Cyprus, Greece, Indonesia, Malaysia, Morocco, the Philippines and Yemen – responded to the Americans and Soviets with their own proposal entitled 'Draft articles on navigation through the territorial sea including straits used for international navigation'.[41] The preambular comments explained that because such straits were formed wholly or partly of territorial seas, the principle of innocent passage should be applied to both 'as an entity'.[42]

This proposal, while invoking the 'traditional régime for navigation through the territorial sea',[43] had novel elements. It embellished and clarified the idea of passage through straits, stating that it must be 'continuous and expeditious'[44] – a formula that was picked up and carried through to the law of the sea convention. But even if passage conformed to these criteria, states bordering straits could enact laws to address new concerns, namely, preventing pollution and setting up sea lanes and traffic separation schemes to enhance navigational safety[45] (while 'taking into account' the recommendations of relevant international organisations[46]). Furthermore, they could require not only warships but also vessels perceived as posing less conventional threats – ships engaged in research on the marine environment and 'ships with special characteristics' such as nuclear-powered or nuclear-carrying

[39] 'Brief no. 2: third United Nations Law of the Sea Conference' (u.d., c. May 1974), p. 3: CAB 148/150, TNA.
[40] 'Statement of Shen Wei-Liang, representative of the People's Republic of China' (u.d., c. August 1972), p. 7: FCO 76/446, TNA.
[41] UN Seabed Committee, A/AC.138/SC.II/L.18 (27 March 1973).
[42] Ibid., p. 1.
[43] Ibid.
[44] Ibid., p. 2.
[45] Ibid., pp. 3–4.
[46] Ibid., p. 4.

vessels – to seek prior notification or authorisation.[47] Finally, they listed various prohibited activities by warships in straits, two of which took a more restrictive view of the law than had *Corfu Channel*: namely, 'intimidation or displaying of force' and 'assuming combat position by the crew'.[48] (The ICJ, as may be recalled, had tolerated the British show of force and made allowance for crews at action stations.)

These innovations aside, the straits states argued that the American and Soviet attempts to overturn the existing innocent passage regime were discriminatory because unlike other coastal states, straits states would be prevented from exercising sovereignty over their territorial sea. This point was made most forcefully by the Malaysian delegate Lal Chand Vohrah, who said: 'We ask no more than what international law accords other States, that is, the right to claim sovereignty over their land territory, air space and territorial sea subject to the right of user States for innocent passage.'[49]

The powers took a hard line against the eight-power proposal. The American delegate John Norton Moore declared his delegation to be 'deeply disappointed' with it,[50] especially the distinction being made between merchant vessels on one hand, and warships and 'ships with special characteristics' on the other. What Moore did not mention was that the Americans' concern about the passage regime in straits and their concern about the movement of 'ships with special characteristics' was intimately connected: at the time, their deployment of nuclear weapons on naval vessels at sea was nearing an all-time high, with around a quarter of its nuclear stockpile mounted on submarines, aircraft carriers, battleships, cruisers, destroyers, frigates and supply ships. This build-up would peak in 1975, when 6,191 nuclear weapons were afloat on US naval vessels whose movement from ocean to ocean depended on unrestricted passage though straits.[51]

The British, another sea-borne nuclear power, also fixed on the designation of 'ships with special characteristics', the consequences of which,

[47] Ibid., pp. 6, 7.
[48] Ibid., p. 8.
[49] 'Statement ... of the Malaysian representative' (5 April 1973), p. 2: CIA-RDP08C01297R 000300090002-0, CIAHC.
[50] S. N. Nandan, Report of the Fijian delegation on the Seabed Committee (u.d., c. mid-1973), p. 15: folder 1, box 69, Mss82-6, Satya Nandan papers, UVLSL.
[51] H. Kristensen, 'Declassified: nuclear weapons at sea', *Federation of American Scientists* (3 February 2016) at: fas.org.

they thought, would be more restrictive than the existing innocent passage regime.[52] According to a ministry of defence paper:

> Such a regime would require us to identify which ships were armed with or carrying nuclear weapons; it would not only give the coastal state the right to ask about the kind of weapons carried but could also be interpreted as enabling the coastal state to search the ship. A special regime for ships carrying nuclear weapons might further result in some important routes being closed altogether to such vessels, and it is therefore unacceptable, both because it would deprive HM [Her Majesty's] Ships of their sovereign immunity and because of the severe penalties which it would impose on our operational capacity.[53]

*

A major factor influencing this debate was the emergence of a package deal, which began to take shape in the final Seabed Committee session in July–August 1973, and would form the basis of negotiations at the next UN law of the sea conference, scheduled to open in November–December 1973.[54] In this package, the maritime powers initially offered to endorse a twelve-mile territorial sea if the coastal states agreed to unrestricted navigation through straits. The coastal states were unimpressed with this proposal – many had by then claimed a twelve-mile territorial sea and had no wish to bargain for something that they had already acquired.[55] A year later, as will be seen, the Americans would put more on the table: the powers would endorse the twelve-mile territorial sea *and* a 200-mile economic zone if the coastal states would agree to unrestricted navigation through straits *and* a satisfactory navigational regime within the economic zone.[56]

One delegate with a keen sense of the forces at play over the package deal was the Fijian delegate Satya Nandan, a moderate within the G77 who would later play a central role in the framing of the straits articles in the convention. He recognised that if the straits states pushed back too hard against the powers over passage through straits, they might lose the

[52] 'Law of the Sea: straits' (25 June 1973), p. 5: FCO 76/726, TNA.
[53] 'Annex C: position paper on surface passage of warships' (u.d., c. May 1974), p. 6: CAB 148/150, TNA.
[54] UNGA Res. 3029(XXVII) (18 December 1972).
[55] S. N. Nandan, Report of the Fijian delegation on the Seabed Committee (u.d., c. mid-1973), p. 9: folder 1, box 69, Mss82–6, Satya Nandan papers, UVLSL.
[56] Stevenson's speech setting out the revised package at the conference is at: UNLOSC III, vol. 1, A/Conf.62/SR.38 (11 July 1974), p. 160.

support of other coastal states who were banking on claims to an economic zone. Nandan noted:

> The Latins and the Africans place great importance [on] the economic resources of the sea and the seabed. They would, I fear, be prepared to bargain with major-powers for the economic zone and give away the straits.[57]

He also observed that the Americans were already trying to strike deals with some of the straits states, reporting, for example, that, 'the US . . . has made quiet approaches to Chile and Argentina implying that it could bargain away economic resources for "free transit" through straits'.[58]

Tanker Trouble

The straits states were concerned about two issues. The familiar issue was the movement of warships along their coastlines, with the attendant problem of threats to national security. The newer issue was the movement of vessels carrying hazardous cargoes – among them, nuclear arms, nuclear waste and high volumes of oil and gas – which, if dislodged by an accident, could potentially devastate their marine environment and undermine their economic security. These concerns were well founded, given recent events in and around the English Channel. In March 1967, a very large Liberian-registered tanker *Torrey Canyon* grounded on a reef in the Channel's approaches, breaching its tanks and disgorging an 106,000 tonne spume of oil that turned the sea black, destroyed sea life, and ruined coastlines in England, France, the Channel Islands and Spain.[59] Attempting to contain the damage, the British government took the legally controversial decision to bomb *Torrey Canyon* – a foreign-flagged vessel on the high seas – with the aim of setting the remaining oil alight. This failed, as did efforts to disperse the spill with detergents, which killed off even more sea life and provided a textbook example of what not to do in the future.

More accidents followed in the Channel, culminating in an especially bad run over four months in 1970–1971. In October 1970, the oil tanker

57 S. N. Nandan, Report of the Fijian delegation on the seabed committee (u.d., c. mid-1973), p. 18: folder 1, box 69, Mss82-6, Satya Nandan papers, UVLSL.

58 Ibid.

59 Figures about the size of the spill vary. This estimate comes from a French report cited in: IMCO, 'Reports on nine studies' (3 October 1973), p. 16: MP/CONF/INF.14/3, International Maritime Organization Archives [hereafter, IMO Archives].

Allegro, trying to avoid another vessel, ploughed into another tanker, *Pacific Glory*, killing fourteen seamen and setting the sea alight.[60] Then in January 1971, in the Channel's narrowest section – the Dover Strait/Pas de Calais – the tanker *Texaco Caribbean* exploded and sank after colliding with the cargo ship *Paracas* in thick fog, killing eight.[61] The next day, the cargo ship *Brandenburg* collided with the wreck of *Texaco Caribbean*, killing twenty.[62] And the following month, *Niki* collided with the wrecks of *Texaco Caribbean* and *Brandenburg*, killing twenty-two.[63]

The *Torrey Canyon* disaster prodded the UN's London-based Intergovernmental Maritime Consultative Organization (IMCO) into action. This body, which presided over shipping engaged in international trade, endorsed the world's first voluntary traffic separation scheme, established in the Dover Strait in June 1967. There, a lane west of Sandettie Bank was reserved for deep-draught vessels of seventeen metres or more transiting towards Europe, while a radar surveillance system at St Margaret's Bay warned other shipping in the area of potential hazards, including vessels travelling the wrong way.[64] Four years later, IMCO's maritime safety committee unanimously agreed to the British request, made in response to the accidents involving *Brandenburg*, *Niki*, *Paracas* and *Texaco Caribbean*, that the 1967 Dover Strait scheme be made compulsory.[65] Steps were also taken to update the IMCO-sponsored regulations governing collisions to include traffic separation schemes, with rules incorporated into the 1972 convention for preventing collisions at sea.[66]

The Dover Strait scheme provided a template for some of the other traffic separation schemes endorsed by IMCO. But the legal questions regarding straits used for international navigation were far from settled, even between the powers. How might day-to-day safety measures endorsed by IMCO and introduced by Britain and France in the Dover Strait sit with the free transit regime then being envisaged by the United States and the USSR? As the British official D. W. Wills explained, there

60 R. Mason, UK House of Commons, *Hansard* (1 March 1971), vol. 812, col. 1221. (Also, IMCO, 'Report of a spillage of oil from a collision between … "Pacific Glory" and "Allegro"' (15 April 1971), p. 1: OP IX/4/2, IMO Archives.)

61 Ibid.

62 Ibid.

63 Ibid.

64 'Brief 11: navigation in the English Channel' (15 July 1971), pp. 2, 3: FCO 76/334, TNA.

65 Ibid., p. 1.

66 Rules 1(d) and 10, Convention on the International Regulations for Preventing Collisions at Sea (signed 20 October 1972, EIF 15 July 1977) 1050 UNTS 16, 22, 25–26.

were plenty of situations in which a straits state might wish to ignore a free transit regime and restrict vessels' passage through the strait:

> For navigational safety reasons we might want to require ships to stop in the event of a serious collision or dense fog or an exceptionally low tide. We might want to forbid the passage of deep draught ships or require them to transit the Strait only at certain states of the tide. We might want to impose speed limits or exclude from our inshore zone ships above a certain size or ships not bound to or from a UK port. We also want clearly to have the right to levy charges on a ship using the Dover Strait area in respect of services provided of shipping generally even if those services were not used by that particular ship; examples are broadcasts to shipping by a Channel Navigation Information Service, or special hydrographic surveys or additional navigation aids provided to assist the safe passage of ships through the Strait. To this extent the expression 'free transit' might give rise to difficulties.[67]

That said, British officials recognised that if Britain held out for controls over the Dover Strait, they would find it hard to argue against other straits states imposing similar restrictions.[68] They were clearly on the horns of a dilemma.

Eastward-Bound Oil

When the legal debate about navigation through straits gathered momentum, attention fixed on the Malacca-Singapore straits, which carried seaborne cargo between the northern Indian Ocean and the South China Sea. The decades following the war had seen a sharp increase in traffic, driven by oil. The opening up of oilfields in the Gulf, the shift from coal to oil as a major source of energy, and the surge in global energy consumption meant that ever-greater numbers of tankers were transporting oil through the Malacca-Singapore straits to Japan and other points east. This shift obviously greatly affected the three bordering states of Indonesia, Malaysia and Singapore, whose territorial seas overlapped each other's in the straits.[69] The movement of oil brought with it opportunities and risks, which affected them in different ways: Singapore, with its optimally located harbour, port and refineries, benefited more than Indonesia and Malaysia, which had less port capacity and their own

[67] D. W. Hills to H. Whitaker (6 June 1973): FCO 76/725, TNA.

[68] 'Sea bed committee of the United Nations' (12 May 1971), p. 2: FCO 76/329, TNA.

[69] The fourth state bordering the Malacca Strait is Thailand, with a short stretch of territorial sea abutting the northern high seas section.

oil and gas sectors to promote. All three faced the problem of oil spills, however, and even though the straits were also a major artery for container vessels, naval flotillas and fishing fleets, the debate about navigational safety and pollution control was viewed primarily through the prism of oil transportation.

In the seventies, the Malacca-Singapore straits were far less congested than the Dover Strait, but were nevertheless highly congested in their narrower sections, being transited, according to one Malaysian estimate, by some 4,500 foreign vessels a month,[70] or around 54,000 a year. A significant proportion of these vessels were oil tankers, which were by then among the largest and potentially most dangerous commercial vessels in the world. Japanese owners and shipbuilders, seeking to exploit economies of scale, led the way in constructing some of the largest tankers, including scores of very large crude carriers (VLCCs) with a deadweight tonnage (dwt) of 200,000–250,000.[71] These vessels were patently unsafe. In the days before mandatory safety features such as double hulls, segregated tanks, oily-water separators and duplicate controls, the VLCCs were, as Noël Mostert put it, 'outsize floating balloons that, if punctured, could release … up to half a million tons of crude oil'.[72] This led Elizabeth Young to conclude that punctured or not, tankers operating under the lax standards of the time represented a significant threat to straits states' environmental security:

> No under-insured, ill-equipped, ill-navigated, chartless, flag-of-convenience-registered, 250,000-ton tanker can ever be 'innocent' in the English Channel or the Malacca strait, or should it find itself there, in the Canadian Arctic.[73]

The Malacca-Singapore straits were particularly ill-suited to accommodating these massive vessels. Towards the southern end, the straits were narrow, just 1.7 miles wide in the narrowest navigable section, and shallow, with scores of spots along the route being less than twenty-

[70] 'Statement made by the Honourable Tan Sri Dato Haji Abdul Kadir bin Yusof' (10 August 1974), p. 4: box 16, RG 43, Records of international conferences, commissions, and expositions, Law of the Sea Conference, NARA. By comparison, the Dover Strait saw the passage an estimated 300,000 vessels a year: Institution of Navigation, *The separation of traffic at sea* (1966), p. 2: NAV II, IMO Archives.

[71] The Japanese also constructed two off-the-scale 'ultra-large' vessels, *Globtik Tokyo* and *Globtik London* of 483,000 dwt each, launched in 1972 and 1973, whose size kept them out of the shallower straits.

[72] N. Mostert, *Supership* (London: Macmillan, 1975), p. 20.

[73] E. Young, 'New laws for old navies', *Survival* 16 (1974), 262, 265.

three metres deep.[74] To complicate matters, the sandy seabed was littered with reefs, shoals and wrecks, and was prone to unpredictable movement, creating metres-high underwater sand ridges. In addition to those hazards, the straits were not only congested but also criss-crossed by different streams of traffic – through traffic, cross traffic, port traffic – as well as being a fishing ground, attracting fishing craft with all their gear. Given that a fully loaded 200,000–250,000 dwt tanker was mostly underwater, with a draught of twenty-one meters and an under-keel clearance in some places of just two to three metres, and given that it would need three miles and twenty minutes to come to an emergency stop, the margin for error in the confined waters of the Malacca-Singapore straits was perilously thin. As the director of the International Association of Independent Tanker Owners later stated, these straits were 'a very high risk waterway'.[75] Measures for preventing accidents, with the attendant potential for oil spillages, crew fatalities and damage to marine life, were urgently needed. But who would pay the financial and political costs – would it be the straits states or should it be the straits users?

Of the straits users, Japan was by far the most important commercial player. Its economy was so dependent on the movement of oil through the Singapore-Malacca straits – often described as a 'lifeline' – that a symbiotic relationship had emerged between itself as the main user, and the three adjacent straits states. All parties recognised the benefits of surveying the straits, introducing a traffic separation scheme, and improving navigational aids such as radar and lights, but they differed over how they should be implemented.

In London, IMCO's subcommittee on safety of navigation became a forum for the discussion between them. In December 1966, Singapore produced recommendations for improvements to navigational aids, proposing, for example, to intensify the light at One Fathom Bank and to place a Racon or direction-finding beacon on the lighthouse to assist

[74] Numbers differed because surveys covered different areas, but one survey, conducted by *Koyo Maru*, detected twenty areas of water less than twenty-three metres deep, while another, conducted by *Hydra*, found seventy areas 'of possible danger to deep draught ships': Japan, 'Matters related to routeing and traffic separation' (20 August 1969), p. 2: NAV VIII/3(a)/2, IMO Archives; and UK, 'Matters related to traffic separation…' (1 July 1971), p. 1: NAV XI/3(a)/8, IMO Archives.

[75] T. A. Meyer, 'Tanker design features and the safety of navigation', *Singapore Journal of International and Comparative Law* 2 (1998), 517, 517.

westbound traffic moving into the Malacca Strait.[76] In November 1967, Japan followed up with a proposal to introduce special sea lanes in the straits, making it obligatory, for example, for deep-draught vessels travelling eastwards to pass through the Phillip Channel.[77] What was most notable about this proposal, however, was that it pushed for IMCO to establish sea lanes in consultation with the 'countries concerned' with these straits – in other words, not only the three straits states but also Japan, as a straits user:

> Japan, as one of the major countries having a large number of big tankers has naturally a deep interest in the establishment of sea lanes in the Malacca and Singapore Straits. In view of this fact, the Government of Japan proposes that IMCO, in consultation with the Governments of the countries concerned, should establish sea lanes in the above-mentioned Straits and should take the necessary steps in connexion with the establishment of such sea lanes.[78]

The Indonesian participant in this discussion, M. T. Dompas, responded extremely cautiously to this latter proposal. He stated that while his government agreed in principle with the aims of reducing hazards and collisions, such measures 'shall in no circumstances interfere with the rights and integrity of a State in its territorial waters'.[79] Furthermore, his government could not 'at the present stage or within the foreseeable future, bear the costs resulting from the establishment of the proposed sea lanes, such as additional navigational aids, hydrographic surveys to be conducted, the clearing of submerged obstructions, etc'.[80]

Yet coaxed along by IMCO, the Malacca-Singapore straits states and Japan edged towards an accommodation. In 1968, the Japanese proposed carrying out a hydrographic survey of the straits as a prelude to a traffic separation scheme. This was carried out by the vessel *Koyu Maru* in January–March 1969, entirely funded by the Japanese and conducted with the straits states' consent and participation.[81] More surveys were

[76] Singapore, 'Recommendations for improved navigational aids in the Malacca Strait and Singapore Strait' (December 1966), pp. 1–2: NAV IV/2/Add.4, IMO Archives.

[77] Japan, 'Establishment of special routes or lanes' (November 1967), p. 1: NAV IV/2/Add.2, IMO Archives.

[78] Ibid.

[79] 'Report of the working group on traffic separation' (7 December 1967), p. 8: NAV IV/WP.4/Rev.1, IMO Archives.

[80] Ibid.

[81] Japan, 'Matters related to routeing and traffic separation' (20 August 1969), p. 2: NAV VIII/3(a)/2, IMO Archives.

planned, but the latent political strains within the relationship soon came to the fore. The straits states, while insisting on retaining complete control over all activities in the straits, also insisted that the Japanese should bear all costs of measures designed to enhance the safety of passing tankers. Aafter all, they argued, the outlay involved was small compared to the billion-plus-yen saving Tokyo made each year from using this route rather than longer and therefore costlier routes through the other Indonesian straits.[82] The Japanese, meanwhile, began to chafe at the obligation to submit to the straits states' control over projects that they were funding themselves, and gravitated towards the idea of passing responsibility for navigational matters in the said straits to an international body – namely, IMCO – to spread the political and financial costs among a wider group of states.

The disagreements between Japan and the straits states over the straits' management came to a head in 1970–1971. In October 1970, Mr. Hazama, the Japanese delegate, urged IMCO's subcommittee to not only endorse safety measures but also to internationalise the Malacca-Singapore straits:

> In order to install and maintain these aids to navigation, it is necessary to set up an international co-operative system which includes three littoral countries and major shipping countries. In view of [the] urgency of the necessity of an implementation of the traffic separation scheme in the Straits, it is recommended that the necessary international action for the installation and maintenance of navigational aids be taken as soon as possible.[83]

The other members of the subcommittee took up this proposal with apparent enthusiasm. The session report stated, for example, that one aspect of the problem – the installation of navigational aids – would, as a matter of urgent necessity, require 'co-operative arrangements at international level' involving consultations between the straits states and an unspecified number of other states 'having an interest in the improvement of safety of navigation in that area'.[84]

[82] By one calculation, Japan saved ¥340 million in oil/petrol carriage and ¥1 billion in bulk trade each year, compared to an outlay of ¥10 billion for various projects over the twenty-six years covering 1968 to 1993: B. A. Hamzah, 'Managing marine pollution in the Straits of Malacca and Singapore: personal observations', *Singapore Journal of International and Comparative Law* 2 (1998), 464, 466.

[83] Japan, 'Ships' routeing' (16 October 1970), p. 2: NAV X/5/4, IMO Archive.

[84] 'Report of the Sub-committee on Safety of Navigation' (16 October 1970), p. 9: NAV X/8, IMO Archives.

The Indonesian and Malaysian representatives strongly resisted these moves towards internationalisation. They thought that the involvement of *any* foreign entities, national or international, would usurp their sovereignty over their territorial seas. And they specifically objected to IMCO playing a role in the process because it was, in their view, a 'ship owners' club' (as one Malaysian official put it).[85] Inviting it to preside over navigation through the straits would, they intimated, be like putting the fox in charge of the chicken coop.

The battle restarted in IMCO's subcommittee in July 1971, when Indonesia and Malaysia took steps to reclaim the initiative from Japan and IMCO. Hasjim Djalal, the head of the Indonesian delegation, brought the discussion of the straits to a sharp halt when he stated:

> I wish to place on record that I am instructed by my Government to impress upon the Sub-Committee that part of the Strait in question is part of the territorial seas of the coastal States. ... My Government therefore cannot accept any idea that might lead to the internationalization of the Strait, in the sense that ... the right to control and to supervise the Strait is taken away from the coastal States. For these reasons, my Government considers that any discussion on the Strait of Malacca leading to the internationalization of the Strait is inappropriate.[86]

This statement, firmly supported by the Malaysian delegation, deterred IMCO from pursuing any further debate about the straits without the straits states' consent. A recommendation for a traffic separation scheme was removed from the record,[87] and thereafter the issue became *sub judice*,[88] making no further appearance in IMCO documents until 1977.

Outside IMCO, the Indonesians followed Djalal's firm words with equally firm action. In September 1971, major-general Ali Murtopo rejected a Japanese proposal to set up a 'multinational taskforce' to dredge the Malacca Strait in preparation for the transit of even larger

[85] D. H. Anderson to M. J. Williams (26 August 1976), p. 2: FCO 76/1358, TNA. The powers countered that the developing countries were not exactly unrepresented in the organisation: some fifty of them had joined it by 1973, including Indonesia, Malaysia and Singapore: 'Airgram A-7576 from the Department of State to all diplomatic posts' (4 September 1973): *FRUS*, 1969–1976, vol. 3-E, *Documents on global issues*, 1973–1976, doc. 6.

[86] 'Report of the Sub-Committee on Safety of Navigation' (14 July 1971), pp. 9–10: NAV XI/9, IMO Archives.

[87] E. F. Oliver, 'Malacca: dire straits', *United States Naval Institute Proceedings* (June 1973), 26, 30.

[88] M. Leifer, *International straits of the world: Malacca, Singapore, and Indonesia* (Alphen aan den Rijn: Sijthoff & Noordhoff, 1978), p. 47.

tankers, on the grounds that dredging would benefit other states but not Indonesia.[89] The Malaysians agreed with this approach, making it clear that they took a dim view of Japan's 'big brother' attitude and its attempts, as one newspaper later put it, to 'boss around in waters which did not belong to it'.[90] Indonesia and Malaysia were both upholding a point of principle, of course, but they were also weighing up the implications of dredging the strait for their own oil and gas export earnings, which were heavily dependent on sales to Japan. As one British official noted, the Malaysians were perhaps not inclined to 'put themselves out to help the Japanese to get oil from the Gulf more easily'.[91]

The three states delivered the most decisive blow to plans to internationalise the straits in November 1971 when they issued a tripartite communiqué declaring their control over them.[92] This declaration had two elements. The first was the three governments' statement that safety of navigation within the straits was 'the responsibility of the coastal states concerned'– or, to put it another way, not the responsibility of others.[93] They further agreed to establish a body to coordinate navigational safety efforts, which would comprise themselves only.[94] The second element addressed international law, declaring that Indonesia and Malaysia had 'agreed that the Straits of Malacca and Singapore are not international straits, while fully recognising their use for international shipping in accordance with the principle of innocent passage'.[95] (Singapore, which inclined towards a freer regime but was beholden to its neighbours, merely took note.) When Indonesia and Malaysia stated that the waters concerned were not international straits, they were not denying, *pace Corfu Channel*, that they connected two parts of the high seas and were used for international navigation but rather were emphasising that they were territorial seas first and straits second.[96]

89 '"No" to Malacca straits plan, Ali Murtopo says', *Indonesian Observer* (25 September 1971).

90 'The need to keep waterway safe', *New Nation* (17 May 1973).

91 W. Turner to D. A. Campbell (6 October 1971), p. 2: FCO 76/256, TNA.

92 Di-terbitkan oleh jabatan penerangan malaysia (PEN: 11/71/106 (Hanluar)), 'Joint statement' (16 November 1971) (and reprinted in: Leifer, *International straits*, p. 47).

93 Ibid.

94 Ibid.

95 Ibid.

96 D. P. O'Connell took issue with this sentence, arguing that it 'acquires meaning only if it is supposed that the right of passage in international straits is greater than, or different from, the right of innocent passage in the territorial sea, so that denying that the Straits of Malacca are international straits would aim at the exclusion of this greater or different

The Japanese, realising that they had pushed too hard for internationalisation, publicly responded in a low-key manner: Maeda Mashida of the Japanese embassy in Kuala Lumpur said his government would 'respect the initiative' but refused to be drawn further on Tokyo's reaction.[97] The debate rippled outwards anyway, raising new questions about who ultimately controlled movement through straits, with the straits states seeming to have the upper hand over straits users. In New Delhi, Congress MPs raised questions in Lok Sabha about what steps the government was taking to 'protect the interest of India for the navigation of her ships' through the Malacca-Singapore straits.[98] And in Beijing, the Norwegian ambassador Per Galby Ravne upbraided China's vice foreign minister Chiao Kuan-hua for supporting the straits states' communiqué, claiming that if the signatories ever closed the Malacca-Singapore and Indonesian straits to foreign traffic, Chinese ships would be forced to sail west by way of 'the South Pole or the Panama Canal'.[99] Why Ravne thought Chinese ships would be compelled to visit the penguins in Antarctica rather than sailing around Australia is not recorded.

Irresistible Forces, Immovable Objects

In spring 1973, the three maritime powers – Britain, the United States and the USSR – invited Japan and France to join them, transforming their triumvirate into the 'group of five'.[100] This group, which orchestrated the campaign against the G77 on the law of the sea and the proposed new international economic order, was the forerunner to the better-known 'group of seven', which would pursue a similar campaign against the G77 across a broader range of issues when it was established two years later. Unlike the G7, however, the G5 included the USSR among its founding members, and initially tried to keep its existence secret, primarily because its members, drawn from both sides of the East–West divide, did not want to appear to be operating as a cabal. Of course, most other conference delegates suspected the group's existence, and the truth came out soon enough, first in 1975, in a footnote to a *Revue générale*

rule' – a reading with which the Indonesians and Malaysians would have concurred: D. P. O'Connell and I. A. Shearer (ed.), *The international law of the sea*, vol. 1 (Oxford: Clarendon Press, 1982), p. 319.

97 'Straits: offer by the Japanese', *New Nation* (17 November 1971).

98 India, *Lok Sabha Debates* (11 May 1972), fifth series, vol. 14, col. 13.

99 UK Embassy Beijing to UK FCO (8 April 1972): FCO 76/451, TNA.

100 'Law of the sea: British policy on straits' (c. 28 June 1978), p. 6: FCO 76/725, TNA.

de droit international public article,[101] and then, the following year, in a *Frankfurter Allgemeine Zeitung* article demanding to know why West Germany was not a member.[102]

Straits dominated the G5's agenda. The group wanted guaranteed access to them, but the American and Soviet 'free transit' idea had been rejected, and they struggled to find a formula to replace it. Meanwhile, the third UN law of the sea conference, due to open at the end of 1973, was drawing ever closer. So in January that year, the British took on the thankless task of coming up with a draft on straits that would satisfy the powers while also being acceptable to the other states. As one British official put it, 'we have to make sure the irresistible force does not meet the immovable object'.[103]

This was easier said than done. They knew that they would have to make at least cosmetic concessions to win around other states, but this brought them up against the 'ultra-hard-line Pentagon view'[104] expressed by Stuart French, who warned that the Americans would walk out of the conference if anything short of high seas freedoms in straits was agreed.[105] The British thought that this uncompromising approach would only alienate the other states, and that a better course would be to mobilise the support of the friendly and less committed nations, and then, one by one, neutralise or isolate those remaining – a tactic known as salami-slicing. The problem they faced, though, was that whenever they came up with drafts that packaged unrestricted passage in a form that might be more acceptable to others, they were slapped down by either the Soviets or the Americans and instructed to start over again.

The British presented their first draft to the G5 in June 1973. It proposed unsuspendable passage for all ships and aircraft through 'multinational' straits – those overlapped by the territorial seas of two or more straits states.[106] This was clearly self-serving: most foreign straits of strategic importance to Britain – such as Gibraltar, Bab-el-Mandeb, Hormuz and Malacca-Singapore[107] – happened to be multinational.

[101] D. H. Anderson, 'UNLOSC: group of five' (28 November 1975): FCO 76/1039, TNA.
[102] M. C. Wood, 'First committee: FRG and the five' (23 March 1976), p. 1: FCO 76/1354, TNA.
[103] 'Ministry of Defence comments on FCO paper' (21 February 1973), p. 3: FCO 76/725, TNA.
[104] H. A. Dudgeon minute (8 June 1973): FCO 76/725, TNA.
[105] H. A. Dudgeon to C. J. Makins (20 June 1973), pp. 2, 3: FCO 76/725, TNA.
[106] 'UK draft articles on straits' (u.d., c. May 1974), p. 1: FCO 76/725, TNA.
[107] Ibid.

It also served a tactical purpose: because it applied to multinational straits only, the number of straits states involved could be kept down, while possibly securing the support of unaffected straits states such as Denmark and Italy.[108] The trouble with this ingenious formula was that by accident or design it disregarded the interests of the USSR, whose manoeuvrability depended on *non*-multilateral straits, such as the entrances to the Aegean Sea. Soviet representative A. A. Kovalev told the British that the reaction against the draft in Moscow had been 'very violent' because it would effectively 'shut the Soviet navy out of the Mediterranean',[109] and that if they persisted with the idea, the Soviets would 'break up the Group of Five'.[110] So that was the end of that plan.

After a rethink, the British circulated a second proposal in August 1973, dealing with both the territorial sea and straits, and recasting the inflammatory idea of free transit as the more neutral-sounding 'transit passage'. This proposal guaranteed extensive rights in straits, but it was packaged as a looser version of the innocent passage regime governing the territorial sea.[111] This time it was the Americans who protested, arguing that it had not broken the link between innocent passage in the territorial sea and transit passage in straits. As John Norton Moore explained, transit passage had to be associated with the high seas rather than with innocent passage 'because it was essential to protect the right of submerged transit and overflight, and to do this without drawing attention to the fact'.[112] To drive the point home, the Americans told the British that they would 'disassociate' themselves from the draft if it were tabled at the conference.[113] So this version was also scrapped.

The phrase 'transit passage' stuck, though, and under the tutelage of the Americans, a proposal began to take shape that was disassociated from innocent passage and straits states' sovereignty, and associated instead with unimpeded passage. At this stage, 'unimpeded' meant freedom from *all* straits state controls, such as the obligation to notify or seek authorisation for the passage of warships, or to submit to coastal

108 H. A. Dudgeon to C. J. Makins (20 June 1973), p. 2: FCO 76/725, TNA.
109 UK delegation to UK FCO (13 July 1973), p. 1: FCO 76/726, TNA.
110 'Brief no. 2: Third United Nations Law of the Sea Conference' (u.d., c. May 1974), p. 5: CAB 148/150, TNA.
111 Ibid.
112 'Note of a meeting held in the FCO' (4 February 1974), p. 3: FCO 76/927, TNA.
113 'Brief no. 2: Third United Nations Law of the Sea Conference' (u.d., c. May 1974), p. 6: CAB 148/150, TNA.

regulations managing navigational safety and pollution.[114] In May 1974, the British reported that:

> The section on straits and the section on innocent passage no longer form part of a conceptual whole. On the insistence of the Americans there are now separate chapters on each subject with very few cross-references. This is because the US believes that, unless passage through straits is kept as a different concept in International Law from innocent passage in the territorial seas, the sanctity of freedom of navigation and overflight in straits will invariably be tainted with coastal states control.[115]

There were still disagreements over the formula, however. The United States tried to restore to the text a reference to the 'high seas' in straits, but the British successfully resisted this: they thought the phrase would antagonise the G77 states and make the straits articles virtually unnegotiable.[116] Between themselves, they grumbled that the American negotiators were clumsy[117] and blind to the fact that most states, if given the choice between accepting the American approach to straits or accepting the treaty without the powers becoming parties to it would choose the latter.[118]

The Conference Begins

When the third UN law of the sea conference opened in New York for its inaugural session from 3–15 December 1973, and then the longer second session in Caracas, held from 20 June to 29 August 1974, the delegates argued over how to decide substantive issues. Would it be by vote or by consensus? They finally agreed to proceed by consensus, retaining the vote only as a last resort. This was set out in a 'gentleman's agreement' stating that,

> the Conference should make every effort to reach agreement on substantive matters by way of consensus; [and] that there should be no voting on such matters until all efforts at consensus have been exhausted.[119]

114 US memo, 'Group of 5 straits meeting' (u.d., c. May 1973), p. 18: FCO 76/725, TNA.

115 'Brief no. 2: third United Nations law of the sea conference' (u.d., c. May 1974), p. 7: CAB 148/150, TNA.

116 Ibid.

117 H. A. Dudgeon minute (8 June 1973): FCO 76/725, TNA.

118 H. A. Dudgeon to C. J. Makins (20 June 1973), pp. 2, 3: FCO 76/725, TNA.

119 UNLOSC III, vol. 3, A/Conf.62/L.1 (3 June 1974), p. 80.

While the idea of using consensus as a decision-making mechanism was not entirely new – it had been used, for example, in negotiations on the 1959 Antarctic treaty – it was the first time it had been used in negotiations involving almost all states over a major multilateral treaty. Its introduction was not without controversy, being insisted upon by the USSR over the protests of some G77 states in the General Assembly, not least because it favoured minority groupings such as the maritime powers who had no hope of securing a majority vote. At Caracas, the Tanzanian delegate Joseph Warioba, expressing the sentiments of the time, counterposed the 'gentleman's agreement' with what he hoped would be 'a people's treaty'.[120]

After the decision on decision-making, the three major conference committees got to work. The first addressed the seabed; the second addressed the other maritime zones; and the third addressed the protection and preservation of the marine environment, marine scientific research, and the development and transfer of marine technology.

The maritime powers considered unimpeded passage through straits (and archipelagos, considered later) to be of foremost importance,[121] and pushed for a speedy resolution of these issues within the second committee. In July 1974, the British, having previously suffered bruising encounters with both superpowers, finally raised a G5-endorsed proposal covering straits used for international navigation. The relevant section began:

> 1. In straits to which this article applies, all ships and aircraft enjoy the right of transit passage, which shall not be impeded.

[120] UNLOSC III, vol. 1, A/Conf.62/SR.26 (2 July 1974), p. 93.

[121] From 1974 onwards, commentators started suggesting that the superpowers' interest in straits declined as the range of missiles increased. USN rear-admiral Max Morris's comments in NATO that same year strongly suggest otherwise:

> A. Nuclear deterrence – [US chiefs of staff] had concluded that unreported (covert), unnotified, unrestricted movement of submarines is essential for defense. Option for submerged transit must be retained not only for present but for long-term future planning ... B. ASW – attack SSN's must retain option to trail hostile submarines in a covert fashion. Therefore[ ], they must not be required to surface ... or be legally restricted in any way in submerged passage through water column (as in economic zone) ... C. Conventional fleet mobility and resupply of alliance – ... high seas freedoms were essential for allied interests for moving cargo as well as for purely military shipping.

(US Mission to NATO to US State Department (23 May 1974), s. 4, p. 2 – s. 4, p. 3: 1974NATO02859, AAD.)

2. Transit passage is the exercise in accordance with the provisions of this chapter of the freedom of navigation and overflight solely for the purpose of continuous and expeditious transit of the strait between one part of the high seas and another part of the high seas or a State bordering the strait.
3. This article applies to any strait or other stretch of water, whatever its geographical name, which:
   (a) is used for international navigation;
   (b) connects two parts of the high seas.
4. Transit passage shall apply in a strait only to the extent that:
   (a) an equally suitable high seas route does not exist through the strait; or
   (b) if the strait is formed by an island of the coastal State, an equally suitable high seas passage does not exist seaward of the island.[122]

This motion retained *Corfu Channel's* definition of international straits – being used for international navigation and connecting two parts of the high seas – but replaced the associated regime of unsuspendable innocent passage with the new regime of transit passage, with the exceptions set out in the fourth paragraph. The words 'shall not be impeded' – note the imperative 'shall' - made clear that under the regime straits states could not restrict passage in peacetime, even on security grounds.

When motivating the proposal, the British delegate Harry Dudgeon presented it as being the 'middle way' between the majority interests of the international community and the minority interests of the straits states, without mentioning the other conspicuous minority interest – that of the maritime powers in transit passage.[123] Dudgeon also avoided comparing less restricted transit passage with more restricted innocent passage, while his American colleague John Norton Moore stressed instead the difference between the uninhibited freedom of the high seas and the inhibited right of transit passage (which obliged vessels to move through a strait solely for the purpose of continuous and expeditious transit, without threatening the security of the coastal state).[124] The other G5 states' public response to the British submission was calculatedly tepid, most likely on the insistence of the Soviets, who repeatedly

[122] UNLOSC III, vol. 3, A/Conf.62/C.2/L.3 (3 July 1974), pp. 185–186.
[123] UNLOSC III, vol. 2, A/Conf.62/C.2/SR.11 (22 July 1974), p. 126.
[124] 'Statement before committee II: the Honourable John Norton Moore' (22 July 1974), p. 2: box 17, RG 43, Records of international conferences, commissions, and expositions, Law of the Sea Conference, NARA.

cautioned members against praising their own initiatives too highly lest other states suspect them of colluding.[125]

Some of the coastal states raised pointed questions about transit passage. The Egyptian delegate, Mohamed Shaffie Abdel Hamid, for example, asked the American delegates how one could be sure that a submerged submarine had refrained from testing weapons while it was moving through a strait.[126] John Stevenson replied that the waters of a strait used for international navigation were so confined that 'no captain of a surface ship, much less of a submarine, would choose to take action threatening the security of a strait State'[127] – an argument that may have given pause to states bordering wider straits. And yet, at the debate's conclusion, Stevenson was cautiously optimistic about the prospects of transit passage, noting that there had been a 'marked shift' in the direction of unimpeded passage, led by the East European states and followed by a few of the Arab states.[128] The process of winning support and breaking down the opposition was under way.

In the interval after the second conference session in Caracas, the powers presented new arguments justifying the need for transit passage. The British instructed their missions abroad to convey the message to foreign governments that it was essential that submarines be able to pass submerged (and thus, they hoped, undetected) through straits because this would maintain a stable balance of mutual deterrence based on the second-strike capability.[129] By the same token, they argued that retaining the 1958 innocent passage regime requiring submarines to surface in straits, as many straits states demanded, was destabilising because,

> The balance of mutual deterrence between the super-powers would rest on a much less secure foundation; and the desire to track missile-firing submarines observed in straits would lead both sides to concentrate military forces in peace-time in the vicinity of straits. These concentrations of forces would themselves be a cause of tension.[130]

[125] 'Discussion of informal single negotiating text: part II' (u.d., c. July 1975), p. 6: FCO 76/1038, TNA.

[126] UNLOSC III, vol. 2, A/Conf.63/C.2/SR.13 (23 July 1974), p. 131.

[127] Ibid., p. 135.

[128] US Embassy Caracas to US State Department (27 July 1974), p. 2: 1974CARACA07083, AAD.

[129] UK FCO to UK Embassy Buenos Aires and other missions (7 February 1975), p. 3: FCO 76/1098, TNA.

[130] Ibid. Another argument, advanced by the West German delegate Elmar Rauch, was that the transit passage regime was beneficial to states bordering strategic straits because it

This argument obviously made no concession to the idea that maximising the range of submarines (and submarine hunters) might increase the risk of conflict, and it received a mixed reception. In Dar-as-Salaam, for example, Joseph Warioba told the British high commissioner Mervyn Brown that while he saw the need for balanced nuclear deterrence he thought the international community should find a better way of maintaining world peace than giving the superpowers a free run through straits.[131] He also dismissed the suggestion that submarines had to transit straits submerged in order to avoid detection, arguing that 'the Americans had admitted that their technology already enabled them to detect underwater vessels passing through the Straits of Gibraltar'.[132] (Warioba may have had in mind the recently reported submarine detection towers installed by the Americans in the Azores to monitor traffic through the strait.[133]) In New Delhi, meanwhile, members of the British high commission argued that it was pointless lobbying Indian officials as instructed because India, as one of the main supporters of the Indian Ocean peace zone, 'could not conceivably accept proposals based on an argument that it was essential for there to be undetected nuclear weapon carrying submarines in the Indian Ocean'.[134]

Nandan's Move

At the next session of the law of the sea conference, held in Geneva from 17 March to 9 May 1975, two developments shaped the negotiations about straits. One development was conference president Shirley Amerasinghe's decision – in response to the problem caused by the lack of a working text – that the three committee chairs should each submit a set of draft articles to him at the end of the session, synthesising the progress of the committee debates up to that point. These drafts, combined, would form a single negotiating text that would provide the basis

kept them out of 'the vicious cycle of escalation in times of crisis and tension': 'Military uses of the ocean', *German Yearbook of International Law* 28 (1985), 229, 247.

131 M. Brown to H. A. Dudgeon (18 February 1975), p. 1: FCO 76/1098, TNA.

132 Ibid.

133 K. Tsipis, 'Antisubmarine warfare', in Stockholm International Peace Research Institute (ed.), *World armaments and disarmament, SIPRI yearbook 1974* (Stockholm: Almqvist & Wiksell, 1974), p. 317.

134 T. C. S. Stitt to UK FCO (5 March 1975): FCO 76/1098, TNA.

for the discussion at the next session. This gave considerable power to the committee chairs, or, in the case of the second committee, to the Fijian rapporteur Satya Nandan, who persuaded the chair Reynaldo Galindo Pohl to delegate the drafting of the articles to him.[135] The other development was British delegate Harry Dudgeon's decision, as part of his campaign to win wider acceptance of transit passage, to join forces with Nandan to co-convene a secret group on straits known as the UK-Fiji group. The aim was to persuade the invited delegates (most of them representing 'moderate' and 'like-minded' straits states[136]) to draft a set of articles endorsing transit passage through straits, which, it was hoped, would then be accepted by the second committee as the basis for the end-of-session text.

This UK-Fiji group got to work, joined by the representatives from Argentina, Bahrain, Denmark, Ethiopia, Iceland, Italy, Kenya, Lebanon, Nigeria, Singapore, the United Arab Emirates and Venezuela, and later Australia, Bulgaria and India.[137] They took as their starting point an amalgam of two motions covering straits submitted in 1974: the British one, already discussed, and another submitted by Nandan on behalf of Fiji.[138] The group's deliberations were off the record, but the chairs helpfully kept the other G5 states abreast of developments. The Americans, for example, were able to report to Washington that Nandan, who was 'feeling heavy pressure on archipelago issue', had been instrumental in winning the group's support for the view that warships should enjoy the same rights as other vessels in straits.[139] Within a few weeks, the G5 received further good tidings. The UK-Fiji group had not only unanimously endorsed the idea of transit passage but had also produced a detailed twelve-article draft on straits incorporating the idea. Meanwhile, the Americans received word, presumably from Nandan himself, that the group's 'text will be one used . . . in preparing single package text' at

[135] Nandan wrote: 'I ended up doing the whole of the Second Committee's Single Negotiating Text although it appears in [Galindo Pohl's] name as Chairman': 'The third session of the conference on the law of the sea' (9 June 1975), p. 2: folder 1, box 69, Mss82-6, Satya Nandan papers, UVLSL.

[136] UK Ministry of Defence, 'Chilean concern about the Law of the Sea' (2 June 1975), p. 1: DEFE 24/955, TNA.

[137] US Mission Geneva to US State Department (19 April 1975), p. 1: 1975GENEVA02754, AAD.

[138] UNLOSC III, vol. 3, A/Conf.62/C.2/L.3 (3 July 1974) and A/Conf.62/C.2/L.19 (23 July 1974).

[139] US State Department to all posts (19 April 1975), p. 4: 1975STATE072297, AAD.

the end of the session,[140] and that it would likely be 'incorporated virtually intact'.[141]

Before any of that could happen, though, the powers still had to shepherd the UK-Fiji group's draft articles through the second committee. The Americans and the Soviets agreed beforehand that they would challenge some of the less important provisions with the aim of helping out Galindo Pohl in the chair who, when confronted by arguments from the other side, could put on the appearance of having steered a centre course between two extreme views.[142]

Representatives of some straits states who had not been invited to join the no-longer-secret UK-Fiji group voiced more genuine dissatisfaction. Canada, Norway and Chile resented being railroaded into accepting draft articles in whose creation they had played no part, and objected to two provisions which they said went beyond the law. One was article 1(3) of the UK-Fiji draft, which stated that transit passage was the exercise of freedom of navigation and overflight 'between one part of the high seas and another part of the high seas or between the high seas and a state bordering the strait'; and the other was article 7, which referred to 'straits in which the regime of transit passage applies in accordance with article 1'.[143] The effect of these, they argued, would be to 'create entirely new categories of . . . straits' by potentially internationalising internal waters on the landward side of straight baselines along indented coastlines overlapped by a strait,[144] affecting, for example, Norway's Indreleia, Canada's Northwest Passage and Chile's portion of the Beagle Channel.[145] This criticism carried weight, and changes were made: Nandan's end-of-session submission to the negotiating text specified that internal waters within an international strait would not be affected by the transit passage regime

[140] US Mission Geneva to US State Department (19 April 1975), p. 1: 1975GENEVA02754, AAD.

[141] US Mission Geneva to US State Department (24 April 1975), p. 1: 1975GENEVA02905, AAD.

[142] US Mission Geneva to US State Department (19 April 1975), pp. 1–2: 1975GENEVA02754, AAD.

[143] US Mission Geneva to US State Department (19 April 1975), s. 1, p. 2, s. 2, p. 2: 1975GENEVA02757, AAD.

[144] US Mission Geneva to US State Department (1 May 1975), p. 2: 1975GENEVA03116, AAD.

[145] The Chileans was also concerned that acceptance of the text would prejudice their position in the ongoing arbitration with Argentina over the Beagle Channel: US Embassy Santiago to US State Department (20 May 1975), p. 2: 1975SANTIA03416, AAD.

'unless they were considered as part of the high seas or territorial sea prior to the drawing of straight baselines'.[146]

Yet despite the complaints about the UK-Fiji articles, it was clear from the debate in the committee that opposition to transit passage was starting to ebb. As the Americans noted,

> Our hard core straits opposition has been reduced to China, Albania, Spain, Oman, Yemen, Democratic Yemen, and the Philippines, while supporters of the UK-Fiji text are growing, notably including some Arabs, Argentina, India, Kenya, the Bahamas, and Fiji . . . Indonesia and Malaysia have been virtually silent, and Morocco launched a colonialism attack on Spain linked to the straits issue.[147]

One reason for the softening of the opposition was that the Americans had signalled their willingness to be flexible about dead-end straits, which would be governed as before by an innocent passage regime. This brought some Arab states onside, because it met their concern about the dead-end Strait of Tiran, and suited those who were themselves dependent on access to straits used for international navigation.[148] Another reason was that the powers insisted that transit passage was a make-or-break issue; without it, none of them would become parties to the treaty.[149] Another reason still was that the powers argued that the straits states opposed the free movement of trade, even though the latter stressed that commercial vessels would be unaffected.[150] Finally, the straits states were under pressure not only from the powers but also from some other coastal states which would not tolerate a hard stance on straits that endangered the promise of a 200-mile economic zone.

Using these levers, the powers' objective of isolating the hardliners within the straits group paid off. Nandan amplified this success by inserting the Fiji-UK group's draft articles into the end-of-session text, and the powers claimed this as 'a major negotiating victory'.[151] From

[146] Article 35, UNLOSC III, vol. 5, A/Conf.62/WP.8/PartII (7 May 1976), p. 157.

[147] US Mission Geneva to US State Department (10 May 1975), p. 3: 1975GENEVA03400, AAD.

[148] 'Current status of the International Law of the Sea negotiations' (10 February 1975), p. 6: CIA-RDP86T00608R000600140001-1, CIAHC.

[149] H. Djalal, 'The developing countries and the Law of the Sea Conference', *Indonesian Quarterly* 9 (1981), 59, 63–64.

[150] Ibid., 64.

[151] US Mission Geneva to US State Department (19 April 1975), p. 1: 1975GENEVA02754, AAD.

now on, their tactics would shift from offensive to defensive, as they sought to prevent any further changes to the text.[152]

After the *Showa Maru* Spill

The Malacca-Singapore straits states' fears about pollution were realised on 6 January 1975, when the 237,000 dwt Japanese supertanker *Showa Maru* ran aground in Indonesian waters eight miles south of Singapore harbour and deposited a two-inch-thick oil slick in the Singapore Strait. The Japanese transport ministry immediately dispatched Tomita Choji, head of the shipping bureau's overseas division, to Singapore to survey the damage and to stave off moves by those affected to use the incident to restrict the larger tankers' passage through the straits.[153] More strandings, collisions and spills followed. On 17 April 1975, the in-ballast Japanese tanker *Tosa Maru* collided with the fully loaded Japanese-owned Liberian-registered tanker *Cactus Queen* near St John's Island off Singapore, causing explosions, setting the sea alight and sinking *Tosa Maru.*[154] On 5 April 1976, the Shell-owned British tanker *Mysella* struck a reef near St John's Island after taking on bunkers at Singapore, ripping open two tanks and polluting Singaporean and Indonesian waters as far south as Pulau Sambu and Pulau Batam.[155] And on 24 July 1976, the Philippines-registered tanker *Diego Silang* was holed in a collision with a Soviet freighter *Vysotsk* and an empty tanker *Brazilian Faith* near Batu Pahat in Malaysia, creating a slick that lodged in the mangrove groves along the coast and ruined the prawning grounds at the mouth of the Sungai Muar.[156]

Spurred by these events, the three straits states pursued two courses of action. The first was to specify a minimum under-keel clearance for the largest tankers as part of traffic separation schemes within the straits; and

[152] The Americans reported, 'The maritime powers, including the U.S., have strongly opposed further negotiations on the straits issue, and resisted the formation of special groups within the [c]onference for further work': US mission to the UN to US State Department (17 September 1976), p. 2: 1976USUNN03795 (pt. 2), AAD.

[153] US Embassy Tokyo to US State Department (8 January 1975), p. 2: 1975TOKYO00224, AAD.

[154] '2 am: two ships ablaze off S'pore', *Straits Times* (18 July 1975).

[155] J. Daniel, 'Clean-up battle as tanker hits reef', *Straits Times* (6 April 1976); and 'Mysella oil spill: mop-up bill for Shell', *Straits Times* (8 April 1976).

[156] 'Singapore alert as oil spill moves south', *Straits Times* (27 July 1976); 'Navy wins oil spill battle', *Straits Times* (29 July 1976); and US Embassy Kuala Lumpur to US State Department (5 August 1976), p. 2 (quoting *New Straits Times*): 1976KUALA04488, AAD.

the second was to establish liability for damages caused by accidents. Talks between the Malaysians and the Japanese in mid-1976 focussed on setting the lower limit of under-keel clearance, with the Malaysians calling for a clearance of four metres and the Japanese for three metres, calculated as two metres plus one metre squat at twelve knots (squat being the effect of the hull sinking deeper into the water at higher speeds).[157]

Both sides edged towards the mid-point of 3.5 metres under-keel clearance. For the Japanese, a four-metre under-keel clearance would affect around eighty of its deep-draught tankers then using the Malacca-Singapore straits route.[158] They would have to either travel light, losing an estimated 16,000 tonnes of oil for each extra metre of clearance,[159] or take the deeper but longer routes through Indonesia's Lombok and Macassar straits, adding thirty hours more time, fuel and operating costs to each journey. According to the Indonesians, the extra cost of transiting the Lombok Strait amounted to less than one-half cent a barrel a day,[160] or if a VLCC was carrying two million barrels, less than $10,000 a day. But this calculation might not have factored in all expenses: another estimate from the same period suggested that once depreciation and other costs had been added to a VLCC's daily running cost of US$6,000–8,000, the overall total rose to US$30,000–50,000 a day.[161]

Meanwhile at the conference, the Malaysians made little headway against the Nandan-authored text endorsing transit passage, which, according to delegation leader Abdul Kadir bin Yusuf, 'shortchanged' the straits states.[162] One problem was that their cause was impeded by the introduction of the 'rule of silence' into the second committee in 1976. This obliged all states not actively opposed to the negotiating text to stay silent, while compelling those who were opposed to drum up vocal support to persuade the chair (now the Venezuelan Andrés Aguilar) to make amendments. The new rule, instigated by the powers to preserve their achievements so far, was presented as a way to speed up the proceedings by cutting down on speeches. In fact, it removed nuance, encouraged inertia and made it easier to cast opponents as a minority,

157 US Embassy Kuala Lumpur to US State Department (6 July 1976), p. 1: 1976KUALA03826, AAD.
158 Djalal, 'The developing countries', 64.
159 'Malaysian amendments to RSNT' (u.d., c. December 1976), p. 1: FCO 76/1356, TNA.
160 UK Embassy Jakarta to UK FCO (7 January 1977), p. 2: FCO 76/1637, TNA.
161 Mostert, *Supership*, p. 25.
162 Editorial, 'Still at sea', *New Straits Times* (7 September 1976).

which, according to the Indonesian delegate Hasjim Djalal, 'certified the death warrant of the struggle of the straits states'.[163]

Another problem was that the straits states' group began to disintegrate under the pressures imposed on its members by the powers, the coastal states and, in a few cases, domestic politics. One casualty was Spain, hitherto the leader of the campaign against transit passage. As delegate José de Yturriaga recalled:

> After the publication of the ISNT [informal single negotiating text of 1975] discouragement spread in the ranks of the Straits States' Group. Even the Spanish delegation, which had been its main sponsor, underwent an internal crisis. The Ministry of the Navy, sensitive to the pressures of the United States and other NATO countries, decided to ... change course towards positions closer to the regime of transit passage. The Ministry of the Air Forces, on the other hand, maintained its firm opposition to the right of transit passage of aircraft over straits. Therefore, the Spanish delegation lost both coherence and cohesion, and had to keep a lower profile in its established position as defender of the *status quo* of the regime of innocent passage. This internal crisis affected the work of the Group. During the IV session of the Conference ... [of 1976] the Group died of natural consumption and its members recovered their freedom of action and acted separately in the defence of their interests.[164]

Among the states striking out on their own was Malaysia, whose officials drew up a list of amendments to the text on straits, which they then distributed to various nations, including Britain, Indonesia, Japan, the United States and the USSR. One change related to articles 39 and 40 of the negotiating text (later, articles 41 and 42 of the convention), which rang alarm bells for the Malaysians because they proposed the effective internationalisation of straits under the tutelage of IMCO.

Article 39(4) specified that '*Before* designating or substituting sea lanes or prescribing or substituting traffic separation schemes, States bordering straits *shall* refer proposals to the competent international organization with a view to their adoption'[165] – this organisation being IMCO. And article 40(1)(a) and (b) reinforced and expanded the obligation to conform to international supervision and standards, stating:

[163] Djalal, 'The developing countries', 64.

[164] J. A. de Yturriaga, *Straits used for international navigation: a Spanish perspective* (Dordrecht: Martinus Nijhoff, 1991), p. 125.

[165] UNLOSC III, vol. 5, A/Conf.62/WP.8/Rev.1/PartII (7 May 1976), p. 159. Emphases added.

> 1. Subject to the provisions of this section, States bordering straits may make laws and regulations relating to transit passage through straits, in respect of all or any of the following:
>
> (a) The safety of navigation and the regulation of maritime traffic, as provided in article 39;
> (b) The prevention of pollution by giving effect to applicable international regulations regarding the discharge of oil, oily wastes and other noxious substances in the strait . . .[166]

This meant that straits states had no independent right to prescribe laws or regulations on safety and pollution in straits; they first had to meet the requirements set by 'the competent international organization' and the 'applicable international regulations'.[167]

Finally, article 40(2) stated that, 'Such laws and regulations shall not discriminate in form or fact amongst foreign ships, nor in their application have the practical effect of denying, hampering or impairing the right of transit passage as defined in this section.'[168] Malaysia hitched its amendment to this last paragraph, proposing to insert after it a new paragraph that declared:

> Notwithstanding the provisions of paragraph 2, where the geographical peculiarities of the straits so determine, the state bordering the strait may make laws and regulations limiting the right of transit passage of such vessels, which because of their insufficient Under-Keel-Clearance, constitute a grave danger to safety of navigation or to the marine environment of that State. Such laws and regulations shall be made in consultation with the competent international organisation.[169]

This proposed change, relating to the making of laws and regulations, is significant for four reasons. First, the Malaysians tacitly accepted (after having previously opposed) the right of transit passage with their acknowledgment of 'the provisions of paragraph 2' of article 40, which

[166] Ibid., pp. 159–160. The reference to 'applicable international regulations' in article 40(1)(b) was to the International Convention for the Prevention of Pollution from Ships of 1973, later modified by the Protocol of 1978 relating to the International Convention for the Prevention of Pollution from Ships [hereafter, Protocol of 1978] (signed 17 February 1978, EIF 2 October 1983) 1340 UNTS 61.

[167] The remaining sub-paragraphs of article 41(1) – (c) permitting the adoption of laws and regulations on fishing vessels, and (d) permitting the adoption of laws and regulations on smuggling – address activities which would negate the right of transit passage.

[168] UNLOSC III, vol. 5, A/Conf.62/WP.8/Rev.1/PartII (7 May 1976), p. 160.

[169] Proposed Malaysian amendments to revised single negotiating text (u.d., c. June 1976), p. 7: FCO 76/1358, TNA.

referred directly to this right. Second, while accepting the principle of transit passage, they attempted to carve out an exception for straits with 'geographical peculiarities' – namely, the shallow and hazardous Malacca-Singapore straits. Third, they sought to make explicit reference to under-keel clearance within the convention itself, rather than confining it to bilateral discussions with, say, Japan. Finally, they held out for 'consultation with' (not prior approval by) 'the competent international organization' (IMCO), when making laws and regulations on under-keel clearance.

The Japanese outright opposed the Malaysian amendment. Officials in Tokyo stated that although the Malaysians had nominally accepted transit passage, their approach was nonetheless 'designed to confer on the states bordering the straits prescriptive competence, after consultation with international body, to establish safety margins of the deep-draught vessels such as very large crude carriers passing through the strait'.[170] This, they said, caused the most serious concern because 'the adverse effects ... on the Japanese economy would be immense'.[171] Not everyone was persuaded that Japan would suffer as much as claimed, however. Hasjim Djalal, by now treaty affairs director at the Indonesian foreign affairs department, thought the Japanese were just 'shadow boxing' over the impact of laws and regulations governing under-keel clearance: he said that if Japanese deep-draught tankers could no longer transit the Malacca Strait, and if they chose not to use the deeper Lombok Strait, they could always be transferred to the Japan-to-Alaska run.[172]

It was undeniable, though, that there were greater economic implications for Japan than for the other powers. In New York, counsellor Iguchi Takeo at Japan's UN mission fretted that the Americans, whom he thought were swayed by a vocal environmental lobby at home, seemed to be more 'flexible' about straits states' restrictions on tankers than they were about restrictions on warships.[173] As a consequence, the Japanese delegates took a very hard line at a G5 meeting in December 1976, warning the Americans and the Soviets that if they made any concessions to Malaysia on tanker traffic, and especially on under-keel clearance, Tokyo in turn might be forced to support calls for submarines to surface

[170] UK Embassy Tokyo to UK FCO (no. 526) (10 June 1976), p. 1: FCO 76/1358, TNA.
[171] Ibid., p. 2.
[172] A. C. Stuart to M. J. Williams (28 March 1977), p. 2: FCO 76/1638, TNA.
[173] UK Embassy Tokyo to UK FCO (no. 525) (10 June 1976), p. 1: FCO 76/1358, TNA.

when transiting straits[174] – Japan's preferred position regarding its own straits.[175]

At the same time, the Japanese were beginning to question whether IMCO could be relied on to hold the line against the straits states, with Iguchi telling the British that he had seen a 'steady erosion of IMCO's position as an organisation protecting the interests of the major maritime powers', and that he was not sure that it could be depended on to back Japan's '2 metres plus squat' position against Malaysia's call for a greater under-keel clearance.[176]

On 24 February 1977, the three straits states increased the pressure on Japan, when they issued a joint statement dealing with the safety of navigation in the Malacca-Singapore straits. This required that all vessels maintain a 3.5 metre under-keel clearance throughout all parts of the straits; that all tankers and large vessels should be adequately covered by insurance and compensation schemes; and that all deep-draught vessels should stay in a designated deep-water route in the Singapore Strait without overtaking other vessels or exceeding a twelve-knot speed limit.[177] The statement also proposed that they coordinate their policies to prevent pollution, and that they delineate three more traffic separation schemes (at One Fathom Bank, Horsburgh Lighthouse, and the Main Strait and Phillip Channel) with the straits-users bearing the costs of implementation.[178] There was no mention of introducing pollution measures in conformity with international regulations, or of submitting the traffic separation schemes for prior approval to IMCO, as specified by the conference negotiating text.

This statement stirred a new round of criticism, to which Hasjim Djalal responded in a meeting with the British embassy counsellor Andrew Stuart in Jakarta. He argued that it was absurd for the shipping companies to claim that the straits states were imposing restrictions on the passage of tankers for 'selfish reasons', when in fact their sole concern

[174] 'Group of V meeting' (20 December 1976), p. 1: FCO 76/1357, TNA.

[175] Tokyo, adhering to the non-nuclear principles prohibiting the creation, possession and presence of nuclear weapons on Japanese territory, disagreed with the other maritime powers about the uninhibited passage of nuclear vessels through straits, but agreed to remain silent in the name of G5 unity. On their silence, see US Embassy Jakarta to US State Department (27 March 1974), s. 1, p. 2: 1974JAKART03748, AAD.

[176] UK Embassy Tokyo to UK FCO (no. 525) (10 June 1976), p. 1: FCO 76/1358, TNA.

[177] 'Joint statement on safety of navigation in the straits of Malacca and Singapore' (24 February 1977), pp. 1–3: FCO 76/1638, TNA.

[178] Ibid.

was to preserve the coastal environment.[179] He also claimed that it made absolutely no difference to the Indonesians whether tankers transited through the Malacca or the Lombok straits because either way the shipping companies paid no dues for doing so.[180] (In fact, it *did* make a difference: the diversion of deep-draught tanker traffic from the Malacca-Singapore straits to the straits of Lombok and Makassar would benefit Indonesia by driving some Singapore-bound traffic towards bunkering facilities at the Javanese port of Cilicap.)

Stuart, obviously not wholly persuaded by Djalal's argument, assured him that although nobody begrudged the straits states their wish for environmental security, the 'purity of their motives' was not the only issue:

> [I]t had also to be considered whether the Schemes proposed by them to protect themselves were reasonable when set against the general international interest in Freedom of Passage; and even whether in some cases the Schemes might lead to an actual increase in insecurity, because the co[a]stal States had not appreciated all the technical factors concerned. This was where IMCO came in. Nobody was trying to prevent the Malacca Straits states from bringing into force a reasonable Traffic Separation Scheme, but if they did so unilaterally, this would be a bad precedent for other, perhaps less well prepared, Schemes in other Straits.[181]

Not for the first time, an envoy from a major shipping state would inform an Indonesian official that international navigation should take priority over national interest.

The Deal with Malaysia

After the three states' joint statement, the Americans decided to take the initiative on behalf of the G5 and broker a deal with the Malaysians (but not with Indonesia, with whom they were also wrangling over navigation through archipelagos).[182] Elliot Richardson, the new leader of the US delegation appointed by Jimmy Carter's administration, and legal adviser Bernard Oxman met with attorney general Abdul Kadir bin Yusuf in

[179] A. C. Stuart to M. J. Williams (28 March 1977), p. 1: FCO 76/1638, TNA.
[180] Ibid.
[181] Ibid., pp. 1–2.
[182] For Indonesian justice minister Mochtar Kusumaatmadja's negative reaction to hearing of the American's agreement with Malaysia: US State Department to US posts (12 April 1977), p. 7: 1977STATE081604, AAD.

Kuala Lumpur on 28–29 March 1977. The Americans sought Malaysia's abandonment of its aforementioned amendment to the text relating to straits.[183] In return, they said they would help Malaysia to secure IMCO's endorsement of a traffic separation scheme through the Malacca-Singapore straits incorporating a 'reasonable' under-keel clearance provision, and they would agree to Malaysia submitting an on-the-record interpretive statement of the straits component of the convention, also covering under-keel clearance.[184] With this offer, the British reported to London, the powers had managed to 'buy off' the Malaysians.[185]

But this was not the end of the story. During the discussion, Kadir and his team managed to breach the apparently watertight transit passage regime by insisting on straits states being allowed to enforce their laws and regulations on safety and pollution against foreign vessels in straits in exceptional circumstances – namely, in the event of a vessel causing or threatening to cause a major pollution incident. (The negotiating text as it stood did not permit straits states to take enforcement measures against a transiting foreign vessel if it contravened navigational safety or pollution control measures and did not voluntarily enter one of the state's ports or offshore terminals, where action was permitted; the state's only recourse would be to transmit information about the vessel's conduct to the flag state and the next port of call.) The Malaysians did not focus on the part of the second committee's text dealing with straits, however, but concentrated instead on the part of the third committee's text dealing with pollution, which in article 42 restated the position on unrestricted transit passage:

> Nothing in Sections 6, 7 and 8 [relating to pollution] shall affect the legal regime of straits used for international navigation.[186]

In 1977, the Malaysians wanted to either delete this article or expand it, and the Americans agreed to a follow-on sentence:

> However, if a foreign ship other than those referred to in section 10 [vessels with sovereign immunity] of this Part of the present Convention has committed a violation of the laws and regulations referred to in subparagraphs 1

[183] US Embassy Kuala Lumpur to US Embassy London (29 March 1977), p. 1: 1977KUALA01938, AAD.

[184] Ibid., pp. 2–3.

[185] K. S. Pitt and S. S. Crew, 'UNLOSC: fourth week' (17 June 1977), p. 4: DEFE 24/1185, TNA.

[186] UNLOSC III, vol. 5, A/Conf.62/WP.8/Rev.1/PartIII (7 May 1976), p. 180.

> *(a)* and *(b)* of article 42 [laws and regulations of states bordering straits relating to transit passage] causing or threatening major damage to the marine environment of the straits, the States bordering the straits may take appropriate enforcement measures and if so shall respect *mutatis mutandis* the provisions of section 7 [legal remedies] of this Part of the present Convention.[187]

In sum, a straits state could take appropriate enforcement measures if a vessel without sovereign immunity caused or threatened 'major damage' to the marine environment in violation of laws and regulations on navigational safety and pollution control. Did this constitute an exception to the transit passage regime? As Hugo Caminos noted, the word 'however' linking the two sentences indicated that it did.[188]

That said, the provision was carefully crafted to restrict the straits states' scope for action. For one thing, it was clear that it was designed to deal only with exceptional circumstances, while also being unclear about the threshold of 'major damage' (thus leaving the door open to the argument that anything less than a *Torrey Canyon*-scale spill would not meet the criterion). For another thing, the revised article was hedged with qualifications. It dealt only with pollution of the marine environment (not the atmosphere above), only with straits (not other bodies of water), and only with pollution from vessels not enjoying sovereign immunity (i.e. not warships). In addition, the cross-reference to article 42(1)(b) indicated that it would cover only discharges (not dumping) from vessels, and only oil, oily wastes and other noxious substances (not 'harmful substances carried by sea in packaged form', sewage and garbage[189]). Finally, the vessel threatening or causing major damage would violate not the convention but the laws and regulations of the straits state – assuming, that is, that the state had already enacted these after referral to the relevant international organisation and in conformity with the applicable international regulations. (One study noted in 2007 that Malaysia had not introduced new laws meeting these criteria, and therefore lacked enforcement powers in the event of major damage in the Malacca Strait.[190])

[187] Article 234, UNLOSC III, vol. 8, A/Conf.62/WP.10 (15 July 1977), p. 40.

[188] 'The legal régime of straits in the 1982 United Nations Convention on the Law of the Sea', *Recueil des Cours de l'Académie de Droit International de La Haye* 205 (1987), 9, 174–175.

[189] These other vessel-source pollutants would later be cited in optional annexes III–V of the Protocol of 1978, 255, 256, 263.

[190] A. Emran, 'The regulation of vessel-source pollution in the straits of Malacca and Singapore' (University of Wollongong Thesis Collection, 2007), p. 134.

After the meeting in Kuala Lumpur, Oxman cabled a report to American diplomatic missions explaining why the second sentence had been added to article 42, and conceding, without saying as much, that an exception to transit passage had been admitted:

> USdel was faced with situation in which it was clear that agreement resulting in withdrawal of Malaysian amendments could not be reached without addressing enforcement question. We considered following factors in reaching a conclusion.
>
> A. We did not wish to amend straits articles, and felt Malaysian pressure would receive strong sympathy at conference which would result in formation of negotiating group on straits in committee II, where others would take advantage of situation to erode the articles.
>
> ...
>
> E. In the absence of some understanding, the straits states might proceed to impose the regulations soon unilaterally, and point to acquiescence in fact over time as recognition of their authority to regulate passage unilaterally, without IMCO approval.
> F. If section [on safeguards including article 42 of the third committee text[191]] were applied mutatis mutandis to straits, *we would strongly limit and qualify the enforcement powers of straits states.*
> G. A change in part [covering pollution] is less risky than one in part [covering straits]. Article 42 ... was being subject to attack anyway, an agreed change could deflect the attacks of extremist straits states.[192]

The way Oxman told it, the Americans were merely tossing the straits states a small bone, but the comment that 'we would strongly limit and qualify the enforcement powers of straits states' gives the game away: a concession had been made. Not only that, but Oxman revealed that it was not the Malaysians who drafted the initial version of the sentence, but the Americans – possibly Oxman himself. He wrote:

> On basis foregoing, we presented Malaysians with a draft amendment to ... article 42. Minister Kadir said it was an improvement over Malaysia's amendment to this article, and met his concerns. We did not rpt [repeat] not elaborate on what enforcement actions would be permissible in light of the other relevant provisions.[193]

[191] UNLOSC III, vol. 5, A/Conf.62/WP.8/Rev.1/PartIII (7 May 1976), pp. 179–180.
[192] US State Department to US posts (12 April 1977), pp. 4–5: 1977STATE081604, AAD. Emphasis added.
[193] Ibid., pp. 5–6.

Oxman did not specify what the 'other relevant provisions' were, and the text did not indicate what enforcement measures were permissible in exceptional circumstances. (Some commentators have since argued that when a vessel threatens or causes major pollution damage in a strait, a state may be guided by the enforcement provisions applicable to the territorial sea.[194]) Thereafter, article 42, as amended, was transported virtually unchanged into the convention as article 233[195] – a testament both to the Malaysians' persistence and to the Americans' pragmatism.[196] Richardson, the delegation's new broom, wanted to get the treaty signed, and the added sentence broke a deadlock.

*

This exception was significant, but nowhere near as significant as the new rule providing for transit passage. Thenceforth, the text, and later the convention, upheld 'freedom of navigation and overflight' in straits used for international navigation, provided that vessels refrained from activities 'other than those incident to their normal modes of continuous and expeditious transit'.[197] The words 'navigation', broadly construed, indicated that the regime covered submarines as well as surface vessels, while the phrase 'normal modes' confirmed that submarines, whose normal mode is underwater, were permitted to transit straits submerged. The hold of article 14(6) of the 1958 convention had been broken.[198]

The new regime gave the powers almost everything they had sought in straits, despite the initial hostility to the idea of free transit. As testimony to the effectiveness of this campaign, almost all of the straits states eventually submitted to the idea of transit passage, including the states bordering the Singapore-Malacca straits. And so, by the alchemy that governs all law-making, the maritime powers' will on navigation solidified into treaty law.

[194] D. R. Rothwell, 'International straits', in D. R. Rothwell *et al.* (eds.), *The Oxford handbook of the law of the sea* (Oxford: Oxford University Press, 2017), pp. 123–124. See also, R. Beckman, 'The international regime governing the safety of navigation and the prevention of pollution in international straits', *Singapore Journal of International and Comparative Law* 2 (1998), 350, 353–354; and Churchill and Lowe, *The law of the sea*, pp. 108–109.

[195] UNCLOS, 493.

[196] The accompanying interpretive statement, drafted by Malaysia in consultation with the powers, could be read as suggesting that article 233 was applicable only to the Malacca-Singapore straits: UNLOSC III: A/Conf.62/L.145 (29 April 1982), p. 250.

[197] Articles 38(2) and 39(1)(c), UNCLOS, 411.

[198] The relationship between the convention and earlier treaties is addressed in article 311 (ibid., 519).

7

The Archipelagic Concept

Division, Unity and Archipelagic Statehood

When Indonesia and the Philippines, inspired in part by the *Fisheries* decision, launched their respective campaigns in the mid-fifties for the recognition of their special archipelagic status, the Indonesian chief justice Wiryono Projodikoro proclaimed that the legal relationship between the land and the sea would undergo a 'radical' transformation.[1] Delegates from the two states stressed the organic relationship between land and sea within an archipelago, contrasting it to the existing law's terrestrial orientation, which assumed that land was central and the sea peripheral. Mochtar Kusumaatmadja, architect of Indonesia's claim to archipelagic statehood in 1957,[2] rejected 'a continent-based approach, a land-based approach, in which islands are viewed as mere accidents of geography' in favour of the ancient Greek approach to the Aegean, 'as a unit with islands in it'.[3] The modern advocates' stress on the unitary sea-land relationship within archipelagos laid the basis for both international claims to specific maritime entitlements and domestic campaigns for national unity.

In the early seventies, Indonesia and the Philippines were joined by newly independent Fiji, whose delegates, Satya Nandan and solicitor-general Donald McLoughlin, would play a vital role in the campaign for

1 Wiryono also noted that the Jakarta government's decision to claim archipelagic status in 1957 'deviated from international law', but he hoped that other states would appreciate Indonesia's claim: 'Brief on the Indonesian claim to sovereignty over all the waters around, between and connecting the islands of the Indonesian republic' (u.d., c. 1959), p. 3: A1209/96 1958/5904, NAA.

2 The Indonesian government distributed an English-language translation, 'Announcement on the territorial waters of the Republic of Indonesia', to foreign missions on 14 December 1957. See, for example, 'Translation of communique redefining Indonesian waters', Australian Embassy Jakarta to External Affairs Canberra (14 December 1957): A1209/80 1958/5106, pt. 1, NAA; and the abridged version in M. M. Whiteman, *Digest of international law*, vol. 4 (Washington, DC: Department of State, 1965), §8, p. 284.

3 'Supplementary remarks', in L. M. Alexander (ed.), *The law of the sea: needs and interests of the developing countries* (Kingston, RI: Law of the Sea Institute and University of Rhode Island, 1973), pp. 172, 173.

recognition of the archipelagic concept. In 1972, they too stressed the dynamic relationship between land and sea within archipelagos:

> Archipelagic states are all by their very composition dependent to a large extent on the resources of the seas that surround them. Whether by way of subsistence fishing, large scale fisheries or mineral and petroleum exploitation, all archipelagic states are to a greater or lesser extent farmers of the seas around them. By their very nature the islands and the seas between them are so closely interrelated as to form the natural heritage of such states upon which they are dependent for the livelihood of their peoples. Their seas are to them as important as lands are to continental states. Equally the control of those seas assumes as much [importance] to them as does the control of its land areas to a continental state.[4]

This approach may have presented a more nuanced idea of the relationship between land and sea than was already evident in treaty law, but it faced significant challenges from the powers, who wished to retain their high seas navigation and fishing rights. In the seabed committee, the American delegation leader John Stevenson told the Fijians that he could not endorse the archipelagic concept because it would shrink the high seas in the Asia and Pacific regions, thereby hampering the United States' strategic ability 'to operate ... and to act on detecting what other people were doing in the area'.[5] The Japanese delegation meanwhile 'attempted to sell us [the Fijian delegation] the idea that [archipelagic] baselines could be accepted to give the political unity to the islands but the resources enclosed would not be subject to sovereignty and that territorial and fishing limits would begin from the coastlines of each of the islands' – or, to put it another way, the Japanese hoped to drastically revise the concept to allow their fleets to fish in parts of archipelagic waters not 'subject to sovereignty'.[6] The Fijians, who were already greatly perturbed by the scale of Japanese, Korean and Taiwanese tuna fishing operations beyond their existing territorial limits dismissed the proposal as 'totally unacceptable'.[7]

From March 1972 onwards, Nandan and McLoughlin pushed the other claimants – Indonesia, Mauritius and the Philippines – to formulate a set of written principles that they could use to advance and clarify

[4] 'Statement by the Fiji delegation on archipelagic principles' (u.d., c. 14 March 1973), pp. 6–7: folder 7/2, box 69, Mss82-6, Satya Nandan papers, UVLSL.

[5] S. N. Nandan, 'B: Informal discussions on the law of the sea...' (4 April 1972), p. 4: folder 1, box 69, Mss82-6, Satya Nandan papers, UVLSL.

[6] Ibid., p. 5.

[7] Ibid.

the archipelagic concept within the seabed committee. These principles were tabled on 6 February 1973, with the first principle stating:

> An archipelagic State, whose component islands and other natural features form an intrinsic geographical, economic and political entity, and historically have or may have been regarded as such, may draw straight baselines connecting the outermost points of the outermost islands and drying reefs of the archipelago from which the extent of the territorial sea of the archipelagic State is or may be determined.[8]

This principle stressed the integrity of the archipelagic state. It also proposed that to qualify for this status, a cumulative target had to be met: a state's component islands and other natural features had to be an intrinsic geographical, economic and political entity, and moreover, historically must have been regarded as such.[9] The British, French and Japanese delegates criticised this formula for lacking sufficient precision and objectivity, and proposed specifying the maximum length of archipelagic baselines and the land-to-water ratio within those baselines. The Fijians resisted, arguing that the requirement for geographic, economic and political integrity already constituted a precise definition, and that adding more criteria would be counterproductive:

> Where the difference of opinion has arisen has been in attempts to add additional tests, namely those of distance between the islands themselves or a land to water ratio, each of which would have the effect of nullifying the very validity of the established criteria of a geographical, political and economic unity. Either an island group is such an entity or it is not . . . For instance if we accepted a test of ten or even twenty-four miles between islands we would be excluding from the definition . . . both the Fiji archipelago and the Tongan archipelago.[10]

[8] UN Seabed Committee, A/AC.138/SC.II/L.15 (14 March 1973), p. 2.

[9] This proposal and its successors, culminating in the definition of an archipelago set out in article 46(b) of the convention (UNCLOS, 414), did not address the question: historically regarded by whom? In the fifties, A. P. Higgins and C. J. Colombos examined an earlier archipelagic claim, namely, 'the British claim to New Guinea and Papua . . . covering more than one hundred miles from the shore, [which] embraces all the numerous scattered islands which are *considered as forming an archipelago and has been generally admitted by other nations*' and suggested that the claim was make primarily on prescriptive or historic grounds: *The international law of the sea*, 2nd rev. ed. (London: Longmans, Green & Co., 1951.), emphasis added. L. Herman also emphasised that the answer could not rest solely with the claimant, and that the test would be that of effective occupation: 'The modern concept of the off-lying archipelago in international law', *Canadian Yearbook of International Law* 23 (1985), 172, 183.

[10] 'Statement by the Fiji delegation on archipelagic principles' (u.d., c. 14 March 1973), p. 2: folder 7/2, box 69, Mss82–6, Satya Nandan papers, UVLSL.

The second and third principles advanced by the archipelagic claimants addressed the regime within the baselines. These stated:

> 2. The waters within baselines, regardless of their depth or distance from the coast, the sea-bed and the subsoil thereof, and the superjacent air space as well as all their resources belong to, and are subject to the sovereignty of the archipelagic State.
> 3. Innocent passage of foreign vessels through the waters of the archipelagic State shall be allowed in accordance with its national legislation, having regard to the existing rules of international law. Such passage shall be through sea lanes as may be designated for that purpose by the archipelagic State.[11]

When evolving these two principles, they focussed on the two linked ideas central to the archipelagic scheme: archipelagic waters, and the exception, sea lanes – ideas that had each figured in discussions going back to the 1950s. The second principle did not refer directly to archipelagic waters, however, but simply to 'waters within baselines'. Explaining this, the Fijians noted that there were several schools of thought on the legal status of these waters. One school – namely, Fiji – proposed that the waters inside and outside the baselines be deemed territorial sea, subject to innocent passage.[12] Another school – the Philippines – proposed that waters inside baselines should be deemed internal waters, subject to sovereignty, and waters outside be deemed territorial waters, subject to innocent passage.[13] Yet another school – Indonesia – adopted a position sui generis, proposing that waters inside baselines be deemed internal waters but subject to innocent passage (albeit under strict coastal state control).[14] The second principle consequently accommodated all views by simply referring to 'waters within baselines', and the 'waters of the archipelagic State'.

The third principle set out the exception to the rule: sea lanes, designated by the state, which foreign vessels would be obliged to use. What can be seen, then, was the novel application of sea lanes to the novel idea of archipelagic waters to the novel idea of an archipelagic state. When motivating the principles, the claimants stressed that they were not opposed to foreign passage as such, but merely to passage though archipelagic waters outside sea lanes without restraint or regard for the

[11] UN Seabed Committee, A/AC.138/SC.II/L.15 (14 March 1973), p. 2.

[12] 'Statement by the Fiji delegation on archipelagic principles' (u.d., c. 14 March 1973), p. 4: folder 7/2, box 69, Mss82–6, Satya Nandan papers, UVLSL.

[13] Ibid.

[14] Ibid., pp. 4–5.

rights of the inhabitants. After all, one of the Fijian delegates said, a subsistence fisherman 'can derive little enjoyment of his right to fish those waters if . . . his canoe is to run the risk of being run down by an alien warship blundering through on an exercise of war'.[15] The idea of confining foreign vessels to sea lanes was thus designed to protect the localised and diverse concerns of the claimants while at the same time meeting the powers' interest in navigational rights.

This set of archipelagic principles set off flurries of concern among some of the other states. Some African and landlocked nations were worried that if the archipelagic states claimed waters within archipelagic baselines *and* economic zones outside them, they might swallow up more ocean than was their fair share. Nandan assured them that archipelagic waters would cover little more than if each island claimed its own economic zone: the difference would be that baselines would give rise to a belt of zone 'free from indentations' rather than there being 'undulating intersecting "scallops"' around the outer islands .[16]

Another challenge came from the Maltese delegate Arvid Pardo, the leading advocate of the internationalisation of the seabed, who feared that archipelagic claims would drastically reduce common heritage. He argued that the claimants' principles mandated the potential closure of tens of millions of square kilometres as internal waters because almost every island group could claim to be an archipelago: he suggested that Hawaii, for example, could be joined to Wake Island 2,000 miles away on the theory that both were part of the same geological ridge formation.[17] This was stretching the point, as the principles clearly stated that an archipelagic state would have to meet economic, political and historical as well as geographical criteria to qualify as such.

The Regime Takes Shape

The Indonesian and Philippines delegates thought the principles would be sufficient to carry them through to the law of the sea conference, but in the months before the final session of the seabed committee of July–August 1973, Nandan pushed them to table a new, more comprehensive motion based on a text he had produced, arguing that if they did not

[15] Ibid., p. 7.

[16] S. N. Nandan, 'Report of the March–April session of the 1973 Seabed Committee' (u.d., c. April 1973), p. 4: folder 1, box 69, Mss82-6, Satya Nandan papers, UVLSL.

[17] Butcher and Elson, *Sovereignty and the sea,*, pp. 216, 217.

present a package themselves, another delegation might steal a march with a text of their own.[18] The Indonesian and Philippines delegates (along with the Mauritian) agreed, but, according to Nandan they then argued over every word.[19] They were dragging their heals, he said, because they expected 'the mountain' – the maritime powers – 'to come to Mohammed'.[20]

He indicated that there were two major disagreements within the claimants' group. On innocent passage, the Fijians wanted to spell out non-innocent actions, whereas the Indonesian and Philippines delegates wanted to leave it to the state concerned to decide on a case-by-case basis. And on the passage of warships and 'ships with special characteristics' (such as nuclear vessels and ships carrying other hazardous cargoes), the Fijians wanted a less restrictive regime, allowing vessels to pass so long as they did not engage in activities unconnected to passage or pose a threat to the archipelagic state, whereas Indonesia and the Philippines favoured a more restrictive regime requiring prior notification or authorisation.[21] These views reflected different national priorities: Fiji wanted to derive the economic benefits of being on the trans-Pacific route between Australasia and North America, whereas Indonesia and the Philippines were concerned about internal security, foreign insurgents and hostile powers.

The four states eventually produced a resolution, but only after Nandan had threatened to break off negotiations and submit his own motion if they had not reached agreement by a deadline in July 1973.[22] (He was serious: he lodged his own text with the committee secretariat, instructing officers to release it unless he withdrew it beforehand 'to ensure that the Philippines and Indonesia did not rush through draft articles of their own behind our backs and thereby gain advantage over us by having theirs issued first'.[23]) Later, Nandan vented his frustration with his fellow claimants in a report to Suva:

> We have deliberately not narrated ... the blow by blow description of table banging and display of temper and attempts at intimidating us that flowed from the Philippines delegation in particular, and the Indonesians.

[18] S. N. Nandan, 'Summer session of the Seabed Committee' (u.d., c August 1973), p. 1: folder 1, box 69, Mss82-6, Satya Nandan papers, UVLSL.
[19] Ibid., p. 2.
[20] Ibid., p. 9.
[21] Ibid., p. 5.
[22] Ibid., p. 4.
[23] Ibid.

> We took all that came our way in our strides and kept our cool, though it was difficult sometimes.[24]

The resultant resolution followed the basic model set out by the principles, but was altogether sharper and more detailed. It stated that its provisions applied 'only to archipelagic States . . . constituted wholly or mainly by one or more archipelagos' – in other words, not to continental states possessing outlying island groups.[25] It proposed that archipelagos form an 'intrinsic geographical, economic and political entity', but changed '*and* historically have or may have been regarded as such' to '*or* which historically have been regarded as such'.[26] It expressly used the phrase 'archipelagic waters' and indicated that the phrase referred to waters enclosed within baselines.[27] It spelt out that the sovereignty of the archipelagic state extended to the airspace above the archipelagic waters, as well as to the water column, seabed, subsoil and all the resources therein. And it expanded considerably on the idea of sea lanes, addressing among other things traffic separation schemes, the scope of laws and regulations, and the alteration of sea lanes.

On passage, the resolution stated that 'innocent passage of foreign ships shall exist through archipelagic waters'.[28] This was a passively constructed formula that made no mention of the exercise of rights, and with the word 'ships' excluded submarines and aircraft. On sea lanes, the resolution proposed one limit after another, stating that the state may restrict innocent passage by foreign ships to designated sea lanes; that the state may constrain the arena of passage by prescribing traffic separation schemes within these sea lanes; that the state may make laws and regulations regarding sea lanes and traffic separation schemes dealing, among other things, with navigational safety and traffic regulation of vessels including ships with special characteristics; and that the state may not ordinarily suspend passage through particular sea lanes 'except when essential for the protection of its security'.[29]

As it turned out, Nandan's concern about another delegation tabling a motion on archipelagos proved to be well founded, because the British unexpectedly submitted one of their own. This proposal, drawn up after

[24] Ibid., p. 5.
[25] UN Seabed Committee, A/AC.138/SC.II/L.48 (6 August 1973), p. 1.
[26] Ibid.
[27] Ibid., p. 2.
[28] Ibid.
[29] Ibid., p. 3.

consultations between Peter Beazley of the Royal Navy's hydrographic office and the US State Department's geographer Robert Hodgson, proposed that routes through archipelagos used for international navigation between one part of the high seas and another, or between the high seas and another state's territorial sea, should be treated 'as if they were straits'.[30] This signalled the start of a tussle between the maritime powers and the archipelagic claimants over the legal status of sea lanes, with the claimants pushing for a territorial seas regime, and the powers pushing for a straits-like regime. Some, including Nandan, wanted to keep the two regimes apart, fearing the highly politicised debate about straits would contaminate the debate about archipelagos.[31] But later, after Suva came around to the idea of largely unrestricted passage through both, he would be instrumental in ironing out most of the differences between them.

Another feature of the British proposal, which would have concerned Fiji in particular, was that it set out a numbers-based method for determining archipelagos, suggesting that no archipelagic baseline should be longer than forty-eight miles and that the ratio of land to sea within the enclosed area should not exceed 1:5.[32] The ensuing negotiations demonstrated that numbers can be slippery things, however. Fiji's own experience demonstrated this. Various foreign hydrographic experts including Hodgson presented Suva with computations of Fiji's land–sea ratio, which ranged widely, from 1:3.0502,[33] to 1:4.88,[34] to 1:6.31,[35] to 1:6.8.[36] Indeed, as will be seen, the numbers applied to archipelagos proved even more prone to political manipulation than the apparently less objective method of assessing them based on their economic, political, geographical and historically perceived integrity.

[30] UN Seabed Committee, A/AC.138/SC.II/L.44 (2 August 1973), p. 2.

[31] S. N. Nandan, 'Report of the March–April session of the 1973 Seabed Committee' (u.d., c. April 1973), p. 2: folder 1, box 69, Mss82-6, Satya Nandan papers, UVLSL.

[32] UN Seabed Committee, A/AC.138/SC.II/L.44 (2 August 1973), p. 1.

[33] R. D. Hodgson to S. N. Nandan (29 May 1974): folder 6, box 69, Mss82-6, Satya Nandan papers, UVLSL.

[34] This was an earlier estimate made by Hodgson, referred to in: E. J. Cooper (Canadian Hydrographic Service) to S. N. Nandan (11 September 1973), p. 2: folder 6, box 69, Mss82-6, Satya Nandan papers, UVLSL.

[35] Ibid., p. 1.

[36] S. N. Nandan, 'Report on the fourth session of the third United Nations Conference on the Law of the Sea' (u.d., c. May–June 1976), p. 28: folder 1, box 69, Mss82-6, Satya Nandan papers, UVLSL.

The US–Indonesian Minuet

After the opening of the law of the sea conference in December 1973, the Americans embarked on bilateral talks with the Indonesians on archipelagos. These discussions, taking place outside the conference, would set the tempo for the negotiations over archipelagos inside it, until the two states reached agreement on the text nearly four years later.

The American delegates, after discouraging the other G5 members and Australia from involving themselves in these bilateral discussions,[37] chose to conduct talks with Indonesia due to its size, strategic position, and, they thought, susceptibility to pressure on sea lane passage (in contrast to the Philippines, with whom discussions on the subject were frosty and intermittent).[38] By 1973–1974, Nixon's officials had abandoned their earlier attempts to bury the archipelagic concept and, though not formally recognising any claims, now directed their efforts to minimising the number of archipelagic states and maximising navigational freedoms through archipelagic waters. In Indonesia, meanwhile, ministers in Suharto's New Order government had been constructing an archipelagic concept that stressed not only national unity but also enforced national homogeneity. As Hasjim Djalal, a key player in the negotiations, argued, without this concept, there was the danger that the republic would succumb to the separatist island-based 'sentimentality' inculcated during the colonial era.[39]

The negotiations between the Americans and the Indonesians began in earnest on 25 March 1974, when Mochtar Kusumaatmadja, then justice minister, hosted a meeting in Jakarta for a visiting American team led by John Norton Moore. Moore set out the Americans' terms. Washington, he said, could accept the archipelagic concept if it was reasonably limited to ocean-bound states, and if foreign vessels and aircraft were given 'unimpeded archipelagic passage' through 'designated passage areas' in archipelagic waters.[40] That was the deal. He also stated that if agreement could not be reached, the United States would come out in opposition to

[37] See, for example, US Mission to the UN to US State Department (16 March 1973), p. 2: 1973USUNN00906, AAD.

[38] US State Department to US Embassy Manila (29 March 1974), p. 2: 1974STATE063021, AAD.

[39] H. Djalal, *Indonesia and the law of the* sea (Jakarta: Centre for Strategic and International Studies, 1995), p. 337.

[40] US State Department to US posts (9 April 1974), p. 2: 1974STATE071502, AAD.

the archipelagic concept.[41] That was the threat. Before that impasse was reached, however, Moore said that it was necessary to set out some objective criteria for defining an archipelago to forestall claims from a multitude of other states. He proposed a maximum land-sea ratio of 1:5, and an eighty-mile maximum length for archipelagic baselines (ignoring the earlier British proposal of forty-eight miles).[42] These two criteria – so clear and simple – would undergo substantial changes over the next few years as the protagonists tugged them this way and that.

Responding, Mochtar observed that Indonesia and the United States were engaged in a 'minuet', with the Indonesians waiting for the Americans' recognition of their archipelagic status and the Americans waiting for the Indonesians' guarantee of archipelagic passage.[43] He also made four eminently political points about Indonesia's concerns about foreign vessels transiting their archipelago (here reported by US ambassador David Newsom):

> a) We [Indonesia] must be realistic about each other's concerns. We know that we can't tell you [the US] not to use nuclear submarines.
> b) One of traditional passages goes near [Buru] island where political opponents of regime are kept. This presents problems.
> c) Passage areas can't be defined in way that appears to divide Indonesia by high seas passageways. This is difficult political problem, but good lawyers could work it out.
> d) It must be clear that we can put up seabed oil installations in passage areas and Malacca Strait.[44]

The Indonesians and Americans met for a second round of talks a few months later, on 31 May–1 June 1974, this time in Washington, where they discussed sea lanes, an idea derived from a Dutch proposal at the 1958 conference. At this meeting, the Americans again stressed that recognition of archipelagic statehood was dependent on *unimpeded* passage – not innocent passage – through sea lanes. They set out three conditions. All vessels would have rights of passage without the requirement of notification or authorisation.[45] All aircraft would have the right

[41] Ibid., p. 5.
[42] Ibid., pp. 2–3.
[43] US Embassy Jakarta to US State Department (27 March 1974), p. 2: 1974JAKART03779, AAD.
[44] Ibid.
[45] US State Department to US Embassy Caracas (15 June 1974), p. 3: 1974STATE128398, AAD.

to overfly sea lanes, having the same rights as they did over the high seas.[46] And sea lanes would have to be wide enough for safety and manoeuvrability, namely, 'not . . . less than 80 percent of waters between islands or 100 miles, whichever is the larger'.[47] This was a much less restrictive regime than innocent passage, as the archipelagic state could not suspend passage, and sea lane rights applied to both vessels and aircraft. To this list of conditions, the Americans added a fourth: if the claimants wanted recognition as archipelagic states they would be expected to support the United States' position on unimpeded transit passage through straits used for international navigation.[48]

The Americans followed up by distributing to each of the archipelagic claimants a draft purportedly to 'promote . . . universal recognition' of archipelagic statehood at the conference.[49] This velvety promise scarcely concealed the ultimatum within. Repeating some of the themes already raised at the meeting with the Indonesians, it began:

> The treaty would specify that the right of passage is a right of transit in archipelagic sealanes through and over the archipelago state – that is, a right of unimpeded archipelagic passage through the archipelago state – in the normal mode for vessels and aircraft (including submerged transit, overflight [a]bove archipelagic sealanes, and normal measures associated with transit), and with no requirement of notification.[50]

This sentence contained three crucial words: the 'right' of passage (passage would not be endowed by the state); 'unimpeded' (sea lanes, once designated, would not be subject to state regulation);[51] and 'normal', which permitted the submerged passage of submarines and the airborne passage of aircraft as well as the surface passage of ships.[52]

The draft then addressed sea lanes. This approach, as will be seen, was driven by the tactical needs of submarine operations – concealment, dispersion and mobility – and the obverse requirements of aircraft and surface vessels engaged in antisubmarine operations. The draft stated:

46 Ibid.
47 Ibid., p. 2.
48 Ibid., p. 4.
49 US Embassy Manila to US State Department (7 June 1974), s. 2, p. 1: 1974MANILA06706, AAD.
50 Ibid., s. 2, p. 3.
51 US Embassy Manila to US State Department (7 June 1974), s. 2, p. 1: 1974MANILA06741, AAD.
52 Ibid., s. 1, p. 3.

> The treaty would provide that archipelagic passage would take place in designated archipelagic sealanes. Such archipelagic sealanes would run from high seas to high seas and would:
>
> 1. include all normal passage routes through archipelagic waters, and within such routes all normal navigational channels and,
> 2. include an area which at all points is not less than the narrower of:
>
>   A. 80 percent of the area between the nearest points of land on the main islands, i.e., not drying rocks or shoals, or B. 100 nautical miles.[53]

They provided clarifying details. They could accept the archipelagic state's right to designate the location of sea lanes, but this would have to meet strict criteria. First, sea lanes would have to include all normal routes, and within them, all normal navigation channels,[54] thereby enabling the dispersal, if necessary, of submarines and surface taskforces across a broad area. Second, sea lanes would have to be wide enough to meet 'vital US security objectives',[55] thus allowing the concentration, if necessary, of large sea and air forces, as well as enabling surface vessels to zigzag to throw off submarine trackers. Finally, sea lanes would have to be designated in accordance with international criteria and subject to compulsory dispute settlement if disagreements arose over, say, the location of 'normal' routes.[56] A final point: the archipelagic state would have the *duty* (as well as a right) to designate sea lanes; if it declined to do so, the Americans took the view that all of its archipelagic waters should be treated as a sea lane.[57]

Looked at from the other side, vessels moving through sea lanes also had duties.[58] They had to act in conformity with the UN Charter by refraining from threats or acts of force – this meant that a threatened archipelagic state would have to invoke the right of self-defence rather than proclaim non-innocence as the legal basis for action. They were also

[53] US Embassy Manila to US State Department (7 June 1974), s. 2, p. 4: 1974MANILA06706, AAD.

[54] US Embassy Manila to US State Department (7 June 1974), s. 1, p. 3: 1974MANILA06741, AAD.

[55] Ibid., s. 1, p. 4.

[56] Ibid., s. 1, p. 3.

[57] '[I]f an archipelago state does not rpt not establish sealanes, archipelagic sealane passage (not rpt not innocent passage) would be the general regime throughout the archipelago': US State Department to US Embassy Berlin (28 February 1978), p. 2: 1978STATE051056, AAD.

[58] US Embassy Manila to US State Department (7 June 1974), s. 2, p. 3: 1974MANILA06706, AAD.

obliged to move continuously and expeditiously through sea lanes except in cases of distress and *force majeure*, and had to comply with international navigational safety and pollution control regulations.

The reaction from Indonesia and the Philippines to the sea lane proposals was not positive. The Philippines delegation head Arturo Tolentino, veteran of the two earlier UN conferences, told the Americans that the problem with their proposal for unimpeded passage through sea lanes was that it created sovereignty-resistant channels within archipelagic waters:

> [W]e cannot accept the proposition that customary routes for navigation and sealanes in archipelagic waters shall be converted, in effect, into channels of high sea, where foreign vessels of all types may pass freely, without control or regulation by the archipelagic state. This proposal would clearly be a negation of sovereignty over those waters, and constitute a legal absurdity. It would so dilute the concept of sovereignty over archipelagic waters as to reduce it to an attractive but empty word.[59]

Tolentino's point was not that these channels *were* high seas, but that they might as well be, because the archipelagic state's capacity to exercise control over them was virtually negligible. The whole point of claiming archipelagic status was to eliminate the high seas channels that destroyed the integrity of the nation state, yet under the new proposals, sea lanes would merely replicate the high seas channels between islands that the states concerned had sought to remove.

Selling the Idea to the G77

While these talks were afoot, the Indonesians faced a decision about how to pursue their campaign for archipelagic status. Two routes presented themselves: they could either submit to the Americans' escalating demands for unimpeded sea lane passage and transit passage through straits, or they could build support within the G77 for their original idea of innocent passage in sea lanes. The Jakarta government tried to keep both options open, and canvassed support for their own approach in a number of Arab and African capitals.[60] These trips must have been successful because on one occasion, Mochtar, playing on American insecurities, told ambassador David Newsom that he estimated that

[59] Tolentino, *The Philippines and the law of the sea*, p. 29.

[60] S. N. Nandan, 'Archipelagos recent developments' (6 March 1975), p. 2: folder 1, box 69, Mss82-6, Satya Nandan papers, UVLSL.

seventy-nine states would support their line (while fourteen would possibly oppose it and ten would definitely oppose it).[61] Seven months later, he told Newsom that Indonesia was making great progress in their campaign and now had enough African, Arab and Asian votes to secure endorsement of their approach at the conference 'even without big power support'.[62]

The difficulty for all the archipelagic claimants, however, was that the G77's support, while broad, was also shallow and likely to ebb away before the convention was signed. With respect to the African states, the Organisation of African Unity's declaration of 1974 endorsing the archipelagic concept[63] was seen as a great coup, but it had not translated into much active support from its members. Many coastal states would back them only as long as their claims did not complicate their own claims to the economic zone under the package deal, and many landlocked and geographically disadvantaged states were primarily concerned about the potential contraction of seabed common heritage. The archipelagic claimants would therefore have their work cut out to hold onto seventy-nine supporters.

Not only that, but they faced two additional problems in their campaign to win support within the G77. One problem, obviously, was the states who might oppose their claims. The other was the continental states who wished to claim outlying island groups as archipelagos.

First, the potential opponents. In March 1974, the archipelagic claimants converged at the G77's conference in Nairobi. Nandan reported that:

> [A] number of South-East Asian states, specifically Thailand, the Khmer Republic, South Vietnam, Singapore and Malaysia, for the first time openly expressed reservations on some aspects of the concept of archipelagos, and in particular its implications on resources available to them and on passage. Thailand and Singapore, for instance, were concerned that they should not be deprived of their traditional fishing grounds in areas which would be enclosed by archipelagic baselines. Malaysia was concerned that it should continue to enjoy direct navigational access to Sabah through waters that would be enclosed within the Indonesian archipelago.[64]

61 US Embassy Jakarta to US State Department (2 August 1974), p. 2: 1974JAKART09512, AAD.

62 US Embassy Jakarta to US State Department (3 March 1975), p. 1: 1975JAKART02614, AAD.

63 Reproduced in: UNLOSC III, vol. 3, A/Conf.62/33 (19 July 1974), p. 63.

64 'Notes of a meeting held in the prime minister's conference room' (11 April 1974), p. 1: folder 1, box 69, Mss82-6, Satya Nandan papers, UVLSL.

Although the claimants had tried to avoid confrontation with some of these critics by steering the issue away from the plenary and into a more manageable working group,[65] they there encountered another opponent, the South Vietnamese delegate, Le Van Loi. The timing was significant. Just a few months earlier, in January 1974, Chinese forces had ejected the South Vietnamese from the Paracel islands. The regime in Saigon, which was by then on its last legs, was concerned that Beijing would follow up its military intervention with a legal claim based on the archipelagic concept. Le thus tried to pre-emptively discredit the idea by submitting a hostile amendment to the archipelagic claimants' working paper. This, he reported back to Saigon, brought trouble in its train:

> Delegations of Indonesia and Philippines pressed me in brutal manner to withdraw my reservations and insisted that RVN [Republic of Vietnam] should support proposed text which was drafted by them in New York. I resisted their diktat. They resorted to threats and blackmail that they will withdraw their political support to RVN in international conference and report to Manila to ask our government to give in to their request.[66]

Eventually Le folded, agreeing to withdraw his objections to the archipelagic proposals in Nairobi but reserving South Vietnam's position in future negotiations.

Shortly afterwards, the debate about archipelagos moved on to the second committee of the conference. There, the archipelagic claimants faced another threat – the continental states who wished to stretch the archipelagic concept to allow them to enclose their outlying island groups as archipelagos. They included Argentina (claiming the British-occupied Malvinas/Falklands), Canada, Chile, Ecuador, France (claiming its Indo-Pacific colonies), Honduras, India, Peru, Portugal and Spain. The problem for the ocean-bound claimants, who emphasised the integrity of their states *as* archipelagos, was that a deluge of claims from continental states *with* archipelagos might unnerve the powers and sink the campaign for recognition of archipelagic status in the convention.

The Indian law minister H. R. Gokhale argued that there were no grounds for a distinction being made between archipelagic states and states with archipelagos:

[65] Ibid.

[66] US Embassy Nairobi to US Embassy Saigon (3 April 1974), p. 2: 1974NAIROB02802, AAD.

> It cannot be argued on good ground that if an archipelago constitutes an independent State, it will be recognised by international law but if it constitutes part of a coastal state, it will not be so recognised, even though it otherwise fulfils all the elements of the definition of archipelago. Nor should an archipelago which is at some distance from the coastal State be denied that status if it would have had that status, had it been located near the coast of that coastal State. In other words, the archipelago of Andaman and Nicobar islands and the archipelago of Lakshadweep should be entitled to the same status as any other archipelago.[67]

The Portuguese delegate Manuel Primo de Brito Limpo Serra, thinking of the Azores and the Madeira island groups, suggested that claims made on behalf of archipelagic states were equally applicable to continental states with archipelagos. 'Application of a different regime to the latter,' he said, 'would mean that the archipelagic part of the territory of mixed States would be regarded as second class territory.'[68]

Raising the Stakes

Talks recommenced between the Indonesians and the Americans on 9–10 December 1974, this time in Jakarta. The Indonesians, having already given away the principle of unimpeded passage through sea lanes, tried to haggle over the width of these sea lanes and the altitude of overflight. The Americans responded by ratcheting up their demands – a tactic that would temporarily rebound on them.

The debate about the width of sea lanes had started a few months earlier, when the Indonesians had proposed ten-mile-wide sea lanes, and the Americans had proposed 100-mile-wide sea lanes.[69] (These figures had prompted a bad-tempered exchange between Mochtar and Moore, each accusing the other of lack of seriousness.[70]) In Jakarta, the Indonesian team led by air-marshal Sudarmono moved upwards to twenty miles, while the Americans, led by Moore and rear-admiral Max Morris, moved downwards to eighty miles.[71] When making the case for

[67] 'Statement by the Honourable Mr. H.R. Gokhale' (3 July 1974), p. 12: box 16, RG 43, Records of international conferences, commissions and expositions, Law of the sea conference, NARA.

[68] UNLOSC III, vol. 2, A/Conf.62/C.2/SR.37 (12 August 1974), p. 266.

[69] US Embassy Caracas to US State Department (13 August 1974), p. 3: 1974CARACA 07731, AAD.

[70] Ibid.

[71] US Embassy Jakarta to US State Department (12 December 1974), s. 1, p. 2: 1974JAKART 14919, AAD.

narrow sea lanes, the Indonesians indicated that they were primarily concerned about their security: they did not want tensions between the powers being played out within the archipelago, and they were sensitive about foreign interventions in their internal affairs. They argued, for example, that wide sea lanes would pass too close to Buru Island,[72] where 12,000 political prisoners, mostly former Partai Komunis Indonesia (PKI) members, were incarcerated. (Sudarmono, who a decade earlier had signed the order banning the PKI, was not uninvested in the issue.)

As an illustration of the multiplicity of Indonesia's security concerns, the American consul in Surabaya in East Java wrote that in the seas to the northeast of the city:

> The Indonesian armada (based in Surabaya) frequently conducts anti-smuggling patrols and other operations in these regions. Moreover, Buru Island is the site of the PKI detention camp, and any unauthorized shore visits on that island could create a major incident. The waters ... are also sensitive because of Indonesian concern about poaching by foreign trawlers. Vessels are often stopped and searched ... East Java waters, particularly the Madura straits, are off-limits to foreign trawling of any kind.[73]

At the time, the movement of foreign naval forces through the archipelago added to Indonesia's concerns, especially around East Timor, where its armed forces were engaged in undermining and then bloodily dispatching the new Fretelin government after Portugal's departure. The Americans backed Jakarta, but only as long as it did not interfere with their navigational rights: in 1978, for example, they protested when the Indonesians closed the Wetar and Ombai straits north of Timor to prevent the resupply by sea of Fretelin forces.[74]

Meanwhile, the Americans made the case for wide sea lanes by playing on Indonesia's fears of covert operations by submarines. They explained that the US Navy's carrier forces needed plenty of operating room so that they could deploy shielding vessels laterally 'to prevent archipelago from becoming lucrative area for su[r]prise attack from unknown submarine lurking outside the lanes'.[75] In other words, they were demanding not

[72] Ibid., s. 2, p. 3.
[73] US Consulate Surabaya to US State Department (14 February 1975), p. 2: 1975SURABA 00114, AAD.
[74] US Embassy Jakarta to US State Department (7 November 1978), p. 1: 1978JAKART 15349, AAD.
[75] US Embassy Jakarta to US State Department (12 December 1974), s. 2, p. 2: 1974JAKART 14919, AAD.

just sea lanes wide enough for passage, but also wide enough for its vessels to enjoy militarily secure passage. The Indonesians were not persuaded that the US Navy would need 80- or 100-mile-wide sea lanes to take evasive action against foreign submarines. Rear-admiral Prasodjo Mahdi, for example, produced a map showing that a bent-screen carrier group would require a sea lane width of fifteen miles, which would easily fit into the twenty-mile width they were then proposing.[76] The Australians, meanwhile, told the Americans they thought a width of twenty-four miles would be quite sufficient for defensive purposes.[77]

This raised another contentious issue: foreign overflight of sea lanes. Indonesia initially took the view that overflight should be resolved not by a law of the sea conference but by a law of the air conference.[78] Later they argued that foreign aircraft would potentially obstruct domestic aircraft, on which the government depended to maintain contact with the more remote islands in the archipelago.[79] The Americans noted that the Indonesian team was not objecting to overflight in principle, but to overflight at the lower altitudes used by domestic traffic.[80] This made the problem much more manageable: all they had to do was to agree a threshold for overflight. The Indonesians proposed unrestricted overflight over 40,000 feet; below that, safety became a concern because, they said, the local air traffic control system was not particularly good.[81] The Americans said that even 30,000 feet was too high for their turboprop aircraft.[82] Moore suggested a minimum altitude of 22,000 feet, and Sudarmono proposed 25,000 feet.[83] The Americans made clear that whatever was decided, they would not accept any requirement for prior notification for aircraft, including block booking arrangements.[84]

[76] Ibid., s. 2, p. 3.
[77] 'Third United Nations Conference on the Law of the Sea . . . [Confidential] report of the Australian delegation' (u.d., c. August–September 1974), p. 17: A2539/3 B1974/15, NAA.
[78] US Embassy Caracas to US State Department (13 August 1974), s. 1, pp. 2–3: 1974CARACA07731, AAD.
[79] US Embassy Jakarta to US State Department (12 December 1974), s. 3, p. 1: 1974JAKART14919, AAD.
[80] Ibid., s. 3, p. 2.
[81] 'US talks with Indonesia and the Philippines' (20 December 1974), p. 1: FCO 76/1088, TNA.
[82] Ibid., p. 2.
[83] US Embassy Jakarta to US State Department (11 December 1974), s. 2, p. 3: 1974JAKART14917, AAD.
[84] 'US talks with Indonesia and the Philippines' (20 December 1974), p. 2: FCO 76/1088, TNA.

To round off the session in Jakarta, the Americans returned to a condition mentioned earlier: the Indonesians would be expected to support the British proposal on transit passage through straits. As Indonesia and the Philippines were archipelagic *and* straits states, the linkage of these two issues tied each country's hands on both. Earlier, Mochtar had told the Americans that his government had 'major political problems' with supporting transit passage because it would sour its relations with the other straits states, especially Malaysia over the Malacca Strait.[85] Moore, apparently oblivious, then suggested that the Indonesians 'make a speech conditionally supporting the British straits articles' and in return the Americans would 'make statement of conditional acceptance of archipelago principle',[86] Mochtar recoiled: it would be 'political suicide' for Indonesia to publicly back the British on the issue.[87]

Later at the Jakarta meeting, Moore returned to the subject, but this time with even more conditions. As well as supporting the Americans and British over transit passage in straits, Indonesia would be expected to open talks with Japan over cable-laying and fishing rights in archipelagic waters, and back the British and French on islands having the same maritime entitlements as continents.[88] Moore's team was pushing too hard, and the Indonesians backed away from further talks.

A Paradox

The Americans, meanwhile, were still working out a definition of an archipelago that included the small number of claimants they were intending to endorse – the Bahamas, Fiji, Indonesia, the Philippines, and later, Papua New Guinea – while at the same time excluding other states. But the criteria they had laid out to the Indonesians at the start,

[85] US Embassy Caracas to US State Department (13 August 1974), s. 1, p. 1: 1974CARACA07731, AAD.

[86] Ibid., s. 2, p. 1.

[87] Ibid.

[88] 'US talks with Indonesia and the Philippines' (20 December 1974), p. 2: FCO 76/1088, TNA. The exhortation to support Britain and France on islands was indirectly connected to archipelagos. At the time, a proposal suggested that an island's entitlement to maritime zones would be dependent on population size. This worried low-population island states, who predicted that they might not be able to claim economic zones for some or all islands, and who were thinking instead about claiming archipelagic status to get around the problem.

namely, 'unimpeded archipelagic passage' plus a 1:5 land-sea ratio and an eighty-mile maximum for baselines – did not please either Fiji or the Philippines.

The Fijians objected because their archipelago did not meet the specifications. In May 1974, Nandan took their concerns about this to the State Department, where he met Moore and geographer Robert Hodgson. They assured him that they had no intention of excluding Fiji, and would make sure that it was included in any future settlement on archipelagos.[89] (Nandan, sensibly, asked Moore to confirm this in writing.[90]) They also told him that Fiji *did* meet the 1:5 criteria because they had reworked the definition and were now counting water between reefs and the coast, and water within atoll lagoons, as 'land'.[91] This manipulation of the definition – cooked up in the Department to meet Fiji's case – would bring its land-sea ratio down to 1:4.88.[92] Nandan, relieved, returned the favour by telling them that Fiji was more amenable than Indonesia and the Philippines to foreign passage through archipelagos, and that he and others would do what they could to persuade other claimants to support the American position.[93]

The other state unhappy about the Americans' criteria was the Philippines, whose officials objected not just to unimpeded archipelagic passage, but also to the 'arbitrary' land-sea ratio and baseline lengths.[94] In their view, a 1:7.3 ratio and 100-mile maximum baseline would be more suitable.[95]

The Philippines was one of the earliest advocates of the archipelagic idea, first broaching the idea in the International Law Commission in 1956, then raising a motion along with Yugoslavia at the 1958 conference. Three years later, in 1961, Manila had enclosed its islands and 'historic waters' as internal waters within baselines, which in turn was

89 Fiji Mission to the UN to Foreign Affairs Suva (8 May 1974), p. 1: folder 1, box 69, Mss82-6, Satya Nandan papers, UVLSL.

90 Fiji Mission to the UN to Foreign Affairs Suva (17 June 1974), p. 2: folder 1, box 69, Mss82-6, Satya Nandan papers, UVLSL. Moore's confirmation appears in: US Embassy Caracas to US State Department (2 July 1974), p. 2: 1974CARACA06018, AAD.

91 US State Department to US Embassy Suva (9 May 1974), p. 2: 1974STATE095957, AAD.

92 Ibid. Later, Nandan, having consulted Suva, feared that the 'unusual' inclusion of atoll waters in the criteria might be used by other states as a stick to beat Fiji: US State Department to US Embassy Suva (16 May 1974), p. 2: 1974STATE102655, AAD.

93 US State Department to US Embassy Suva (9 May 1974), p. 3: 1974STATE095957, AAD.

94 US Embassy Jakarta to US State Department (14 May 1974), p. 2: 1974JAKART 05867, AAD.

95 Ibid.

enclosed by a roughly rectangular box of territorial sea. This, it was argued, had been demarcated by the US-Spain Treaty of Paris of 1898 and the US-UK Philippines-Sabah sea boundary agreement of 1930.[96] It meant that instead of having a uniform strip of territorial sea around each island, the Philippines claimed jurisdiction over waters which extended 293 miles outwards from Polillo island off Luzon and less than three miles outwards from the Turtle islands of Tawi-Tawi to the sea boundary with Sabah in Malaysia.[97] There were thus two grounds for the Philippines' claim to archipelagic status: one based on historic rights and the other based on it being an intrinsic geographical, economic and political entity – each being a fall-back for the other. Philippine delegates therefore felt able to pursue a tougher line on passage rights than other members of the group.

Manila's archipelagic claim, like Indonesia's, was strongly motivated by the desire to curb the activities of rebel movements and associated interventions by foreign states. Its greatest concern was the Islamist Moro rebellion that had ignited in the southern islands of Mindanao and the Sulu archipelago in 1968, and backed, it was suspected, by Malaysia. President Ferdinand Marcos responded to this and another perceived threat – from the Maoist New People's Army, established in 1969 – by declaring martial law in September 1972.

The Americans had to take these security-related factors into account when dictating their criteria for archipelagos. Counsellor Lewis Purnell at the US embassy in Manila noted that the Philippines' archipelagic claim conformed to the 1:5 land-sea ratio and the eighty-mile maximum baselines, except for a long baseline that crossed Mindanao's Gulf of Moro. Purnell explained the security implications:

> Should 80 mile limit on baseline in effect open up gulf as part of high sea, result would cause very serious problem for GOP [Government of Philippines]. Muslim provinces which face onto gulf have been locus of heavy fighting against government for past few years. Although the Philippine Navy has not been very successful in patrolling gulf coast, it is reliably believed that coast is one of the landing areas for weapons,

[96] The Philippines, *Republic Act No. 3046 of June 17, 1961*, printed in: International Law Commission, A/CN.4/99 (20 January 1956), *Yearbook of the International Law Commission* (1956), vol. 2, pp. 69–70.

[97] A. M. Tolentino, 'Proceedings of the Philippines Senate on Bill No. 541', in R. P. M. Lotilla (ed.) *The Philippine national territory: a collection of related documents* (Manila: Institute of International Legal Studies; Foreign Service Institute: c. 1995), p. 282.

> ammunition and men to fight against Philippine armed forces, which assistance has been provided at least with the facilitation of Sabah and possibly with the active involvement of such states as Malaysia and Libya.[98]

Having initially held the Philippines at arm's length in favour of Indonesia, the Americans agreed to discuss the former's archipelagic claims with ministers at a meeting in Manila on 5 July 1974. Solicitor-general Estelito Mendoza pointed out that the Philippines stood to gain a great deal from recognition of the archipelagic concept, but only if the territorial sea remained at three miles.[99] If the territorial sea were extended, his government could abandon its archipelagic status and claim a twelve-mile territorial sea around each of its islands, which would enclose the entire Philippines archipelago except for parts of the Sulu Sea.[100] Foreign vessels would thus be subject to the innocent passage regime (rather than to the less restrictive unimpeded archipelagic passage regime then being advocated by the Americans), giving Manila 'control over almost all waters of its archipelago without any of compromises involved in U.S. proposal'.[101] So arose a paradox: the United States (who had earlier attempted to destroy the archipelagic idea, and still refused to formally recognise any state's claims) was busy defining the concept, while the Philippines (who had played a major role in the creation of the concept) was threatening to walk away.

Slippery Criteria

In the process of trying to mould the archipelagic concept to their own liking, the Americans were also tinkering with the criteria to meet their approved claimants' needs. As the negotiations progressed, the maximum length of archipelagic baselines crept upwards, from the eighty miles initially proposed in May 1974;[102] to eighty miles plus 1 per cent of

[98] US Embassy Manila to US State Department (15 April 1974), p. 1: 1974MANILA04294, AAD.
[99] US Embassy Manila to US Embassy Caracas (6 July 1974), p. 2: 1974MANILA08023, AAD.
[100] Ibid.; and CIA, 'Law of the sea country study: Philippines' (May 1974), p. 7: CIA-RDP79-01054A000100100001-9, CIAHC.
[101] US Embassy Manila to US Embassy Caracas (6 July 1974), p. 2: 1974MANILA08023, AAD.
[102] US State Department to US posts (9 April 1974), pp. 2–3: 1974STATE071502, AAD.

baselines up to a 100-mile maximum in July 1974;[103] to eighty miles with an undecided percentage of baselines up to a 125-mile maximum in 1975;[104] to eighty miles with 1 per cent of baselines up to a 125-mile maximum in 1976;[105] to 100 miles with 3 per cent of baselines up to a 125-mile maximum in 1977, and thereafter in the convention.[106] This process disconcerted the British, with Peter Beazley of the hydrographer's office pointing out in 1974 that if states were allowed 100-mile baselines, Sweden could enclose Gotland, Canada could enclose its coastal islands, Greece could enclose some coastal archipelagos, and Denmark could enclose all of its islands, to the detriment of NATO-related 'defence interests', and with the consequences worsening with each increase in baseline length.[107]

Yet the Americans were not deterred. They had already transformed water into land to accommodate Fiji,[108] and this was not the end of their efforts. Fiji had two far-flung islands, Conway and Rotuma, which were hundreds of miles from the rest, which skewed its land-sea ratio. At this point the Americans abandoned their initial insistence on states enclosing *every* island within archipelagic baselines,[109] enabling Fiji to enclose most of its archipelago without including the outlying islands.[110]

The Americans nonetheless insisted that claimants include within baselines their *principal* island or islands, thus pre-empting a state from enclosing just minor islands as an archipelago – for example, Cuba claiming just the Jardines de la Reina along its southern coast.[111] But this brought another definitional issue in its train: how might 'principal'

103 US Embassy Caracas to US Embassy Singapore (13 July 1974), p. 2: 1974CARACA 06493, AAD.

104 Article 118(2), UNLOSC III, vol. 4, A/Conf.62/WP.8/PartII (9 May 1975), pp. 168–169.

105 Article 119(2), UNLOSC III, vol. 4, A/Conf.62/WP.8/Rev.1/PartII (7 May 1976), p. 171.

106 Article 47(2), UNLOSC III, vol. 8, A/Conf.62/WP.10 (15 July 1977), pp. 11–12; and Article 47(2), UNCLOS, 414.

107 UK Ministry of Defence, 'Baselines – note by the Hydrographer' (u.d., c. early 1974), p. 3: CAB 148/150, TNA.

108 US Embassy Manila to US State Department (7 June 1974), s. 2, p. 1: 1974MANILA 06706, AAD.

109 US Embassy Caracas to US State Department (18 July 1974), p. 1: 1974CARACA06721, AAD.

110 US Mission to the UN to US State Department (13 June 1974), p. 2: 1974USUNN02142, AAD. In 1975, the Americans raised the ratio from 1:5 to 1:9, to the relief of Fiji and the Bahamas, who no longer had to claim lagoon water and the water between the coast and reefs as 'land' to meet the criteria.

111 US State Department to US Mission to the UN (12 June 1974), p. 2: 1974STATE 124371, AAD.

islands be defined? Should it be according to their size, their population or their economic weight? If based on size, most of the largest islands would also contain the main population and economic centres, as with Fiji, Indonesia and the Philippines.[112] But not always. The Bahamas, one of the US-approved claimants, was the exception because its largest island, Andros, was one of the less populated islands in the archipelago, whereas one of its smaller islands, New Providence, was the site of the capital, Nassau, home to 70 per cent of the population.[113]

While using its ratio and baseline criteria to include the approved claimants, the Americans (and the Soviets) also used them to exclude potential claimants, including compact islands states such as Britain and Japan. Thus, in 1974–1975, when British officials were seriously weighing up the prospect of claiming archipelagic status, American officials were devising ways of preventing them from doing so. The latter started tweaking the land-sea ratio, so that archipelagos were now required to sit between maximum and minimum criteria: the already announced land-sea ratio of 1:5 (i.e. mostly sea) and the new ratio of 1:1 (equal parts land and sea).[114] If claimants were also required to include their principal islands, the compact island states would possess more land than water, and therefore fall outside the 1:1 ratio. This, Moore noted, would exclude the United Kingdom, which would have to claim mainland Britain as part of its archipelago, Japan (with Honshu), Malta and Mauritius.[115]

The British were none too pleased about the appearance of the 1:1 ratio. One reason they wanted archipelagic status, legal adviser David Anderson wrote, was because it would 'increase the extent of our internal waters which could be advantageous under the present or a revised CFP [the European Community's Common Fisheries Policy]'.[116] (Whether this was so, given that the negotiating text compelled archipelagic states to 'respect existing agreements with other States' and 'recognize traditional fishing rights of the immediately adjacent neighbouring States', is

[112] US State Department to US Embassy Caracas (3 July 1974), p. 2: 1974STATE139044, AAD.

[113] Ibid.

[114] Moore made an early reference to a 'tentative' proposal of a 1:1 limit in June 1974: US Embassy Manila to US State Department (7 June 1974), p. 2: 1974MANILA06706, AAD.

[115] US State Department to US Embassy Caracas (3 July 1974), p. 3: 1974STATE139044, AAD.

[116] D. H. Anderson, 'Proposed understanding of archipelagic states and straits' (13 February 1975), p. 1: FCO 76/1088, TNA.

a moot point.[117]) Another reason, according to Anderson, was that it would probably allow the British to extend baselines out to the island of St Kilda and other outlying islands, which might strengthen claims to the 'island' of Rockall and over the continental shelf shared with Ireland.[118] (Others were not so sure: enclosing Rockall would require longer baselines than Britain was prepared to accept elsewhere, and would not conform to a provision requiring that baselines did not depart appreciably from the archipelago's configuration.[119])

The British reported that it was 'not clear' where the minimum ratio had come from,[120] but they must have strongly suspected that the Americans were responsible. They probed Bernard Oxman, telling him that they hoped the land-sea ratio could be changed from 1:1 to 1:0.5 in the text, enabling them to claim archipelagic status.[121] Oxman suggested that they raise it with Washington via 'irregular (i.e. defence) channels' – in other words, not via the proper State Department route.[122] He also indicated why the change would likely be rejected: a 1:0.5 ratio would also allow Japan to declare itself an archipelagic state, which, some in the Nixon administration feared, would restrict the United States' capacity to 'deploy nuclear weapons within a Japanese archipelago'.[123] A few weeks later, Oxman gave the British a little more detail:

> He confirmed that the question of deployment of US nuclear armed ships was one of the American worries about Japanese proclamation of archipelagic status, but mentioned two others: (a) The Americans feared an angry reaction by the Chinese because of their claim to the Senkaku islands, which the Japanese might well want to include. (b) Further extension of rights to the maritime powers would make it more difficult to hold others in line.[124]

Behind the scenes, the French privately urged the Americans to not budge on 1:1 – their concern being that if Britain were to acquire

[117] Article 122, UNLOSC III, vol. 4, A/Conf.62/WP.8/PartII (9 May 1975), p. 169.
[118] D. H. Anderson, 'Proposed understanding of archipelagic states and straits' (13 February 1975), p. 1: FCO 76/1088, TNA.
[119] 'UK as an archipelagic state' (u.d., c. December 1975), p. 2: FCO 76/1088, TNA.
[120] Ibid.
[121] UK Mission to the UN to UK FCO (4 December 1975), p. 1: DEFE 24/954, TNA (and, clarifying the land and sea elements of the 1:0.5 ratio, 'UK as an archipelagic state' (u.d., c. December 1975), p. 2: FCO 76/1088, TNA).
[122] Ibid.
[123] Ibid.
[124] UK Embassy Washington to UK FCO (24 December 1975), p. 1: DEFE 24/954, TNA.

archipelagic status it would, they claimed, extend its waters to just two miles from the French coast.[125] As it turned out, the British, deterred by the Americans, shelved their plans.

Quashing Continental Claims

While these developments were unfolding, tensions were mounting inside the archipelagic claimants' group. Nandan complained that in early 1975 their discussions had been 'just going around in circles'.[126] His colleague Donald McLoughlin explained:

> This appeared to be because of a desire on the part of the Philippines to delay the issue in the hopes of gaining greater concessions from the maritime powers. The Indonesians were also playing a game of their own whilst negotiating privately with the United States. Mauritius also complicated the issue by insisting on the omission of any criteria for the definition of archipelagic States based on length of baselines or land to water ratios. The Bahamas, whilst not joining in the discussions between the archipelagic States, submitted proposals which were clearly based on those previously suggested to us by the United States and had obviously been prepared in close consultation with the State Department.[127]

As will be recalled from the discussion of straits, Nandan had at the March–May 1975 conference assumed the chair's responsibility for drafting the second committee's end-of-session text, and this enabled him to gain the upper hand over the less accommodating archipelagic states. He reported:

> I . . . decided that the only way to deal with them was to present them with a *fait accompli* through the single negotiating text which I was already engaged in drafting for the Chairman. Through the medium of the single negotiating text we have extricated ourselves from being hostages to the ploys of Indonesia and the Philippines. As a result the initiative has been taken away from them. Understandably, to some extent, this has hurt their pride.[128]

[125] US Embassy Paris to US State Department (1 March 1976), p. 2: 1976PARIS06097, AAD.

[126] S. N. Nandan, 'The third session of the conference on the law of the sea' (9 June 1975), p. 3: folder 1, box 69, Mss82–6, Satya Nandan papers, UVLSL.

[127] D. McLoughlin to secretary of foreign affairs (17 June 1975), p. 4: folder 11, box 69, Mss82–6, Satya Nandan papers, UVLSL.

[128] S. N. Nandan, 'The third session of the Conference on the Law of the Sea' (9 June 1975), p. 4: folder 1, box 69, Mss82–6, Satya Nandan papers, UVLSL.

Nandan's purported aim was to strike a balance between the interests of the archipelagic claimants and the maritime powers, but in fact he incorporated most of the American proposals regarding passage into the text, with just one restriction added – the requirement that passage through sea lanes be continuous and expeditious.[129] That the text erred in favour of the powers was indicated by the response, summarised by McLoughlin: 'Whilst not acceptable to the Philippines or to Indonesia, as yet, it is generally acceptable to the United States, the U.K., and the U.S.S.R., and follows the concept found in the Bahamas draft.'[130]

While laying the ground for unrestricted passage, Nandan also took care to ensure that all the then archipelagic claimants were covered by the definition. In article 117(2)(a) – which stated that an archipelagic state 'means a State constituted wholly by one or more archipelagos and may include other islands'[131] – the words 'wholly by one' met the needs of Indonesia and the Philippines; the words 'or more' met the needs of Mauritius, made up of three archipelagos; and the words 'may include other islands' met the needs of Fiji with Rotuma and Conway. And in article 117(2)(b), the description of an archipelago as 'a group of islands, including parts of islands'[132] was designed to cover Indonesia's areas of Kalimantan and West Papua, shared with Malaysia and Papua New Guinea respectively.

By Nandan's own account, the text that he produced on archipelagos was a 'giant step' in the campaign for the recognition of the concept.[133] He added that,

> by presenting a balanced acceptable solution on the concept we have now the support of a wider constituency of the Conference which includes maritime powers as well as developing countries. Developing countries are not prepared to sacrifice the acceptance of their exclusive economic zone by the maritime powers for the sake of conservative passage and overflight regimes through straits and archipelagos of a handful of states.[134]

129 Article 124(3), UNLOSC III, vol. 4, A/Conf.62/WP.8/PartII (9 May 1975), p. 169.

130 D. McLoughlin to secretary of foreign affairs (17 June 1975), p. 5: folder 11, box 69, Mss82-6, Satya Nandan papers, UVLSL.

131 UNLOSC III, vol. 4, A/Conf.62/WP.8/PartII (9 May 1975), p. 168.

132 Ibid.

133 Fiji Mission to the UN to Foreign Affairs Suva (3 June 1975), p. 2: folder 1, box 69, Mss82-6, Satya Nandan papers, UVLSL.

134 S. N. Nandan, 'The third session of the Conference on theLaw of the Sea' (9 June 1975), p. 4: folder 1, box 69, Mss82-6, Satya Nandan papers, UVLSL.

The continental states continued pushing to extend the archipelagic concept to their outlying island groups, however, and because this issue was unresolved when Nandan was drafting the text, he had to allow for both a restrictive and an expansive approach to archipelagos.

The restrictive approach, which limited claims to ocean-bound states, appeared in article 117(2)(a), which referred to the archipelagic state being 'constituted wholly by one or more archipelagos'; and in article 117(2)(b), which described an archipelago as islands, waters and other natural features 'so closely interrelated' that they formed 'an intrinsic geographic, economic and political entity'.[135] The words 'wholly' and 'intrinsic . . . political entity' thus excluded continental states from claiming outlying island groups as archipelagos. By contrast, the expansive approach, which allowed continental states to claim outlying island groups as archipelagos, was discernible in the structure of part VII on archipelagos. This was divided into two sections, entitled 'archipelagic states' and 'oceanic archipelagos belonging to continental states', with the latter containing a single article – article 131 – which stated that, 'The provisions of section 1 are without prejudice to the status of oceanic archipelagos forming an integral part of the territory of a continental State.'[136] The question was, would the section heads and article 131 be retained, amended or deleted?

Opposition to the continental states' claims was gathering force, and not just among the ocean-bound claimants. Other states, while grudgingly accepting the claims of the latter, outright rejected the claims of the former. One of these was Algeria, a geographically disadvantaged shelf-locked state, whose delegate Madjid Bencherkh warned that 'certain continental coastal States wanted to take advantage of the situation to grab for themselves more and more ocean space':

> They did not even want to take into account . . . the fact that their claims were in disregard of the rights of other States or, what was more, the fact that the Conference was supposed to ensure respect for the common heritage of mankind so as to assist various countries in their fight against under-development.[137]

The Turkish too had concerns. Their delegate Namik Yolga challenged the idea that continental states could claim outlying archipelagos, his prime concern being potential Greek claims:

[135] UNLOSC III, vol. 4, A/Conf.62/WP.8/PartII (9 May 1975), p. 168.
[136] Ibid., p. 170.
[137] UNLOSC III, vol. 2, A/Conf.62/C.2/SR.37 (12 August 1974), p. 271.

> Continental States which possessed islands should not be mistaken for archipelagic States. To generalize any rule of law was contrary to the interests of the international community and often resulted in injustice. His delegation had distributed a map which illustrated the consequences of applying the regime of archipelagic State in the Aegean Sea. A cursory examination showed that practically the whole sea would become the internal waters of one of two countries, while the other would be excluded from waters which had traditionally been open to it and its economic rights with regard to fishing and the continental shelf would be nullified. Most importantly, one of the two States would be deprived of the right to take measures for its own defence in a sea which was of great importance to it.[138]

Ultimately, it was the maritime powers who were responsible for eliminating the continental states' claims. The British had already raised the alarm about the implications for NATO security of the Scandinavian states enclosing their outlying island groups as archipelagos. The Soviets feared the consequences for the USSR, as well as for Bulgaria and Romania, if Greece did the same near the approaches to the Dardenelles. And the Americans wanted to keep down the number of potential claimants to prevent further encroachments on the high seas. In September 1975, the US delegation distributed to G5 members a paper recommending article 131's deletion because it led to an absurd result 'viz., that despite all the other provisions of the convention, and the express limitation of the archipelago chapter to independent island states, a continental state can argue there is some special undefined status for its oceanic archipelagos'.[139]

The Americans also tried to dissuade the individual continental states involved. Bernard Oxman's discussion with Spanish delegation leader Martín Herrero in April 1976 about its outlying island groups – the Canaries in the Atlantic and the Balearics in the Mediterranean – was one example. Separatists in each of these island groups were agitating for independence from Spain, and Herrero indicated that Madrid hoped to neutralise them by securing archipelagic status for both.[140] Oxman poured cold water on this idea. He directed Herrero's attention to article 117(2)(b) stating that archipelagos were an 'intrinsic ... political entity'

[138] Ibid., p. 272.
[139] US State Department to US Embassy Moscow (11 September 1975), pp. 22–23: 1975STATE215920, AAD.
[140] US Mission to the UN to US Embassy Madrid (13 April 1976), p. 2: 1976USUNN01525, AAD.

and argued that if Spain were to claim the Canaries and Balearics as outlying archipelagos this might produce the opposite political effect to the one Madrid intended, by spurring the separatist movements to claim that they possessed independent statehood by virtue of having acquired archipelagic status.[141]

Taking another tack, Oxman also claimed that the two island groups, which were both partly dependent on fishing, would be materially worse off with archipelagic status than they would be if Spain claimed exclusive economic zones for each constituent island. This was because the text specified that states would be obliged to recognise the 'traditional' (i.e. historic) fishing rights of neighbouring states in archipelagic waters,[142] but not in the exclusive economic zone.[143] He added that the ocean-bound archipelagic states were willing to concede traditional fishing rights in archipelagic waters because they wanted to build support for their campaign – hence Indonesia's agreements with, say, Thailand.[144] But Oxman failed to draw attention to another fishing-related disparity between archipelagic waters and the exclusive economic zone: in archipelagic waters, there was no obligation on a coastal state to give other states access to the surplus allowable fish catch if it lacked the capacity to harvest the entire catch itself, whereas article 51(2) imposed at least a nominal obligation on coastal states with a surplus to give access to fish in the exclusive economic zone.[145]

Shortly after this discussion, the Soviet delegate in the second committee delivered the coup de grâce to the provisions favouring the continental states' claims. He proposed changing the title of part VII from 'archipelagos' to 'archipelagic states' so that it would be inapplicable to continental states, and deleting the now-superfluous section heads and article 131.[146] The change was supported by the East Europeans, other shipping and long-distance fishing states, the landlocked and geographically disadvantaged states, and those states neighbouring others with outlying archipelagos – namely, Algeria, Bulgaria, Byelorussia, East Germany, Egypt, Hungary, Iraq, Israel, Liberia, Malta, Morocco,

141 Ibid., p. 3.
142 Article 122, UNLOSC III, vol. 4, A/Conf.62/WP.8/PartII (9 May 1975), p. 169.
143 US Mission to the UN to US Embassy Madrid (13 April 1976), pp. 2–3: 1976USUNN 01525, AAD.
144 Ibid., p. 3.
145 UNLOSC III, vol. 4, A/Conf.62/WP.8/PartII (9 May 1975), p. 160.
146 US Mission to the UN to US State Department (28 April 1976), p. 2: 1976USUNN01783, AAD.

Nicaragua, Pakistan, Poland, Senegal, Thailand, Tunisia, Turkey, Ukraine and United Arab Emirates.[147] The ocean-bound archipelagic claimants, who also opposed the continental states claims, kept a diplomatic silence: why speak out when the USSR was doing their work for them?

Axes, Not Lanes

Throughout most of 1975 and 1976, the Indonesians continued to hold the Americans at arm's length, with Mochtar telling David Newsom that he was doubtful about the usefulness of further bilateral meetings because Indonesia was bound by the decisions of the archipelagic group.[148] Newsom weighed up Indonesia's receptivity to strong American persuasion to act otherwise, and concluded that,

> Our ability to take a firm line on major issues is dependent in part on continuation of US assistance to Indonesia, which is important to ou[r] leverage here. Inverse, however, does not apply; we would be unlikely [to] secure Indonesian support by any direct threat to cut off assistance.[149]

Discussions restarted in March 1977, with two factors contributing to their resumption. First, the Americans had by then managed to neutralise most of the conference opposition to transit passage through straits, which made it easier for Indonesia to consider publicly endorsing the idea. Second, the Indonesians managed to reconceptualise sea lanes in a way that suited both themselves and the Americans. President Suharto was reportedly responsible, suggesting to Mochtar that foreign vessels could move along an axis line rather than through a sea lane corridor – a line which, as Butcher and Elson pointed out, removed nothing from Indonesian sovereignty.[150]

In the talks, both parties took axis lines to be a given and moved on to the question of how far vessels could deviate from them. The Indonesians proposed twenty miles either side, the Americans proposed thirty miles, and they compromised on twenty-five miles, giving transiting vessels a fifty-mile leeway (double the width that the Australians had estimated to

[147] Ibid., pp. 2–3.

[148] US Embassy Jakarta to US State Department (14 November 1975), p. 2: 1975JAKART 14013, AAD.

[149] US Embassy Jakarta to US State Department (12 April 1976), p. 4: 1976JAKART04755, AAD.

[150] Butcher and Elson, *Sovereignty and the sea*, p. 350.

be sufficient for naval operational purposes). Their agreement on this appeared in the negotiating text as the following:

> Sea lanes shall be defined by a series of continuous axis lines from the entry points of passage routes to the exit points. Ships and aircraft in archipelagic sea lanes passage shall not deviate more then 25 nautical miles to either side of such axis lines during passage, provided that ships and aircraft shall not navigate closer to the coasts than 10 per cent of the distance between the nearest points on islands bordering the sea lane.[151]

As the Americans pointed out, this formula allowed an archipelagic state to angle an axis line so that it avoided a particular rock or island,[152] meeting the Indonesians' concern about keeping traffic away from Buru Island, and, according to senior official Sufri Jusuf, preventing its 'nearest potential enemy' – China – from too closely approaching Indonesia's islands once it had developed a larger naval fleet.[153]

This brought the Indonesians and Americans to the delicate issue of overflight along the axes. The discussion fixed on civil aviation. The Indonesians argued that they should not be expected to concede overflight to foreign commercial airlines without being assured that Indonesia's own airlines – Garuda in particular – would be given reciprocal rights over foreign states. The British, who at the time were planning to run Concorde over Indonesia on a London-to-Melbourne route, dug in their heels. 'It seems likely that the Indonesians are laying claim to bargaining rights for later use, and we have some interest in smoking them out', wrote one official.[154] They stated that if the Indonesians wanted foreign overflight rights, they should strike bilateral deals and sign up to the International Air Services Transit Agreement.[155] They also pointed out that the Indonesians were not proposing true reciprocity: if they wanted to overfly British territory, the British should have the right to overfly Indonesian territory, not just the sea lane axes.[156] The Americans reassured the British that they would resist reciprocity on

[151] Article 53(5), UNLOSC III, vol. 8, A/Conf.62/WP.10 (15 July 1977), p. 12.
[152] See, for example, UK Mission to the UN to UK FCO (11 July 1977): DEFE 24/1185, TNA.
[153] US Embassy Jakarta to US State Department (12 January 1977), pp. 3–4: 1977JAKART 00534, AAD.
[154] UK Trade and Industry Department to UK Mission to the UN (u.d., c. late June 1977), p. 1: DEFE 24/1185, TNA.
[155] Ibid., p. 2.
[156] UK FCO to UK Mission to the UN (23 June 1977), p. 1: FCO 76/1673, TNA.

the grounds that it would not win support at the conference, even from other archipelagic claimants,[157] and, as they predicted, no reciprocity clause appeared in the conference text.

A final point of disagreement was over the scope of an archipelagic state's duty to interact with IMCO over the designation, prescription or substitution of sea lanes and traffic separation schemes. This debate was overshadowed by the debate about IMCO's role in straits, and both parties knew that any concession made on archipelagos would have a knock-on effect on straits and vice versa. Indonesia therefore argued, as it also did on straits, that states should be obliged to share information with IMCO, nothing more. The Americans, however, insisted that archipelagic states should seek prior approval from the organisation for the designation of sea lanes and traffic separation schemes. This view prevailed. In the negotiating text, the imperative 'shall' indicated that prior permission had to be sought from IMCO:

> In designating or substituting sea lanes or prescribing or substituting traffic separation schemes, an archipelagic State shall refer proposals to the competent international organization with a view to their adoption. The organization may adopt only such sea lanes and traffic separation schemes as may be agreed with the archipelagic State, after which the archipelagic State may designate, prescribe or substitute them.[158]

The negotiations on archipelagos concluded in July 1977, when the Indonesians and Americans ironed out their remaining differences and agreed the provisions that would appear in the end-of-session conference text. Max Morris may have described the final round of talks as a 'terrible and unusual punishment',[159] but in the end, the Americans conceded little beyond the principle itself. It took them six years, but they had finally managed, in British words, to 'bring the Indonesians to heel'.[160] The Bahamas, Fiji and Papua New Guinea supported the new articles in the text; only the Philippines registered dissent. To all intents and purposes, the negotiations over archipelagos were over.

*

[157] K. S. Pitt and S. S. Crew, 'UNLOSC: seventh week' (8 July 1977), p. 1: DEFE 24/1185, TNA.
[158] Article 53(9), UNLOSC III, vol. 8, A/Conf.62/WP.10 (15 July 1977), p. 13.
[159] S. S. Crew, 'The Pentagon position' (1 July 1977): DEFE 24/1185, TNA.
[160] K. S. Pitt and S. S. Crew, 'UNLOSC: seventh week' (8 July 1977), p. 1: DEFE 24/1185, TNA.

In July 1977, Mochtar took the news of the agreement back to Jakarta, where, after reporting to Suharto, he addressed the Indonesian press on a triumphant note. After decades of campaigning for recognition, he said that Indonesia had 'finally obtained approval of US, USSR and almost all other states for its archipelago concept' which 'has now become part of new international law'.[161] The convention's provisions, he added, meant that worldwide, Indonesia would be the 'third biggest gainer' after the United States and the USSR of jurisdiction over adjacent waters. This was indeed a great achievement for Indonesia, and for the other archipelagic states.[162]

He did not, however, mention the considerable concessions Jakarta had made over passage rights. In 1972, during the initial debates in the seabed committee, Indonesia had claimed all waters within archipelagic baselines as internal waters, subject to innocent passage and thereby excluding aircraft and submerged submarines. By 1977, they had conceded fifty-mile-wide IMCO-dictated sovereignty-proof sea lanes through which all foreign vessels could pass by any means they chose – below, above and on the surface. Not only that, but the rules and regulations governing navigational safety and pollution control within sea lanes were determined not by the archipelagic state, but by external international entities. Together these concessions represented a significant erosion of the unitary concept of the archipelago in which sea and land together constituted an indivisible whole.

161 US Embassy Jakarta to US State Department (27 July 1977), p. 1: 1977JAKART09921, AAD. Nandan concurred with this, stating that the archipelagic concept had the same status as the exclusive economic zone 'as an established rule of international law as it has evolved at the Conference': 'Report by Fiji on the sixth session of the third United Nations conference on the law of the sea' (u.d., c. July–August 1977), p. 4: box 30, Mss82-6, Satya Nandan papers, UVLSL. The Americans disagreed: the archipelagic claimants would have to wait for the convention to enter into force before their position was recognised: US State Department to US Embassy Jakarta (20 August 1977), p. 2: 1977STATE198669, AAD.

162 US Embassy Jakarta to US State Department (27 July 1977), p. 1: 1977JAKART09921, AAD.

8

New International Orders

The Exclusive Economic Zone, the Continental Margin and Marine Scientific Research

The group of seventy-seven's campaign for a new international economic order gathered force in the early seventies, buoyed by OPEC's successful stand on oil prices and encouraged by the prospect of seabed exploitation. In 1974, it raised two General Assembly resolutions – the 'Declaration on the establishment of a new international economic order' and the associated 'Charter of economic rights and duties of states' – setting out a blueprint for this new order.[1] But by then, unbeknownst to all, the group's campaign had already peaked, and the next decade would be marked by its retreat, which would be played out at the law of the sea conference.

Even at its high point, the G77 was a far from unified bloc. As Julius Nyerere noted at a group meeting held in Arusha:

> The Group of 77 does not share an ideology. Some of us are avowedly 'scientific' socialists, some just plain socialists, some capitalist, some theocratic and some fascist! ... Some countries represented here are currently engaged in a war with each other. Our national income per capita varies from about 100 to 2,000 USD a year. Some of us have minerals, some do not. Some of us are landlocked, and others are isolated in huge oceans.[2]

Had Nyerere continued on law of the sea themes, he might have added that some had narrow continental shelves and others wide continental margins; some backed equitable solutions to maritime delimitation and others backed equidistance; some favoured anti-pollution measures and others, such as the open-registry states, opposed them; some were oil exporters and many were oil importers. Indeed, it was only

1 UNGA Res. 3201(S-VI) (1 May 1974); and UNGA Res. 3281(XXIX) (12 December 1974).

2 J. K. Nyerere, *Freedom and a new world economic order* (Dar es Salaam: Oxford University Press, 2011), p. 58.

nationalism, he said, that compelled them to stick together as a group.[3]

As the developing countries embarked on the conference negotiations from 1973 onwards, their differences could not be ignored. Most significant of all was the split, almost down the middle, between the coastal states and the landlocked and geographically disadvantaged states over access to resources in the economic zone. (Mohammed Bedjaoui went so far as to say that the creation of the geographically disadvantaged group 'broke up' the G77.[4]) Not only were these factions pulling in different directions, but the G77's original purpose was being distorted by the new demands being placed upon it. When it had formed a decade earlier, it had set itself the monumental task of rectifying the economic inequalities created by colonialism and imperialism; now, with the emergence of the geographically disadvantaged states within its ranks, it was expected to rectify geographical inequalities as well.

The powers took note, and pressed their advantage. Within four years of the opening of the conference, they had managed to transform the debate about economic rights, of foremost concern to the developing world, into a debate about navigation and communication rights, of interest primarily to those at the cutting edge of nuclear deterrence. As a result, the exclusive economic zone and the continental shelf regimes set out in the convention were shaped as much by the requirements of security as by resource management – a new order for sure, but not on the lines envisaged for the new international economic order.

A Divided Group

Early portents of the G77's disarray could be seen in the UN seabed committee. When it began its work on substantive issues in 1969, there were already tactical differences between the coastal state members over the scope of claims to resource zones. One group, the 'territorialists', made up mostly of South American states, claimed either sovereignty over a 200-mile territorial sea or jurisdiction over a 200-mile maritime zone. The other group, the 'patrimonialists', initially hailing mainly from Central America and the Caribbean, advocated a patrimonial sea adjacent to a twelve-mile territorial sea, in which states would assert 'sovereign rights' (not sovereignty) over resources but not the whole zone.

[3] Ibid.
[4] Bedjaoui, *Towards a new international economic order*, p. 260.

At heart, their disagreement was over economic security, with the territorialists arguing that jurisdiction or sovereignty over the maritime zone was a necessary safeguard against the encroachments of foreign states, and the patrimonialists contending that 'sovereign rights' over resources would be sufficient protection.

Also in the seabed committee, the landlocked states joined forces with the geographically disadvantaged states, doubling the group's size. Of these, the landlocked states were the older presence at law of the sea gatherings: at the 1958 conference, they had ensured that the high seas convention referred to 'coastal and *non*-coastal States' enjoying high seas freedoms, and that states with no sea coast 'should have free access to the sea'.[5] The newer presence in the group, the self-styled 'geographically disadvantaged' states, emboldened by West Germany's pleadings during the 1969 *North Sea Continental Shelf* case, claimed their status based on their restricted access to the sea. They made several attempts to define themselves, and to exclude the wrong sort of claimant (their definitional difficulty being that disadvantage is both relative and varied), before edging towards an agreed formula in 1976.[6] All the while, the coastal states briefed against them: Fernando Zegers, the delegate for Chile – a country with almost no continental shelf – said that the disadvantaged shelf-locked states' demands sounded to him 'like a man with one car complaining that he did not have a second'.[7]

During these sessions, the landlocked and geographically disadvantaged states began to coordinate their work in secret meetings convened by Anton Prohaska of landlocked Austria and Tommy Koh of geographically disadvantaged Singapore.[8] Initially their aim was to prevent the codification of any expanded national jurisdiction that would eat into international resources such as seabed minerals or high seas fisheries. The African members (including Burundi, Chad, Lesotho and Mali) were primarily concerned about claiming their full share of common heritage revenues derived from the exploitation of seabed minerals, while wealthier European states possessing long-distance fishing fleets (such as

[5] Articles 2 and 3, High Seas Convention, 84. Emphasis added.

[6] See, for example, Singapore's proposal reported in: US Mission to the UN to US State Department (23 April 1976), p. 2: 1976USUNN01719, AAD.

[7] R. L. Harry, 'Record of conversation' (11 August 1971), p. 3: A1838/376 1734/4 pt. 1, NAA.

[8] 'Circular airgram CA-2554 from the Department of State to all diplomatic posts' (28 May 1971): *FRUS*, 1969–1976, vol. E-1, *Documents on global issues*, 1969–1972, doc. 393.

Austria, Poland and East Germany) were more concerned about retaining high seas fisheries. As for security, the geographically disadvantaged states sought to prevent their naval vessels from being boxed in by the extension of neighbouring maritime zones – an issue potentially affecting, among others, Singapore and the two Germanys.

In 1971, the landlocked and geographically disadvantaged states' leaders solicited the support of the United States (which at the time opposed recognition of the economic zone) while cautioning American officials against embracing them too publicly lest this 'destroy them as a group'.[9] This entreaty did not bear long-term results: the Americans were much more interested in playing the G77 landlocked and geographically disadvantaged off against the G77 coastal states than in permanently aligning themselves with one or the other.

Within the G77, various efforts were made to find common ground between the major rival groups – namely, between the territorialists and the patrimonialists, and between the coastal states and the landlocked and geographically disadvantaged states. In 1972, two declarations emerged out of these efforts, which, it transpired, would together become a blueprint for the future exclusive economic zone. The Santo Domingo Declaration on the 'patrimonial sea', agreed by ten Caribbean and Central American states, sought to bridge the gap in the region between patrimonialists and territorialists.[10] The Yaoundé Declaration on the 'economic zone', drafted by African experts, sought compromise between Africa's coastal states and landlocked and geographically disadvantaged states.[11]

Both declarations endorsed a territorial sea of up to twelve miles.[12] Neither committed to the proposed economic zone's breadth, although the Santo Domingo Declaration stated that it should not exceed 200 miles, and should be subject to international agreement (not unilateral declaration).[13] Both asserted strong rights over resources, but not over the economic zone itself: the Yaoundé Declaration claimed 'exclusive jurisdiction' over 'living and non-living' resources, and the Santo

9 Ibid.

10 'Text of the Declaration of Santo Domingo approved by the meeting of ministers of the specialized conference of the Caribbean countries on the law of the sea' (7 June 1972), reprinted in: GOAR, A/8721 (1972), pp. 70–73.

11 'Conclusions in the general report of the African states regional seminar on the law of the sea, held in Yaoundé' (20–30 June 1972), reprinted in: GOAR, A/8721 (1972), pp. 73–76.

12 GOAR, A/8721 (1972), pp. 71, 74.

13 Ibid., p. 71.

Domingo Declaration claimed 'sovereign rights' over 'renewable and non-renewable' resources.[14] Finally, both declarations specified that other states' exercise of the freedoms of navigation, overflight and the laying of cables and pipelines would not be prejudiced in the economic zone,[15] which meant that the coastal states there had 'functional, but not spatial sovereignty'.[16] These approaches signalled the eventual demise of the territorialist position on 200-mile territorial seas, except as a maximal negotiating stance – and, of course, as a bogey to unnerve the maritime powers.

That said, the two declarations dealt differently with the relationship between the economic zone and the continental shelf over the exploration and exploitation of resources. The Santo Domingo Declaration envisaged the patrimonial sea coexisting with the continental shelf regime, absorbing the shelf into the economic zone's jurisdiction as far as it extended, but recognising the applicability of the continental shelf regime to shelf extending beyond it[17] – this being a sop to the wide-continental-margin Atlantic seaboard Latin American states. The Yaoundé Declaration, by contrast, envisaged an integrated economic zone that would absorb the whole continental shelf: inside the zone, all resources would fall under its jurisdiction; outside it, seabed resources would be managed by the international authority.[18] This spoke to the many mainland African coastal states with narrow continental shelves who would lose nothing from the incorporation of their shelves into an economic zone, and to the continent's many landlocked and geographically disadvantaged states who wished to maximise seabed common heritage. In addition, the Yaoundé Declaration offered the latter the right to exploit the living resources of the neighbouring economic zone, and the landlocked the right to transit through neighbouring coastal states, provided that exploitation was carried out by enterprises 'effectively controlled by African capital and personnel'[19] – a reminder that in Africa as elsewhere, commercial imperatives, protectionist or otherwise, drove the debate about the exploitation of maritime resources.

[14] Ibid., pp. 74, 75, 71.
[15] Ibid., pp. 72, 74.
[16] A. Aguilar Mawdsley, 'Law of the Sea: the Latin American view', in G. Pontecorvo (ed.), *The new order of the oceans* (New York: Columbia University Press, 1986), p. 178.
[17] GOAR, A/8721 (1972), p. 72.
[18] Ibid., pp. 75–76.
[19] Ibid., p. 74.

These concessions did not produce the hoped-for emollient effect among the landlocked and geographically disadvantaged states, however. This group within the G77, led by Afghanistan, Singapore and Uganda, noted that the Yaoundé Declaration did not offer them the right to explore (as distinct from exploit) the economic zone or to exploit its *non*-living resources. This prompted them in May 1974 to produce a declaration of their own – the Kampala Declaration – calling for these rights, as well as the right to transit and to use port facilities on an equal basis with the coastal states.[20] Their repudiation of the idea of an *exclusive* economic zone caused a row with the coastal states at the G77's conference at Nairobi shortly afterwards. As a result, the developing countries failed to agree a common platform before the start of negotiations on substantive issues at the second conference session, held in Caracas in June–August 1974. Thereafter at the conference, they would outnumber the powers and their allies, but would remain deeply divided within their own ranks.

Recognising the Economic Zone

At the Caracas session, the G5 powers tried to make the previously discussed package deal more enticing by abandoning their opposition to the economic zone. Throughout the earlier UN seabed committee sessions they had resisted the idea of the zone because they thought that it might develop into a de facto territorial sea, and because it would diminish the area of high seas open to their long-distance fishing fleets. But they changed tack at the conference, and offered to accept a twelve-mile territorial sea and a 200-mile economic zone in return for transit passage through straits and unimpeded navigation through the economic zone.[21] (The powers' acceptance of the zone entailed no great hardship to themselves: they would lose some long-distance fishing rights elsewhere but would gain the largest economic zones in the world.)

The Americans played the economic zone card just in time, as many delegates were arguing that it had already acquired the status of customary international law.[22] This assumption spurred seventy-one more states

[20] Reprinted in: UNLOSC III, vol. 3, A/Conf.62/23 (2 May 1974), p. 2.

[21] Oxman, *From cooperation to conflict*, pp. 10–11.

[22] Reynaldo Galindo Pohl pointed out that although the ICJ's *Fisheries jurisdiction* decisions handed down on 25 July 1974 did not recognise the exclusive economic zone as custom, this was likely because the Court had had 'neither the time nor the opportunity to

to claim new 200-mile zones in the years 1975–1979, with a surge of claims in the period after the 1974 session, and again after the United States' claim to a 200-mile conservation zone in 1976.[23] Acceptance of the designation '*exclusive* economic zone' would take a little longer: it first appeared in the negotiating text in 1975, but was subject to debate up until 1977 (hence our use of the generic term 'economic zone' in the account of the discussions up to that point.)

The landlocked and geographically disadvantaged states, swept along by this current, also submitted to the idea of the economic zone, their assumption being that collectively they would get a better deal over transit and fishing in neighbouring states' zones than they would from bilateral agreements. Their acceptance raised a host of new questions. Should they have the right to access the economic zone or merely the dispensation to do so subject to coastal state consent? Should access be confined to the economic zone of the neighbouring coastal state or to all economic zones in a sub-region or region? Should access be to all fisheries or only to the surplus catch in the economic zone? Should landlocked and geographically disadvantaged states' access to surplus catch be more extensive than that of other states? And should all landlocked and geographically disadvantaged states or just the developing countries from this group have access to the economic zone? In a motion submitted during the Caracas session, some members of the group made another statement of intent, claiming the right (not the privilege) to participate in the exploration and exploitation of living *and* non-living resources in neighbouring states' economic zones 'on an equal and non-discriminatory basis'.[24]

At this stage, the landlocked and geographically disadvantaged states had much to play for. If the negotiations went their way, they stood to gain a substantial share of living resources from neighbouring states' economic zones. In addition, the developing countries among them would secure a share of the revenues from the exploitation of common heritage on the seabed. And, to cap it all, they would likely bear fewer of the responsibilities shouldered by neighbouring coastal states, such as

examine the many declarations in support of the EEZ' at the contemporaneous Caracas session: 'The exclusive economic zone in the light of negotiations of the third United Nations conference on the law of the sea', in F. Orrego Vicuña (ed.), *The exclusive economic zone: a Latin American perspective* (Epping: Bowker Publishing, 1984), p. 57.

23 W. T. Burke, 'National legislation on ocean authority zones and the contemporary law of the sea', *Ocean Development and International Law* 9 (1981), 289, 292.

24 UNLOSC III, vol. 3, A/Conf.62/C.2/L.39 (5 August 1974), p. 216.

patrolling waters to prevent fishing, customs and immigration law violations; contending with the effects of oil spills, wrecks and other marine accidents; and paying for navigational lights, buoys, surveys and salvage operations.

The coastal states fought back. When the landlocked and geographically disadvantaged states opposed references to the word 'exclusive' in the exclusive economic zone, a coalition of Arab, African and Latin American coastal states argued that if 'exclusive' were deleted, it should be replaced by the word 'national'.[25] And when in 1976 the landlocked and geographically disadvantaged states sent a letter to the conference president stating that the texts on the table did not 'take account of the legitimate rights and interests of the States members of the Group',[26] the Peruvian delegate Alfonso Arias Schreiber responded with a letter of his own, asserting, not entirely in jest, the rights of the 'geo-economically disadvantaged' coastal states who had the misfortune of possessing long coastlines, broad continental shelves, and landlocked states as neighbours.[27]

The coastal state delegates, for less-than-benign motives, probed the fissures between the landlocked and the geographically disadvantaged members of the group. They managed to maintain their cohesion, but obviously had different preoccupations (the landlocked, unlike the geographically disadvantaged, were concerned with transit rights), and different tactical options available to them (if the negotiations were to fail, the landlocked would not have the option of making unilateral claims to the sea). They also had different economic profiles: two thirds of the landlocked states were developing countries, of whom a half were among the poorest,[28] belonging to what Samir Amin called the 'fourth world';[29] while two thirds of the geographically disadvantaged states were

[25] US Mission to the UN to US State Department (8 May 1976), s. 6, p. 4: 1976USUNN 02022, AAD.

[26] UNLOSC III, vol. 5, A/Conf.62/BUR/SR.15 (22 March 1976), p. 82.

[27] UNLOSC III, vol. 5, A/Conf.62/BUR/SR.17 (5 April 1976), p. 87.

[28] The landlocked signatories of the aforementioned letter to the president were: Afghanistan, Austria, Bhutan, Bolivia, Botswana, Burundi, Byelorussia, Central African Republic, Chad, Czechoslovakia, Holy See, Hungary, Laos, Lesotho, Lichtenstein, Luxembourg, Malawi, Mali, Mongolia, Nepal, Niger, Paraguay, Rwanda, San Marino, Swaziland, Switzerland, Uganda, Upper Volta and Zambia: UNLOSC III, vol. 5, A/Conf.62/BUR/SR.15 (22 March 1976), p. 82.

[29] S. Amin, and W. H. L. Anderson (trans.), *Empire of chaos* (New York: Monthly Review Press, 1992), p. 30, fn. 6.

wealthier nations, hailing from either Northern Europe or from the Gulf region.[30]

Paul Engo of Cameroon (a geographically disadvantaged state, although not a listed member of the claimants to this status) was among those who drew attention to the disparity between rich and poor within the group, arguing: 'One cannot seriously submit . . . that the land-locked States of Europe share a profound community of interest with those in my native Continent.'[31] He emphasised, for example, the difference between the European and African landlocked states' physical access to the coast: while the European states had 'an effective infrastructure of railway lines, road systems and air services linking their respective nations', the African states did not, even if the coastal states were prepared to grant them access.[32] (He did not mention it, but one place where such infrastructure was lacking was Tanzania, which in 1964 possessed just 300 kilometres of tarmacked roads; hardly enough to support the transit requirements of the five surrounding landlocked states of Burundi, Malawi, Rwanda, Uganda and Zambia.[33]) Engo and others' comments along these lines must have touched a raw nerve in the group. Later, the Ugandan delegate Ibrahim Wani, alluding to the transit issue for the African landlocked states, wrote: 'The group was chaired by the Austrian delegation for some time and one noticed the obvious emphasis put on the question of access to the resources of the EEZ rather than on transit and access to the sea, which should have received equal – if not more – attention.'[34]

Abandon the Shelf?

Another question preoccupying the delegates at Caracas was the relationship between the economic zone and the continental shelf. Many states

[30] The geographically disadvantaged signatories of the aforementioned letter to the president were: Bahrain, Belgium, Bulgaria, East Germany, Ethiopia, Finland, Gambia, Iraq, Jamaica, Jordan, Kuwait, Netherlands, Poland, Qatar, Singapore, Sudan, Sweden, United Arab Emirates, West Germany and Zaire: UNLOSC III, vol. 5, A/Conf.62/BUR/SR.15 (22 March 1976), p. 82.

[31] 'Statement in plenary session by Paul Bamela Engo' (2 July 1974), p. 12: box 16, RG 43, Records of international conferences, commissions, and expositions, Law of the Sea Conference, NARA.

[32] Ibid.

[33] Nyerere, *Freedom and a new world economic order*, p. 87.

[34] I. J. Wani, 'An evaluation of the Convention on the Law of the Sea from the perspective of the landlocked states', *Virginia Journal of International Law* 22 (1982), 627, 629, fn. 9.

took the view that the 1958 continental shelf convention had been overtaken by events, with some arguing that it had been made obsolete by newer commitments to the economic zone or to an internationalised seabed, and others that it had been discredited by its tilt towards wealthy states with wide, shallow continental shelves. Change was required, but states differed over what form it should take, and how the continental shelf should coexist with the economic zone. Given that both would grant the coastal states sovereign rights over seabed resources, should the economic zone regime extinguish, co-exist with, or overlap the continental shelf regime?

Some called for the complete abandonment of the continental shelf concept in favour of the economic zone. Some envisaged the two regimes operating in tandem, with either a water/shelf split[35] (the economic zone regime for water-based resources, the shelf regime for seabed-based resources) or an inner/outer split[36] (the economic zone regime for all resources within 200 miles, the continental shelf regime for shelf resources beyond 200 miles). Others saw two regimes overlapping on sovereign rights to exploration and exploitation while also retaining their distinct features – this being the approach that would ultimately be adopted in the convention.

The most conspicuous difference in approach was between the landlocked and geographically disadvantaged states, who wanted coastal state jurisdiction to stop at 200 miles irrespective of whether the geological shelf stopped before or went beyond that limit, and the wide-margin states who wanted coastal state jurisdiction to extend to either 200 miles or to the edge of the continental margin, whichever was further. The landlocked and geographically disadvantaged states, demonstrating impressive unity of purpose, queued up to argue that the economic zone, which at least had a defined limit, should override the existing continental shelf convention. Helmut Tuerk of Austria opened the debate, stating that 'the legal content of the term "continental shelf" should be absorbed by the new legal notion of "economic zone"'.[37] He was followed by Víctor Godoy of Paraguay ('The idea of a 200-mile economic zone meant that the rules governing the continental shelf were no longer in force'[38]);

35 Argentina's position, cited by Spain: UNLOSC III, vol. 2, A/Conf.62/C.2/SR.17 (26 July 1974), p. 148.
36 El Salvador's position: UNLOSC III, vol. 2, A/Conf.62/C.2/SR.18 (29 July 1974), p. 149.
37 UNLOSC III, vol. 2, A/Conf.62/C.2/SR.17 (26 July 1974), p. 143.
38 Ibid., p. 145.

Antoine Fattal of Lebanon ('The concept of the continental shelf should be replaced by that of the economic zone'[39]); Moufid Chehab of Egypt ('The idea of the exclusive economic zone ... would thus subsume the idea of the continental shelf'[40]); Mooki Molapo of Lesotho ('The colonial [shelf] concept ... should now be superseded by the concept of the economic zone'[41]); and Lucius Caflisch of Switzerland (the 'establishment of an exclusive economic zone ... would necessarily involve the disappearance of the regime provided for in the Geneva Convention on the Continental Shelf'[42]). And so on, with delegates from Gambia, Ghana, Kenya, Lesotho, Mali, Malta, Nepal, Tunisia and West Germany making the same point.

Their reason for wishing away the continental shelf concept, or at least restricting it to 200 miles, was that if wide-margined coastal states were permitted to claim both an economic zone *and* the continental shelf and the margin beyond it, they would encroach unreasonably upon the international seabed regime. Chao Hick Tin of Singapore thus argued that:

> Every State, whether coastal or land-locked, should be entitled to a fair share of the resources of the sea in accordance with the principle of the common heritage of mankind. If that principle was to have any meaning, as great an area as possible of the continental margin and the sea-bed should be reserved for the international regime. Even the establishment of the economic zone would be a crippling blow to the international regime ... If the coastal States were granted the right to the continental margin beyond the economic zone, leaving the international regime with merely the abyssal plains and other parts of the deep ocean basins, the concept of the common heritage of mankind would be as good as buried.[43]

Patrick Robinson of Jamaica made a similar point, citing a figure from a report by the UN secretary-general:

> a claim of coastal State jurisdiction up to the 3,000-metre isobath – which coincided approximately with the outer edge of the continental margin – would leave only 7 per cent of the off-shore mineral resources to the international zone. Was that the best endowment that could be offered the

39 Ibid., p. 148.
40 UNLOSC III, vol. 2, A/Conf.62/C.2/SR.18 (29 July 1974), p. 154.
41 UNLOSC III, vol. 2, A/Conf.62/C.2/SR.20 (30 July 1974), p. 164.
42 Ibid., p. 157.
43 UNLOSC III, vol. 2, A/Conf.62/C.2/SR.18 (29 July 1974), p. 151.

> international community? If so, it was questionable whether the International Sea-Bed Authority would be economically viable.[44]

On the other side, the group of wide-margin states led by Argentina, Australia and Canada (and also including Britain, India, the United States and the USSR), argued from the outset that the conference's role was not to abolish the legal concept of the continental shelf, but to determine its outer margin.[45]

The first touchstone for their campaign was the exploitability criterion appearing in the 1958 continental shelf convention.[46] This had given parties to the convention – who were now responding to the lure of oil and gas on their own continental shelves and to the oil shocks emanating from the Gulf – grounds to issue licences to commercial operations to explore the continental shelf at considerable distances out to sea. Australia, Canada, New Zealand and the United States (as well as non-parties Indonesia, Nicaragua and Taiwan) had, for example, licensed oil companies to survey seabed areas extending up to 400 miles out and 3,000 metres down, sometimes covering parts of the abyssal plain beyond the continental slope.[47] The Thai delegate Arun Panupong stated that in line with the 1958 convention (to which Thailand was a party):

> Long-term concessions had been granted to numerous companies and enterprises, both foreign and domestic, for the exploration of the continental shelf and the exploitation of its resources. Moreover, Thailand had entered into several international agreements on continental shelf boundaries with two of its neighbours. In short, an intricate web of legal relationships, both private and public, had already been established on the basis of the existing regime of the continental shelf.[48]

These wide-margin states argued that their rights could not, and more to the point, *should not* be reversed: 'there was no reason of equity why a coastal State should be deprived of an area over which it had existing rights', argued the Australian delegate, Ralph Harry – especially when the

44 UNLOSC III, vol. 2, A/Conf.62/C.2/SR.20 (30 July 1974), p. 167.

45 Australia's position: UNLOSC III, vol. 2, A/Conf.62/C.2/SR.17 (26 July 1974), pp. 146–147.

46 Convention on the Continental Shelf [hereafter, Continental Shelf Convention] (signed 29 April 1958; EIF 10 June 1964) 499 UNTS 311, 312.

47 'Limits to national jurisdiction for the purposes of exploration and exploitation of the seabed' (16 January 1970), p. 14: CAB 148/114, TNA; and 'Memorandum from the assistant legal adviser for East Asian and Pacific Affairs (Aldrich)' (29 May 1969): *FRUS*, 1969–1976, vol. E-1, *Documents on global issues*, 1969–1972, doc. 340.

48 UNLOSC III, vol. 2, A/Conf.62/C.2/SR.19 (30 July 1974), p. 159.

area under other states' jurisdiction 'was being maintained or even extended'.[49]

The second touchstone for the wide-margin states' arguments was the ICJ's 1969 *North sea continental shelf* decision that coastal states exercised rights over the continental shelf area 'that constitutes a natural prolongation of its land territory'.[50] The Court did not define 'natural prolongation', but when considering the shelf's extent, they argued that it should constitute the continental shelf, the continental slope, and the continental rise (the shelf debris at the bottom of the slope on the abyssal plain). This, the Argentinian delegate Elsa Kelly de Guibourg stated, was the only approach that was 'in harmony with the concept of the natural prolongation of the territory of the coastal State'.[51] But the problem with this argument, as the Swiss delegate Lucius Caflisch pointed out, was that the selective focus on 'natural prolongation' ignored the Court's holdings on the 'adjacency' test set out in article 1 of the 1958 continental shelf convention:

> Indeed, the Court, in paragraph 41 of its judgment, had said that by no stretch of the imagination could a point on the continental shelf situated about 100 miles, or even much less, from a given coast, be regarded as adjacent to that coast in the normal sense of 'adjacency'. That statement clearly contradicted the idea that the sea-bed extending beyond 200 miles to the outer limit of the continental margin, *de lege ferenda*, belonged to the continental shelf adjacent to the territorial sea.[52]

The delegates thus applied themselves to the question of where the continental margin ended and the international seabed regime began. Should the line be drawn at the last grain of sand on the continental rise, or might some other measure be devised? While this debate was unfolding, some landlocked and geographically disadvantaged states begun to calculate how they might claw back some concessions from the wide-margin states if the latter's campaign for a margin beyond 200 miles proved to be successful. At Caracas, they proposed a split regime governing the continental shelf, consisting of an inner zone within 200-miles, and an outer zone beyond 200 miles in which the coastal state would be obliged to hand over to the international authority

[49] UNLOSC III, vol. 2, A/Conf.62/C.2/SR.17 (26 July 1974), p. 147.

[50] *North Sea Continental Shelf (Federal Republic of Germany v Denmark; Federal Republic of Germany v Netherlands)* (Merits) [1969] ICJ Rep 3, 22.

[51] UNLOSC III, vol. 2, A/Conf.62/C.2/SR.18 (29 July 1974), p. 150.

[52] UNLOSC III, vol. 2, A/Conf.62/C.2/SR.19 (30 July 1974), pp. 157–158.

a percentage of revenues earnt from exploitation, to be shared out among states on similar lines as common heritage revenues. Patrick Robinson of Jamaica argued that this distribution would not entail mixed ownership of or mixed jurisdiction over the continental shelf: 'it would simply require that a contribution should be made out of the income derived from exploitation beyond 200 miles in favour of the international community'.[53]

This approach pointed to the eventual compromise: the wide-margin states would retain their sovereign rights over resources on the outer continental shelf (the margin edge of which should not exceed 350 miles from the territorial sea baseline or 100 miles from the line of the 2,500-metre isobath) while dispensing a percentage of revenues derived from non-living resources to other states,[54] thus going some way towards meeting the demands of the landlocked and geographically disadvantaged states. Some wide-margin states such as New Zealand and Canada signalled early on their acceptance of this idea in principle, leaving the battle over percentages and grace periods for later.[55] Others such as Australia and Britain held out against the idea for longer, their intransigence, John Stevenson noted, being a 'peculiar wrinkle' in Gough Whitlam and Harold Wilson's governments' 'professed support for LDCs'.[56]

As it turned out, securing revenues from the exploitation of the margin proved to be the landlocked and geographically disadvantaged states' only major success during the negotiations. By contrast, the group failed to make any headway against the coastal states over the economic zone. Despite their early declarations of intent, they could not find a way to compel the coastal states to share *any* of the resources of the economic zone, living or non-living; they had to be content with nominal access to the surplus living catch subject to the coastal states' laws and regulations.[57] This showed that despite their numbers and careful coordination, they suffered from two weaknesses. First, three-quarters of them were from the 'third' or 'fourth' worlds, or were mini- or micro-states, or both, and this, as Barry Buzan pointed out, meant that they were susceptible to pressure (or inducements) from the neighbours and

[53] Ibid., p. 168.
[54] Articles 76(5) and 82, UNCLOS, 429, 431.
[55] US Embassy Caracas to US State Department (30 August 1974), s.7, p. 4: 1974CARACA08511, AAD.
[56] Ibid.
[57] Article 62(2) and (4), UNCLOS, 421–422.

regional blocs on whom they relied for transit and other rights.[58] Second, the group – and especially the landlocked, as Buzan also indicated – lacked the fall-back option of unilateral action.[59] Moreover, if they failed to achieve what they wanted from the conference, they were unlikely to be able to reclaim it by any other method without precipitating a crisis.

Military Activities

While the debate about the relationship between the economic zone and the continental shelf was developing at the conference, the powers were privately digesting the potential impact on their military activities. At the heart of this concern was submarines – the movement of their own, and the detection of everyone else's. As far as the naval powers were concerned, these activities depended on being able to operate freely within the economic zone and on the continental shelf.

Modern integrated submarine detection systems, like the nuclear-powered and -armed submarines that inspired their use, evolved rapidly from the fifties onwards. Both the Americans and the Soviets devoted considerable resources to finding and tracking foreign submarines: using acoustic soundwaves such as active or passive sonar; electromagnetic light and radio waves such as radar and infrared; and magnetic anomaly detectors. Each of these technologies had strengths and weaknesses, so they were often used in combination – passive sonar, for example, was good for picking up the presence of a submarine a hundred miles away, but not for identifying its direction of travel, whereas active sonar was good at fixing the precise position of a submarine, but only at short range. These technologies could be either static or mobile; being either tethered to the sea floor, or attached to underwater installations, or mounted onto submarines and ships, or distributed onto the water by helicopters and fixed-wing aircraft.

The Americans led the field with passive sonar technologies capable of monitoring wide swathes of open ocean – the Soviets, according to the CIA, came a very poor second.[60] The centrepiece of their system was the seabed-based submarine 'sound surveillance system', or SOSUS, which consisted of hydrophone arrays linked by cable to coastal monitoring

58 B. Buzan, *Seabed politics* (New York: Praeger, 1976), p. 142.

59 Ibid.

60 'Soviet antisubmarine warfare: current capabilities and priorities' (September 1972), pp. 49, 58–59, 65: DOC0005512850, CIAHC.

stations (hence the US delegates' insistence on retaining the high seas freedom to lay cables in the exclusive economic zone and on the continental shelf). In the fifties, after experiments carried out off Puerto Rico and Eleuthera in the Bahamas, the Americans deposited SOSUS arrays along their own East and West coasts. Later, they laid arrays across the Bear Island-Norway and the Greenland-Iceland-UK (GIUK) gaps, with cables running to adjacent NATO states, to monitor Soviet submarines heading for the Atlantic; and across the Kurile-Japan straits, with cables running to Japan, to monitor Soviet submarines moving into the Pacific. Still later, as the Stockholm International Peace Research Institute reported in 1979, the Americans' SOSUS passive sonar combined with other detection technologies, operated by themselves and their allies, could track Soviet submarines moving through the North Atlantic and North Pacific:

> Submarines departing from Murmansk to the Atlantic Ocean and the Barents Sea will have been monitored by photographic, and perhaps electronic, reconnaissance satellites, and the progress of the Atlantic submarines will have been successively monitored by Norwegian Orions, sea-bottom sonar between Norway and Bear Island . . ., the well-documented SOSUS barrier across the GIUK gap (generally regarded as having 100 per cent detection capability), and by British Nimrod ASW aircraft. Once the submarines have passed out of the British area of responsibility into the Atlantic proper, they are monitored by US Navy systems. SOSUS installations on Bermuda and the Azores, SURTASS [surveillance towed array sensor systems] and remotely emplaced RDSS [rapidly deployable surveillance system] buoys will follow them in the mid-ocean 'holding areas', and US coastal SOSUS will detect any that come within 'Yankee'-class firing range. . . . The SSBNs ['ship, submersible, ballistic, nuclear' ballistic missile submarines] in the Pacific will be subject to a similar pattern of surveillance, although perhaps less thorough. They will be monitored by fixed sonars as they pass through the various Japanese straits, and then monitored by SOSUS, Japanese aircraft and US Orions. If necessary Australian and New Zealand Orions will assist.[61]

Size-wise, the SOSUS hydrophone arrays, which provided the backbone to the Americans' submarine detection system, were very large pieces of equipment. In the early sixties, for example, the US Navy indicated that

[61] O. Wilkes, 'Strategic anti-submarine warfare and its implications for a counterforce first strike', in Stockholm International Peace Research Institute (ed.), *World armaments and disarmament, SIPRI yearbook 1979* (London: Taylor & Francis, 1979), p. 445.

the arrays being laid on the seabed measured 1,800 feet (549 metres) across.[62] By the early seventies, the United States and its NATO allies started to mount hydrophones on underwater towers, including three 130-metre towers in waters just off the Azores to monitor submarine traffic moving through the Strait of Gibraltar.[63] By the end of the decade, they had developed vessels capable of towing arrays several miles behind them and transmitting data by satellite – the system known as SURTASS. Given the size and detectability of some of this equipment, laying static devices in the waters adjacent to a submarine-possessing hostile state was a risky proposition: hydrophone arrays, for example, still needed to be connected by cable to friendly onshore facilities, and if discovered, would be vulnerable to destruction and to legal challenges.[64] Even off their own coasts, the arrays were occasionally put out of action because their cables were cut by anchors and caught up in fishing gear – sometimes by accident but sometimes, it was suspected, by design; in 1974, the US Senate armed services committee considered a *Washington Post* article alleging that Soviet trawlers were deliberately cutting SOSUS cables with their trawls.[65]

In 1975, the Americans Max Morris and John Norton Moore addressed NATO delegates in Brussels, where they stressed that SOSUS was essential for maintaining the alliance's military edge over the USSR. As Morris stated: 'If we lost SOSUS, either through treaty or sabotage, we woul[d] lose much of our ability to track Soviet submarines.'[66] Moore explained that this was why they should insist on retaining high seas

[62] U.S. Navy: *Watch in the sea* [part one]: *the story of Project Caesar* (u.d., c. early 1960s), 9:23 at: www.youtube.com.

[63] M. Howe, 'Nato group establishes underwater testing range in the Azores for communications research', *New York Times* (5 March 1972); and K. Tsipis, 'Antisubmarine warfare', in Stockholm International Peace Research Institute (ed.), *World armaments and disarmament, SIPRI yearbook 1974* (Stockholm: Almqvist & Wiksell, 1974), p. 317.

[64] One argument might be that laying SOSUS devices to collect intelligence about traffic through a maritime zone is different from laying cables to transport information across it: V. Lowe, 'The commander's handbook on the law of naval operations and the contemporary law of the sea', in H. B. Robertson (ed.), *The law of naval operations* (International law studies, vol. 64) (Newport, RI: Naval War College Press, 1991), p. 113.

[65] The article – J. Anderson, 'U.S. military communications archaic', *Washington Post* (5 February 1973) – referred to the activities of Soviet trawlers *Autovon* and *Autosevocom*: US Senate committee on armed services, *Fiscal year 1974: Authorization for military procurement, research and development, construction authorization for the Safeguard ABM, and active duty and selected reserve strengths* (17 April 1973), p. 1050.

[66] US Mission to NATO to US State Department (8 March 1975), s. 6, p. 2: 1975NATO 01298, AAD.

rights in the economic zone.[67] He advised NATO states to remain silent about SOSUS at the conference, and to oppose any attempts by the coastal states to enumerate within the text 'precise rights' relating to the zone.[68] 'The best way to protect NATO security interests in SOSUS,' he continued, 'would be to make clear that aside from certain economic activities other existing high seas freedoms permitted under international law remain permitted rights in the economic zone'.[69] They hoped that the question of whether it was lawful to deploy hydrophone arrays (and other devices) in another state's economic zone or on its continental shelf without involving the coastal state would remain unclarified, allowing the powers to infer that what was not expressly prohibited would be permitted. The delegates representing NATO's members took Morris's advice, and by and large kept silent about military activities in the conference debates.

Other countries did not operate under the same constraints. At the Caracas session, Mexico tabled a motion in the second committee proposing that, 'No state may construct or deploy military installations or devices on the continental shelf of another state without its consent'.[70] Within hours it had attracted the support of several dozen other delegations. A week later, Mexico and Kenya introduced an even stronger thirty-six-power redraft proposing that, 'No State shall be entitled to construct, maintain, deploy or operate on or over the continental shelf of another State any military installations or devices or any other installations for whatever purposes without the consent of the coastal State.'[71] Ronald Purves, a well-placed Canadian observer, noted that Mexico's move was 'one of the more dramatic moments' of an already momentous session, and that the Americans responded in equal measure – by letting it be known that they would rather see the conference collapse than accept what was on offer.[72]

[67] Ibid., s. 1, p. 3.

[68] Ibid.

[69] Ibid.

[70] Reproduced in: US Embassy Caracas to US State Department (7 August 1974), p. 3: 1974CARACA07512, AAD; and, with slightly different wording, US Embassy Caracas to US State Department (15 August 1974), p. 2: 1974CARACA07850, AAD.

[71] UNLOSC III, vol. 3, A/Conf.62/C.2/L.42/Rev.1 (13 August 1974), p. 220.

[72] R. G. Purver, 'Canadian foreign policy and the military uses of the seabed', in B. J. Johnson and M. W. Zacher (eds.), *Canadian foreign policy and the law of the sea* (Vancouver: University of British Columbia Press, 1977), p. 245.

Along with the threat, John Stevenson made every possible effort to make the motion disappear. He argued that the issue was a diversion, and that the second committee was not the appropriate forum for the discussion of arms control.[73] He made 'strong private representations' to the Venezuelan chair Andrés Aguilar to drop references to it in a document on the continental shelf.[74] He recommended instructing the US ambassador in Mexico City to raise the matter with foreign secretary Emilio O. Rabasa.[75] He pressed Mexican delegation leader Jorge Castañeda and others to back down. And he rallied Western allies to oppose the motion. All this had the desired dampening effect, with Richardson reporting:

> After strong US private representation to Mexico . . . and others, Mexico introduced proposal on behalf of over 30 cosponsors requiring coastal state consent for military installations on cont[in]ental shelf in low-key fashion. Only other co-sponsors to speak was Gu[ ]yana, which said it supported Mexican proposal because this was correct interpretation of cont[in]ental shelf convention (probably implying that Mexican proposal could be dropped, and disagreement over interpretation of shelf convention continued). US, UK, FRG, Japan, and Turkey spoke against Mexican proposal, urging that question be taken up in arms control forum. Uruguay said Argentine proposal for coastal state control over installation, without mentioning military installations specifically, was more appropriate.[76]

'I Like Russian Tactics'

In the final year of Gerald Ford's Republican administration, the US Congress faced down the executive and enacted a 200-mile fishing conservation zone, signed into law on 13 April 1976.[77] Washington officials feared this would reduce the incentive for other states to sign up to the convention. They also feared that it would reduce their bargaining power over some of the remaining issues on the table, such as seabed exploitation and marine scientific research. They were not the

[73] US Embassy Caracas to US State Department (17 August 1974), p. 2: 1974CARACA 07946, AAD.

[74] US Embassy Caracas to US State Department (15 August 1974), p. 2: 1974CARACA 07850, AAD.

[75] Ibid.

[76] US Embassy Caracas to US State Department (20 August 1974), s. 1, p. 3: 1974CARACA 08037, AAD.

[77] *Fishery Conservation and Management Act of 1976*, PL 94-265, 94th Congress, H.R. 200 (13 April 1976).

only ones expressing these concerns. According to Bernard Oxman, the Soviets seemed 'shocked at and betrayed' by the Congressional action because they felt that the basis for their cooperation with the United States was 'opposition to unilateral claims by coastal states'.[78] In Washington, Soviet deputy foreign affairs minister Semyon P. Kozyrev met with secretary of state Henry Kissinger (referred to below as 'Secretary'). He began diplomatically enough by counting off the powers' successes at the conference thus far: straits, archipelagos, the territorial sea, pipelines and cables.[79] Then he got to the point:

> KOZYREV: ... There are some problems in the Economic Zone regime, however. Some States, which in the past have been reasonable, are now making problems. Some have hardened their positions on the Economic Zone to justify their national legislation. The fisheries law of the United States [hereafter referred to as 'the law'] played a negative role in this. We have always attached high importance to a common approach by the U.S. and the USSR on all basic Law of the sea issues. On many issues we have moved together and have had good impact. The departure of the United States from this common approach, in taking unilateral law of the sea action, has had a negative impact.
>
> SECRETARY: Is there anything else in addition to the law?
>
> KOZYREV: Yes, there are other things, too. Law of the sea issues have an international character and should be solved internationally. I recall your April 8 statement but your law does not tally with your statement.
>
> SECRETARY: I like Russian tactics. They beat me over the head for fifteen minutes, so it takes me at least ten minutes to catch up; but, seriously, we opposed the law. What else has shown unilateral tendencies by the United States?
>
> KOZYREV: The law has hardened developing countries positions and has not brought any benefit to the conference.
>
> SECRETARY: We can't do anything about it now.
>
> KOZYREV: Many developing countries are now firmer on the Economic Zone regime, demanding exclusive jurisdiction and they have hardened their positions on the deep seabed and scientific research.

[78] Oxman, *From cooperation to conflict*, p. 15.

[79] 'Memorandum of conversation' (13 August 1976), p. 2: *FRUS*, 1969–1976, vol. E-3, *Documents on global issues*, 1973–1976, doc. 37.

SECRETARY: I was against the law, but Senator Pell here was for it, so you should yell at him.[80]

Kissinger's flippancy must have been exasperating, but it was symptomatic of the growing schism between the United States and the USSR on the law of the sea. As Kozyrev noted, the two powers had achieved what they initially had set out to do – restricting the territorial sea and maximising freedom of navigation. Without the need for further collaboration, their relationship started to unravel.[81] This loosened the ties holding the G5 together, and before long, the Americans, *primus inter pares*, would find themselves not only fighting rear-guard actions against the Soviets, but also against their erstwhile Western allies.

Throughout this process, all states paid close attention to the negotiations over the economic zone. Would waters within the zone remain as high seas, allowing states complete freedom of action except over resources, or would they become sui generis, giving the coastal state sovereign or jurisdictional rights over all except navigation and communications? The Americans fought for the economic zone to retain its high seas character, but by 1976 it was clear that a more nuanced strategy might be required. In this scenario, US delegates would publicly agree to a compromise – presented by a state that was not a major power but with whom they were privately colluding – which would hint at the economic zone's sui generis form while retaining its high seas content. The Americans had already identified three states as candidates for this role: Australia, Canada and Norway. 'Australia is making considerable attempts to help us on sensitive military-related issues,' John Stevenson had noted back in 1974, 'and it is clear that we will have to rely to some extent on them and Canada to carry the ball on certain issues where a US intervention would be a red flag.'[82] The economic zone was one of these issues.

In August 1976, the American delegation reported some movement along these lines:

> For the time being, on certain issues – e.g., high seas status of the economic zone – we are telling the opposition to make a proposal,

[80] Ibid., pp. 2–3.
[81] US Mission to the UN to US State Department (10 August 1976), s. 1, p. 1: 1976USUNN03172: AAD.
[82] US Embassy Caracas to US State Department (27 July 1974), s. 2, p. 3: 1974CARACA07083, AAD.

> because it is clear that maritime power initiative will not have as good a chance of succeeding; we are working behind the scenes with sympathetic members of opposing groups (e.g., Australia in the coastal state group).[83]

The Australian delegate Keith Brennan duly presented a proposal on the economic zone that suited the Americans.[84] Shortly afterwards, Bernard Oxman discussed the next steps in the campaign with Stuart French and Stevenson's successor, Vincent Learson.

> *OXMAN:* . . . Australia is going to sound people out on [Brennan's proposal], but my guess is that it won't work.
>
> *LEARSON:* The next step is to get [Stuart] French to write some words that do the same thing in another way. We need to give the 77 the appearance of a victory. We can't say that the Economic Zone is the high seas in so many words, but we can find some language that will do essentially the same thing. I think we can work this one out.
>
> . . .
>
> *FRENCH:* What we need is language that gives the 77 what they need cosmetically, but for all practical purposes give high seas status to the Economic Zone.[85]

The Castañeda Initiative

The new regime governing the exclusive economic zone was finally constructed at the end of the climactic May–July 1977 session. This began, much like all the previous committee sessions, as a three-way fight between the maritime powers, the coastal states and the landlocked and geographically disadvantaged states. In June, the Americans insisted on the existing text being changed to refer to the exclusive economic zone having the status of the high seas.[86] The Peruvian Alfonso Arias Schreiber dismissed this attempt to amend the text as a 'waste of time'.[87] The landlocked and geographically disadvantaged states threatened to

83 US State Department to US delegation (7 August 1976), p. 2: 1976STATE196781, AAD.

84 US Mission to the UN to US State Department (8 May 1976), s. 7, p. 4: 1976USUNN 02022, AAD.

85 'Memorandum for the record' (27 August 1976), p. 2: *FRUS*, 1969–1976, vol. E-3, *Documents on global issues*, 1973–1976, doc. 40.

86 K. S. Pitt and S. S. Crew, 'UNLOSC: fourth week' (17 June 1977), p. 2: DEFE 24/ 1185, TNA.

87 Ibid.

block the preparation of a text if they did not secure the preferential fishing rights they were seeking.[88] So far, predictable enough.

In early July, faced with the prospect of yet another deadlocked session, the Mexican delegation leader Jorge Castañeda invited a small group of delegation heads to a private dinner. He proposed that they produce a text that would cut through the knot of three entangled issues: the legal status of the economic zone; marine scientific research in the economic zone; and dispute settlement provisions relating to the economic zone. A slightly larger group was then formed, and its more-or-less secret discussions continued from 2 to 12 July 1977.[89] The Americans, who had a hand in the initiative, envisaged something similar to the UK–Fiji straits group: as well as encouraging a G77 delegate to lead the talks, and excluding most of the more radical coastal states, they hoped to draft a compromise between themselves and those occupying the centre ground, which would then be presented to the other delegates in the committee as a fait accompli.

Once the group was up and running, Castañeda chaired most of the meetings, and co-rapporteurs Helge Vindenes (Norway) and Andrés Rozental (Mexico) drafted the text.[90] The core group of regular attendees was made up of Australia, Brazil, Britain, Canada, India, Mexico, Nigeria, Norway, Singapore, the United States and the USSR. It included four G77 coastal states, three maritime powers and one geographically disadvantaged state. US delegation head Elliot Richardson played a leading role in the discussions, indicating the importance of the subject for the Americans. Delegates from Egypt, Kenya and Tanzania attended intermittently, as did the second and third committee chairs, Andrés Aguilar and Alexander Yankov (whose committees covered, respectively, the exclusive economic zone, and marine scientific research in the exclusive economic zone).[91] Arias Schreiber had not been invited because of the Peruvian government's radical stance on the economic zone, but he got wind of the meetings and invited himself.[92]

The most important issue addressed by the Castañeda group was the status of the exclusive economic zone. While the powers sought high seas

[88] UK Mission to the UN to UK FCO (9 June 1977), p. 2: FCO 76/1666, TNA.
[89] D. Logan, 'Note on negotiations on the legal status of the economic zone' (u.d., c. July 1977), p. 1: FCO 76/1643, TNA.
[90] Ibid., pp. 1–2.
[91] Ibid., p. 1.
[92] Ibid.

rights, the G77 members (adopting a proposal put forward by Aguilar[93]) wanted an economic zone sui generis: neither territorial sea nor high sea. The two sides eventually settled on a new formula, which appeared in articles 55 and 86 in the text produced at the end of the 1977 session.[94] Article 55 began: 'The exclusive economic zone is an area beyond and adjacent to the territorial sea, subject to the specific legal regime established in this Part.'[95] Because it nowhere stated that the economic zone was legally distinct from the high seas, the word 'specific' could be read either as recognising the zone's sui generis nature, or as referring to any legal regime applicable to the zone, including the high seas. This latter possibility was removed by reading article 55 alongside article 86, which stated that the high seas provisions 'apply to all parts of the sea *that are not included in the exclusive economic zone*, in the territorial sea or in the internal waters of a State, or in the archipelagic waters of an archipelagic State'[96] – a formula that would, following on the heels of custom, confirm the shrinkage of the high seas by a third.

For all that, Richardson and his colleagues took two important steps to ensure that the exclusive economic zone did retain many high seas features. Their first move was to take up Keith Brennan's helpful proposal to insert a 'no sovereignty' clause into article 55 of the exclusive economic zone part of the text,[97] which would match the 'no sovereignty' clause in the high seas part (stating: 'Accordingly, no State may validly purport to subject any part of them to its sovereignty'[98]). This change would foreclose any coastal state claims to an exclusive economic zone that had the character of a territorial sea. But when Arias Schreiber started attending the meetings, he demanded the deletion of this new 'no sovereignty' clause, to which Bernard Oxman acceded,[99] leaving article 55 to read:

93 UNLOSC III, vol. 5, A/Conf.62/WP.8/Rev.1/PartII (7 May 1976), p. 153.

94 On citations, the Castañeda text's amendments to the 1976 committee texts are reproduced in: US Mission to the UN to US State Department (16 July 1977), s.1, p. 1 – s. 4, p. 2: 1977USUNN02276, AAD. These articles were incorporated substantially unamended into the text produced in 1977: UNLOSC III, vol. 8, A/Conf.62/WP.10 (15 July 1977). For clarity about the numbering and the cross-references to other articles, all the articles quoted above come from the 1977 text.

95 Ibid., A/Conf.62/WP.10, p. 13.

96 Ibid., p. 17. Emphasis added.

97 D. Logan, 'Note on negotiations on the legal status of the economic zone' (u.d., c. July 1977), p. 3: FCO 76/1643, TNA.

98 Article 76(1), UNLOSC III, vol. 5, A/Conf.62/WP.8/Rev.1/PartII (7 May 1976), p. 165.

99 D. Logan, 'Note on negotiations on the legal status of the economic zone' (u.d., c. July 1977), p. 4: FCO 76/1643, TNA.

> The exclusive economic zone is an area beyond and adjacent to the territorial sea, subject to the specific legal regime established in this Part, under which the rights and jurisdictions of the coastal State and the rights and freedoms of other States are governed by the relevant provisions of the present Convention.[100]

Oxman, moving to a fall-back position, proposed that within the high seas part of the text, the 'no sovereignty' clause in article 76(1) would be turned into a new standalone article – article 89 – stating: 'No State may validly purport to subject any part of the high seas to its sovereignty.'[101] This would be linked back to the exclusive economic zone by the new article 58(2) in the exclusive economic zone part stating that, 'Articles 88 to 115 [on the high seas] and other pertinent rules of international law apply to the exclusive economic zone in so far as they are not incompatible with this Part'[102] – thereby achieving by a roundabout route what the uncut article 55 had done directly.[103] The French delegation, informed of these developments, opposed this, pointing out that the coastal states would deny that article 89 was applicable to the exclusive economic zone by way of article 58(2) because it was possibly incompatible with new article 55 (which stated that the exclusive economic zone was 'subject to the specific legal regime established in this Part'), and likely incompatible with new article 56 (on the rights, jurisdiction and duties of the coastal State in the zone).[104] In short, the French thought it was a clumsy manoeuvre that would fool precisely nobody.

Expanding Freedoms

The powers' second move to retain high seas freedoms in the exclusive economic zone related to the existing article 46(1) on the rights and duties of 'foreign' states there, which read:

> In the exclusive economic zone, all States, whether coastal or land-locked, enjoy, subject to the relevant provisions of the present Convention, the freedoms of navigation and overflight and of the laying of submarine

[100] UNLOSC III, vol. 8, A/Conf.62/WP.10 (15 July 1977), p. 13.
[101] Ibid., p. 18.
[102] Ibid., p. 13.
[103] On the discussion, see: D. Logan, 'Note on negotiations on the legal status of the economic zone' (u.d., c. July 1977), pp. 4–5: FCO 76/1643, TNA.
[104] Ibid., p. 8.

> cables and pipelines and other internationally lawful uses of the sea related to navigation and communication.[105]

This final clause was the sum of differing viewpoints. In earlier sessions, the Americans had added the words 'and other internationally lawful uses of the sea' to it with the aim of legitimising military activities in the economic zone.[106] In response, the Argentinian delegate Arnoldo Listré had added the words 'related to navigation and communication', presumably with the aim of reining in the scope of these 'other' uses.[107] Now in the Castañeda group, Richardson and Oxman made it clear that they wanted more high sea freedoms in the exclusive economic zone than allowed for by article 46(1). What they had in mind was a more capacious new text – new article 58(1) – which read:

> In the exclusive economic zone, all States, whether coastal or land-locked, enjoy, subject to the relevant provisions of the present Convention, the freedoms referred to in article 87 of navigation and overflight and of the laying of submarine cables and pipelines, and other internationally lawful uses of the sea related to these freedoms such as those associated with the operation of ships, aircraft and submarine cables and pipelines, and compatible with the other provisions of the present Convention.[108]

States already vested with the named freedoms in the exclusive economic zone – navigation, overflight and so on – were now also endowed with further freedoms, 'such as those associated with the operation of ships, aircraft and submarine cables and pipelines', which might not necessarily be classed as 'related to navigation and communication' (as specified in the earlier version). The American commentator Horace Robertson suggested that naval manoeuvres, for example, were not covered by 'navigation' but were covered by 'associated with the operation of ships, aircraft'.[109] Yet these further freedoms were not fully enumerated, and the nature of their association with the named freedoms was not specified. Indeed, even if they had been itemised, any list of further freedoms would still be open-

105 UNLOSC III, vol. 5, A/Conf.62/WP.8/Rev.1/PartII (7 May 1976), p. 160.

106 D. Logan, 'Note on negotiations on the legal status of the economic zone' (u.d., c. July 1977), p. 3: FCO 76/1643, TNA.

107 Ibid.

108 UNLOSC III, vol. 8, A/Conf.62/WP.10 (15 July 1977), p. 13.

109 H. B. Robertson, 'Navigation in the exclusive economic zone', *Virginia Journal of International Law* 24 (1984), 865, 877.

ended, as indicated by the words 'such as' in this article, and the phrase '*inter alia*' in article 87(1).[110]

Finally, regarding this article, the word 'operation' did a good deal of heavy lifting because it could be interpreted as either the mechanical function or the naval undertaking. The powers assumed that 'operation' in the second sense validated military activity within the exclusive economic zone, especially when read in conjunction with article 237,[111] which used the same terminology ('operations', 'operational capabilities' and 'operated') in relation to the immunity of warships and other state vessels and aircraft.[112]

At a NATO meeting convened a few months after article 58(1)'s introduction into the text, the West Germans probed the Americans for more information about the sort of military activities allowed in the exclusive economic zone. They tabled a paper setting out their own reading of the text:

> we believe that article 58 in connection with articles 86 and 87 of the ICNT [informal composite negotiating text of 1977], covers all normal military uses of ships, aircraft, submarine cables and pipelines, especially by the text 'uses of the sea ... such as those associated with the operation of ships, aircraft and submarines cables and pipelines'. This comprises especially the navigation of ships of armed navies and of submarines, overflight by military aircraft, naval and air manoeuvres, exercises, weapons tests, reconnaissance and surveillance, landing exercises, the take-off and the taking on board of aircraft, detection of mines. On the other hand, it appears doubtful whether, for example, 'dormant weapons systems' in foreign economic zones are covered by para. 1 of art. 58 of the ICNT since they do not have anything directly to do with the operation of warships and aircraft and the laying of submarine cables and pipelines. Reconnaissance systems, on the other hand, seem to be covered by para. 1 of article 55 of the ICNT.[113]

The Dutch followed the Germans, noting that the wording of the clause 'internationally lawful uses of the sea ... associated with the operation of ships, aircraft' could encompass 'many things', but they could still foresee problems with reconnaissance systems because these, unlike

[110] UNLOSC III, vol. 8, A/Conf.62/WP.10 (15 July 1977), pp. 13, 17.
[111] Ibid., p. 41.
[112] US Mission to NATO to US State Department (25 October 1977), s. 1, p. 3: 1977USNATO10323, AAD.
[113] Ibid., s. 1, p. 3 – s. 2, p. 1.

dormant weapon systems, were not connected with the operations of ships.[114]

The Americans responded that the text preserved existing rights regarding the military uses of the oceans, setting out a regime that was 'qualitatively the same' in the high seas and the exclusive economic zone as long as these rights were exercised with due regard to the rights and duties of the coastal state in the latter.[115] Turning to specific articles, they noted that the freedoms set out in article 58(1) were 'very broad indeed',[116] and that article 60, which gave the coastal state the exclusive right to construct and regulate artificial islands, installations and structures, 'does not rpt not include under coastal state jurisdiction the types of devices referred to in the FRG paper' (i.e. dormant weapons systems).[117]

> This fact, along with the broad language of article 58, para 1, supports our belief that the right of military use in the economic zone has been preserved. We further believe that this was commonly understood by those who negotiated the text.[118]

*

Although the Americans and their allies had made most of the running in the Castañeda group, they were not home yet. Delegates who had not been invited to join were bound to raise criticisms, and it was by no means guaranteed that the committee chairs Aguilar and Yankov would incorporate the Castañeda text unamended into their respective end-of-session texts. But time – or rather the lack of it – was on the powers' side. The group released the text to the other delegations on 12 July 1977, just three days before the session broke up, leaving insufficient time for considered debate about the proposals.

When Aguilar broached discussion about the 'anonymous' Castañeda text in the second committee, it drew a strong response.[119] Some

114 US Mission to NATO to US State Department (16 November 1977), p. 2: 1977USNATO11437, AAD.

115 US State Department to US Mission to NATO (12 December 1977), pp. 2–3: 1977STATE296069, AAD.

116 Ibid., p. 2.

117 Ibid., p. 3.

118 Ibid.

119 US Mission to the UN to US State Department (16 July 1977), s. 4, p. 2: 1977USUNN02276, AAD.

delegates objected to their exclusion from the decision-making process, including the Uruguayan, who was 'somewhat incensed by the procedure which had been employed in the formulation of the new text'.[120] Others complained about substance, including Arias Schreiber, who argued that article 58(1) gave even more freedom to foreign states in the exclusive economic zone than they already enjoyed on the high seas,[121] and that its references to the 'operation of ships, aircraft' should be preceded by the words 'peaceful' or 'normal'.[122] Landlocked Zambia and Bolivia complained that the text seemed to be designed to satisfy only the interests of the coastal states and the maritime powers, but not the interests of the third major group at the conference – the landlocked and geographically disadvantaged states.[123]

Yet the prevailing inclination was to accept the Castañeda text. The West Germans pushed Aguilar to incorporate it into the text,[124] and Elliot Richardson pressed even harder, stating that if it was an improvement, Aguilar had a *duty* to incorporate it[125] at this 'most critical moment of the conference'.[126] Aguilar obliged, adding it to the end-of session text without amendment.

This was not the first time the powers had bounced the second committee into accepting provisions agreed by an unrepresentative group. But while the powers' methods were hardly democratic, they were certainly effective, resolving both the form and the content of the exclusive economic zone. Keith Brennan, who had played an important supporting role to the Americans, privately acknowledged that the United States had won a 'signal victory' by preserving high seas rights within this new jurisdiction.[127]

120 Ibid., s. 4, p. 3.

121 Ibid.

122 H. G. Darwin, 'Second committee consultative group: status of EEZ' (12 July 1977), p. 1: FCO 76/1643, TNA.

123 US Mission to the UN to US State Department (16 July 1977), s. 5, p. 3: 1977USUNN 02276, AAD.

124 H. G. Darwin, 'Second committee consultative group: status of EEZ' (12 July 1977), p. 2: FCO 76/1643, TNA.

125 Ibid.

126 US Mission to the UN to US State Department (16 July 1977), s. 5, p. 2: 1977USUNN 02276, AAD.

127 Australian High Commission London to Foreign Affairs Canberra (23 September 1977), p. 2: A10463/3 801/10/2 pt. 5, NAA.

Consent for Research

It was a different story in the third committee. This body, whose drafting responsibilities overlapped with those of the other committees, dealt not with zones but with activities – namely, marine scientific research, technology transfer, and the protection of the marine environment. The stumbling block for many delegates was the Castañeda text's liberal approach to scientific research in the exclusive economic zone, which, they thought, gave foreign states too much leeway. The issue of coastal state consent for research became a flashpoint in relations between the researching and the researched states. The former, led by the United States, claimed the right to carry out research unhindered in or on other states' economic zones or continental shelves provided that it was not connected to the exploration and exploitation of resources. The latter, led by Brazil, India and Kenya, argued that the researching states should seek permission from the coastal state before embarking on *any* scientific research there, whether its purpose was resource-related or not.

When considering the issue, the existing law did not offer very much guidance. It was accepted that states should secure permission to carry out research in others' territorial seas, and that they had a free hand on the high seas so long they did not interfere unreasonably with others' activities, but what of the intervening zones? The point of reference for the debate was article 5(8) of the 1958 continental shelf convention, which read:

> The consent of the coastal State shall be obtained in respect of any research concerning the continental shelf and undertaken there. Nevertheless, the coastal State shall not normally withhold its consent if the request is submitted by a qualified institution with a view to purely scientific research into the physical or biological characteristics of the continental shelf, subject to the proviso that the coastal State shall have the right, if it so desires, to participate or to be represented in the research, and that in any event the results shall be published.[128]

This article set down several markers: it established that consent should be sought from the coastal state for research on the continental shelf; that the coastal state 'shall not normally withhold its consent' for 'purely scientific research'; and that 'purely scientific research' (bolstered by article 5(1)'s reference to 'fundamental oceanographic … scientific research') set up a distinction based on intent between 'pure' research dedicated to the

[128] Article 1, Continental Shelf Convention, 316.

advancement of knowledge for its own sake and 'applied' research directed towards exploration and exploitation for commercial ends.

Yet article 5(8), while being the most detailed of the research-related provisions in the 1958 conventions, was also the most ambiguous. For one thing, the obligation to seek permission for 'any research concerning the continental shelf and undertaken there' could either be read restrictively, as addressing only research *about* the shelf carried out *on* the shelf (such as coring or dredging), or it could be read expansively, as also allowing research *about* the shelf conducted from elsewhere (such as remote sensing by satellites) and research *from* the shelf directed elsewhere (such as shelf-based monitoring of currents). For another thing, the phrase 'in any event' could suggest that the publication of research should take place irrespective of whether the coastal state had participated in the research, or it could suggest that it take place irrespective of the circumstances being abnormal, the research mixed, or the institution unqualified. Furthermore, the words 'normally', 'purely' and 'qualified' were bound to give rise to widely differing interpretations.

When focussing on consent for research on the continental shelf, the conference delegates adopted a selective approach to article 5(8). The G77 coastal states, when insisting that all foreign scientific research should be subject to consent and possible refusal, tended to ignore the article's injunction to 'not normally withhold its consent'. And the powers, when arguing that research unrelated to resources should be either unrestricted or subject at most to prior notification, were inclined to overlook the article's injunction to seek consent for 'any research concerning the continental shelf'.

When presenting the case for a consent-free regime for non-resource related research, the powers couched their argument in the language of universalism, declaring that scientific investigation on the continental shelf and in the economic zone was valuable to all states, and especially those unable to conduct research of their own. Even so, they managed to convey this uplifting message in negative, and at times slightly threatening, terms. In 1974, John Stevenson observed that scientific research was 'difficult, time-consuming and expensive', and the only way to make sure that those who could afford it shared it with others 'would be to create a regime which would guarantee that research was conducted for the universal benefit'.[129] In the same debate, the Swedish

[129] UNLOSC III, vol. 2, A/Conf.62/C.3/SR.8 (19 July 1974), p. 341.

delegate Jarl-Ove Strömberg argued that imposing controls on research 'would delay and might even obstruct a final understanding of many of the natural processes of the oceans',[130] while the British delegate Donald Logan predicted that controls would lead to the 'reduction, and perhaps complete cessation, of marine scientific research'.[131] (The Spanish delegate José de Yturriaga responded to Logan's bold claim with a bold claim of his own, saying that 'no State, as far as his delegation knew, had complained that research activities were being impeded, slowed down, or paralysed'.[132])

The researching powers also claimed that a consent regime in the economic zone would be tantamount to claiming a 200-mile territorial sea because it would extend coastal state control over the whole zone, rather than simply over resources. In 1976, for example, the West German delegate, Hermann Knoke, remarked:

> It appeared from the statements made by representatives of Kenya, the United Republic of Tanzania, Brazil and Peru that they regarded the concept of the economic zone as very similar to that of the territorial sea. Yet in the beginning there had not been any question of the economic zone being a zone under the exclusive jurisdiction of coastal States when it came to scientific research. If such had been the case, the international scientific community would have been up in arms.[133]

Some scientists were indeed up in arms, but the powers' campaign for a consent-free regime was frustrated by two developments. First, the G77 coastal states, whether patrimonialist or territorialist, maintained a united front on research, eventually forcing the powers to retreat from their position in exchange for concessions elsewhere in the package. Second, under this pressure, the researching powers' own unity cracked in 1976, with the USSR breaking ranks and joining the developing countries' campaign for a complete consent regime, and France and Japan either endorsing or being prepared to accept a qualified consent regime. At this point, the Americans grumbled that the only states they could still rely on for support were West Germany and the Netherlands.[134]

[130] Ibid., p. 344.
[131] UNLOSC III, vol. 6, A/Conf.62/C.3/SR.29 (10 September 1976), p. 93.
[132] Ibid., p. 94.
[133] Ibid.
[134] US Mission to the UN to US State Department (17 September 1976), s. 8, p. 1: 1976USUNN03795, AAD.

The United States tried to reclaim lost ground in 1977. When the session opened, Elliot Richardson distributed to other delegation heads a statement by the US National Research Council (NRC) oceans policy committee, representing American oceanographers, which set out a science-without-borders position:

> Nature knows no artificial boundaries. Ocean phenomena do not stop at national boundaries, or stop at the edge of the continental shelf. Scientific curiosity does not cease as one moves from deep water to shallow water, or from one area of the deep sea into the economic zone.[135]

The NRC committee argued that the study of regional phenomena – from monsoons in the Indian Ocean, to upwelling in the Gulf of Guinea, to El Niño in the West Pacific – should not be held back by 'artificial boundaries':

> Since marine scientific research yields knowledge of social utility, it is difficult to understand how any State can erect barriers that restrict mankind from learning what must be known about the ocean in order to optimize its use for the benefit of all. Because ocean phenomena do not respect national boundaries, if an individual coastal State has control over marine scientific research projects in its zone, it can control the flow of benefits of that proposed research to neighbouring States.[136]

The committee then gave examples of the damaging effects of states impeding American oceanographic research:

> A few years ago, the Woods Hole Oceanographic Institution made a series of studies along the continental shelf of West Africa. Permission was requested from all the necessary coastal States for the *R/V Atlantis II* to perform the research. The primary purpose was to accumulate knowledge about the geologic history of the West African continental margin area and the geologic structure of the shelf. At the same time the study provided some evidence about which shelf areas might be more likely than others to have oil and gas resources. Two coastal states refused to allow the Woods Hole ship to work on their continental shelf. Although the program was not a failure because of these two refusals, the results were incomplete and interpretations more difficult. The problem is somewhat analogous to attempting to solve and then interpret a jigsaw puzzle

[135] National Research Council (US), 'The marine scientific research issue in the law of the sea negotiations' (u.d., c. May 1977), p. 2: FCO 76/1634, TNA. (This was reprinted as: Ocean Policy Committee of the Commission of International Relations NAS-NRC, 'The marine scientific research issue in the law of the sea negotiations', *Science* 197 (15 July 1977), 230-233.)

[136] Ibid.

> with a number of missing pieces. The larger the number of missing pieces the more difficult the task and the more likely the interpretation will be wrong, even in those areas where the research was completed. An analogous program off the coast of East Africa and the Arabian Sea has never been carried out because of the negative response to preliminary enquiries from a significant number of States in the region.[137]

This account likely referred to the *R/V Atlantis II*'s research cruise off West Africa in 1972–1973. But who were the unnamed states who refused to allow it to conduct research on their continental shelves? Two decades later, Judith Fenwick, also based at Woods Hole, surveyed all clearance requests sought by American research vessels over this period, and showed that two West African states did not consent to requests in 1972. One state was Liberia, which did not actively *refuse* a research cruise, as the NRC committee claimed, but simply omitted to approve one due to unspecified 'coastal state problems'.[138] The other state was neighbouring Sierra Leone, which permitted a port call but declined a research cruise 'because of state of emergency'.[139] Given the political and security situation in these states in 1972, their response to the requests was perhaps understandable.

Another theme, which was absent from the committee's account, was a plain fact of international life – the law of the sea. In law, maritime boundaries, however 'artificial' (as the committee put it), could not be ignored. While the scientific argument for borderless science was compelling, so too was the legal argument upholding coastal state authority over adjacent maritime zones. The US State Department, as distinct from the NRC committee, was well aware of its legal obligations towards foreign states. In 1973 it cited three instances in which it felt obliged to ask another state's permission to conduct research. The first was for research conducted in the territorial sea – but only a territorial sea out to three miles,[140] in line with the United States' then non-recognition of claims beyond that limit. The second was for fisheries-related research in a fishing zone – but only out to twelve miles,[141] in line with the United States' own twelve-mile fishing zone declared in 1966. The third was for

137 Ibid., p. 5.

138 J. Fenwick, *International profiles on marine scientific research* (Woods Hole, MA: Woods Hole Oceanographic Institution, 1992), p. 85.

139 Ibid., p. 132.

140 US State Department to US Embassy Quito (4 October 1973), p. 3: 1973STATE197620, AAD.

141 Ibid.

research that entailed actual physical contact with the continental shelf – the Americans opting for a narrow interpretation of article 5(8)'s phrase, 'concerning the continental shelf and undertaken there'.[142]

Bearing these obligations in mind, one can speculate as to why the East African states also mentioned in the committee's account might have responded negatively to preliminary enquiries about similar research on their continental shelves. They may have wanted to discourage research for security reasons, because it might have entailed an American vessel working over the continental shelf just outside their territorial sea (or even inside their territorial sea if it was of a width unrecognised by the United States). They might also have discouraged it for resource-related reasons, withholding consent in accordance with the 1958 convention if the research had an obvious 'applied' science purpose – as did the *R/V Atlantis II*'s research off West Africa, which as the committee stated, had gathered evidence of continental shelf areas likely to contain oil and gas.

Science and Security

The less powerful coastal states rejected the consent-free research regime, arguing that the main beneficiaries would be the researching powers, not the international community. As the Peruvian delegate Juan Miguel Bakula said in 1976, 'To defend the principle of freedom of marine scientific research was to give to those who might avail themselves of that freedom the means to dominate those who were not able to do so.'[143] For this reason, the coastal states stressed that while they supported scientific research, they also supported its control, and that being pro-science and pro-control were not incompatible. There was no reason, they argued, why the requirement on a foreign state to seek permission would impede scientific research.[144] Their case for a consent regime was two-fold: first, without controls, the powers might try to use scientific research as a cover for gathering military or resource-related intelligence detrimental to the coastal states' security; and second, without controls, the powers would withhold from the coastal state samples, data and analyses, and control over the publication of research results.

[142] Ibid.

[143] UNLOSC III, vol. 6, A/Conf.62/C.3/SR.29 (10 September 1976), p. 93.

[144] See L. J. Kateka of Tanzania and I. C. Jain of India (UNLOSC III, vol. 4, A/Conf.62/C.3/SR.23 (2 May 1975), pp. 108, 109), and Inam-ul-Haq of Pakistan (UNLOSC III, vol. 6, A/Conf.62/C.3/SR.30 (14 September 1976), p. 97).

Regarding national security, there was a fine line between marine scientific research and intelligence gathering, and it was not unknown for the powers to engage in the latter under the guise of the former.[145] The classic example was the *USS Pueblo*, an American electronic surveillance spy-ship masquerading as an environmental research vessel, with civilian oceanographers used as part of the vessel's cover. In January 1968, the North Korean authorities captured *Pueblo*, along with the crew and the oceanographers, who had been taking samples just before their arrest. Pyongyang claimed the vessel was within its territorial sea; the Americans insisted that it was on the high seas. If the North Korean claim was true, *Pueblo*'s passage was rendered non-innocent by the gathering of intelligence and samples without permission.[146] The law governing espionage *outside* the territorial sea was unsettled, but the subterfuge raised questions about the bona fides of other research vessels: as Judith Kildow wrote a few years later, the *Pueblo* incident threatened the credibility of all American marine scientists.[147]

Of course, all states, being security conscious, paid attention to foreign vessels active around their coastlines, whether they are conducting research or not. American research vessels attracted particular attention because of their numbers and their global reach, because of the sophisticated and unusual equipment towed or carried by some, and because of many other states' heightened sensitivity to any American presence in their waters. When, for example, the State Department asked its Conakry embassy to apply for permission to the Guinean government for the *R/V Atlantis II*'s continental shelf research in 1973, the embassy advised against it: Guinean and Soviet warships and fighter planes patrolled the

[145] As pointed out by J. A. Sanders of Guyana (UNLOSC III, vol. 2, A/Conf.62/C.3/SR.7 (18 July 1974), p. 340), P. Pojani of Albania (UNLOSC III, vol. 2, A/Conf.62/C.3/SR.9 (19 July 1974), p. 351), and Lo Y. J. of China (UNLOSC III, vol. 6, A/Conf.62/C.3/SR.30 (14 September 1976), p. 96).

[146] Some suggested that even if the ship was on the high seas, and had been conducting genuine marine scientific research, it might still have been on the wrong side of the law had it carried out continental shelf-related research without North Korea's permission (an argument that might have carried more weight had North Korea been a party to the continental shelf convention): J. Knauss, US Senate Subcommittee on Ocean Space of the Committee on Foreign Relations, *Activities of nations in ocean space*, ninety-first congress, first session (Washington, DC: US Government Printing Office, 1969), p. 110.

[147] J. A. T. Kildow, 'Nature of the present restrictions on oceanic research', in W. S. Wooster (ed.), *Freedom of oceanic research* (New York: Crane, Russak & Co., 1973), p. 20.

coastline on the look-out for any dubious-looking foreign vessels, 'of which the Atlantis will surely be one'.[148]

So too elsewhere. In 1977 there was alarm in American embassies in both Jakarta and Rangoon over the route of the Scripps Institution of Oceanography's ship *R/V Thomas Washington*, which was sailing from Indonesia towards the Andaman Sea, possibly through waters claimed by Burma (and, it seems, out of radio contact). Rangoon was highly distrustful of foreign vessels and took a hard line, especially with those suspected of fishing: in the mid-seventies, they impounded a Southeast Asian Fisheries Development Center research vessel and imprisoned its crew.[149] Would *R/V Thomas Washington* enter Burmese waters, and if so, had Rangoon's permission been given? That the vessel was loaded up with explosives intended for use in geo-physical tests in the Andaman Sea would have further complicated matters. As the Jakarta embassy reported:

> Ship not involved in fishing, but as it is doing geophysical research, it carries explosives for refraction studies. These number thousands of 8 lb. TNT blocks and 20 lb. chains of 8 two and half pound blocks, and hundreds of smaller units. If ship challenged by Burmese navy, explosive cargo may cause more misunderstandings than any fish cargo.[150]

As it turned out, the vessel entered Burmese waters with permission and without incident.

Of all the areas of interest to American marine scientists, the USSR's coastal reaches proved to be among the most inaccessible. In 1967, Moscow refused permission for the University of Washington's *R/V Thomas G. Thompson* to carry out research on its continental shelf on the grounds it was a really naval vessel and therefore not from 'a qualified institution with a view to purely scientific research', as specified by article 5(8).[151] The Soviets also turned down most other American requests up until 1988, when *R/V Thomas Washington*, now in colder waters than Burma's, began research on the USSR's continental shelf in the Bering Sea.[152]

148 US Embassy Conakry to US State Department (23 March 1973), p. 1: 1973CONAKR 00439, AAD.

149 US Embassy Rangoon to US Embassy Singapore (2 March 1977), pp. 1–2: 1977RA NGOO00600, AAD.

150 US Embassy Jakarta to US Embassy Rangoon (3 March 1977), p. 2: 1977JAKART02723, AAD.

151 Kildow, 'Nature of the present restrictions', p. 14.

152 L. R. Monroe, 'Undersea mapping aboard Scripps vessel: scientists hope ship will cut U.S.-Soviet ice', *Los Angeles Times* (16 August 1988), at: latimes.com.

At the same time, the Soviets, with a large stake in scientific research themselves, were curious, and sometimes conspicuously so, about the technology on board American research vessels. In 1975, *R/V Thomas Washington* put into the Indonesian port of Surabaya, where the US counsel-general Richard Howland organised a tour of the vessel for local notables. He recounted:

> During visit . . . Soviet consul general Kondratiev toured ship with consular corps and Indonesian dignitaries. While IBM 1800 computer was processing and displaying data obtained from orbiting satellite, Kondratiev bluntly asked for piece of computer print-out paper, grabbed it from table and put it in his pocket. . . . Scientists present in computer room did not wish to risk scene with Indonesian dignitaries present by asking Kondratiev to return document. They believe it was routine display of vessel's position, docked in Surabaya harbor . . . Usually aloof and diffident, Kondratiev was extremely aggressive interrogating scientists about equipment aboard ship, and visibly strained to hear replies. He got jubilantly drunk during reception at my home that evening, suggesting he may believe he scored intelligence coup.[153]

When it came to economic security, any research with a potential resource-related dimension was a touchy subject, especially when carried out by market competitors. In 1970, the Bahamas turned down a request by the Florida Institute of Oceanography for the *R/V Joie de Vivre* to conduct physical, chemical and biological work in its waters because, Kildow noted, it was 'suspected that the request was connected with efforts of the Florida commercial fishing industry to obtain local information that could be used in fisheries talks'.[154] And in the late seventies, after a long-running dispute between Mexico and the United States over tuna quotas in the Eastern Pacific, the Mexican fisheries ministry blocked two American research cruises in 1980–1981 because, Fenwick observed, their proposed research entailed the study of tuna migration patterns.[155]

As a result, states began to introduce their own controls before agreement had been reached at the conference over marine scientific research. In 1969, Artur da Costa e Silva's military government responded to the appearance of unauthorised vessels in Brazil's waters by issuing a decree setting out conditions for research on the continental shelf and in its

[153] US Consulate Surabaya to US State Department (11 February 1975), p. 1: 1975SURABA 00113, AAD.

[154] Kildow, 'Nature of the present restrictions' p. 17.

[155] Fenwick, *International profiles*, p. 95.

territorial waters. (Vessels intercepted by the Brazilian navy included the *Michale Kegostrov*, sponsored by Moscow's Academy of Sciences, in the Ilhe de Trinidade's territorial sea,[156] and a ship run by Teledyne Corp, Houston, which had allegedly taken electronic soundings in Brazilian waters without permission.[157]) The Brazilian seabed committee delegate Ramiro Saraiva Guerreiro explained why his government felt that these steps were necessary:

> With regard to scientific research, it was not always possible to distinguish between pure research and research for economic or military purposes. In the last analysis, every particle of scientific knowledge could be translated into terms of economic gain or national security and, in a technological society, scientific knowledge meant power. Consequently, it was imperative that coastal states should exercise some form of control over scientific research off their coasts, even when it was carried out under the auspices of purely scientific institutions.[158]

Reclaiming Data

Another concern for coastal states was how to compel foreign states and institutions to share data, samples, working methods and editorial control over publication. Some delegates from newly independent states recalled how the powers had stripped them of data as well as physical resources during the colonial period, including the period just before independence. The Guinean delegate Sébo Maurice Gbilimi – doubtless recalling the French departure from his country in 1958, when they had shipped government records wholesale back to Paris, as well as ripping out road signs, lightbulbs and telephones – remarked: 'It was a well-known fact that many documents relating to scientific research carried out during the colonial period were missing from certain developing countries.'[159] Instead of adding to humankind's knowledge, as Stevenson had proposed, these findings languished, inaccessible, in the former colonial powers' archives. To put an end to this, Gbilimi asked that data, samples and reports be shared with the coastal state while the research

156 R. G. Tallboys, 'Brasil and the territorial sea' (30 September 1971), p. 2: FCO 76/262, TNA.

157 M. N. Franssen, 'Oceanic research and the developing nation perspective', in W. S. Wooster (ed.), *Freedom of oceanic research* (New York: Crane, Russak & Co., 1973), p. 189.

158 GOAR, A/AC.138/SR.54 (22 March 1971), p. 109.

159 UNLOSC III, vol. 2, A/Conf.62/C.3/SR.9 (19 July 1974), p. 352.

was in progress, and that the publication of certain findings acquired from marine areas under national jurisdiction 'be subject to the prior consent of the coastal State'.[160]

If the researching powers could be unhelpful (or worse) about sharing research data, then so could some of the major research institutions. The US embassy in Brasilia reported that Brazilian officials referred to this when tightening restrictions on research 'to correct abuses of past foreign scientific activities in Brazil which resulted … in knowledge of Brazil unavailable to Brazilians and scientific specimens in foreig[n] institutions not duplicated here'.[161] The report added that the Brazilians had cited the Washington-based Smithsonian Institution as 'one culprit'.[162]

If so, the Smithsonian was not the only one. Some institutions omitted to pass any data or findings back to the coastal state; some held it back for years after the research had been carried out; and some shared only meagre two-page summaries of their findings. In 1974, India's hydrographer, Frank Fraser, cited the country's 'many bad experiences with research organisations', one of whom took nine years to hand over promised raw data.[163] In 1976, Nigerian officials had to enquire about the whereabouts of some remaining atlases, microfilms and the analyses of the sediments from the continental shelf collected by Woods Hole's *R/V Atlantis II* on the West African cruise that had taken place back in 1973.[164] And in 1977, Indonesian officials made clearance for the Scripps vessel *R/V Thomas Washington* conditional on receipt of raw and processed data from the proposed cruise, and also, tellingly, on receipt of copies of the data from *previous* Scripps cruises through Indonesian waters.[165]

Given some institutions' unwillingness to share their data and conclusions, it is hardly surprising that a number of coastal states instituted

160 Ibid.

161 US Embassy Brasila to US State Department (22 March 1978), s. 2, p. 1: 1978BRASIL 02304, AAD.

162 Ibid.

163 US Embassy Bangkok to US State Department (4 June 1974), s. 2, p. 1: 1974BANGKO 09054, AAD.

164 US Embassy Lagos to US State Department (5 January 1976), p. 1: 1976LAGOS00093, AAD. As an indication of the data's value, the Nigerians used it, among other things, as the basis for determining their conference position on the continental margin: US Embassy Lagos to US State Department (15 February 1977), p. 1: 1977LAGOS01804, AAD.

165 US Embassy Jakarta to US State Department (20 January 1977), p. 1: 1977JAKART 00932, AAD.

strict rules to ensure that material gathered on foreign cruises was shared with them. Chile, for example, insisted that the processing and analysis of data and samples be conducted at a Chilean institution, and that data and results be handed over before the vessel left the country.[166] If research vessels knowingly or otherwise broke the rules, some coastal states arrested research vessels and confiscated their samples. This happened after Brazil first agreed to, but then refused permission for the University of Miami vessel *R/V Pillsbury* to conduct continental shelf and biological research around the Arquipélago de São Pedro e São Paulo in the central Atlantic in 1967.[167] The refusal arrived after the vessel had departed and was out of radio contact, so the research went ahead as planned, but when *Pillsbury* put into Recife afterwards, the Brazilian authorities impounded the rock samples.[168] Whether the British would have done the same had they got wind earlier of the US National Science Foundation ship *D/V Glomar Challenger* drilling a hole on the continental shelf off the UK-claimed mid-Atlantic rock Rockall without their consent[169] is an open question.

The high-handedness of research institutions showed itself in other ways. Article 5(8) of the 1958 continental shelf convention mandated participation of coastal state scientists in research cruises if the coastal state so desired, and this arrangement usually went without a hitch. But not always: in 1979, the Papua New Guinean government nominated two scientists to join the Scripps ship *R/V Alpha Helix* while it was in their waters, one being John Pernetta, a specialist in echinoderm fauna such as spiny starfish. The Scripps cruise leader questioned Pernetta's involvement because there was already an echinoderm specialist from the Smithsonian on board, and said that two people studying the same taxonomic groups would duplicate each other's work.[170] He therefore suggested a (carefully worded) alternative: how about Pernetta 'participating in the sampling program to collect this material?'[171] The Smithsonian specialist would then assess all the samples in Washington

[166] Fenwick, *International profiles*, p. 26.
[167] Kildow, 'Nature of the present restrictions', p. 16.
[168] Ibid.; and Franssen, 'Oceanic research', p. 188.
[169] Fragment on marine scientific research on the continental shelf (u.d., c. April 1976), p. 3, para. 19: DEFE 24/957, TNA.
[170] US State Department to US Embassy Port Moresby (23 May 1979), p. 2: 1979STATE 131541, AAD.
[171] Ibid., p. 3.

before returning them to Papua New Guinea for study.[172] Would Pernetta's research interests be met by this?[173] The foreign affairs department in Port Moresby made it very clear that they would not: 'The Department as well as the fisheries authorities are disinclined to believe the sincerity of the original invitation unless its purpose was merely to provide the ship with a modicum of free scientific labour.'[174] Scripps immediately backed down: Pernetta could carry out his own research as originally proposed.[175]

Recalling the obligation in article 5(8) to publish scientific results, another bugbear for some coastal states was the question of editorial control over the publication of research – this being participation of a different kind. Sometimes researchers turned up something of significance that the state did not want revealed to commercial competitors or unfriendly neighbours. And sometimes they uncovered information of no short-term application, but which the state thought might become more important in the future, such as the genetic subjects of modern-day bioprospecting. They knew for sure that knowledge once acquired could not be unacquired, and so some coastal states tried to make pre-publication editorial clearance a condition of granting licences for research. This resulted in article 61 of the 1976 conference negotiating text, which stated that: 'The results of a research project bearing substantially upon the exploration and exploitation of the living or non-living resources of the economic zone and on the continental shelf of a coastal State shall not be published or made internationally available against the express wish of that State.'[176]

The researching states were not sympathetic to these coastal state concerns. They reminded delegates that article 5(8) of the 1958 convention imposed an obligation on parties to the convention to publish. They suggested that states who benefited from foreign institutions carrying out research that they could not afford to carry out themselves should not prevent others from having access to the results. The Americans and the West Germans led this campaign, stating that editorial restrictions were

[172] Ibid.
[173] Ibid.
[174] US Embassy Port Moresby to US State Department (6 June 1979), p. 2: 1979PORTM 00817, AAD.
[175] US State Department to US Embassy Port Moresby (7 June 1979), p. 1: 1979STATE 146135, AAD.
[176] UNLOSC III, vol. 5, A/Conf.62/WP.8/Rev.1/PartIII (7 May 1976), p. 182.

unconstitutional,[177] and represented unwarranted interference in academic freedom. The Americans, for example, openly denounced 'censorship', and took action to remove article 61.[178] The major research institutions took a similar anti-censorship line, doubtless keeping in mind that publication was essential for maintaining their research profile and fulfilling contractual funding obligations.

One of the states the Americans clashed with over publication was Trinidad and Tobago. In 1976, Port of Spain officials gave permission for the American naval vessel *USNS Hayes* to carry out research in its waters, but only 'subject to the condition that the results of research performed in Trinidadian territorial waters or on its continental shelf are the property of the government of Trinidad and Tobago and can be published only with its prior approval'.[179] An American embassy officer remonstrated: the restrictions 'created real difficulties for U.S. government' and might compel *USNS Hayes* to cancel the Trinidadian section of the cruise. Also,

> He reminded the ministry officer that the just-concluded cruise of the 'Oregon II' [in the Gulf of Paria] had performed valuable and economically useful research for the T&T ministry of agriculture, lands and fisheries and that the restrictive policy . . . on marine scientific research might prevent such fruitful cooperation in the future.[180]

This approach did not sway the Port of Spain authorities, so the Americans cancelled the cruise.[181]

Excluding Hydrographic Surveys

The coastal states' campaign for consent for marine scientific research came together at the conference in 1976. They thought that the 1975 negotiating text was inadequate and imprecise, especially article 14 of the relevant part, which stated:

[177] 'Article 61' (2 June 1977), pp. 1–2: FCO 76/1635, TNA.
[178] US State Department to US Embassy Port of Spain (21 October 1978), p. 2: 1978STATE 267572, AAD.
[179] US Embassy Port of Spain to US State Department (14 May 1976), p. 1: 1976PORTO 01263, AAD.
[180] Ibid., pp. 1–2.
[181] US State Department to US Embassy Port of Spain (18 May 1976): 1976STATE122183, AAD.

> Marine scientific research beyond the territorial sea, in the economic zone and on the continental shelf, shall be conducted by States as well as by appropriate international organizations in such a manner that the rights of the coastal State, as provided for in this Convention, are respected.[182]

In 1976, they replaced the anodyne obligation to respect rights with a more muscular injunction: 'Marine scientific research activities in the economic zone or on the continental shelf shall be conducted with the consent of the coastal State in accordance with the provisions of this Convention'.[183]

The following year the powers pushed back, introducing qualifications to the consent regime by way of the Castañeda text dealing with research in the exclusive economic zone, which the Bulgarian third committee chair Alexander Yankov incorporated into the 1977 negotiating text. First, article 60(2)'s negative imperative that the state 'shall not withhold its consent'[184] was transformed into new article 247(3)'s positive imperative that the state 'shall, in normal circumstances, grant its consent'.[185] (The phrase 'in normal circumstances', carried over from article 5(8), put the onus on the coastal state to prove, among other things, that circumstances were abnormal if consent was refused.) Second, a clause was added obliging coastal states to establish rules and procedures ensuring that consent 'will not be delayed or denied unreasonably'.[186] Third, the old article 61 giving coastal states control over the publication of results relating to exploration and exploitation was deleted.[187] And finally, article 253 in the new text retained the idea of implied consent, stipulating that research could commence after six months of a valid application for permission if the coastal state had not responded within four months.[188]

Another of the powers' successes was the exclusion of hydrographic surveys from the consent regime. Led by the United States and Britain, they argued that the hydrographic services' work – usually involving the collection of data on depths, tides, currents, salinity and underwater topography – should be exempted because the navigational charts and tables based on them enhanced mariners' safety and was beneficial to all states. What was not spelt out was that these surveys were also essential

182 UNLOSC III, vol. 4, A/Conf.62/WP.8/PartIII (9 May 1975), p. 177.
183 Article 60(1), UNLOSC III, vol. 5, A/Conf.62/WP.8/Rev.1/PartIII (7 May 1976), p. 182.
184 Ibid.
185 UNLOSC III, vol. 8, A/Conf.62/WP.10 (15 July 1977), p. 42.
186 Article 247(3), ibid.
187 UNLOSC III, vol. 5, A/Conf.62/WP.8/Rev.1/PartIII (7 May 1976), p. 182.
188 UNLOSC III, vol. 8, A/Conf.62/WP.10 (15 July 1977), p. 43.

for defensive and offensive naval planning, and they informed, among other things, decisions about the concealment and detection of submarines, the planning of amphibious landings and defences, and the laying of mines and planning of mine-countering operations. The naval powers were obviously keen to exempt hydrographic surveys from the consent regime because if they had to seek permission from a coastal state, their activities would obviously be known to it.

Some senior figures privately went even further, contending between themselves that no research with a military application – not just hydrographic surveys – should be subject to coastal state scrutiny. This issue arose in Washington in 1976 during a three-way discussion between Defense Secretary Robert Ellsworth, Henry Kissinger ('Secretary') and Bernard Oxman about military research carried out under other states' jurisdiction. Ellsworth stated that his department needed a free hand to conduct 'certain kinds of experiments':

> *SECRETARY:* But under the present text, we have to inform the coastal states of our scientific research. Is that agreeable to Defense?
>
> *ELLSWORTH:* Not if scientific research includes the kind of research we conduct.
>
> *OXMAN:* Defense can't even accept prior notice.
>
> . . .
>
> *SECRETARY:* So then we're saying the Defense activity falls outside of scientific research.[189]

Needless to say, this argument would never see the light of day at the conference, because the powers had no wish to draw attention to their military activities within other states' jurisdictions, or to further excite the coastal states' interest in sharpening the 'peaceful purposes' provisions.

By the end of the 1977 session, the powers had managed to separate hydrographic surveys and marine scientific research – although the practical difference between the two was unclear as neither was defined in the text. The distinction made by the negotiators was purely legal: foreign states and competent international organisations were obliged to seek consent for research conducted in the exclusive economic zone or on the continental shelf, but not for hydrographic surveys. They were also obliged to publish

189 'Memorandum for the record' (27 August 1976), p. 3: *FRUS*, 1969–1976, vol. E-3, *Documents on global issues*, 1973–1976, doc. 40.

and disseminate the results of research, and to share these results with the coastal state,[190] but this did not apply to the results of hydrographic surveys. Furthermore, research had to be carried out 'in order to increase scientific knowledge of the marine environment for the benefit of all mankind',[191] whereas hydrographic surveys for military purposes directed against foreign threats were by their very nature partisan.

The exclusion of hydrographic surveys from the marine scientific research regime was signalled by omission. While articles 19(2)(j), 21 (1)(g), 40 and 54 – relating to passage through the territorial sea, straits and archipelagos – referred to both hydrographic surveys and scientific research,[192] there was no mention of surveys carried out in the exclusive economic zone or on the continental shelf. As Peter Beazley of the Royal Navy's hydrography service observed, this indicated

> that hydrographic surveying . . . can rightly be viewed as distinct from scientific research, and that there is therefore no restriction on [hydrographic] work in the EEZ or on the continental shelf, neither is there to be any requirement to seek prior consent. Nevertheless Hydrographer believes that care must be taken not to overstress this right lest too obvious an insistence on it should see it swept away.[193]

Because the practical distinction between marine scientific research and hydrographic surveys was not addressed, the resultant grey area created difficulties for the surveying powers. For example, British officials worried that when the Royal Navy carried out acoustic, gravity and magnetic surveys on other states' continental shelves, the coastal state might misconstrue this activity either as being exploration for resources or as being carried out to substantiate a disputed continental shelf claim – the Republic of Ireland's dispute with Britain being hinted at in this instance.[194] And because the results of hydrographic surveys were usually not disclosed publicly for security reasons, establishing the surveying vessel's bona fides could present problems. Peter Beazley noted, for example, that when the Royal Navy's Admiralty Research Laboratory carried out acoustic tests by detonating

[190] Articles 245(1) and 250(1)(b), UNLOSC III, vol. 8, A/Conf.62/WP.10 (15 July 1977), pp. 41, 42.

[191] Article 247(3), ibid., p. 42.

[192] Ibid., pp. 8, 11, 13, referring respectively to 'research or survey activities', 'Marine scientific research and hydrographic surveys', and 'research and survey activities'.

[193] P. B. Beazley, 'UNLOSC . . . effect on Hydrographer's operations' (3 November 1977), p. 1: FCO 76/1634, TNA.

[194] Ibid., p. 2. The *Aegean continental shelf* case involving Greece and Turkey, which also raised the problem of contested claims to the continental shelf, was ongoing at the time.

explosive charges on other states' continental shelves, 'it would be difficult to claim that it was not scientific research . . . without disclosing its purpose'.[195] But if its military purpose *was* divulged, it would not necessarily make the survey more acceptable to the coastal state, unless it happened to be a fellow member of a military alliance.[196] If an objection was made, Beazley concluded, defence-related hydrographic surveys 'either cannot be made or a decision must be made to obtain them clandestinely'.[197]

Yankov's Consent Regime

At the end of the 1977 session, after Yankov had released the text, Elliot Richardson held a press conference and outlined some of the powers' achievements:

> The provisions of the text dealing with scientific research were improved. An effort by some delegations to increase the degree of coastal state control of scientific research in the economic zone was defeated. In the new text, the conditions for conducting scientific research are set out clearly, and are likely to be copied into national laws, thus regularizing what has until now been a capricious situation. Also, we successfully eliminated a clause that could have obliged the U.S. to restrict publication of scientific data after the fact and without the consent of scientists, which was highly offensive to our concepts of free science and free speech.[198]

This positive presentation failed to mention one important thing. Although Yankov had incorporated the relevant parts of the Castañeda text on marine scientific research into the text, he had also made a few additions of his own, which had the effect of firming up the consent regime. This move blindsided the Americans and their allies.

The first of these changes was Yankov's insertion of a new paragraph into the text – article 247(1) – which read:

> Coastal States, in the exercise of their jurisdiction, have the right to regulate, authorize and conduct marine scientific research in their exclusive economic zone and on their continental shelf in accordance with the relevant provisions of the present Convention.[199]

This insertion, using the loaded word 'right' in relation to regulation and authorisation, replicated a proposal he had made the previous year,[200]

[195] Ibid., p. 1.
[196] Ibid., pp. 1–2.
[197] Ibid., p. 2.
[198] US State Department to all posts (20 July 1977), p. 3: 1977STATE169685, AAD.
[199] UNLOSC III, vol. 8, A/Conf.62/WP.10 (15 July 1977), p. 42.
[200] UNLOSC III, vol. 6, A/Conf.62/L.18 (16 September 1976), p. 142.

which had been supported by many coastal states but had been rejected by the Americans, British and West Germans.

Yankov's second change was to add to article 265(a) on the settlement of disputes three words: 'a right or'. In the relevant part the article states:

> disputes relating to the interpretation or application of the provisions of the present Convention with regard to marine scientific research shall be settled in accordance with section 2 of Part XV of the present Convention, except that the coastal State shall not be obliged to submit to such settlement [of] any dispute arising out of:
>
> (a) the exercise by the coastal State of *a right or* discretion in accordance with article 247;[201]

The effect of these two additions was to exclude from compulsory dispute settlement the coastal states' *right* (not just 'discretion'[202]) to grant consent for scientific research, thereby strengthening their grip over the consent regime. The British explained the implications:

> The text which emerged from the discussions unfortunately was amended by the Chairman of the Third Committee in such a way as to render the settlement of dispute provisions almost ineffective. This was a great blow, for we were relying on researching states' recourse to a disputes settlement procedure to balance the inevitable drift towards a full consent regime. We consider the ICNT to be worse, in total, than the RSNT [revised single negotiating text of 1976] but it was the best that could be obtained given the increasing weight of op[in]ion against the researching states' view, particularly after the Soviet Union at the previous session had changed its position to support the coastal states' view.[203]

The Americans were just as negative, telling their allies that the text was 'bad', and that the battle over marine scientific research had been 'lost'.[204]

Yankov's insertions into the 1977 text seem to have been motivated by two factors, one demonstrably true, the other based on speculation.

201 UNLOSC III, vol. 8, A/Conf.62/WP.10 (15 July 1977), p. 44. Emphasis added.

202 In the Castañeda text, the same provision had not excluded from compulsory dispute settlement a coastal state's 'right to regulate, authorize and conduct marine scientific research'; but merely excluded 'its discretion to withhold its consent in accordance with article 60' – this article setting out when consent *had* to be sought from the coastal state, such as research involving drilling or the use of explosives, or of 'direct significance' for exploration or exploitation: US Mission to the UN to US State Department (16 July 1977), s. 3, p. 2: 1977USUNN02276, AAD.

203 J. R. S. Guinness, 'UNLOSC: policy options' (26 September 1977), p. 1: FCO 76/1634, TNA.

204 'Brief: UNLOSC: bilateral talks with the Americans' (c. 13 September 1978), p. 5: FCO 76/1634, TNA; and, J. R. S. Guinness, 'CIA report on UNCLOS' (8 September 1977), p. 2: FCO 76/1675, TNA.

Demonstrably, many coastal states supported his amendments on marine scientific research, giving credence to his argument that the text reflected the prevailing view in the committee, and that no consensus could be reached without these changes being made.[205] Speculatively, the Americans presumed that Yankov had made the amendments under pressure from the Soviets, who supported a consent regime. The Americans' subsequent campaign against Yankov's amendments, shaped by these suspicions of Soviet involvement, explains why they spent nearly as much time lobbying Soviet ministers as they did trying to persuade Yankov to delete his additions. They even offered the Soviet delegation head Semyon P. Kozyrev a quid pro quo: they could work together to reinstate the aforementioned 'no sovereignty' clause in article 55 (which the Soviets wanted to retain) in exchange for the Soviets seeing to it that Yankov's additions were removed.[206] The Soviets did not take up the proposal, which suggests that the Americans had misread them. Perhaps they had less influence over Yankov than the Americans thought, or perhaps they were more interested in protecting the consent regime than chasing the lost cause of the 'no sovereignty' clause.

Over the following year, the Americans called repeatedly for a return to the Castañeda text on marine scientific research, but in May 1978, Richardson reported that the chances of this happening were slim, and that despite 'heavy lobbying' the Soviets seemed disinclined to compel Yankov to remove his additions.[207] The latter frustrated Richardson, who reported that

> Soviets in the past have shown little compunction about directing Yankov to make substantive revisions. Conference procedures at this session make it more difficult for them to alter text, but they could encourage him to make some favorable modifications were they to decide to be helpful.[208]

By then, the discussions between the Americans and Soviets on marine scientific research had become entangled with those about the renewal of the US–USSR Agreement on Cooperation in Studies of the World

[205] US Mission Geneva to US State Department (3 May 1978), s. 2, p. 3: 1978GENEVA06700, AAD.

[206] D. Logan, 'Note on negotiations on the legal status of the economic zone' (u.d., c. July 1977), p. 6: FCO 76/1643, TNA.

[207] US Mission Geneva to US State Department (5 May 1978), s. 2, p. 3: 1978GENEVA06882, AAD.

[208] US Mission Geneva to US State Department (9 May 1978), s. 1, p. 3: 1978GENEVA07023, AAD.

Ocean.[209] That same month, Aleksander P. Metal'nikov of the USSR's oceanic committee told American delegation advisers that his government would review their position on marine scientific research after the end of the 1978 session, and that their attitude would be influenced by the American position on the World Ocean Agreement.[210] Norman Wulf, the American delegate to the third committee, protested that Metal'nikov's attempt to shift the burden onto the United States was 'ridiculous' because it was unlikely that more changes would be made to the text after the session had ended.[211] Within a few weeks, the fight had moved to Moscow. This time, Metal'nikov met American embassy officials and insisted that the Soviet delegates had 'done their part' in the committee by not objecting to Wulf's attempts to restore the Castañeda text.[212] This was not what the Americans wanted to hear. They reported that the Soviets had 'made no effort to move Yankov at LOS on MSR [marine scientific research] issue and that they will pull out of deep sea drilling project . . . if US does not renew Oceans Agreement'.[213] Over the ensuing years, the third committee refused to budge over consent, despite a wobble by Yankov and a walk-out by Wulf.[214] The offending additions were retained, appearing in the convention as articles 246(1) and 297(2)(a)(i).[215]

*

The conference sessions between 1973 and 1977 had been tumultuous, and had placed enormous strains on both the G77 and the G5. The G77 countries, riding into the proceedings on the wave of assertiveness inspired by OPEC's stand in 1973, hoped to lay the basis of a more equitable world order by drawing on common heritage and by formalising claims to the exclusive economic zone. But the divisions within the

209 Agreement on Cooperation in Studies of the World Ocean (EIF 19 June 1973 by signature, in accordance with article 8 (1)) 917 UNTS 55, 57.

210 US Mission Geneva to US State Department (9 May 1978), p. 1: 1978GENEVA07023, AAD.

211 Ibid.

212 US Embassy Moscow to US State Department (6 June 1978), p. 2: 1978MOSCOW12753, AAD.

213 US Embassy Moscow to US State Department (25 May 1978), p. 2: 1978MOSCOW11733, AAD.

214 W. Wertenbaker, 'A Reporter at large: The law of the sea – I', *New Yorker* (1 August 1983), 38, 56.

215 UNCLOS, 497, 513.

group, and the pressures exerted on it by the powers, meant that they achieved less than expected. The coastal state members managed to secure consent over marine scientific research, but they lost out to the powers over military activities in the exclusive economic zone. The landlocked and geographically disadvantaged state members were able to obtain a share of the revenues from wide margin resources but lost out to the coastal states over guaranteed fishing surpluses in the exclusive economic zone. By 1977, after four grinding years of negotiations, the prospects of forging unity within the group, and for building the foundations of a new international economic order, seemed to be more elusive than ever.

Over the same period, the powers within the G5, operating as a bulwark against the G77, made a strong start to the conference, securing their interests on the territorial sea, then on straits, and then on the exclusive economic zone and archipelagos. Consensus worked in their favour, allowing them, as a minority, to prevail over the majority. But having secured their initial objectives, the rationale for their continuing partnership within the G5 faded away. The cohesion of the group was tested in 1976, when the US Congress declared a 200-mile conservation zone, and tested again by internal disagreements over marine scientific research and seabed mining. The powers consequently became more unpredictable in their relations with each other, and less able to bring collective pressure to bear on the other states involved in the negotiations. Both the G5 and the G77 would bring these divisions with them as they entered the final stretch.

9

The Bitter End

The Seabed Mining Controversy and the Signing of the Convention

The negotiations were dragging. Before the opening of the conference in 1973, the Peruvian Alfonso Arias Schreiber had turned to his neighbour on the UN seabed committee benches, the Philippines' delegate Arturo Tolentino, and asked him how long he thought the forthcoming conference would last. Tolentino estimated seven years. 'You are very optimistic', replied Arias Schrieber.[1] In the event, it took nine. As soon as the question of the exclusive economic zone was settled in July 1977, some four years in, the delegates turned their attention to seabed mining – the issue that would dominate proceedings for the next five years.

Those of every stripe proclaimed the vital importance of seabed exploitation. Some took a positive view, saying it would underwrite a new international economic order, or exemplify the virtues of free enterprise on Earth's final frontier. Others warned of a fundamental threat to land-based mining industries. But for all the rhetoric, the truth was that nobody involved knew how profitable seabed exploitation might be, or the technological challenges involved, or the effect on commodities markets in decades to come. Because of this uncertainty, no state wanted to put itself at a disadvantage and forego future rewards, and the negotiations were therefore hard-fought and protracted.

The text that eventually emerged from the seabed negotiations managed to displease everyone. The G77 states were the main losers: instead of the realisation of universal common heritage they had to make do with rights to half of the exploitable seabed mining sites, exercised in special reserved areas under the auspices of the international authority. The G5 powers did better, although they paid a high price for their success: some of the provisions were unlikely to stand the test of time, and in the process of working them out they lost sight of what they had originally

[1] Tolentino, *The Philippines and the law of the sea*, p. 79.

set out to gain from the conference.[2] They fell out with one another, and when the final text was put to a vote, some voted against or abstained. The G5 laid the blame on a few G77-inspired clauses, but its problems were almost entirely self-inflicted. This was acknowledged by Paul Fifoot, a British Foreign and Commonwealth Office legal adviser, who asked:

> (a) . . . If there is a need for an international authority, should it not be deferred until sea bed mining becomes more probable?
> (b) Can any body attempt to draft rules for sea bed mining 15 years before there is any experience of it?
> (c) Does a production policy tied to nickel have any real meaning?
> (d) Is it necessary to create an Enterprise and reserved sites in order to assist the Third World?[3]

Fifoot concluded: 'I appreciate that all this structure was in fact the creation of the west, but the whole thing got out of hand.'[4]

The Parallel System

There were problems from the start. One of the earliest issues concerned the mandate of the international authority. In the UN seabed committee, the developing countries had campaigned for a strong authority presiding over all seabed activities, while the industrial states pushed for a weaker one, empowered mainly to issue licences to private mining operators. Neither side was prepared to give way, so after the conference opened in 1973, the United States mooted a solution known as the parallel system – a proposal that would in effect replace the unitary concept of common heritage with a dualistic arrangement governing the exploitation of the seabed. Under it, a state- or privately-run mining concern would propose two viable mine sites to the international authority. The authority would 'reserve' one of these sites to be exploited by both the Enterprise (its operating arm) and the developing countries, and it would license the other site to the applicant mining concern to exploit for itself. The advantage of the system, supporters argued, was that the industrial states and developing countries would each have access to their own designated sites without interference from the other. The disadvantage, opponents countered, was that the supposedly indivisible common heritage of mankind would henceforth be divided by half. As the delegate

[2] Oxman, *From cooperation to conflict*, p. 24.
[3] P. Fifoot, 'UK statement at Jamaica' (30 November 1982), p. 2: FCO 76/2448, TNA.
[4] Ibid.

from Algeria asked: 'Are we here to reserve 50 percent of the seabed area for private corporations?'[5]

The parallel system was of course designed to serve the interests of the United States, whose companies were already weighing up the prospects of seabed exploitation. But it was not the only potential beneficiary. The system also suited the most developed of the developing countries such as Brazil and India. Although none of these had yet thrown their hat into the ring, they could in theory make or sponsor an application to mine the international authority's 'reserved' site in the knowledge that the original applicant had already decided that it was viable and had already provided the authority with supporting exploratory data.[6] Armed with this intelligence, the leading developing countries would be well placed to secure funding, and to enter into joint ventures with industrial state ventures seeking access to reserved sites.

A State Department briefing confirmed this, arguing that the parallel system would give (some) states what they most wanted.[7] The industrial powers and their companies would gain exclusive access to mine sites[8] – this being the Americans' main concern. The leading developing countries would gain access to the international authority's reserved sites without having to compete with the powers.[9] And the least developed countries, who were unlikely to embark on seabed mining, would, at least in theory, get a larger cut of the authority's seabed revenues than would other states.[10] (The briefing made no reference to those that would gain nothing from the arrangement, such as the smaller industrial states and the mid-range developing countries.) It concluded that the main effect would be to 'give an advantage on questions of access to the most developed of the developed states in one group, and to the most developed of the developing states in another'.[11]

One of these leading developing countries was Brazil. At the start of the conference, the Brazilians had called for a strong international authority, but by early 1976 their stance on this issue had softened. The

[5] Quoted in J. N. Barkenbus, *Deep seabed resources: politics and technology* (New York: Free Press, 1979), p. 118.

[6] US State Department to US Embassy Brasilia (15 February 1976), p. 2: 1976STATE 037578, AAD.

[7] Ibid., p. 3.

[8] Ibid.

[9] Ibid.

[10] Ibid.

[11] Ibid.

Americans, observing this shift, speculated that Brazil was trying to expedite the conclusion of the convention by facilitating agreement between the Americans and the developing countries, influenced by two seabed-related factors.[12] First, if the conference failed to conclude a seabed regime, the US Congress would likely step in to enact legislation favouring unilateral seabed mining, which would have harmful consequences for Brazil's land-based manganese production; and second, Brazilian companies might well have been thinking of embarking on seabed mining (as part of international consortia) and, under convention proposals, would by virtue of their being from a developing country be given access to the international authority's reserved sites under the parallel system.[13]

Brazil's concerns created the basis for an alignment with the Americans, who, with their objectives on the issue of navigation nearly met and a presidential election looming, also had an interest in quickly wrapping up the negotiations. In February 1976 the Brazilian delegation head Sergio Thomson-Flores privately approached the Americans with what the latter called 'an extremely interesting compromise package'.[14] Thomson-Flores said that his government was offering to 'use of its influence within the group of 77 . . . to have most of the U.S. positions regarding the regime and international organization for the deep seabed accepted by the LDC's' if in return, Washington accepted the following provisions, designed to protect Brazil's manganese and nickel industries:

- the international seabed resource authority would be empowered to participate in any relevant commodity arrangements in which all affected states participate as the principal means of protecting LDC producers of nickel, copper, manganese and cobalt from economic consequences of deep seabed mining.
- 50 [per cent] of the area of the deep seabed would be reserved for direct mining by the authority or LDC's, while the other 50 would be opened to all states and their nationals
- for the initial 15-year period, deep seabed mining would be limited to the growth segment in world nickel demand. (The U.S. has publicly stated that it is highly unlikely that such mining would exceed that growth segment in the foreseeable future.)

12 US State Department to US Embassy Brasilia (10 February 1976), p. 2: 1976STATE032213, AAD.
13 Ibid.
14 Ibid., p. 5.

- compensation would be provid[ed to] LDC producers severely hurt by deep seabed mining.[15]

While the Americans were mulling the proposal, Thomson-Flores demonstrated his seriousness by drawing together the secret 'Brazil group' from among the delegates attending the conference's first committee on the seabed. This group operated on much the same lines as the UK-Fiji group on straits and, later, the Castañeda group on the exclusive economic zone: a chosen few would meet outside the conference to produce a draft which, they hoped, would then be bundled through the relevant committee and into the negotiating text. In this case, the Brazil group's eleven members included two powers, the United States and France, plus Brazil itself, Chile, Jamaica, Kenya, Mexico, Norway, Peru, Singapore and Sri Lanka.[16] While many of the developing countries in this group would have preferred a strong international authority, they had each calculated that a managed accommodation with the Americans within a treaty was preferable to a largely unregulated free-for-all. (All the Latin American members, for example, feared the consequences for their land-based mining industries of direct competition from seabed operators extracting copper, manganese and nickel if no international regulatory framework was agreed.) At the March-May 1976 session they therefore pushed for the parallel system, and, the Americans reported, 'exercised a constructive and moderating influence on the progress of the negotiation and the preparation of draft articles'.[17]

A few of the group's members, including Thompson-Flores himself, traded on their countries' radical reputation on other law of the sea issues to garner acceptance for what were, in effect, American modifications of the seabed text. They were assisted in this by the first committee chair, Paul Engo of Cameroon, who, according to the Americans, went along with the Brazil group and agreed to pass its conclusions off as his own. The US delegation reported:

> From very commencement of session, procedures utilized in Committee I (C-I) have been effective in leading towards revision of [I]SNT [informal single negotiating text of 1975] in manner favorable to US interests. Although sharply criticized by some LDC's for holding private intersessional consultations, chairman Engo has privately sanctioned activities of secret rpt secret Brazil group ... and adhered to his commitment to

[15] Ibid., pp. 5–6.
[16] US State Department to US delegation (10 August 1976), p. 5: 1976STATE198538, AAD.
[17] Ibid.

> distribute only those texts negotiated in this group to C-I as his personal work product. Members of secret Brazil group have in all instances defended pre-arranged compromises worked out in group and have effectively played out agreed tactical scenarios in C-1 informal meetings.[18]

One important area of activity concerned the basic conditions governing the prospecting, exploration and exploitation of the seabed area and its resources, set out in annex I. The Americans again:

> While key details remain to be negotiated in secret Brazil group, US ... has gained agreement of group to new draft annex I altered markedly in our favor. New annex I provides for parallel exploitation system in which enterprise operates under same basic conditions as other contractors; entire area being open to activities in area; single contracts covering all stages of operations; and issuance of contracts on essentially first-come basis. Details of profit-sharing remain to be negotiated but secret Brazil group appears to accept basic outlines of profit-sharing approach considered favorable by US industry advisors.[19]

When Paul Engo produced his end-of-session text incorporating the parallel system in May 1976,[20] it was not well received by some of the other G77 delegates. Those from Algeria, Ecuador, Egypt and Iraq criticised it for draining power away from the international authority, while the Tunisian delegate called it a 'step backward', and the Kuwaiti delegate dubbed it 'a black paper'.[21] (The oil and gas producers among them wanted a strong authority to protect their land and off-shore energy industries if large deposits were discovered under the deep seabed.) Some delegates' criticisms took a more personal turn: Engo, according to one report, was rumoured to have allowed the American delegate Leigh Ratiner to draft the text 'in exchange for U.S. aid to Cameroon',[22] while the G77 members of the Brazil group were condemned as 'sell outs' for trying to divide the developing countries on the issue.[23] The Americans noted that as a consequence, those involved had been discredited within

[18] US Mission to the UN to US State Department (15 April 1976), s. 1, p. 3: 1976USUNN 01573, AAD.

[19] Ibid., s. 2, p. 2.

[20] See article 22, UNLOSC III, vol. 5, A/Conf.62/WP.8/Rev.1/PartI (6 May 1976), pp. 131–132.

[21] 'Group of 77 position on law of the sea issues' (August 1976), pp. 1–2, CIA-RDP82S00697R000400160021-6, CIAHC.

[22] US Embassy Nassau to US State Department (6 August 1976), p. 2: 1976NASSAU01244, AAD.

[23] US State Department to US delegation (10 August 1976), p. 4: 1976STATE198538, AAD.

the G77 and would, at least temporarily, be 'neutralized as effective players' in the ongoing negotiations.[24]

At the next session, in August–September 1976, a group of states opposed to the parallel system tried to whip the other G77 members into line. Algeria, Tanzania and others stressed the benefits of unity (if the world's raw material producers acted in concert, they could bring the new international economic order within reach) and the perils of disunity (they would fall prey to the multinationals' market-driven agenda on the seabed). They also argued that the parallel system was a form of *apartheid*[25] – the wealthy states with their mining conglomerates and the impoverished states with the Enterprise. Persuasion was apparently backed up with coercion: according to the Malaysians, a group of North African oil and gas producers including Algeria, Libya and Tunisia threatened to deny oil loans to countries that did not back their position.[26]

Kissinger's Offer

The Americans, meanwhile, sought to consolidate their gains. In September 1976, Henry Kissinger made a highly publicised pitch for the parallel system before a select group of conference delegates, to whom he offered what seemed to be a better deal than the one already on offer. If the developing countries agreed that industrial states and companies should have *guaranteed* access to seabed mining sites under the parallel system, he said, the Americans would provide the Enterprise with start-up funding and mining technology to enable it to commence its operations at the same time. Thus,

> We are offering to put the Enterprise into business and to give it technology for the sake of achieving an acceptable treaty. The United States will acquire no commercial benefits from putting our business competitor into operation.[27]

Kissinger naturally presented this as an act of generosity, but he was not giving anything away: instead, he was demanding more – namely, exclusive access for predominantly Western consortia to mineral-rich portions

[24] Ibid., p. 6.
[25] M. C. Wood, 'UNLOSC: first committee' (4 June 1977), p. 2: FCO 76/1670, TNA.
[26] 'UK record of discussion with Malaysia' (24–25 January 1977), p. 3: FCO 76/1637, TNA.
[27] 'Memorandum of conversation' (1 September 1976), p. 11: *FRUS*, 1969–1976, vol. E-3, *Documents on global issues*, 1973–1976, doc. 44.

of the seabed for the purposes of extraction. This obviously denied mine-sites and resources to the rest of the international community.

What was apparent to those attending the meeting was that Kissinger's proposal, while heavy on guaranteed access for the industrial states, was light on detail about the proposed funding and technology for the Enterprise. He claimed he could 'easily find the financing' if they agreed to his terms, but declined to expand further: 'I am not going to go into any of the specifics of this concept today'.[28] While some delegates welcomed his commitment to providing technology and funding, others feared that he might not deliver on his promises. The Malaysians noted the absence of other states' commitment to the idea,[29] and the British observed that the US Treasury had recommended against subsidising seabed mining, which was what Kissinger was proposing, because seabed minerals were not essential to American security.[30]

Within a few months, Kissinger was on his way out of government, but his promise of a seabed-access-for-technology-transfer deal gave impetus to the debate about the conditions governing access to the seabed, and the obligation on states and mining concerns to transfer technology to the Enterprise. At the end of the 1977 session, Engo, still committee chair, produced an end-of-session text reflecting the shifting balance of forces between the industrial states and the less accommodating G77 states which retained the parallel system but strengthened the powers of the international authority. The American delegation head Elliot Richardson denounced the text as 'fundamentally unacceptable', and his delegation threatened to walk out.[31] This caused a stir: even the Venezuelan President Carlos Andrés Pérez got involved, saying that the Americans' departure would threaten the dialogue between North and South.[32]

Transfer of Technology

The law of the sea conference was not the only UN forum where the idea of technology transfer was mooted, but it was the most important as far

[28] Ibid., p. 10.
[29] 'UK record of discussion with Malaysia' (24–25 January 1977), p. 3: FCO 76/1637, TNA.
[30] H. J. Ivey, 'Note of a discussion with US Treasury officials' (6 August 1976), p. 3: FCO 76/1378, TNA.
[31] US State Department to all posts (5 October 1977), p. 3: 1977STATE239529, AAD.
[32] US Embassy Caracas to US State Department (21 October 1977), p. 1: AAD.

as the G77's campaign for a new international economic order was concerned. By 1977, any residual faith in the common heritage idea had gone, having been seen off by the parallel system. The settlement on the exclusive economic zone signalled the victory of the coastal states' national approach to development in coastal waters over the landlocked and geographically disadvantaged states' dependence for their development on the internationalised seabed. The G77 leadership had been casting around for an idea which would promote unity, and technology transfer seemed to fit the bill. For one thing, it was an idea that all its members could support. For another, it advanced the cause by offering a route to development that transcended the national/international paradigm. If the industrial states were obliged by the proposed law of the sea convention to transfer technology to the Enterprise, a body operating on behalf of the developing countries, they might also be obliged to transfer technology straight to the developing countries working in reserved seabed sites. And if technology was transferred to developing counties operating on the seabed, a precedent might be set for transfers in non-maritime settings. As the promise of common heritage ebbed away, here was another mechanism for the achievement of the movement's wider developmental aims.

From the outset, and for precisely the same precedent-setting reasons, the Western industrial states were extremely cautious about the transfer of technology. When the issue arose in the UN seabed committee in 1973, the French delegate argued that provision should be made to and assist the developing countries with training, but because the patents protecting commercial technology were owned by private enterprises, not by states, the transfer of patented technology was beyond the competence of the committee.[33]

The Chilean delegate Hernán Santa Cruz rejected this argument, observing that technology was the key to the development of fisheries and the seabed, and therefore within the committee's remit.[34] He also explained that the developing countries were keen to secure the equitable distribution of technology, including patented technology, because they wanted to reduce their dependence on unsatisfactory arrangements with foreign companies involving 'discrimination, restriction in supplies,

[33] US Mission Geneva to US State Department (23 July 1973), s. 1, p. 3: 1973GENEVA03833, AAD.

[34] Ibid., s. 2, p. 1.

excessively long contracts'.[35] Not only that, but for all the talk, the training on offer often did not meet the recipients' needs.[36] Similar complaints were subsequently raised at the conference, where the Cameroonian delegate Jacques Booh noted that the developing countries were being palmed off with inferior goods from the industrial states, with some spending large sums importing technology 'which was in some cases already outmoded'.[37]

The G77's campaign to enshrine technology transfer in the convention served three connected purposes: to ensure that the transferred technology met the needs of the Enterprise's seabed operations; to give the developing countries indirect access to this technology by providing opportunities for joint ventures with the Enterprise; and, most important of all, to establish a convention-based precedent for transferring technology directly to the developing countries. In line with these aims, a group of states led by Madagascar, Mauritius, Nigeria and Tanzania succeeded in April 1979 in introducing into the text a new stand-alone article – article 5 of annex II – that set out the obligations on a state or company applying for a seabed mining site to transfer technology to the Enterprise if requested to do so by the international authority.[38] At its heart was article 5(1)(c), which specified that the applicant should make the transfer 'on fair and reasonable commercial terms and conditions' if the same or equivalent technology was not available on the open market.[39] Assuming that the parallel system was instituted, the purpose of this proposal was not to secure technology at preferential rates below the market price, but to prevent states and corporations from withholding the best technology from the Enterprise.

The industrial states disliked article 5 for many reasons. These included the absence of time limits on the obligation to transfer technology,[40] the absence in article 5(1)(a) of the word 'non-proprietary' before 'equipment',[41] the imposition under article 5(1)(b) of penalties if an owner refused to transfer technology,[42] and the breadth of the definition of 'technology' in article 5(5), even though it no longer included the

[35] Ibid.
[36] Ibid.
[37] UNLOSC III, vol. 2, A/Conf.62/C.3/SR.7 (18 July 1974), p. 340.
[38] UNLOSC III, vol. 8, A/Conf.62/WP.10/Rev.1 (28 April 1979), annex II, article 5, pp. 2–4.
[39] Ibid., p. 3.
[40] 'Group of five: record of meeting' (13 December 1979), p. 6: FCO 76/1911, TNA.
[41] US State Department to US Embassy Bonn (1 May 1979), p. 2: 1979STATE110349, AAD.
[42] Ibid., p. 3.

references to 'blueprints and patents' or 'processes' found in earlier proposals.[43] Yet despite these qualms, they were prepared to put up with the article. One reason for this was that it reassured the developing countries, who, the Americans reported, feared that without legal compulsion the mining operations would 'conspire to keep the technology from the Enterprise'.[44] The other reason was that article 5 would be largely superfluous anyway: technology companies as profit-making concerns had few motives for withholding their wares, and many motives for selling to the Enterprise, provided the Enterprise could afford to pay.

Even so, the industrial states, taking a belt and braces approach, set about hedging article 5 with qualifications. As already mentioned, the Enterprise was bound to *first* seek technology on the open market, and on fair and reasonable terms.[45] Also, any transfers of technology would be subject to *commercial* terms and conditions, and applicable to commercial production.[46] Also, the definition of technology was tightened, with 'specialised' inserted before 'equipment' and 'viable' before 'system'.[47] Also, there would be a ten-year limit on undertakings to provide technology,[48] which meant that the Enterprise would have treaty-mandated access, if it was required, to only the first generations of technology but not to subsequent upgrades. And finally, disagreements over terms would be subject to compulsory dispute settlement.[49]

There was, however, one clause in article 5 which the industrial states absolutely opposed. Article 5(1)(e), called the 'Brazil clause' after its sponsor, mandated that technology should be transferred directly to developing states operating in the international authority's reserved mining sites, stating that every applicant for a mining site other than the Enterprise shall:

> Undertake the same obligations as those prescribed in subparagraphs (b), (c) and (d) [regarding transfer to the Enterprise] for the benefit of a developing country or a group of developing countries which has applied for a contract under article 8 provided that these obligations shall be limited to the exploitation of the reserved part of the Area proposed by

[43] 'Group of five: record of meeting' (13 December 1979), p. 6: FCO 76/1911, TNA; and an earlier proposal: UNLOSC III, vol. 4, A/Conf.62/C.3/L.12/Rev.1 (24 April 1975), p. 198.
[44] 'US delegation report: ninth session' (u.d., c. April 1980), p. 10: FCO 76/1989, TNA.
[45] Article 5(3)(a), annex III, UNLOSC III, vol. 17, A/Conf.62/122 (7 October 1982), p. 206.
[46] Article 5(3)(a), (b), (d); article 5(4); article 5(5); and article 5(7), ibid.
[47] Article 5(8), ibid.
[48] Article 5(7), ibid.
[49] Article 5(4), ibid.

> the applicant, and provided that activities under the contract sought by the developing country or group of developing countries would not involve transfer of technology to a third country or the nationals of a third country.[50]

The industrial states wanted this clause deleted for two reasons. First, and most importantly, it would create a precedent for the transfer of technology direct to developing countries. (Both the Japanese and the Americans observed that it was the only provision in the text that imposed a compulsory obligation on an applicant to provide for them.[51]) And second, they argued, it was not in keeping with the objective of article 5, which was to ensure that the Enterprise, and only the Enterprise, had access to technology.

The Brazil clause came with a backstory. In 1978, before it appeared in the text, Elliot Richardson did his best to dissuade the Brazilians from proposing it, visiting Brasilia to press the point. There, the story took an interesting turn. Foreign minister Antonio Azeredo da Silveira immediately raised the Brazil clause with him, pointing out that it had actually been worked out between Sergio Thompson-Flores and the American deputy delegation head George Aldrich in 1976 when they had been working together to sell the parallel system to the G77.[52] Richardson confirmed that Thompson-Flores and Aldrich had indeed discussed the issue but that 'it had been understood that Aldrich could not promise that what he and Thompson-Flores worked out would be acceptable to Richardson or the U.S. government'.[53] (When these comments got back to Thompson-Flores, he was reportedly 'livid' – either because he thought Aldrich had misled him or because Richardson was welching on a deal – and said that as far as he was concerned, the parallel system could 'go down the drain'.[54])

The Brazilians had good reason for sponsoring the clause: as one of the leading developing countries, they hoped to capitalise on the obligation to transfer technology not just to the Enterprise but also (as the clause put it) 'for the benefit of a developing country or a group of developing

[50] Article 5(1)(e), annex II, UNLOSC III, vol. 8, A/Conf.62/WP.10/Rev.1 (28 April 1979), p. 3.
[51] 'UNLOSC group of five meeting' (u.d., c. 3–4 December 1980), p. 5: FCO 76/1978, TNA.
[52] US Embassy Brasilia to US State Department (25 July 1978), p. 1: 1978BRASIL05790, AAD.
[53] Ibid.
[54] US Mission to the UN to US State Department (23 August 1978), s. 1, p. 3: 1978USUNN03259, AAD.

countries which has applied for a contract' if they ever pursued seabed operations themselves.[55] Richardson tried to persuade Azeredo da Silveira that the clause would be unnecessary because Brazilian firms would be more likely to seek joint ventures with the Enterprise or a foreign company than to go it alone, and that these links would give it access to the technology by another route.[56] American ambassador Robert Sayre kept up the pressure after Richardson's departure, arguing that the clause would be unhelpful to Brazil because by the time it was ready to embark on seabed mining it would have left the ranks of the developing countries, to which the clause was directed, and joined those of the industrial states, to which it was not.[57]

Despite this pressure, the Brazilian government decided to sponsor the clause anyway, and, once it had been inserted into the negotiating text, the G77 states ensured that it remained there. In 1980, the G5 members considered what sort of action could be taken to dilute the clause in case they failed to get it deleted. The American and Japanese representatives considered imposing a restrictive definition of the term 'developing country'[58] – a proposal that, had it been taken up, might have greatly prolonged the discussion. The British representative suggested chipping away at the clause's mandatory character.[59] And the American suggested limiting transfer obligations to those companies that had already secured a contract.[60] They did not, however, manage to delete it completely from the text that was opened for signature in 1982.[61]

By that stage, technology transfer had become a lightning rod not only for the G77 states but also for Western neoliberal critics of the conference proceedings. The American presidential counsellor Edwin Meese wrote that it would be 'a chilling precedent which would in effect nationalize private property with no guarantee of just compensation'.[62] The British thinktank director Michael Ivens claimed that 'we will be obliged to hand

[55] Article 5(1)(e), annex II, UNLOSC III, vol. 8, A/Conf.62/WP.10/Rev.1 (28 April 1979), p. 3.

[56] US Embassy Brasilia to State Department (27 July 1978), p. 2: 1978BRASIL05790, AAD.

[57] US Embassy Brasilia to State Department (13 March 1979), p. 2: 1979BRASIL02177, AAD.

[58] 'UNLOSC group of five meeting' (u.d., c. 3–4 December 1980), p. 5: FCO 76/1978, TNA.

[59] Ibid., p. 4.

[60] Ibid., p. 5.

[61] Article 5(3)(e), annex III, UNLOSC III, vol. 17, A/Conf.62/122 (7 October 1982), p. 206.

[62] E. Meese, 'Seabed mining and the law of the sea treaty' (1 November 1982), p. 4: box 10, Law of the sea, William Barr papers, Ronald Reagan Presidential Library, Digital Library Collections [hereafter, RRPL].

over our technological secrets to the Soviets and other nations'.[63] And the British industrialist Ian MacGregor told Margaret Thatcher that the profits accrued by states from 'compulsory acquisition of . . . technology' could be passed on to UN bodies and even to the Palestine Liberation Organization (PLO) and the South West Africa People's Organisation (SWAPO).[64]

Of course, there would be no Gadarene rush into seabed mining by the developing states, never mind by the PLO or SWAPO. Even the Brazilians, who were better placed than most among the developing countries, described the prospect of their nation going it alone as 'future-ology'.[65] But the utility or otherwise of article 5 on technology transfer would never be put to the test, because fourteen years after the convention was signed, and months before it would enter into force, a US-backed UN-sponsored amendment would sweep it away.[66] By this time, the new international economic order, which some had once believed to be within reach, now appeared to be less achievable and more anachronistic than at any time since the concept's inception.

The Second Front

While the United States was holding the line against the developing countries over technology transfer and other issues, it also faced formidable challenges from the industrial states of the North.

The first of these challenges came from Western land-based mineral producers led by Canada and Australia, the largest and the fourth largest global producers of nickel, who sought automatic seabed mineral production limits or anti-subsidy provisions to protect their industries. These states also won the support of some developing land-based mineral producers, who, while pushing for a strong international authority, were inclined to hedge their bets. In 1976, the Americans agreed a temporary ceiling for seabed nickel production, based on an estimated yearly market growth of 6 per cent for twenty years from 1980 or the start of commercial

63 M. Ivens, 'UN Convention on the Law of the Sea', *Financial Times* (15 November 1982).

64 I. MacGregor to M. Thatcher (8 November 1982), pp. 1–2: box 10, Law of the sea, William Barr papers, RRPL.

65 US Embassy Brasilia to US State Department (27 July 1978), p. 3: 1978BRASIL05861, AAD.

66 'Agreement relating to the Implementation of Part XI of the UN Convention on the Law of the Sea of 10 December 1982': UNGA Res. A/RES/48/263 (17 August 1994).

production, with the option of a five year extension.[67] Although this arrangement was condemned by US mining interests as being antithetical to market principles, American officials privately indicated that its effect would be cosmetic, not real:[68] projected seabed mining capacity over the first decades of commercial production was unlikely to hit a compounded 6 per cent until after the arrangement had been terminated. The issue was eventually resolved when the United States and Canada came to an agreement over nickel quotas, this being embedded in the detailed provisions set out in article 151 of the convention.[69]

A second and equally dangerous challenge came from within the G5 itself. Three members of the group – France, Japan and the USSR – were among those who saw themselves as potential competitors to the United States over seabed mining sites and market share. Their campaigns to level up the playing field with the Americans took the form of either anti-monopoly clauses or quotas limiting the number, percentage and size of seabed sites available to states and companies. Japan wished to ensure that in competitive bidding, its companies would not be shut out of good sites during the second generation of seabed mining, and wanted preference given to states such as itself that were heavily dependent on mineral imports.[70] And the USSR wanted to shield its copper and nickel industries (then ranking second and third in global production) from competition, while also ensuring that there were not 'too many American flags in any one [seabed mining] spot' in case the United States gained too much influence in certain ocean areas.[71]

Yet of all the advocates of anti-monopoly clauses and quotas, the French were the most persistent. As with Canada, Australia and the USSR, nickel strongly influenced French thinking: its dependency New Caledonia was the second largest producer after Canada. In 1975, Giscard d'Estaing's government instructed its delegation to put the G5

[67] Article 9(4)(ii) and annex I, para. 21, UNLOSC III, vol. 5, A/Conf.62/WP.8/Rev.1/PartI (6 May 1976), pp. 129–130, 142.

[68] US Mission to the UN to US State Department (16 August 1976), p. 2: 1976USUNN03256, AAD.

[69] UNCLOS, 452–454.

[70] US Mission to the UN to US State Department (29 April 1976), s. 2, p. 2: 1976USUNN01811; and US Mission to the UN to US State Department (5 August 1976), p. 2: 1976USUNN03119, AAD.

[71] US State Department to US Embassy Bonn (14 July 1978), p. 2: 1978STATE178263, AAD.

on notice that it was considering introducing 'some kind of world-wide anti-trust law which would prevent any State or group of States having a monopoly of sea-bed exploitation'.[72] The French followed this up in 1976 with a proposal designed to prevent single states or entities from securing additional seabed contracts if their operations exceeded a certain percentage of production. In their words (with blanks still to be decided):

> After the conclusion of — contracts for the exploitation of resources of the area, any new application for a contract presented by a state party shall be refused by the economic planning commission when the total num[ ]ber of contracts already concluded by this state or already applied for … will assure to that state party an overall capacity for extraction greater than — percent of the annual production of minerals recovered from the mineral resources of the Area.[73]

The Americans resisted. They described the idea of imposing a percentage limit on the annual production of individual states as arbitrary and unacceptable[74] – no less troublesome than the general production limits being proposed by Canada. If the French measures were introduced, American enterprises would face an unpleasant choice: either they would have to submit to what they saw as a rigged system, or they would have to transfer their technology and capital to foreign 'flag of convenience' operations designed to get around it. Aside from the impact on profits, the overall effect, it was argued, would be twofold: it would choke off free enterprise, and it would restrict the United States' access to strategic minerals.

Among those Americans who laid stress on the proposed measures' ill effects on free enterprise was the first committee delegate Leigh Ratiner – a staunch advocate of US mining interests. When in 1975 the British initiated a discussion at the conference about quotas, Ratiner 'responded violently' and 'threatened that if we pursued this line, there would be no transfer of technology to UK companies'.[75] (The British backed away from their pro-quota position.) Among those Americans more inclined

[72] 'Group of five meeting, New York' (u.d., c. late September 1975), p. 4: FCO 76/1039, TNA.

[73] US Mission to the UN to US State Department (12 April 1976), s. 1, p. 4: 1976USUNN 01507, AAD.

[74] US Mission to the UN to US State Department (30 April 1976), p. 3: 1976USUNN01858, AAD.

[75] D. A. Lamont to E. C. Glover (15 July 1975): FCO 76/1038, TNA.

to emphasise the security ramifications if mineral supplies to the United States were curtailed was William Scranton, US ambassador to the UN. In 1976, for example, he pointed out that the United States, unlike France, did not enjoy 'secure production' of strategic minerals such as nickel and cobalt,[76] and that restrictive provisions 'would force American companies to seek contracts under the auspices of other countries, thus reducing substantially politically secure supplies of raw materials'.[77]

The United States stood almost alone in opposing these proposals, with only West Germany supporting its stance. To manage this problem, the Americans adopted a three-pronged approach: they took a consistently hard line, making it clear that it was a 'no-sign' issue for Washington;[78] they made efforts to keep the issue off the agenda of the first committee;[79] and if all else failed, they did what they could to water down their opponents' proposals.

Of these approaches, the hard line was the most conspicuous. In April 1976, Ratiner warned the other industrial states that if the negotiating text included quotas, then the US Congress might pass legislation endorsing unilateral seabed mining by American firms[80] – a threat given extra heft by Congress's decision that same month to declare a 200-mile fishing conservation zone. He also delivered an 'emotional' blast against quotas in the first committee, directing a good deal of it towards the European Community.[81] The French delegate later took Ratiner to one side: why attack the European Community, whose members vigorously disagreed among themselves over the seabed? Ratiner admitted that he had really meant to say 'European *countries*', meaning France and the USSR, who, he said, had been exerting 'intense pressure' on the developing countries to support their campaign for quotas.[82]

[76] US Mission to the UN to US State Department (12 April 1976), s. 2, p. 5: 1976USUNN01507, AAD.

[77] US Mission to the UN to US State Department (10 August 1976), s. 2, pp. 4–5: 1976USUNN03172, AAD.

[78] Ibid., s. 1, p. 3.

[79] US Mission to the UN to US State Department (12 April 1976), s. 2, p. 3: 1976USUNN01507, AAD.

[80] See, for example, US Mission to the UN to US State Department (30 April 1976), pp. 1–2: 1976USUNN01857, AAD.

[81] M. C. Wood to M. J. Williams (9 April 1976), p. 1: FCO 14/651, TNA.

[82] Ibid., p. 2. Emphasis added. The Americans reported, for example, that: 'We understand that the Soviets have persuaded both Mexico and India that a state quota would assist these countries in attracting seabed mining investments by forcing capital and technology

Alongside the hard line, the Americans tried to settle the fears of the other industrial states by talking up the number of potential mine sites available on the seabed. In April 1976, Kissinger stated that 'arbitrary' limitations on seabed mining were quite unnecessary because 'there are many more productive seabed mining sites than conceivably can be mined for centuries to come'.[83] Three weeks later, Ratiner told European Community delegates that their concerns about a single state monopolising seabed mining were unjustified because there would be close to 500 prime sites available.[84] A week after that, the Americans quietly revised their figures downwards, informing the G5 that restrictions would be unnecessary because there would be around 300–400 sites to exploit.[85] These estimates did not take into account the production limits being proposed by Canada: in 1978, the Americans privately estimated that if production controls were imposed during the first phase of seabed mining, US-led consortia would mine three to four sites and the Enterprise and the rest of the world would have ten to fourteen sites to share between them.[86]

Société Le Nickel

When in 1978 American officials made a high-level approach to the French government to persuade it to drop its proposals, foreign minister Louis de Guiringaud refused to give way. The French position, he explained, had been set out many times previously, including before parliament, with the aim of permitting 'the maintenance of a certain equilibrium among the various miners of international deep seabed multimetal nodules'.[87] He continued:

> Our difference of opinion is restricted, in fact, to the setting up, upon the granting of the first contracts, of a mechanism which would permit avoiding the monopolization of all available sites by the existing consortia.

out of industrialized countries that have used up their quota': US State Department to US delegation (7 August 1976), p. 4: 1976STATE196813, AAD.

83 US State Department to all posts (8 April 1976), p. 17: 1976STATE084997, AAD.

84 US Mission to the UN to US State Department (30 April 1976), p. 2: 1976USUNN01857, AAD.

85 US Mission to the UN to US State Department (8 May 1976), s. 2, p. 2: 1976USUNN02022, AAD.

86 US State Department to US Mission Geneva (11 May 1978), p. 4: 1978STATE119888, AAD.

87 US Embassy Paris to US State Department (7 August 1978), p. 2: 1978PARIS24673, AAD.

> This precaution appears essential to us because of the limitation on deep sea production required by land mineral producers [in article 151]. This production limitation will result in strictly limiting the number of exploitable sites. Consequently, it is our intention to take measures as soon as the first contracts are awarded against any monopolization by consortia controlled by a specific country.[88]

Meanwhile, Claude Riffaud of the research organisation, Centre national pour l'exploitation des océans, provided some context to de Guiringaud's comments. He told the American representative Jacob Myerson that even if the number of potential mine sites outnumbered the capacity to mine them, as the Americans were claiming, the quality of the sites differed.[89] (It was well known that the Clarion-Clipperton site in the Southeast Pacific, for example, was potentially richer in nodules than sites elsewhere.) He added that the French thought that an anti-monopoly clause was necessary in the convention because American firms already knew where the very best sites were located and would submit applications to exploit them before French enterprises had developed the technical capacity to make their own competitive bids.[90]

Riffaud also indicated that French ministerial thinking was greatly influenced by the nickel crises in New Caledonia. The combined impact of the fall in world nickel prices and the expansion of production capacity had created significant problems for the New Caledonian economy, and in particular, the French mining company, Société Le Nickel. Consequently, the French government had every incentive to try to control, and if possible impede, the development of any seabed mining industry. As he explained (and Myerson reported),

> the French viewed nickel to be the primary metal determining the economic viability of deep seabed mining operations closely followed by cobalt. All other metals including copper ... would be economic by-products. Consequently, the French neither envisaged nor favored early exploitation of deep seabed minerals.[91]

In 1980, the French proposed amendments designed to strengthen anti-monopoly clauses that had already been introduced into the negotiating text. Their attention focussed on articles 6 and 7 of annex II. With respect

88 Ibid.
89 US Embassy Paris to US State Department (20 November 1978), p. 1: 1978PARIS38065, AAD.
90 Ibid., pp. 1–2.
91 Ibid., p. 2.

to article 6(3)(d)(i), they proposed that the international authority should approve a plan of work (subject to the usual uniformity and non-discriminatory requirements) except if it was submitted or sponsored by a state that had an earlier plan in progress, and the plans together covered more than 20 per cent of a moveable circular area of 400,000 square kilometres or gave the state more than two plans within this area.[92] This circular area covered both non-reserved and reserved sites,[93] so that states trying to avoid anti-monopoly provisions by entering into joint ventures with the Enterprise would still be counted. If more than one state sponsored a plan, all states would be counted.[94] As for article 7(4), France, mindful of the production limits set out in article 151, wanted priority given to applications from states with no approved plans of work over those with two or more approved plans, wherever they were situated.[95]

In response, the Americans made further amendments,[96] which were then incorporated into the April 1980 text. These deleted France's change to article 7(4), and made substantial alterations to the French changes to article 6(3)(d)(i). The latter now stated that the international authority should approve plans of work unless:

> (d) The proposed plan of work has been submitted or sponsored by a State Party which already holds:
>
> > (i) plans of work for exploration and exploitation of polymetallic nodules in non-reserved sites that, together with either part of the proposed site, would exceed in size 30 per cent of a circular area of 400,000 square kilometres surrounding the centre of either part of the area covered by the proposed plan of work[97]

This knocked the sharp edges off the French proposal. First, it increased the maximum percentage of a state's operations within the 400,000 square kilometre area from 20 to 30 per cent, transforming the provision from onerous to acceptable. Second, it omitted from percentage calculations plans of work covering reserved sites, counting only non-reserved sites. Third, it indicated with the words 'already holds' that non-reserved sites meant only those sites that the state held at the time of application,

92 'U.S. delegation report: ninth session' (u.d., c. April 1980), p. 14: FCO 76/1989, TNA.
93 UNLOSC III, vol. 14, A/Conf.62/C.1/L.28 and Add.1 (23 August 1980), p. 162.
94 Ibid.
95 Ibid.
96 'U.S. delegation report: ninth session' (u.d., c. April 1980), p. 15: FCO 76/1989, TNA.
97 UNLOSC III, vol. 8, A/Conf.62/WP.10/Rev.2 (11 April 1980), p. 155.

not abandoned or worked-out sites that the state had held previously. And finally, the reference to polymetallic nodules excluded other exploitable non-living resources on the seabed such as mineral crusts and oozes. The American formula turned out to be the final one, appearing in the convention with drafting tweaks as article 6(3)(c)(i) of annex III.[98]

From Carter to Reagan

In September 1980, in the final months of the Carter administration, Elliot Richardson delivered a speech to the American Mining Congress about the progress of the seabed negotiations. He compared the end-of-session text produced by Paul Engo in 1977 – over which his delegation had threatened to walk out – to the latest version to illustrate how much ground the United States had made up since:

> Thanks to a lot of ingenuity and even more very hard bargaining, the present draft convention is vastly better ... Since 1977, roughly 135 changes have been made in the seabed mining provisions; 120 of these are improvements from our point of view.[99]

When published, Richardson's remarks were carefully picked over by those participating in the conference as well as by the restless gallery of critics in Washington. There was no denying that the American delegation had mostly got its way on seabed issues. Not only did it manage to spike the guns of the technology transfer and anti-monopoly clauses, but it also held the line on production ceilings, the review conference, and the distribution of votes on the international authority's Council. Richardson also emphasised that the draft text's financial provisions were 'no worse than other tax systems', and that the up-front costs of seabed mining were 'modest in proportion to the size of the investment involved'.[100] He also pointed out that private enterprises had been prepared to accept more onerous contractual arrangements than those set out in the negotiating text, and gave the example of six foreign companies' recent oil exploration contracts with state-run Pertamina in Indonesia.[101]

[98] UNCLOS, 532.

[99] E. Richardson, 'Seabed mining and law of the sea', *Department of State Bulletin* 80 (December 1980), 60, 60–61.

[100] Ibid., 62.

[101] R. B. Keating to J. Lehman (21 December 1982), p. 2: box 10, Law of the sea, William Barr papers, RRPL.

In the meantime, the common heritage idea had receded. The Western states had once seen it as a useful counterweight to the coastal states' unilateral claims, but they had later abandoned it in favour of the parallel system. And some G77 members had once seen it as a rallying point for a new international economic order but had later shifted their attention to technology transfer. As a result of this slippage on both sides, the text had little to say about common heritage, and nothing to say about the distribution of its fruits to the developing countries. Article 136 of the convention simply asserts that: 'The Area and its resources are the common heritage of mankind.'[102] Article 140(1) states that activities in the Area – not the distribution of benefits – should be carried out 'for the benefit of mankind as a whole' while 'taking into particular consideration the interests and needs of developing States and of peoples who have not attained full independence or other self-governing status'.[103] Article 140(2) *does* address distribution, but makes no special provision for the developing countries, merely stating that the international authority 'shall provide for the equitable sharing of financial and other economic benefits derived from activities in the Area . . . on a non-discriminatory basis'.[104] This opens up the possibility that the industrial states might receive the same or even more than the developing countries because benefits would be either shared on a 'non-discriminatory basis' (i.e. the same for all) or shared on an 'equitable' basis, with the major operators possibly claiming a bigger slice because they provided most of the investment.

Towards the end of the conference, the G77 states proposed that common heritage was *jus cogens*[105] – not because of any residual investment in the principle, but as a tactical means of discouraging the Americans from embarking on seabed mining operations outside the terms of the convention. The United States responded by not only rejecting the argument,[106] but also by repudiating the common heritage idea itself. Delegate Robert Keating, for example, argued that common heritage 'fits quite happily into the global socialists['] tool kit as a theory of property' and was 'leading the United Nations itself into commerce in a way its Charter can never have intended, there to dominate the free

[102] UNCLOS, 446.
[103] Ibid., 447.
[104] Ibid.
[105] F. Zegers, UNLOSC III, vol. 17, A/Conf.62/SR.189 (8 December 1982), p. 67.
[106] UNLOSC III, vol. 17, A/Conf.62/WS/37 and Add.1-2 (8 March 1983), p. 243.

enterprise resource markets'.[107] Meanwhile, in the drafting committee, the powers took steps to prevent the G77 countries from declaring common heritage to be a peremptory norm, by replacing the word 'can' with the word 'shall' in article 311(6), which now read that parties 'agree that there shall be no amendments to the basic principle relating to the common heritage of mankind set forth in article 136'.[108]

In a final session to the conference, the Iranian delegate Jamshid Momtaz delivered a requiem for the principle as applied to the seabed, when he observed that the 'protection of the industrialized countries' investments' seemed to have prevailed over the protection of common heritage.[109]

*

When Ronald Reagan assumed office in January 1981, the new delegation head, James Malone, announced a pause in the Americans' participation in the negotiations while the new administration reviewed the negotiating text. A few months later, at the Asian-African Legal Consultative Committee (AALCC) session in Colombo, observers Alvaro de Soto of Peru and Sergio Thompson-Flores of Brazil mounted a 'vigorous' and 'vitriolic' attack on the American move,[110] with Thompson-Flores questioning whether a decade's work should be sacrificed 'merely to satisfy the wishes of just one delegation'.[111] He pointed out that many parts of the package on which the administration were now passing judgment were originally American proposals, including the parallel system itself.[112] He also warned that the administration might call for the renegotiation of issues 'on the same terms and conditions as in 1970', while embarking along with other industrial states on seabed mining.[113] According to one observer, Thomson-Flores seemed to be suggesting that the developing countries should pre-empt this by wrapping up the

107 R. B. Keating to J. Lehman (21 December 1982), p. 3: box 10, Law of the sea, William Barr papers, RRPL.
108 UNLOSC III, vol. 17, A/Conf.62/122 (7 October 1982), p. 203.
109 UNLOSC III, vol. 16, A/Conf.62/SR.159 (30 March 1982), p. 17.
110 I. Sinclair, 'UNLOSC: discussions at AALCC session' (3 June 1981), p. 1: FCO 76/2139, TNA.
111 'Draft minutes of the second meeting of the twenty-second session of the Asian-African Legal Consultative Committee' (25 May 1981), p. 10: FCO 76/2139, TNA.
112 Ibid., p. 9.
113 Ibid.

negotiations and getting the convention signed without American participation.[114]

Meanwhile, behind the scenes, Leigh Ratiner and James Malone met with other G5 members to spell out everything they thought was wrong with the seabed provisions. The list was long, and many objections had a sharp political ring to them. Ratiner did most of the talking. Article 150(d) ensuring the supply of minerals to consumers, he said, smacked of 'central economic planning'.[115] Article 150(g) protecting developing countries from adverse effects tended towards 'economic adjustment assistance for certain developing countries'.[116] Article 150(i) covering conditions such as import duties would be unacceptable to the US Senate as a 'matter of philosophy'.[117] Article 151 on production controls was 'dramatically opposite to the guiding principles of the New Administration'.[118] Article 6 annex III on anti-density and anti-monopoly provisions, although hatched within the G5, 'had *never* been acceptable to the US Congress'.[119] And article 161 on the composition, procedure and voting on the international authority's Council was defective because there was no guaranteed seat for the United States, the votes allocated to the industrial states were insufficient, and these votes could be split between competing states.[120] And so he continued, clause by clause.

The other G5 representatives, some of whom had been involved in the negotiations for years, were not especially sympathetic. One veteran, Semyon Kozyrev, noted that the Americans were objecting to a text that gave them more than 2 per cent of the seabed, which he thought was 'pretty generous'.[121] Ratiner replied that only 2 per cent of the seabed 'was not fair for a country that consumed 20% of the world's resources'.[122] Another veteran, the French delegate Guy Ladreit de Lacharrière, then turned to the newly appointed Malone and asked him what *his* solution

[114] I. Sinclair, 'UNLOSC: discussions at AALCC session' (3 June 1981), p. 1: FCO 76/2139, TNA.

[115] 'First committee experts' meeting' (24 June 1981), p. 2: FCO 76/2170, TNA.

[116] Ibid.

[117] Ibid.

[118] Ibid.

[119] Ibid., p. 5. Original emphasis.

[120] Ibid., pp. 2, 3, 4.

[121] Ibid., p. 5. Kozyrev is quoted as saying 'oceans', but it is clear from the context and Ratiner's response that he meant seabed.

[122] Ibid.

was to the Council voting question – would it be 'the tyranny of the G77 or paralysis'?[123] Malone's response could not have inspired much confidence:

> [He] said they had no solution. They would like more determinative power on an affirmative basis for themselves and less determinative power on a negative basis for others. Apart from that platitude he confessed to total mental paralysis on this point.[124]

After a year-long hiatus, the Americans returned to the conference in March 1982, bringing with them a sixty-eight page dossier of proposed amendments to the seabed proposals, known as the 'green book'. The new conference president, the Singaporean Tommy Koh, recalled:

> I had to persuade the Conference to give Reagan a year. One whole year to decide to reconsider its position with respect to the draft treaty that we have negotiated. And then they came back with a long list of unreasonable demands for changes. Was a very tough time that last year.[125]

The 'green book' set off a loud chorus of criticism. Siddiquer Rahman of Bangladesh said the amendments were so sweeping 'that they called into question all the major substantive aspects of the compromises that had been achieved on the provisions governing the sea-bed'.[126] Ukraine's Yuriy Kochube added that it would be hard to find 'even one delegation' who found its contents acceptable.[127] The Americans, as its authors, were forced to run the gauntlet: Pakistan's delegate Inam-ul-Haque, speaking on behalf of the G77, condemned them for an 'act of bad faith';[128] Kozyrev criticised them for their 'obstructionism';[129] the GDR's Gunter Görner for their 'destructive attitude';[130] Fiji's Satya Nandan for their 'unrealistic demands';[131] and China's Shen Wei-liang for their 'unrealistic and unwise' approach.[132] The Holy See's delegate Mgr. Cheli was moved to enter the debate, stating that 'material wealth should be used to unite

[123] Ibid., p. 6.
[124] Ibid.
[125] Koh Tommy Thong Bee transcript (6 June 1998), reel 7, p. 79: Acc. no. 002021, National Archives of Singapore.
[126] UNLOSC III, vol. 16, A/Conf.62/SR.162 (31 March 1982), p. 42.
[127] UNLOSC III, vol. 16, A/Conf.62/SR.161 (31 March 1982), p. 36.
[128] UNLOSC III, vol. 16, A/Conf.62/SR.156 (8 March 1982), p. 5.
[129] Ibid.
[130] UNLOSC III, vol. 16, A/Conf.62/SR.159 (30 March 1982), p. 20.
[131] Ibid., p. 17.
[132] UNLOSC III, vol. 16, A/Conf.62/SR.161 (31 March 1982), p. 32.

men rather than divide them'[133] – a remark that seemed more applicable to the celestial realm than to the ocean floor.

So the Americans withdrew the 'green book' and replaced it with new set of amendments,[134] co-sponsored by other Western industrial states, which many denounced as being a reheated version of the same thing. One co-sponsor, Britain, was prepared to go out on a limb in their support of the Americans not just because they had similar views on seabed mining but also because they were anxious to mend fences with Washington during the ongoing Malvinas/Falklands crisis.[135] They paid a price for this support, however. Their delegation head John Powell-Jones reported that any influence the delegation had earlier commanded had dissipated because it was now regarded as 'a mere satellite of the United States with whom separate communication is pointless'.[136] Consequently,

> [Tommy] Koh has ... not found it necessary to speak to me during the past ten days, and rather pointedly refused to attend a reception which I am giving this evening ... Keith Brennan of Australia, with whom I have enjoyed very close co-operation has clearly turned the cold shoulder since our decision on co-sponsorship ... It is also noticeable that the United States having achieved their objective have become noticeably offhand with this delegation which they now feel can be taken for granted.[137]

The real losers, however, were not the British, but the developing countries. The Tanzanian Joseph Warioba, whose delegation had presented the first comprehensive proposal on the international authority nearly a decade earlier, explained how they had lost out. He recalled that the G77 had earlier accepted the parallel system, but with misgivings since some (Tanzania included) 'felt that the system would lead to a kind of *apartheid* by which the Area would be divided into two halves, one for the rich few and one for the impoverished many'.[138] Yet, he added,

> They were none the less consoled by the proposal to establish an Enterprise through which the poor majority would be able to participate in the

[133] UNLOSC III, vol. 16, A/Conf.62/SR.162 (31 March 1982), p. 50.

[134] UNLOSC III, vol. 16, A/Conf.62/L.121 and L.122 (both 13 April 1982). Another proposal – L.104 – advanced by a group of smaller Western powers on the same date was widely seen as serving the same American-led agenda.

[135] W. J. Adams to J. E. Powell-Jones (23 April 1982): FCO 76/2456, TNA.

[136] J. E. Powell-Jones to W. J. Adams (21 April 1982): FCO 76/2456, TNA.

[137] Ibid.

[138] UNLOSC III, vol. 16, A/Conf.62/SR.169 (15 April 1982), p. 95.

> exploitation of the resources of the Area, and would be guaranteed both technology and financial capital and areas of established commercial value which had already been surveyed. It was also proposed that the parallel system would operate for a period of not more than 20 years, after which there would be a review conference with the option of changing the system.[139]

He noted how the American proposals aimed to further tighten the industrial states' control over both sides of the parallel system: by removing power from the international authority and vesting it in the contracting states in non-reserved areas; and by exercising power through the Council (on which they would possess permanent membership and a veto) over the authority's reserved areas.[140] The outcome in the text, Warioba pointed out, was that contrary to the assurances made by Kissinger in 1976, there was insufficient protection for land-based producers, there was no indication of who would transfer technology to the Enterprise, most of the burden of financing the Enterprise had passed to the developing countries, and the review conference would be unable to change the parallel system even if it was untenable.[141] In short, he said, the Tanzanian delegation felt 'betrayed by the succession of promises that had been broken over the previous eight years'.[142]

Warioba's appraisal may have been accurate enough, but the G77 states were nonetheless still prepared to make further concessions on the seabed to persuade the United States and its co-sponsors to sign up to the convention. They agreed, for example, to accept a preparatory investment protection plan that would give 'pioneer investors' who invested in seabed operations before the convention entered into force guaranteed access to mining sites after it took effect. They were also, according to Koh, prepared to agree to amendments to the existing seabed text to meet the industrial states' concerns.[143] Yet when presented with these proposed concessions, Ratiner demanded even more changes to the text on some of the most bitterly contested issues. He reported that these were:

> a) Voting in the preparatory commission [for the international authority];
> b) An improved solution to the review conference problem;
> c) A change in voting system in the Council;

[139] Ibid.
[140] Ibid.
[141] Ibid.
[142] Ibid.
[143] UK Mission to the UN to UK FCO (22 April 1982), p. 1: FCO 76/2410, TNA.

d) A better solution to the NLM [national liberation movement] problem (article 140);
e) Assembly powers;
f) Transfer of technology on which the present article 5.3 [the Brazil clause] was wholly unacceptable.[144]

Not all of these concessions were granted, and, at the penultimate session held in New York, the Americans expressed their displeasure by insisting on overriding the consensus procedure and putting the draft convention text to a vote. It was passed 140-4-17 (with Israel, Turkey, the United States and Venezuela voting against). Rounds of applause followed: most states had emphatically endorsed the outcome of a treaty-making project that spanned over half a century. James Malone, as representative of the host nation, should, according to the diplomatic tradition, have then delivered some congratulatory remarks, but he swiftly departed from the conference chamber leaving Koh to wrap up the proceedings by himself.

Of those who voted against, the United States did so because it apparently disapproved of a few seabed provisions; Venezuela because of delimitation issues with Colombia; Turkey because of disputes with Greece; and Israel because the 'benefit of mankind' provision set out in article 140(1) allowed non-self-governing 'peoples' (including the Palestinians) to share in common heritage.[145] Of those who abstained, the largest group, made up of the USSR and eight Eastern bloc states, opposed the US-sponsored preparatory investment protection provision, which, they argued, withheld pioneer status from the USSR and others until they had signed the convention while giving it to some Western members of seabed mining consortia even if they had not signed.[146] The remaining abstainers, almost all from Western Europe, included Britain and West Germany, who abstained in solidarity with the United States while resisting Washington's pressure to vote against.[147]

Walking Away

The final session of the conference took place at the Rose Hall Beach Hotel in Montego Bay in Jamaica in December 1982. The Americans

144 Ibid., p. 2.
145 UNLOSC III, vol. 17, A/Conf.62/122 (7 October 1982), p. 175.
146 S. P. Kozyrev, UNLOSC III, vol. 16, A/Conf.62/SR.177 (28 April 1982), p. 136.
147 UK delegation to UK FCO (29 April 1982); and J. W. D. Gray, 'UNLOSC' (30 April 1982): FCO 76/2411, TNA.

hoped that 'sun, surf, and sand' would entice the delegates 'out of their smoke-filled rooms where they would otherwise be mapping out interpretive strategies', and that they might all enjoy 'a quiet, nonconfrontational closing session'.[148] This was wishful thinking. The session was every bit as tense as the previous ones and most of the criticism was again directed towards the United States.

The Americans' reluctance to support the convention had long been evident. It started during Carter's administration, gathered pace during Reagan's, and culminated in their vote against the text at the earlier session in 1982. Both administrations looked instead to customary international law to justify their maritime activities. In 1979, Carter's administration inaugurated the 'freedom of navigation operations' programme to claim, and try to establish, as custom the same navigational and overflight rights as those set out in the negotiating text. Then, when Reagan's administration followed, it calculated that the parts of the convention of which they approved could also be claimed under evolving custom (to which, of course, the conference proceedings had contributed), and the parts of which it disapproved could be safely ignored, as it would not be a party to the treaty. (Another calculation was that while exempting itself, the United States could nevertheless reap the greatest benefit of the convention – stability – because most other states, as parties, would be bound in relation with each other.)

Given the prominence of custom in the Americans' thinking, their objective at the final session in December 1982 was to talk up the customary character of the rights pertaining to most parts of the text, while talking down the customary character of issues relating to the seabed. The other states resisted this selective invocation of custom, which is why so much of the debate about the proposed treaty on the table before them was instead devoted to a different source of law. In his closing statement, Tommy Koh, responding to the Americans, stated that the conference was not a codification conference, that many new ideas were enshrined in the text, and that consequently

> The argument that, except for Part XI [on the seabed], the Convention codifies customary law or reflects existing international practice is factually incorrect and legally insupportable. The regime of transit passage through straits used for international navigation and the regime of archipelagic sea lanes passage are only two examples of the many new concepts

[148] J. R. Henriksen, 'Memorandum for "WG-9" members' (15 November 1982), p. 2: FCO 76/2448, TNA.

> in the Convention. Even in the case of article 76, on the continental shelf, the article contains new law in that it has expanded the concept of the continental shelf to include the continental slope and the continental rise. This concession to the broad-margin States was in return for their agreement to revenue-sharing on the continental shelf beyond 200 miles. It is therefore my view that a State which is not a party to this Convention cannot invoke the benefits of article 76.[149]

Turning to the seabed provisions, the G77 members and others asserted that it would be illegal for non-parties to engage in seabed mining outside the convention, and that national legislation or bilateral treaties incompatible with its provisions would therefore be invalid. Bernard Oxman claimed the United States and its allies – Britain and West Germany – had been 'backed into a corner' on the issue.[150] Yet the suggestion that the G77, among others, was able to dictate terms to them was demonstrably not the case. On the contrary, they made concession after concession to the Americans to induce them to become parties to the convention. In the final days, several delegates made reference to this, including the Surinamese representative Lucien Henar, who argued that the G77 could not make any further concessions without the whole package unravelling, and that 'the major industrialized States cannot just pick up their marbles and walk away, just because they did not get everything they might have wanted'.[151] In reality, though, the powers could indeed pick up their marbles and walk away – and this they duly did.

On 10 December 1982, the final day of the final session, the convention was opened for signature. Some 119 states and other entities signed on the day – 117 states, the Cook Islands as an associated state, and the United Nations Council for Namibia. Fiji deposited an instrument of ratification that day too, it being the first state to ratify the convention. The delegates gave Arvid Pardo, the great advocate of seabed common heritage, a standing ovation for his efforts, if not for the outcome. It had taken four international conferences and fifty-two years to reach agreement on all the cardinal points of the law of the sea. Now, it seemed, the task was finally finished.

[149] UNLOSC III, vol. 17, A/Conf.62/SR.193 (10 December 1982), pp. 135–136.
[150] Oxman, *From cooperation to conflict*, p. 25.
[151] UN press release, SEA/502 (7 December 1982), p. 2.

Afterword

There was no guarantee that the 1973–1982 law of the sea conference would succeed. Indeed, the outcome of the previous conferences strongly suggested that it might not. Delegates frequently predicted its imminent collapse, and the maritime powers, who had most to lose from its failure, were among the most pessimistic. At a low point in 1978, Elliot Richardson estimated the chances of a successful conclusion to be one in three, while the British delegate Ronald Arculus put them at one in five.[1]

The Kenyan delegate Frank Njenga had already given warning of what might ensue if the negotiations broke down:

> Kenya would in the event of a collapse of the conference declare a 200 miles territorial sea because its neighbours to the north and south had declared broad territorial seas and he thought others would do likewise. Moreover, the African and Asian states would concert to lay claim to the seabed out to the middle of the ocean in order to establish the basis for a political and legal confrontation with U.S.A.[2]

A global free-for-all posed considerable risks to the powers, who wished to protect their navigational rights. Yet throughout the negotiations they continually damaged their own cause with their high-handedness. The Americans were especially prone to this. Their delegations – under pressure to fight for the interests of a divided Congress, rival government departments, and the US oil, mining and fishing industries – frequently undermined the integrity of the proceedings by threatening to walk out if their demands were not met. As early as 1971 they considered withdrawing from the seabed committee over non-acceptance of their trusteeship

1 'Record of meeting between Mr Ronald Arculus and Mr Richard Cooper' (5 July 1978), p. 2: DEFE 24/1459, TNA.

2 Australian delegation to Foreign Affairs Canberra (3 March 1977), pp. 1–2: A104633 801/10/2, pt. 5, NAA.

proposal.[3] At the start of the conference, they contemplated pulling out if their preferred rules of procedure were not accepted,[4] or if they failed to secure seats on the general and drafting committees.[5] Thereafter, they threatened to walk out of discussions about straits used for international navigation, about the status of the economic zone, about marine scientific research, and about the regime governing the seabed. This carried on right up until 1982, when, despite having secured most of their objectives, and calculating that they could rely on custom, the Americans voted against the final text.

Power Politics

The negotiations demonstrated the barriers faced by the developing countries in their long-standing campaign to challenge the powers and level out the differences between North and South. In 1958–1960, they lobbied for wider territorial seas and exclusive fishing zones while capitalising on the tactical differences between the powers. Over the next decade, the momentum created by the campaign for change in international law contributed to the creation of the G77, which emerged as a prominent force within the United Nations. Yet for all its assertiveness, and its commanding voting majority, the G77 was unable to realise its aim of using the law of the sea negotiations to institute a new international economic order. The common heritage concept soon lost its sparkle, and by the mid-seventies the group found it difficult to regroup around new objectives: attempts to rally members around technology transfer proved to be too little, too late.

The powers were on a different trajectory. After their low point at the 1960 conference, they made three crucial adjustments to their strategy. First, at the instigation of the USSR, they formed a united front: from 1967 onwards, the USSR and the United States set aside their maritime differences and joined forces with other powers within the G5. Second, they engineered the shift from voting to consensus-based decision-making, which served their own interests as a minority, while providing the mechanism for locking states with widely differing interests into the treaty-making process until agreement was reached. And third, they

[3] F. G. K. Gallagher, 'Seabed / law of the sea' (24 May 1971), p. 2: FCO 76/341, TNA.
[4] H. A. Dudgeon, 'UN Conference on the Law of the Sea: rules of procedure' (2 May 1974), p. 2: FCO 76/923, TNA.
[5] 'Note on a meeting . . . on tactics' (23 January 1974), p. 2: FCO 76/927, TNA.

adopted a more calculating approach to deal-making, arriving at the conference with the 'package', which held out the promise of recognition of the economic zone. Although some developing countries criticised the powers for their self-serving insistence on consensus, and waved away the package deal as merely promising what was already theirs, these tactics nevertheless enabled the powers to deflect the claim that they had stitched up the law of the sea – an accusation that had been levelled against them over the 1958 conventions. They could now argue that all states had taken part in the creation of the new treaty, and all had gained something from the package deal: either directly in the form of an economic zone, or indirectly in the shape of a stable and universally applied ocean regime.

When looking back at all four conferences from the powers' perspective, it can be seen that their campaign for navigational manoeuvrability peaked not during the first two post-war conferences when the United States and the other Western powers dominated the United Nations, but in 1975–1977 during the final conference – ironically, the period when the G77 appeared to be at its most forceful. In those three years, the powers secured, in succession, recognition in the negotiating text of the twelve-mile territorial sea limit in 1975, transit passage through straits in 1976, and both high seas navigational rights in the exclusive economic zone and the right of archipelagic sea lane passage in 1977. Their later fallings-out, though unwelcome, were manageable so long as these earlier achievements were not reversed.

From late 1977, once the powers had secured recognition of their navigational rights and the G77 coastal states had done likewise with the exclusive economic zone, the focus of the conference shifted to the regime governing seabed exploitation. This issue assumed importance because no state wanted to be left behind should seabed mining later prove to be a viable proposition. Yet despite professing great interest in this new frontier, the delegates were rarely candid about their real order of priorities regarding non-living resources: most countries were far more preoccupied with access to oil and gas – tapped from dry land or from the continental shelf – than with access to deep seabed minerals. And mining companies – wherever they operated in the world – would for the foreseeable future make most (if not all) of their profits by extracting hard minerals from dry land rather than from the sea floor.

By the latter half of the conference, there was, along with the seabed, two other pressing issues still to be resolved. One was compulsory dispute settlement. States had agreed in principle to both binding mechanisms and optional exceptions back in 1974,[6] but even so, the detailed discussions about what sort of third-party settlement, and in what legal forum, carried on for the duration of the proceedings. The other issue was maritime boundary delimitation. As with dispute settlement, states had begun to consider the issue early in the conference, but thereafter split down the middle over whether delimitation should be decided on the basis of equidistance or of equitability.[7] (As it transpired, the convention would reflect this impasse by offering placeholders derived from custom and the 1958 conventions, and proposing, unhelpfully, that delimitation of both the exclusive economic zone and the continental shelf be 'effected by agreement on the basis of international law'.)[8]

By late 1980, however, even these long-running and intractable issues were being wrapped up, and delegates expected to conclude their work in 1981. But then the Americans, at the behest of the Reagan administration, took a year to review the text, and when they returned to the conference in 1982 they turned the tables on the other states by insisting on a vote rather than agreement by consensus, to make the point that they disagreed with a handful of seabed provisions. By this stage the G77 countries had internalised the powers' policy of assimilation: one of their main criticisms of the United States' negative vote was that it was a betrayal of the consensus-based negotiations that had preceded it.

The Beneficiaries

Once the convention was signed and the dust had settled, many commentators declared that it had established a new order in the oceans. A few even hailed it as a revolution. Clearly, there were major innovations driven by politics and technology, but the convention's emphasis was on establishing order, not bringing about revolutionary change.

It could be argued that all states were beneficiaries of the convention because they had agreed a regime that set out standards on jurisdictional issues that had previously been unsettled. Even the 'losers' – the landlocked states who failed to secure automatic fishing rights in others' exclusive economic zones, and the researching states compelled to seek

6 For a summary of positions in 1974, see: UNLOSC III, vol. 3, A/Conf.62/L.7 (27 August 1974), pp. 85–92.
7 See, for example, the different positions adopted in an early debate about the delimitation of the continental shelf: UNLOSC III, A/Conf.62/C.2/SR.20 (30 July 1974).
8 Articles 74 and 83, UNCLOS, 427, 431.

permission to conduct research in foreign waters – would have lost out more dramatically under an unregulated system entailing exclusion from unilaterally declared 200-mile territorial seas.

And yet, some states clearly did much better than others. The biggest winners were the powers. In straits used for international navigation they gained greater rights than those they had enjoyed under the previous innocent passage regime. And in the exclusive economic zone they secured virtually the same navigational rights as they had previously had on the high seas. As a result, the US Navy has been one of the most consistent supporters of the convention's navigational regime: a Judge Advocate General's Corps report published in 2011 quotes leading naval figures to this effect and explains that the convention 'provides legal certainty in the world's largest maneuver space, and preserves essential navigation and overflight rights'.[9]

In addition to these navigational advantages, the powers and their allies also managed to acquire some of the most extensive exclusive economic zones (and continental margins) in the world, easily offsetting the effects of their own long-distance fishing fleets losing access to zones elsewhere. These states – Australia, Britain, Canada, France, Japan, New Zealand, the United States and the USSR – not only secured the zones granted to their own territories, but also the zones granted to any island dependencies, however distant or remote. As Arvid Pardo observed in 1979, the American dependencies in Micronesia, with a population of 120,000, 'would obtain control of marine areas comparable in size to those obtained by all the other nations of continental Asia with the exception of India'.[10] Meanwhile, the British dependency of Pitcairn Island, with a population of eighty-six, 'would control a marine area more than double the size of that controlled by the Federal Republic of Germany'.[11]

By contrast, the G77, with its failed attempt to use seabed resources and revenues to kickstart the new international economic order, gained far less from the convention. Even at the height of its campaign on maritime issues in the early seventies, the group was hampered by the split between the coastal states on one side, and the landlocked and

[9] US Navy Judge Advocate General's Corps, *The convention on the law of the sea*, at: www.jag.navy. See also, Department of State factsheet, 'The Law of the Sea Convention: in our national security interest' (1 July 2011), at: 2009-2017.state.gov.

[10] Pardo, 'Law of the sea conference', p. 146.

[11] Ibid.

geographically disadvantaged states on the other. The landlocked states, among them some of the least developed of the developing countries, did worst of all. They expected access to common heritage and campaigned for rights to resources within the exclusive economic zones of other states but came away from both virtually empty-handed.

One reason the G77 failed to achieve its global aspirations was that as the conference progressed, they were undone by precisely the economic trends that the new international economic order was designed to eradicate. By the early eighties most of its members were experiencing the ill effects of falling investment and rising debt. As the Tanzanian delegate Joseph Warioba later wrote:

> For many of the developing countries, the 1980's have been viewed as a lost decade for development . . . Economic and social infrastructure have been eroded to a large extent, wiping out the gains made in the provision of basic needs resulting from investments in the social and economic spheres in the 1960's . . . The external imbalances in some industrialised countries whose economies have a large impact on the world economy, have contributed towards economic instability and led to higher interest rates. For developing countries, external indebtedness has emerged as a major factor in economic stagnation.[12]

Over the same 'lost decade', the United States and its allies started to back away from the UN-sponsored bodies and processes through which the new international economic order had been advocated. Warioba again:

> The demand of the developing countries which questioned the dominant economic and political role of the North led the major powers of the West to be critical of the United Nations System. They began to use their political and economic power to cripple the UN and its machinery. The idea of global negotiations on a new international economic order was killed at the Cancun Summit in 1981 and since then the North has refused to deal with major economic issues within the United Nations System, and instead they prefer the Bretton Woods institutions which are under their control.[13]

Although the Western powers were turning their backs on some parts of the UN, the organisation still had a final, crucial role to play in the story of the seabed regime. In 1994, months before the convention was due to

[12] J. S. Warioba, 'The reform of the United Nations system in the context of the law of the sea and the United Nations conference on the environment and development', *African Journal of International and Comparative Law* 7 (1995), 426, 427.

[13] Ibid., 435.

enter into force, the General Assembly, prodded along by the United States, delivered the final blow to the G77's hopes by unanimously passing the 'Agreement relating to the Implementation of Part XI of the UN Convention on the Law of the Sea of 10 December 1982'.[14] The agreement's provisions, enumerated in the annex, substantially amended the seabed regime set out in the convention, removing any remaining constraints on the powers' exploitation of the area. (The euphemistic use of 'implementation' in the title – rather than the more accurate 'amendment' – was designed to remove from states who had already ratified the convention the obligation to go back to their legislatures for endorsement of the changes.)

The Western origins of the agreement were evident in the preambular paragraphs. One of these presented a justification for the agreement's provisions: namely, 'political and economic changes, including market-oriented approaches'.[15] Another offered the facilitation of 'universal participation' in the convention – by which it meant the prospect of the non-party Western powers becoming parties.[16] Finally and most significantly, it affirmed that the agreement would be interpreted and applied along with part XI of the convention on the seabed 'as a single instrument'.[17]

Many of the proposed alterations wiped out the contested seabed provisions in the convention, including those dealing with technology transfer, production policies, Council voting, the review conference, and contractors' fees. One need only consider the sheer number of those containing the phrase 'shall not apply' to understand the scale of the changes. It appears in the sentence: 'The provisions of article 151, paragraphs 1 to 7 and 9 . . . of the Convention [on seabed mining production policies] shall not apply.'[18] And in: 'The provisions relating to the Review Conference in article 155, paragraphs 1, 3 and 4, of the Convention shall not apply.'[19] And in: 'The provisions of article 161,

[14] UNGA Res. A/RES.48/263 (passed 28 July 1994; resolution text dated 17 August 1994); and Agreement relating to the Implementation of Part XI of the United Nations Convention on the Law of the Sea of 10 December 1982 [hereafter, Implementation Agreement] (adopted by the General Assembly on 28 July 1994, entered provisionally into force on 16 November 1994) 1836 UNTS 3.

[15] Implementation Agreement, 43.

[16] Ibid.

[17] Article 2(1), ibid., 44.

[18] Annex, s. 6, para. 7, ibid., 62.

[19] Annex, s. 4, ibid., 60.

paragraph 1, of the Convention [on the composition of the Council] shall not apply.'[20] And in: 'The provisions of article 161, paragraph 8 (b) and (c), of the Convention [on required voting majorities in the Council] shall not apply.'[21] And in: 'The provisions of article 162, paragraph 2 (j), of the Convention [on the Council's approval of plans of work] shall not apply.'[22] And in: 'The provisions of . . . article 162, paragraph 2 (q) of the Convention [on selection of applicants for production authorisations] . . . shall not apply'.[23] And in: 'The provisions of . . . article 165, paragraph 2 (n) . . . of the Convention [on production ceilings and issuance of production authorisations] shall not apply.'[24] And in: 'The provisions of Annex III, article 5, of the Convention [on transfer of technology] shall not apply.'[25] And in: 'The provisions of . . . Annex III, article 6, paragraph 5 [on the authority adopting rules for deciding which plans of works should be approved], and article 7 [on the authority's selection among applicants for production authorisations], of the Convention shall not apply.'[26] And in: 'The provisions of Annex III, article 13, paragraphs 3 to 10, of the Convention [on fees to be paid by the contractor] shall not apply.'[27] Finally, 'The obligation of States Parties to fund one mine site of the Enterprise as provided for in Annex IV, article 11, paragraph 3, of the Convention shall not apply and States Parties shall be under no obligation to finance any of the operations in any mine site of the Enterprise or under its joint-venture arrangements.'[28] With these and numerous other changes, the United States and its allies settled the seabed issue completely in favour of the major industrial powers.

Selective Approaches

The 1982 convention succeeded in establishing stability and predictability, but it failed to curb the tendency to cherry-pick. This problem arose after the 1958 conference, when states could choose which, if any, of the resultant conventions they wished to become party to and submit

[20] Annex, s. 3, para. 16, ibid., 59.
[21] Annex, s. 3, para. 8, ibid., 57.
[22] Annex, s. 3, para. 11(b), ibid., 58.
[23] Annex, s. 6, para. 7, ibid., 62.
[24] Ibid.
[25] Annex, s. 5, para. 2, ibid., 61.
[26] Annex, s. 6, para. 7, ibid., 62.
[27] Annex, s. 8, para. 2, ibid., 64.
[28] Annex, s. 2, para. 3, ibid., 56.

reservations to some of those they chose. This created a complicated and patchy network of obligations between states. To avoid a repeat of this, the 1982 convention was conceived as a single comprehensive treaty, with reservations not being permitted. But this did not resolve the issue because states soon found other ways to opt out of provisions that did not suit them. One method, pursued by the United States and others, was to simply not sign. Another approach was to make use of the 'limitations' and 'optional exceptions' to compulsory dispute settlement set out in articles 297 and 298.[29] But the most common method was to become a party to the convention and then quietly overlook the inconvenient parts of it. Ashley Roach and Robert Smith's book *Excessive maritime claims*, first published in 1994 (the year the convention entered into force) and written from an American perspective, chronicled the non-compliance of other states on a wide range of provisions including those dealing with cable repairs, fishing violations, artificial islands, archipelagos, airspace, baselines, innocent passage, basepoints, historic bays and delimitation.[30] The first edition was a substantial 376 pages; the most recent, published in 2021, ran to 867 pages.[31] The selective approach has clearly become increasingly prevalent, and one is almost tempted to deduce from the most frequent transgressions on certain issues the emergence of new custom.

In situations where the selective approach did not provide the desired outcome, some states were inclined to proclaim that the law validated their policies anyway, even if this meant resorting to questionable interpretations of a text or contentious claims about the emergence of custom. This trend had already become apparent during the conference. In 1982, the Canadian drafting committee chair Alan Beesley rebuked the American, British and West German delegations (who were already indicating that they might not become parties to the convention) for making tendentious claims about what was custom and what was not:

> It is argued in some quarters that the common heritage is not a customary principle of law, but merely a provision in a Draft Convention which will have no binding force unless and until the Convention comes into force. Curiously, it is also argued by the proponents of this very view, that the freedom of transit regime in international straits is already an accepted

29 UNCLOS, 513–516.

30 J. A. Roach and R. W. Smith, *Excessive maritime claims* (Newport, RI: Naval War College, 1994).

31 J. A. Roach, *Excessive maritime claims: fourth edition* (Leiden: Brill Nijhoff, 2021).

> principle of customary law. The proponents of such interpretations or policy options are obviously unfamiliar with the fundamentals of treaty law. They might find great difficulty in attempting to operate on the basis of treaty provisions they accept, while rejecting the Convention as a whole because of other provisions they do not like.[32]

Of course, opinions on these positions differed. Notably, the straits states, including Canada, tended to present their case the other way around, asserting that common heritage was custom and transit passage through straits was not.

*

Throughout the various conferences, states shaped and reshaped legal concepts relating to the oceans. They invented the 'continental shelf', 'transit passage', the 'exclusive economic zone', 'archipelagic waters' and 'the seabed'. They reformulated the contiguous zone and fishing limits. They toyed with and then abandoned innocent passage in straits used for international navigation. They extended the continental shelf to the limit of exploitability and then halted it at the margin edge. And with a single stroke of a pen, they shrank the high seas by a third.

These achievements were the culmination of a process that had begun during the interwar decades, when Britain's decline as an imperial power provided the initial impulse to codify the law of the sea. The project was given new impetus by the global power that supplanted Britain – the United States – but by the time the convention was concluded in 1982 the latter was itself in decline. The treaty was inevitably a product of its times, and just as inevitably it has been scrutinised and reinterpreted in the light of changing circumstances: in the present Asian century, there have already been calls for a 'new type of international relations'.[33] Although the future is unknowable, one thing is certain: the geopolitical forces currently gathering momentum will inevitably generate pressure for further changes to the law governing the sea.

[32] 'Statement by J. Alan Beesley, Ambassador of Canada' (1 April 1982), p. 9: FCO 76/2409, TNA.

[33] Press release: 'Xi Jinping calls for the building of new type of international relations with win-win cooperation at the core' (23 March 2013), at: id.china-embassy.gov.cn.

BIBLIOGRAPHY

Sources of Archival Material

Archives National de France, Paris.
Archivo Central, Ministerio de Relaciones Exteriores del Perú.
Bundesarchiv Koblenz, Germany.
Central Intelligence Agency Historical Collections (online).
Foreign Relations of the United States (online).
India Office Records, British Library, London.
International Maritime Organization Archives, London.
Library and Archives Canada, Ottawa.
The National Archives, Kew, United Kingdom.
National Archives and Records Administration, Maryland, United States.
National Archives and Records Administration's Access to Archival Databases (online).
National Archives of Australia, Canberra.
National Archives of India, New Delhi.
National Archives of Singapore.
Nehru Memorial Museum and Library, New Delhi.
Public Records and Archives Administration Department, Accra.
Ronald Reagan Presidential Library, Digital Library Collections (online).
University of Virginia Law School Library UNLOSC III Collection (Satya Nandan papers).

Other Primary Sources

Historic Hansard Archives, UK (online).
International Law Commission, 'Articles concerning the law of the sea with commentaries', *Yearbook of the International Law Commission* (1956) (New York: United Nations, 1956), vol. 2, 264–301.
International Law Commission, *Yearbook of the International Law Commission* (1952) (New York: United Nations, 1958), vol. 1.
League of Nations, *Conference for the codification of international law –*

vol. I – plenary meetings, C.351.M.145 (1930).
League of Nations, *Conference for the Codification of International Law – bases of discussion – vol. II – territorial waters*, C.74.M.39 (1929).
League of Nations, *Conference for the Codification of International Law – vol. III, minutes of the second committee*, C.351 (b). M.145 (b) (1930).
Parliament of India Lok Sabha Digital Library (online).
United Nations Law of the Sea Conferences,
legal.un.org/diplomaticconferences/1958_los/
legal.un.org/diplomaticconferences/1960_los/
legal.un.org/diplomaticconferences/1973_los/

Digests

Crocker, H. G., *The extent of the marginal sea: a collection of official documents and views of representative publicists* (Washington, DC: US Government Printing Office, 1919).
United Nations Legislative Series, *Laws and regulations on the regime in the high seas*, vol. 1 (New York: United Nations, 1951).
Whiteman, M. M., *Digest of international law*, vol. 4 (Washington, DC: Department of State, 1965).

Treaties

Agreement on Cooperation in Studies of the World Ocean (entered into force [EIF] 19 June 1973 by signature, in accordance with article 8(1)) 917 UNTS 55.
Agreement relating to the Implementation of Part XI of the United Nations Convention on the Law of the Sea of 10 December 1982 (adopted by the General Assembly on 28 July 1994, provisionally EIF on 16 November 1994) 1836 UNTS 3.
The Antarctic Treaty (signed 1 December 1959, EIF 23 June 1961) 402 UNTS 71.
Charter of the United Nations (signed 26 June 1945, EIF 24 October 1945), *Documents of the United Nations Conference on International Organization* (New York: United Nations Information Organizations, 1945–1955), vol. 15, p. 335.
Convention between the United States of America and the United Kingdom respecting the Regulation of the Liquor Traffic (signed 23 January 1924, EIF 2 May 1924) 27 LNTS 181.
Convention on the Continental Shelf (signed 29 April 1958; EIF 10 June 1964) 499 UNTS 311.
Convention on Fishing and Conservation of the Living Resources of the High Seas (signed 29 April 1958, EIF 20 March 1966) 559 UNTS 285.

Convention on the High Seas (signed 29 April 1958, EIF 30 September 1962) 450 UNTS 82.

Convention on the International Regulations for Preventing Collisions at Sea (signed 20 October 1972, EIF 15 July 1977) 1050 UNTS 16.

Convention on the Territorial Sea and the Contiguous Zone (signed 29 April 1958, EIF 10 September 1964) 516 UNTS 206.

Convention regarding the Régime of Straits (signed 20 July 1936, EIF provisionally on 15 August 1936 and definitively on 9 November 1936, in accordance with article 26) 173 LNTS 213.

Declaration on the Maritime Zone (signed and EIF 18 August 1952) 1006 UNTS 323.

International Convention for the Prevention of Pollution from Ships of 1973, modified by the Protocol of 1978 relating to the International Convention for the Prevention of Pollution from Ships (signed 17 February 1978, EIF 2 October 1983) 1340 UNTS 61.

Optional Protocol of Signature concerning the Compulsory Settlement of Disputes (signed 29 April 1958, EIF 30 September 1962) 450 UNTS 169.

Statute of the International Court of Justice (signed 26 June 1945, EIF 24 October 1945), *Documents of the United Nations Conference on International Organization* (New York: United Nations Information Organizations, 1945–1955), vol. 15, p. 355.

Treaty on Principles Governing the Activities of States in the Exploration and Use of Outer Space, including the Moon and Other Celestial Bodies (signed 27 January 1967, EIF 10 November 1967) 610 UNTS 205.

Treaty on the Prohibition of the Emplacement of Nuclear Weapons and Other Weapons of Mass Destruction on the Sea-Bed and the Ocean Floor and in the Subsoil Thereof (signed 11 February 1971, EIF 18 May 1972) 955 UNTS 115.

United Nations Convention on the Law of the Sea (signed 10 December 1984, EIF 16 November 1994) 1833 UNTS 397.

Cases

ARA Libertad (Argentina v Ghana) (Provisional Measures) ITLOS (2012) ITLOS Rep 21.

Church v Hubbart (1804) 6 US 187.

Corfu Channel (United Kingdom v Albania) (Merits) [1949] ICJ Rep 4.

(Pleadings) [1950] ICJ Pleadings III 166.

(Pleadings) [1950] ICJ Pleadings IV 9.

Fisheries (United Kingdom v Norway) (Judgment) [1951] ICJ Rep 116.

(Pleadings) [1951] ICJ Pleadings IV, 8.

M/V 'Saiga' (No. 2) (St Vincent and the Grenadines v Guinea) (Judgment) [1999] ITLOS Rep 10.

North Atlantic Coast Fisheries (Great Britain/United States) (Proceedings) (1910) PCA XI 1593 (Washington, DC: Government Printing Office, 1912).

North Sea Continental Shelf (Federal Republic of Germany v Denmark; Federal Republic of Germany v Netherlands) (Merits) [1969] ICJ Rep 3.

S.S. 'I'm Alone' (Canada/United States) III RIAA, 1609.

The Tenyu Maru (1910) 4 Alaska Reports 129.

Books, Chapters and Articles

Aguilar Mawdsley, A., 'Law of the sea: the Latin American view', in G. Pontecorvo (ed.), *The new order of the oceans* (New York: Columbia University Press, 1986), pp. 158–198.

Alvarez, A., 'Impressions left by the first Hague conference for the codification of international law', *Transactions of the Grotius Society* 16 (1930), 119–129.

Amin, S., and W. H. L. Anderson (trans.), *Empire of chaos* (New York: Monthly Review Press, 1992).

Anand, R. P. (ed.), *Law of the sea: Caracas and beyond* (The Hague: Martinus Nijhoff, 1980).

Origin and development of the law of the sea: history of international law revisited (The Hague: Martinus Nijhoff, 1982).

Andrews, W., 'DOD delays decision on advanced ICBM', *Aerospace Technology* (11 September 1967), 16.

Arntzen, S., 'Fiskerigrensesaken mellom England og Norge for den internasjonale domstol i Haag', *Tidsskrift for Rettsvitenskap* 2 (1952), 113–136.

Austin, C. F., 'Rock site – a way into the sea', *Sea Frontiers* 13 (1957), 342–352.

Barkenbus, J. N., *Deep seabed resources: politics and technology* (New York: Free Press, 1979).

Baslar, K., *The concept of the common heritage of mankind in international law* (The Hague: Martinus Nijhoff, 1997).

Beckman, R., 'The international regime governing the safety of navigation and the prevention of pollution in international straits', *Singapore Journal of International and Comparative Law* 2 (1998), 350–392.

Bedjaoui, M., *Towards a new international economic order* (Paris: UNESCO/Holmes & Meier, 1979).

Bethlehem, D., 'The secret life of international law', *Cambridge Journal of International and Comparative Law* 1 (2012), 23–36.

Booth, K., Military implications of the changing law of the sea', in J. K. Gamble (ed.), *Law of the sea: neglected issues* (Honolulu: University of Hawaii Law of the Sea Institute, 1979), pp. 328–397.

Bourquin, M., 'La portée général de l'arrêt rendu le 18 Décembre 1951 par le Cour Internationale de Justice dans l'affaire Anglo-Norvégienne des pêcheries', *Nordisk Tidsskrift and International Ret og Jus Gentium* 22 (1952), 101–132.

'Brazil straitjackets foreign research', *Scientific Research* (17 February 1969), 15.

Brown, E. D., 'The 1994 agreement on the implementation of part XI of the UN Convention on the Law of the Sea: breakthrough to universality?', *Marine Policy* 19 (1995), 5–20.

'The lessons of the *Torrey Canyon*: international law aspects', *Current Legal Problems* 21 (1968), 113–136.

Burke, W. T., 'National legislation on ocean authority zones and the contemporary law of the sea', *Ocean Development and International Law* 9 (1981), 289–322.

Butcher, J. G., and R. E. Elson, *Sovereignty and the sea: how Indonesia became an archipelagic state* (Singapore: National University of Singapore Press, 2017).

Buttigieg, J., 'Arvid Pardo – a diplomat with a mission', *Symposia Melitensia* 12 (2016), 13–28.

'The common heritage of mankind: from the law of the sea to the human genome and cyberspace', *Symposia Melitensia* 8 (2012), 81–92.

Buzan, B., 'Negotiating by consensus: developments in techniques at the United Nations conference on the law of the sea', *American Journal of International Law* 75 (1981), 324–348.

Seabed politics (New York: Praeger, 1976).

Cable, J., *Gunboat diplomacy 1919–1991: political applications of limited naval force*, 3rd ed. (Basingstoke: Macmillan, 1994).

Caminos, H., 'The legal régime of straits in the 1982 United Nations Convention on the Law of the Sea', *Recueil des cours de l'Académie de droit international de La Haye* 205 (1987), 9–246.

Carty, A., 'The Corfu Channel case – and the missing Admiralty orders', *Law and Practice of International Courts and Tribunals* 3 (2004), 1–35.

Castañeda, J., 'Negotiations on the exclusive economic zone at the third United Nations Conference on the Law of the Sea', in J. Makarczyk (ed.), *Essays in international law in honour of Judge Manfred Lachs* (The Hague: Martinus Nijhoff, 1984), pp. 605–623.

Chimni, B. S., 'The new regime of the oceans: illusion and reality', *Indian Journal of International Law* 22 (1982), 69–89.

Churchill, R. R., and A. V. Lowe, *The law of the sea*, 3rd ed. (Manchester: Manchester University Press, 1999).

Clingan, T. A., 'Emerging law of the sea: the economic zone dilemma', *San Diego Law Review*, 14 (1977), 530–547.

Craven, J. P., 'Sea power and the sea bed', *United States Naval Institute Proceedings* 92 (April 1966), 36–51.

Dean, A. H., 'Achievements at the law of the sea conference', *Proceedings of the American Society of International Law* 53 (1959), 186–197.

'Freedom of the seas', *Foreign Affairs* 37 (1958), 83–94.

'The second Geneva Conference on the Law of the Sea: the fight for freedom of the seas', *American Journal of International Law* 54 (1960), 751–789.

Dickinson, E. D., 'Jurisdiction at the maritime frontier', *Harvard Law Review* 40 (1926), 1–29.

Djalal, H., 'The developing countries and the Law of the Sea Conference', *Indonesian Quarterly* 9 (1981), 59–72.

Indonesia and the law of the sea (Jakarta: Centre for Strategic and International Studies, 1995).

Dupuy, R.-J., *The law of the sea: current problems* (Leiden: A. W. Sijhoff, 1974).

Eichelberger, C. M. (ed.) (report for the Commission to Study the Organization of the Peace), *New dimensions for the United Nations: the problems of the next decade* (Dobbs Ferry, NY: Oceana, 1966).

Emran, A., 'The regulation of vessel-source pollution in the straits of Malacca and Singapore' (University of Wollongong Thesis Collection, 2007).

Engo, P. B., 'Issues of first committee at UNCLOS III', in A. W. Koers and B. H. Oxman (eds.), *The 1982 Convention of the Law of the Sea* (Honolulu: University of Hawaii Law of the Sea Institute, 1983), pp. 33–52.

Evensen, J., 'The Anglo-Norwegian fisheries case and its legal consequences', *American Journal of International Law* 46 (1952), 609–630.

'Present military uses of the seabed and foreseeable developments', *Cornell International Law Journal* 3 (1970), 121–132.

Fagin, B., *Fishing: how the sea fed civilization* (New Haven, CT: Yale University Press, 2017).

Fenwick, J., *International profiles on marine scientific research* (Woods Hole, MA: Woods Hole Oceanographic Institution, 1992).

Ferreira, P. S., 'The role of African states in the development of the law of the sea at the third United Nations conference', *Ocean Development & International Law* 7 (1979), 89–129.

Fincham, C., and W. van Rensburg, *Bread upon waters: the developing law of the sea* (Jerusalem: Turtledove Publishing, 1980).

Fitzmaurice, G. G., 'The case of the *I'm Alone*', *British Year Book of International Law* 17 (1936), 82–111.

'The law and procedure of the International Court of Justice, 1951–54: general principles and sources of law', *British Year Book of International Law* 30 (1953), 1–70.

'The law and procedure of the International Court of Justice, 1951–1954: points of substantive law I', *British Year Book of International Law* 31 (1954), 371–429.

'Some results of the Geneva conference on the law of the sea', *International Comparative and Law Quarterly* 8 (1959), 73–121.

François, J. P. A., 'La deuxième conference sur le droit de la mer', *Nederlands Tijdschrift voor Internationaal Recht* 7 (1960), 249–254.

'Second International Conference on the Law of the Sea', *United Nations Review* 6 (1960), 12–14.

Franssen, M. N., 'Oceanic research and the developing nation perspective', in W. S. Wooster (ed.), *Freedom of oceanic research* (New York: Crane, Russak & Co., 1973), pp. 179–200.

Frommer, A. M., 'The British hovering acts: a contribution to the study of the contiguous zone', *Revue belge de droit international* 16 (1981–1982), 434–458.

Fulton, T. W., *The sovereignty of the sea* (Edinburgh: William Blackwood & Sons, 1911).

Galindo Pohl, R., 'The exclusive economic zone in the light of negotiations of the third United Nations conference on the law of the sea', in F. Orrego Vicuńa (ed.), *The exclusive economic zone: a Latin American perspective* (Epping: Bowker Publishing, 1984), pp. 31–59.

'Latin America's influence and role at the third conference on the law of the sea', *Ocean Development & International Law* 7 (1979), 65–87.

Gidel, G. C., *Le droit international public de la mer: le temps de paix*, 3 vols. (Chateauroux: Mellottee, 1932–1934).

'La mer territoriale et la zone contiguë', *Recueil des cours de l'Académie de droit international de La Haye* 48 (1934), 133–278.

Goodier, J. L., 'How to mine marine minerals', *World Mining* (July 1967), 44–47.

Green, L. C., 'The Anglo-Norwegian fisheries case, 1951', *Modern Law Review* 15 (1952), 373–377.

Gutteridge, J. A. C., 'The 1958 Convention on the Continental Shelf', *British Year Book of International Law* 35 (1959), 102–123.

Hamzah, B. A., 'Managing marine pollution in the straits of Malacca and Singapore: personal observations', *Singapore Journal of International and Comparative Law* 2 (1998), 464–467.

Heinzen, B., 'The three-mile limit, preserving the freedom of the seas', *Stanford Law Review* 11 (1959), 597–664.

Herman, L. L., 'The modern concept of the off-lying archipelago in international law', *Canadian Yearbook of International Law* 23 (1985), 172–200.

Higgins, A. P., and C. J. Colombos, *The international law of the sea*, 2nd rev. ed. (London: Longmans, Green & Co., 1951).

Hill, N., 'Shipping subsidies as an international problem', *International Affairs* (London) 12 (1933), 327–343.

Johnson, D. H. N., 'The Anglo-Norwegian fisheries case', *International and Comparative Law Quarterly* 1 (1952), 145–180.

Joyner, C. C., 'Legal implications of the concept of the common heritage of mankind', *International and Comparative Law Quarterly* 35 (1986), 190–199.

Keith, K. J., '"Naval secrets", public interest immunity and open justice', in K. Bannelier *et al.* (eds.), *The ICJ and the evolution of international law: the enduring impact of the Corfu Channel case* (London: Routledge, 2011), pp. 124–146.

Kildow, J. A. T., 'Nature of the present restrictions on oceanic research', in W. S. Wooster (ed.), *Freedom of oceanic research* (New York: Crane, Russak & Co., 1973), pp. 5–28.

Kirton, A. G., and S. C. Vasciannie, 'Deep seabed mining under the law of the sea convention and the implementation agreement: developing country perspectives', *Social and Economic Studies* 51 (2002), 63–115.

Klein, N., *Maritime security and the law of the sea* (Oxford: Oxford University Press, 2011).

Koh, T. T. B., 'The territorial sea, contiguous zone, straits and archipelagos under the 1982 Convention on the Law of the Sea', *Malaya Law Review* 29 (1987), 163–199.

Kusumaatmadja, M., 'The concept of the Indonesian archipelago', *Indonesian Quarterly* 4 (1982), 12–26.

'Supplementary remarks', in L. M. Alexander (ed.), *The law of the sea: needs and interests of the developing countries* (Kingston, RI: Law of the Sea Institute and University of Rhode Island, 1973), 172–177.

Leifer, M., *International straits of the world: Malacca, Singapore, and Indonesia* (Alphen aan den Rijn: Sijthoff & Noordhoff, 1978).

Leonardo, L., 'Overlapping entitlements between the continental shelf beyond 200 nautical miles and the exclusive economic zone' (University of Woolongong Thesis Collection, 2019).

Li, Y., *Transfer of technology for deep sea-bed mining: the 1982 Law of the Sea Convention and beyond* (Dordrecht: Martinus Nijhoff, 1995).

Long, D. M., *The Soviet merchant fleet – its growth, strategy, strength and weaknesses* (London: Lloyd's of London Press, 1986).

Lowe, A. V., 'The commander's handbook on the law of naval operations and the contemporary law of the sea', in H. B. Robertson (ed.), *The law of naval operations* (International Law Studies, vol. 64) (Newport, RI: Naval War College Press, 1991), pp. 109–147.

'The development of the concept of the contiguous zone', *British Year Book of International Law* 52 (1981), 109–169.

Mangone, G. J., *Law for the world ocean – Tagore law lectures* (London: Stevens & Sons, 1981).

McLaughlin, R., 'Dangerous waters and international law: the *Corfu Channel* case, warships, and sovereignty irritants', in K. Bannelier *et al.* (eds.), *The ICJ and the evolution of international law: the enduring impact of the Corfu Channel case* (London: Routledge, 2011), pp. 164–180.

Mendelson, M. H., Review Essay: 'The flux and reflux of the law of the sea', *Oxford Journal of Legal Studies* 5 (1985), 285–291.

Mero, J. L., *The mineral resources of the sea* (Amsterdam: Elsevier Oceanography Series, 1965).

Meyer, T. A., 'Tanker design features and the safety of navigation', *Singapore Journal of International and Comparative Law* 2 (1998), 517–526.

Miles, E. L., *Global ocean politics: the decision process at the third United Nations conference on the law of the sea: 1973–1982* (Boston: Martinus Nijhoff, 1998).

'Some socio-cultural problems involved in expanding use of marine protein concentrate for human consumption', in Mershon Center for Education in National Security/Carnegie Endowment for International Peace (eds.), *Second conference on law, organization and security in the use of the ocean* (Columbus, OH: Ohio State University, 1967), pp. 3–33.

Moore, J. N., 'The regime of straits and the third United Nations conference on the law of the sea', *American Journal of International Law* 74 (1980), 77–101.

Morell, J. B., *The law of the sea: an historical analysis of the 1982 treaty and its rejection by the United States* (Jefferson, NC: McFarland & Co., 1992).

Morgan, G. R., and D. J. Staples, *The history of industrial marine fisheries in southeast Asia*, RAP Publication 2006/12 (Bangkok: Food and Agriculture Organisation, 2006).

Mostert, N., *Supership* (London: Macmillan, 1975).

Nandan, S. N., and D. H. Anderson, 'Straits used for international navigation: a commentary on part III of the United Nations convention on the law of the sea 1982', *British Year Book of International Law* 60 (1989), 159–204.

Njenga, F. X., 'Historical background of the evolution of the exclusive economic zone and the contribution of Africa', in G. Pontecorvo (ed.), *The new order of the oceans* (New York: Columbia University Press, 1986), pp. 125–157.

Nordquist, M. H., *et al.* (eds.), *United Nations Convention on the Law of the Sea 1982: a commentary*, 7 vols. and supplementary documents (Dordrecht: Martinus Nijhoff, 1985–).

Noyes, J. E., 'Treaty interpretation and definitions of the law of the sea convention: comments on "Defining terms in the 1982 Law of the Sea Convention"', *California Western International Law Journal* 32 (2002), 367–383.

Nyerere, J. K., *Freedom and a new world economic order* (Dar es Salaam: Oxford University Press, 2011).

O'Connell, D. P., 'International law and contemporary naval operations', *British Year Book of International Law* 44 (1970), 19–86.

'The law of the sea', *Journal of the Royal Society of Arts* 124 (1976), 367–379.

O'Connell, D. P.,and I. A. Shearer (ed.), *The international law of the sea*, 2 vols. (Oxford: Clarendon Press, 1982, 1984).

Ocean Policy Committee of the Commission of International Relations NAS-NRC, 'The marine scientific research issue in the law of the sea negotiations', *Science* 197 (15 July 1977), 230–233.

OECD, 'OECD study on flags of convenience', *Journal of Maritime Law and Commerce* 4 (1973), 231–254.

Oliver, E. F., 'Malacca: dire straits', *United States Naval Institute Proceedings* (June 1973), 26–33.

Oxman, B. H., *From cooperation to conflict: the Soviet Union and the United States at the third UN conference on law of the sea* (Seattle: Washington Sea Grant/ Institute for Marine Studies, University of Washington, 1985).

'The preparation of article 1 of the Convention on the Continental Shelf', 3 pts., *Journal of Maritime Law and Commerce* 3 (1972) 245 (pt. 1), 445 (pt. 2), 683 (pt. 3).

Panel of Oceanography, President's Science Advisory Committee, *Effective use of the sea* (Washington, DC: US Government Printing Office, 1966).

Pardo, A., 'Law of the sea conference – what went wrong', in R. L. Friedheim (ed.), *Managing ocean resources: a primer* (Boulder, CO: Westview Press, 1979), pp. 137–148.

Pardo, A., and C. Q. Christol, 'The common interest: tension between the whole and the parts', in R. St. J. Macdonald and D. M. Johnston (eds.), *The structure and process of international law: essays in legal philosophy doctrine and theory* (The Hague: Martinus Nijhoff, 1983), pp. 643–660.

Pirtle, C. E., 'Military uses of ocean space and the law of the sea in the new millennium', *Ocean Development & International Law* 31 (2000), 7–45.

Proelss, A., *United Nations Convention on the Law of the Sea: a commentary* (Munich: C. H. Beck, Hart, Nomos, 2017).

Purver, R. G., 'Canadian foreign policy and the military uses of the seabed', in B. J. Johnson and M. W. Zacher (eds.), *Canadian foreign policy and the law of the sea* (Vancouver: University of British Columbia Press, 1977), pp. 203–254.

Rao, P. C., *The new law of maritime zones, with special reference to India's maritime zones* (New Delhi: Milind Publications, 1983).

Rauch, E., 'Military uses of the ocean', *German Yearbook of International Law* 28 (1985), 229–267.

Reisman, W. M., and C. P. Skinner, *Fraudulent evidence before public international tribunals* (Cambridge: Cambridge University Press, 2014), pp. 54–77.

Richardson, E. L., 'Seabed mining and law of the sea', *Department of State Bulletin* 80 (December 1980), 60–64.

Roach, J. A., *Excessive maritime claims*, 4th ed. (Leiden: Brill Nijhoff, 2021).

Roach, J. A., and R. W. Smith, *Excessive maritime claims* (Newport, RI: Naval War College, 1994).

Robertson, H. B., 'Navigation in the exclusive economic zone', *Virginia Journal of International Law* 24 (1984), 865–916.

Rothwell, D. R., 'International straits', in D. R. Rothwell *et al.* (eds.), *The Oxford handbook of the law of the sea* (Oxford: Oxford University Press, 2017), 114–133.

Tanaka, Y., *The international law of the sea*, 2nd ed. (Cambridge: Cambridge University Press, 2015).

Thurstan, R., *et al.*, 'Origins of the bottom trawling controversy in the British Isles: 19th century witness testimonies reveal evidence of early fishery declines', *Fish and Fisheries* 15 (2014), 506–522.

Tolentino, A. M., *The Philippines and the law of the sea: a collection of articles, statements, and speeches* (Manila: Secretariat to the Cabinet Committee on the Law of the Sea Treaty by the Development Academy of the Philippines Press, c. 1982).

'Proceedings of the Philippines Senate on Bill No. 541', in R. P. M. Lotilla (ed.), *The Philippine national territory: a collection of related documents* (Manila: Institute of International Legal Studies, Foreign Service Institute, c. 1995).

Treves, T., 'Military installations, structures, and devices on the seabed', *American Journal of International Law* 74 (1980), 808–857.

Tsipis, K., 'Antisubmarine warfare', in Stockholm International Peace Research Institute (ed.), *World armaments and disarmament, SIPRI yearbook 1974* (Stockholm: Almqvist & Wiksell, 1974), pp. 303–325.

United States Department of the Navy, Office of the Chief of Naval Operations, *Strategic concepts of the U.S. Navy*, NWP 1 (A) (Washington, DC: Naval Warfare Publications, 1987).

'US explains its votes on seabed resolutions', *Department of State Bulletin* 62 (26 January 1970), 89–95.

Van Dyke, J. M., 'Transit passage through international straits', in A. Chircop, T. McDorman and S. Rolston (eds.), *The future of ocean regime-building: essays in tribute to Douglas M. Johnston* (Leiden: Martinus Nijhoff, 2009), pp. 177–232.

Van Dyke, J. M., and C. Yuen, 'Common heritage v. freedom of the seas: which governs the seabed?', *San Diego Law Review* 19 (1982), 493–551.

Vicuña, F. O., 'National laws on seabed exploitation: problems of international law', *University of Miami Inter-American Law Review* 13 (1981), 139–156.

Visscher, C. de, and P. E. Corbett (trans.), *Theory and reality in public international law* (Princeton, NJ: Princeton University Press, 2015).

Waldock, C. H. M., 'The Anglo-Norwegian Fisheries case', *British Year Book of International Law* 28 (1951), 114–171.

Wani, I. J., 'An evaluation of the convention on the law of the sea from the perspective of the landlocked states', *Virginia Journal of International Law* 22 (1982), 627–666.

Warioba, J. S., 'The reform of the United Nations system in the context of the law of the sea and the United Nations conference on the environment and development', *African Journal of International and Comparative Law* 7 (1995), 426–444.

Wertenbaker, W., 'A reporter at large: the law of the sea – I', *New Yorker* (1 August 1983), 38–65.

'A reporter at large: the law of the sea – II', *New Yorker* (8 August 1983), 56–82.
Whitaker, J. S., 'Outside the mainstream', *The Atlantic* (October 1982), 18–26.
Wilberforce, R. O., 'Some aspects of the Anglo-Norwegian fisheries case', *Transactions of the Grotius Society* 38 (1952), 151–168.
Wilkes, O., 'Strategic anti-submarine warfare and its implications for a counter-force first strike', in Stockholm International Peace Research Institute (ed.), *World armaments and disarmament, SIPRI yearbook 1979* (London: Taylor & Francis, 1979), pp. 427–452.
World Bank, *Price prospects for major primary commodities*, vol. 4 (Washington, DC: World Bank, 1984).
Young, E., 'New laws for old navies', *Survival* 16 (1974), 262–267.
Yturriaga, J. A. de, *Straits used for international navigation: a Spanish perspective* (Dordrecht: Martinus Nijhoff, 1991).
Zedalis, R. J., 'Peaceful purposes and other relevant provisions of the revised composite negotiating text: a comparative analysis of the existing and the proposed military regime of the high seas', *Syracuse Journal of International Law and Commerce* 7 (1979), 1–36.

Newspapers and Periodicals (ordered by publication title)

'Buzzing of ships confirmed by Indonesian', *Canberra Times* (15 April 1959).
'Icelandic attack on "gunboat diplomacy"', *Daily Telegraph* (6 October 1959).
Ivens, M., 'UN Convention on the Law of the Sea', *Financial Times* (15 November 1982).
'"No" to Malacca straits plan, Ali Murtopo says', *Indonesian Observer* (25 September 1971).
Monroe, L. R., 'Undersea mapping aboard Scripps vessel: scientists hope ship will cut U.S.-Soviet ice', *Los Angeles Times* (16 August 1988).
'Freedom of the high seas – another international lost cause?', *Manchester Guardian* (4 February 1958).
'The need to keep waterway safe', *New Nation* (17 May 1973).
'Straits: offer by the Japanese', *New Nation* (17 November 1971).
'Still at sea', *New Straits Times* (7 September 1976).
Howe, M., 'Nato group establishes underwater testing range in the Azores for communications research', *New York Times* (5 March 1972).
'I'm Alone skipper describes cruises', *New York Times* (30 December 1934).
Mann Borgese, E., 'The complexities of a sea change', *New York Times* (1 October 1976).
'Nuclear test area set', *New York Times* (15 February 1958).
'U.S. fights curb on ships' flags', *New York Times* (3 April 1958).
'2 am: two ships ablaze off S'pore', *Straits Times* (18 July 1975).
Daniel, J., 'Clean-up battle as tanker hits reef', *Straits Times* (6 April 1976).

'Mysella oil spill: mop-up bill for Shell', *Straits Times* (8 April 1976).
'Navy wins oil spill battle', *Straits Times* (29 July 1976).
'Singapore alert as oil spill moves south', *Straits Times* (27 July 1976).
'Defense: Polaris goes to work', *Time* (28 November 1960).
'Environment: squeezing more out the seas', *Time* (29 July 1975).
'Oceanology: journey to inner space', *Time* (17 September 1965).
'Action of Peru ridiculed', *The Times* (27 November 1954).
Lauterpacht, H., 'Freedom of the seas', *The Times* (8 January 1952).
Bain, G., 'Fight for 12-mile fishing limit', *Toronto Globe and Mail* (7 May 1958).
'Next: an arsenal of new weapons for U.S.', *US News & World Report* (16 October 1967).
Anderson, J., 'U.S. military communications archaic', *Washington Post* (5 February 1973).
'Fleetwood concerned about fishing limits', *West Lancashire Evening Gazette* (21 February 1958).

INDEX

www.ingramcontent.com/pod-product-compliance
Ingram Content Group UK Ltd.
Pitfield, Milton Keynes, MK11 3LW, UK
UKHW020729060225
454750UK00007B/68

9 781108 840149